CRIMINAL JUSTICE INFORMATION

HOW TO FIND IT, HOW TO USE IT

by
Dennis C. Benamati
Phyllis A. Schultze
Adam C. Bouloukos
Graeme R. Newman

ORYX PRESS
1998

The rare Arabian Oryx is believed to have inspired the myth of the unicorn. This desert antelope became virtually extinct in the early 1960s. At that time several groups of international conservationists arranged to have 9 animals sent to the Phoenix Zoo to be the nucleus of a captive breeding herd. Today the Oryx population is over 1,000, and over 500 have been returned to the Middle East.

© 1998 by The Oryx Press
4041 North Central at Indian School Road
Phoenix, Arizona 85012-3397

Published simultaneously in Canada
Printed and Bound in the United States of America

∞ The paper used in this publication meets the minimum requirements of American National Standard for Information Science—Permanence of Paper for Printed Library Materials, ANSI Z39.48, 1984.

Library of Congress Cataloging-in-Publication Data

Criminal justice information: how to find it, how to use it / by
Dennis C. Benamati . . . [et al.].
    p. cm.
  Includes bibliographical references and index.
  ISBN 0-89774-957-X (alk. paper)
    1. Criminal justice, Administration of—Research. 2. Criminal
justice, Administration of—Information services. 3. Information storage and
retrieval systems—Criminal justice, Administration of.
4. Information retrieval. I. Benamati, Dennis C.
HV7419.5.C75   1998
364'.07'2—dc21   97-39576
                                                               CIP

Contents

List of Illustrations

Preface

THE NEW INFORMATION ENVIRONMENT

The information explosion is upon us. Due in part to the growth of the Internet as a means of disseminating information, the number of sources in criminal justice has grown enormously in the past five years alone. Although traditional library tools such as the catalog and the periodicals index were once enough to access most published information, these tools were designed for an era of printed sources—books and periodicals. While they were once the first stop in a search for information, the growth of the Internet and electronic sources has rearranged information seeking behavior. Researchers, even professional reference librarians, are just as likely to access the World Wide Web as they are to approach a catalog or index. In addition, recently published research guides for criminal justice have lost some of their value. The authors of outstanding sources such as O'Block's *Criminal Justice Research Sources* (1992) and Lutzker and Ferrall's *Criminal Justice Research in Libraries* (1986) could not have foreseen just how much the information environment would change in the late 1990s.

Neither could these guides have foreseen the isolation in which the researcher can now work. Information is now available from any location—home, office, or classroom—and at any time of day or night. Traditionally, the researcher had to go to a library to access information. There, he or she could find a librarian to assist with locating information and formulating queries. Today, the researcher does not have to be in the same room or building to access Internet and online information sources. The librarian, who would have normally assisted with the research, is remote or may not be on duty. Thus, the concept of the library as a physical location has lost some of its meaning.

We have written *Criminal Justice Information: How to Find It, How to Use It* to accommodate these fundamental changes in the way that criminal justice information is accessed and disseminated. We hope that this new guide will provide the distant researcher with guidance in the use of resources—guidance that would have traditionally been provided by a reference librarian at a library.

We intend for *Criminal Justice Information* to serve a wide audience—from the curious citizen to the advanced scholar—including criminal justice researchers (high school to graduate students and professors); criminal justice professionals, such as police officers and federal, state, and local policy makers; legal professionals; and governmental and nongovernmental organizations.

A NEW APPROACH TO INFORMATION GATHERING

Our publisher has suggested that we provide the researcher with a "roadmap" of how to use this book. It is a well-meant suggestion, to which we reply as follows: In the original *Star Trek* series there was an episode in which Captain Kirk makes a reference to Vulcan, Mr. Spock's home planet. As he refers to Vulcan, he points straight ahead toward the bow of the starship. Mr Spock, in his inimitable way, points off toward the right and replies, "Actually Captain, Vulcan is in that direction." This scene is more memorable for what it does not say about the voyages of the Starship Enterprise than for what it does say. A more insightful script would have had Mr. Spock point to the right but also down a bit, thus giving the viewer a better taste of the three-dimensional nature of space and challenging us to shed our linear notion of travel.

A roadmap is an altogether inadequate analogy to demonstrate how we would like our readers to use this guide. Indeed, for several reasons we encourage our readers to shed the bias that research and information gathering are linear processes. This perception has been part and parcel of a culture that has taught and related information linearly for generations. The media in which our culture and knowledge are recorded—primarily books but also audio and video recordings—are linear because they are borne of the limited technologies of the printing press, tape recorder, and camera. But these technologies have changed, and with them so has the representation of information and knowledge in our culture.

The World Wide Web is only one of the many media through which information is disseminated and acquired in a nonlinear manner. In fact, the Web is only the latest technological development that goes back through self-paced study and several generations of instructional media. The Web has received all the attention because it has had the greatest impact on instruction in schools and universities, challenging us to learn and acquire information in new ways.

Research methods are already changing. If you have spent an afternoon browsing around the Web, clicking here and there, you are using a process quite different from traditional research scholarship. You may move right or left, up or down, and perhaps never completely read a piece of text before moving on to the next. You may acquire bits of information rather than whole concepts and, through the technology of hypertext, *link* to other bits of information located at different sites on different servers. You are no longer confined to the printed resources held within the walls of libraries. Your starting point is often the first Web site or other resource that provides relevant information. The location of the next piece of information you gather is often determined by the previous site you visited and the *links* provided there.

Various metaphors illustrate the way information is gathered in a networked world, including following your nose through a sea of information. But perhaps the best metaphor for the twenty-first century and for using this book, is one of *berrypicking*. The researcher picks a berry, or discovers an initial piece of information, then picks the next berry depending upon what he or she learns from the first and each subsequent berry.

Throughout our efforts to compile and write *Criminal Justice Information*, we were reminded of, and certainly frustrated by, the fact that new sources and new means of accessing them are constantly becoming available. New editions of older works are being published and new methods of accessing information are being marketed. Although we have attempted to gather as many information sources as possible in this work, our focus is on process more than resources. Indeed, the nature of the new information environment is such that the researcher can only rely upon its fluidity. Thus, our objective in writing this work is to outline the process of researching criminal justice.

SCOPE OF INFORMATION SOURCES, MEDIA, AND TOPICS

This guide is not meant to be nor could it hope to be an exhaustive criminal justice reference source. However, we do feel that it is an ambitious and reasonably complete attempt to organize the varied types and sources of criminal justice information available. These sources include statistical reports, directories, agency reports, foundation reports, academic monographs and periodicals, professional organization documents, specialized bibliographies, *grey literature* (government documents), databases (electronic and hard copy), and other online information.

We have also included many Internet and World Wide Web sites—a difficult task due to the nature of the Internet. Internet and Web sites come and go, move, and may even be left unattended. Although we have tried to list only the most authoritative and reliable sites, the fluidity of the Internet is such that we suggest you approach sites forgivingly. In addition to Internet sites, many resources we have discussed are online databases. Thus, we felt it important to include a discussion of the pleasures and pitfalls of using catalogs and online sources, controlled vocabulary and full-text searching.

Some sources are covered in several chapters; this overlap is intentional since the same sources are useful for different kinds of information and their use may be colored by the context in which they are used.

Finally, in the chapters where we describe printed sources, we have also included Library of Congress subject headings for the topics and types of materials listed. If your library does not own the specific sources listed here, these subject headings may help you locate others that we did not include. Please note that in using these headings, we had to take certain liberties. Whenever a subject heading includes the italicized term *Geog.*, your catalog may subdivide the subject by geographic entity. Thus, in the heading "Female offenders—*Geog.*" you may wish to add the name of a country or U.S. state, thus forming Female offenders—New York" or "Female offenders—United States," if it advances your research. Likewise the term *Subject* is added to some headings, for example, "*Subject*—Statistics." In this case, you would add the subject appropriate to your research, for example, "Criminal justice, administration of—Statistics."

ARRANGEMENT OF CHAPTERS

The movement from linearity to a new liquid information space is an evolving one, but not so the publication of books, even today. Despite our best intentions, we are bound to the present format and linear display of information. You are not, however, bound to use this source in that way, and we encourage you not to do so. Our intention is to provide the reader with a reference book that can be accessed from any point in the berrypicking research process, not a book to be read from cover-to-cover. Even more to the point, as mentioned earlier in this preface, we suggest that you use this work as a series of guideposts through a process of research.

Context. As with any endeavor, it is imperative that the researcher understand the context within which the research is being carried out. Thus we have begun our work with a introductory chapter on the evolution of criminal justice as a "discipline." Where the discipline has been and where it is are important to an understanding of all the related subjects and information that goes into criminal justice research. It is in understanding the context of research in this interdisciplinary field that one is able to make cognitive *links* from criminal justice to all its related disciplines— criminology, sociology, psychology, public administration, etc. Making these links and pulling in relevant information from other disciplines often makes the difference between an "A" paper and a "B" paper. This is why you will find information sources from related subjects as well as criminal justice.

Authorities. After an introduction to criminal justice, we discuss the most-often-used but least-acknowledged sources of information: peers, colleagues, and authorities in the field. In an environment often characterized as "information overload," we consider it essential for the researcher to be ready and able to assess the authoritative value of the wide variety of sources now available. For the first time in a criminal justice research guide, the issues and tools needed to determine the authority of information are discussed. Researchers must recognize that authority and the traditional ways of determining authority are being challenged by the Internet. The power to disseminate information has been redistributed, and anyone with a computer, a modem, and $10 a month can publish. Thus, the information seeker can no longer assume that information they read, especially information on the Internet, has been evaluated by someone with knowledge of the field. In chapter 2, but also through-

out this work, we hope that the reader will find clues and suggestions for evaluating information.

Basic Information. As an interdisciplinary discipline, no one individual is likely to be an authority in all of its component parts. For that reason, we have included chapter 3, "Sources of Basic Information." When venturing into unknown territory, it is a good idea to understand the "lay of the land," and it is no less so in doing research. Sources of basic information help the novice and authority alike to acquire a basic understanding and vocabulary of criminal justice and its related disciplines as well as their bibliographies.

Literature Search I. Your literature search begins in chapter 4, "Tools for Identifying, Locating, and Retrieving Books, Documents and Other Information Sources." In this chapter, we provide the reader with assistance in determining the scope of his or her research and suggestions on how to overcome some of the pitfalls of using catalogs and databases. We have also included a discussion of the tools for finding "published" sources of information. Among these tools we have included a survey of online catalogs— fee-based and free on the Internet, sources for identifying online information, and coverage of printed bibliographies.

Literature Search II. Your literature search continues in chapter 5, "Periodicals, News Services, Indexes, and Abstracts." Here we have chosen to open with a description of the different kinds of periodical literature available to the criminal justice researcher and to put the novice on notice of the considerable difference between scholarly and popular literature. We have, nonetheless, advised that popular literature, newspapers, and other timely sources of information have their place. We have also provided the reader with information about how to find periodical literature through indexes, abstracts, and online services and advised that even these resources can provide a filtering mechanism for information.

Statistical Information. Criminal Justice makes liberal use of statistical information in certain areas of research. In chapter 6, "Statistical Sources," we have endeavored to identify the most important sources of statistical information and the indexes and other sources that can be used to locate statistical information wherever it may be published. It is also in this chapter that we begin to make reference to "grey literature"—those sources that tend to fall out of the mainstream of publication.

Government Publications and Grey Literature. Chapter 7, "Governmnent Agencies as Generators of Criminal Justice Information," is process oriented. The volume of literature on locating government information is such that we would do justice to the subject only by making reference to the other sources that deal with it. But the process of locating government information within the context of criminal justice research is lacking except for our modest attempt here.

Legal Research. Legal Research in the context of criminal justice is treated in chapter 8. Here our emphasis is again process oriented. Rather than treating the subject as thoroughly as we might be inclined, we have given the criminal justice researcher who may do occasional legal research a strategy for performing this complex and sometimes baffling exercise.

International Criminal Justice Information. International resources are the topic of chapter 9. As international communication and travel have become easier, crime has increasingly become an international concern. International governmental and nongovernmental agencies have blossomed in number. Chapter 9 is

intended as a means of guiding the reader through this complicated arena of research.

ACKNOWLEDGMENTS

The authors gratefully acknowledge the assistance of the following people:

Mr. Srinivasa Reddy and Mr. Matthew H. Fleming of the United Nations Crime Prevention and Criminal Justice Branch, Vienna.

Evelina and Suzette Lemelin and Alicia and Marcus Benamati.

Ms. Marta Cwik of the Marist College Library.

Staff of the Coleman Karesh Law Library, University of South Carolina School of Law. Especially the advice and assistance of Professor Marsha Baum, Mr. Joseph Cross, Ms. Anna Hoebeke, and Ms. Karen Taylor.

Staff of the Reference Department of the Thomas Cooper Library, University of South Carolina.

The views expressed by Mr. Bouloukos are those of the author and do not necessarily reflect those of the United Nations.

Chapter 1

Criminal Justice Research in an Evolving Information Environment

CRIME AND "CRIMINAL JUSTICE"

Crime and *criminal* are among the most loaded words in the English lexicon. They conjure images and stereotypes that are at once difficult to identify yet ubiquitous. In the video culture of the 1990s, crime and criminals are featured in prime-time television viewing. They figure strongly in almost all news reports and programs. The word *justice* is equally difficult, used constantly in political speeches and by political action interest groups. Yet there has been little agreement on what the word *justice* means—the familiar arguments can be traced at least as far back as Plato's *Republic*. And when we put the words together, to make the expression criminal justice, we do not mean that justice is criminal. Rather, criminal justice is a term that is best defined by the educational programs that have emerged to teach it, which are now widespread throughout the United States.

The term *criminal justice* was first employed in 1963 to name the first school of criminal justice in the United States (that still exists) at the State University of New York at Albany. Its mission was to educate students at the graduate level in all aspects of crime, criminals, corrections, policing, and law. A curriculum was designed that covered the social, economic, and psychological factors relating to the causes of crime and the processing and punishment of offenders. This curriculum eventually became known as the Albany Model.

The Albany Model divides the curriculum into five parts: the nature of crime, law and social control, planned change in criminal justice, the administration of criminal justice, and research methods and statistics in criminal justice. The faculty of the school was drawn from a variety of disciplines including sociology, psychology, public administration, and law. There are now approximately 600 research centers and universities in the United States that specialize in the field of criminal justice. While the Albany Model's way of organizing the criminal justice curriculum has been copied, applied, and changed throughout the United States, its essential thrusts—interdisciplinary and the concept of criminal justice as a system—have survived.

It is the interdisciplinary nature of criminal justice that presents the researcher with the greatest challenge. And woven into this problem is the confusion between two major terms, *criminal justice* and *criminology*.

"CRIMINAL JUSTICE" VERSUS "CRIMINOLOGY"

Were it not for certain historical events, the term *criminology* might have become the most common name for majors and programs in criminal justice in the United States. The first separate school set up to study and teach in the realm of crime and justice was the School of Criminology at the University of California at Berkeley. Its aim was to produce professionally trained scholars who had studied the problems of crime, criminals, and the processing of criminals from an interdisciplinary perspective. However, as a result of the political unrest on college campuses throughout the United States in the 1960s, the Berkeley school suffered severe setbacks and was eventually closed. In part, the collapse of the Berkeley school affected the naming of the new graduate program about to be set up at Albany. New York legislators wanted to avoid any association with the Berkeley criminology school. They chose "School of Criminal Justice." Therefore one view is that there is no substantive difference between the terms *criminal justice* and *criminology*.

The purists, however, would argue otherwise. The term *criminology* was first coined in 1885 by the Italian criminologist Raffaele Garofalo in the title of his book *Criminologia*. Garofalo was most concerned with the causes of crime, although he also tried to express the policy and processing implications of his theory. A judge and lawyer by training, Garofalo argued, along with the positivists (those who were attempting at the time to apply the principles and methods of the natural sciences to the study of human and social behavior), that a scientific approach was needed to understand the causes of crime and that from this understanding policy implications for the punishment and treatment of criminals would follow. Garofalo's prime concern was with the actual origins or causes of crime; he only looked at the actual processing of offenders secondarily. He was, as were the positivists, more interested in applying the new techniques and methods of science to discover the causes of crime than to examine the processing of offenders. It is largely the heritage of this positive school of criminology that lends weight to the meaning of *criminology* as having more to do with the nature or causes of crime rather than the processing of offenders.

Strangely, Cesare Beccaria, who is widely considered the father of criminology and whose treatise *On Crimes and Punishments* (1764) became the manifesto of criminal justice in the eighteenth-century enlightenment, wrote essentially about the processing of offenders and only secondarily about the causes of crime. Beccaria is sometimes credited with having founded the classical school of criminology in Italy, which the Italian positivists took pains to criticize.

The origins of criminology in the United States also proceeded from the positivists, though these were French rather than Italian. For historical reasons, criminology was first taught within or as part of the sociology curriculum in major universities. (See exhibit 1.1.) As a result, American sociological study was dominated by an empirical orientation first effectively promoted by the Chicago School of Sociology in the 1940s and 1950s, which studied successive waves of migration to urban America often with a focus on delinquency, culture conflict, and crime. While the particular topics of study today are widely diverse, the dominance of empirical positivism in American sociology remains.

The sociological approach is still strong today as criminology is often taught in sociology departments, even in universities that have separate departments of criminal justice. Yet, if we examine the definition of *criminology* put forward by Sutherland and Cressy in the 10th edition (1978) of their textbook *Criminology*, arguably the most widely adopted textbook in criminology in the United States for at least 30 years, following the publication of its first edition in 1924, we find a very broad definition of criminology, that encompasses just about everything that would be subsumed under "criminal justice."

> Criminology has three interrelated divisions, as follows: (1) the sociology of criminal law, which is an attempt at the systematic analysis of the conditions under which penal laws develop and also at explanation of variations in policies and procedures used in police departments and courts; (2) the sociology of crime and social psychology of criminal behavior, which is an attempt at systematic analysis of the economic, political, and social conditions in which crime and criminality are either generated or prevented; and (3) the sociology of punishment and correction, which is an attempt at systematic analysis of policies and procedures for reducing the incidence of crime. (Sutherland and Cressey, 1978, 3.)

Thus, although criminologists in the U.S. generally define their mission as searching for the sociological causes of crime, it is still open to them to adopt a broader view that approaches closely that of criminal justice.

While some interdisciplinary schools and faculties have been established outside the United States, they

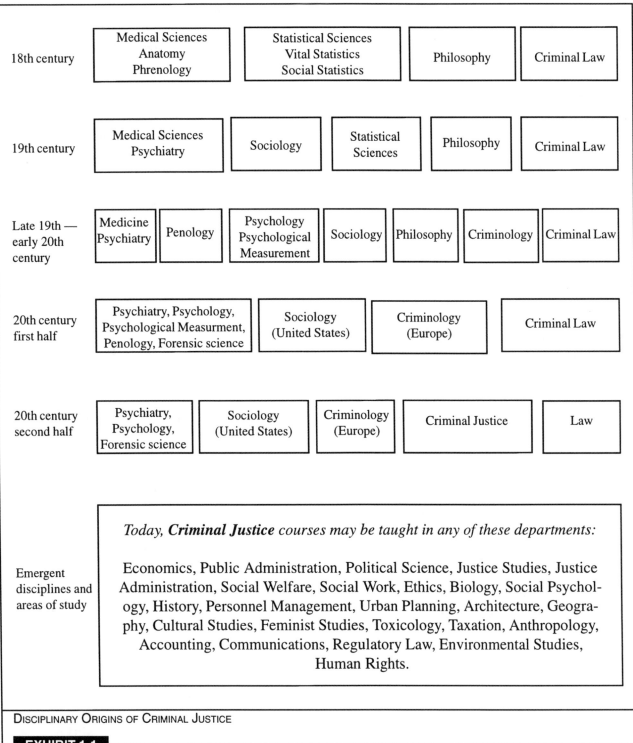

18th century	Medical Sciences / Anatomy / Phrenology	Statistical Sciences / Vital Statistics / Social Statistics	Philosophy	Criminal Law	

19th century	Medical Sciences / Psychiatry	Sociology	Statistical Sciences	Philosophy	Criminal Law

Late 19th — early 20th century	Medicine / Psychiatry	Penology	Psychology / Psychological Measurement	Sociology	Philosophy	Criminology	Criminal Law

20th century first half	Psychiatry, Psychology, Psychological Measurment, Penology, Forensic science	Sociology (United States)	Criminology (Europe)	Criminal Law

20th century second half	Psychiatry, Psychology, Forensic science	Sociology (United States)	Criminology (Europe)	Criminal Justice	Law

Emergent disciplines and areas of study	*Today,* **Criminal Justice** *courses may be taught in any of these departments:* Economics, Public Administration, Political Science, Justice Studies, Justice Administration, Social Welfare, Social Work, Ethics, Biology, Social Psychology, History, Personnel Management, Urban Planning, Architecture, Geography, Cultural Studies, Feminist Studies, Toxicology, Taxation, Anthropology, Accounting, Communications, Regulatory Law, Environmental Studies, Human Rights.

DISCIPLINARY ORIGINS OF CRIMINAL JUSTICE

EXHIBIT 1-1

have tended to adopt the term *criminology* more often than *criminal justice*. In fact, it would be reasonable to say that the term *criminal justice* is distinctly American, and only very recently has it taken on an international flavor. For example, the name of the United Nation's main department for the study of criminal justice was, until a few years ago, the United Nations Branch for Prevention of Crime and Treatment of Offenders. It is now the United Nations Crime Prevention and Criminal Justice Division. Similarly, the name of the United Nation's interregional institute was originally the United Nations Social Defense

Research Institute. It is now the United Nations Inter-regional Criminal Justice Research Institute.

The disciplinary basis of the study of crime and punishment also differs by country. In Italy, for example, the tradition is to teach criminology within departments or schools of medicine. It is beyond imagination that criminal justice courses would ever find their way into schools of medicine in the United States. In countries with a British tradition of higher education, criminology and criminal justice courses have traditionally been taught in schools of law. The most renowned school at Cambridge, England, is called the Institute of Criminology, not criminal justice. However, its faculty represents a variety of disciplines not altogether different from those represented at the School of Criminal Justice at the State University of New York at Albany.

THE SHIFTING BOUNDARIES OF CRIMINAL JUSTICE

Today it is not uncommon to find schools and departments of criminal justice in a variety of academic programs. While there are many schools of criminal justice in United States universities, there are many departments of criminal justice that find their homes in quite a few modern disciplines such as political science, social work or social welfare, public administration, urban affairs, and sociology. Some may also have a slightly different name such as "Law and Society", "Justice Studies," or "Legal Studies." That criminal justice programs are found in such a variety of academic homes and sometimes under a different name reflects a basic fact about the field: its boundaries are constantly shifting and expanding, and there is an ongoing debate as to what is and what should be its proper core or subject matter.

For this reason, any attempt to provide the beginning researcher with a guidepost to the literature of criminal justice must be highly suspect. The way in for some, may be the way out for others. Even the conception of a problem as a criminal justice issue assumes a great deal. For example, would you notify the police if you saw toxic chemicals spilling into a local river? And, if you did, would the police, sirens sounding, rush down to the scene of the crime? Probably not. Rather, you would probably report the case to the local department of environmental conservation, or its equivalent. Yet, in the past 10 years such an event has come to be seen as well within the purview of criminal justice studies, even if it is initially seen or

even dealt with by agencies that are not traditionally thought of as law enforcement agencies. This type of white-collar crime and an enormous range of behaviors—lawful and unlawful—such as Wall Street fraud, political corruption, international terrorism, peace-keeping, human rights, and urban design for crime prevention now fall under the rubric of legitimate topics of study in criminal justice programs throughout the United States.

The boundaries of criminal justice continue to shift, almost always widening, and rarely shrinking.

From this brief semantic tour, we are inclined to view the two terms *criminology* and *criminal justice* as essentially referring to the same body of subject matter. If there are differences, it is more likely that these reflect the different academic and disciplinary histories of particular countries or educational traditions.

CRIMINAL JUSTICE AS A SYSTEM

Criminal justice is now widely regarded as a "system" that has developed a massive bureaucracy. As a result, it has generated, and continues to generate, huge amounts of published and unpublished material. Prior to President Johnson's Crime Commission of 1968, which set the research agenda for many decades to follow, the main generators of criminal justice information were researchers in the academic setting. Although programs in criminal justice have grown phenomenally since then, the amount of research and the number of publications produced by academic researchers has been surpassed by the voluminous amount of material published by criminal justice agencies at the local, state, federal, and international levels. In addition, there are government bureaucracies not directly related to criminal justice that put out massive amounts of information on such topics as environmental pollution, worker health and safety, and tax evasion. Depending on your particular interest within criminal justice, you may be led to a government agency that does not have in its title or even its function operations concerned with criminal justice.

APPROACHES TO RESEARCH IN CRIMINAL JUSTICE

The criminal justice system is often regarded as a process that moves systematically and logically from arrest to sanction. For example, criminal justice textbooks typically begin with a flowchart of the criminal justice system that shows the movement of cases or offenders through the many paths of criminal justice, beginning with the first contact with police and ending with some final outcome. This simplification is useful for beginning students, but you can see from the diverse topics now included in criminal justice that this linear approach to criminal justice can oversimplify and narrow your research agenda.

With the rapid emergence of the Internet and the World Wide Web as information sources, Web surfing has become a popular approach to obtaining information. This method is anything but linear: it depends on following your nose through a sea of information and can take you in many directions. It is, therefore, very important that the researcher have a research agenda or plan of attack in mind.

For the Beginning Researcher

Thinking of the process of conducting criminal justice research as linear can be particularly useful for a beginning researcher. Lutzker and Ferrall's *Criminal Justice Research in Libraries* (1986) and O'Block's *Criminal Justice Research Sources* (1992), two leading resource guides in criminal justice, outline this approach. *Criminal Justice Research in Libraries* offers an explicit 12-stage process for locating and producing criminal justice information on page 17.

1. Choose a topic
2. Draft an outline
3. Master the arrangements and procedures of the library to be used
4. Consider the information flow
5. Establish parameters
6. Maintain a research record
7. Build a bibliography
8. Locate the needed materials
9. Master a citation format
10. Choose and use a method for taking notes
11. Revise the outline
12. Write the paper

Similarly, *Criminal Justice Research Sources* suggests a 14-step plan on pages 1 to 8.

1. Introduction of the problem
2. Statement of the problem
3. Statement of purpose
4. Significance of the study
5. Theoretical framework
6. Hypothesis
7. Definitions and terms
8. Limitations
9. Delimitations
10. Assumptions
11. Review of literature
12. Research design
13. Presentation and analysis of data
14. Construction of the bibliography

Either or a combination of these two approaches should serve the beginning researcher well. However, for the more ambitious or advanced researcher a different approach is necessary since these models have a number of shortcomings.

For the Advanced Researcher

Criminal justice information has been classified according to the linear schemes common to the traditional library. The most significant example of this linearity is the taxonomic Library of Congress subject headings. These headings change very slowly in comparison to the information environment and may often be behind the times. While the organizational or classification system they are based on may make finding material a little easier, it also brings with it considerable restraints:

> A requirement of a classification that is designed for arranging criminal justice material on a shelf is that each class is subordinate to one and only one more general class. The requirement holds also for a classification designed for a manual or classified catalog, since the only possible way of ordering cards in a catalog is linearly. Tree structures represent very simple kinds of orderings, which are both procrustean and unnatural. From the point of view of the structure of knowledge, it is unnatural to require a class to have one and only one superordinate class as it is to require classes to be mutually exclusive or to have clear boundaries. (Svenonius, 1988, 40.)

It could be argued that the process of locating and generating criminal justice information must mirror the complexity of the information environment. That is, not only do criminal justice researchers need to gather theoretical notions from various disciplines, but they must also locate the substance of those notions (e.g., articles, books, databases), which may reside in diverse locations and forms. In order for this search and retrieval process to be comprehensive and sound, researchers may need to abandon the linear model of conducting research.

This traditional linear scheme rests on the assumption that there is a "realm of conceptual order common to both documents and user's intellectual processes which if delineated will provide a useful . . . matching procedure" (Miksa, 1988, 83). That is, it is assumed that research queries naturally correspond to library classification schemes. The focus is on the "matching process . . . [while] the intellectual process behind the query . . . remain[s] . . . on the periphery" (Miksa, 1988, 83). For a match to take place (i.e, for the researcher to locate the exact material needed to answer the query), the user must generate a near flawless query. For example, a researcher may be interested in the relationship between police officers and citizens. How should a researcher begin with such a broad topic? The traditional approach would direct the user to the library's card catalog. A quick perusal of the cards listed under *police* may lead to a series of subheadings, but none of these might be directly applicable to the research query. Arguably, the vagueness of a topic or research query can severely limit the number and quality of materials found. However, equal blame should be placed on the confining nature of subject classification itself, which does not allow for idea expansion nor development.

In contrast to the traditional model, Miksa proposes a model to make the matching process more complete by "promoting idea exploration and clarification rather than simply document retrieval" (1988, p. 84). As we saw in the example above, a criminal justice researcher rarely has a perfectly formulated query. A researcher is most likely to begin with a simple query that evolves and develops a more narrow focus. In the example above, the researcher may have actually wanted to explore the relationship between the race of a police officer and the public deference shown to him or her, the general hypothesis being that the average citizen shows varying degrees of respect toward a police officer based on the officer's race. An interactive, dynamic searching strategy could have helped the researcher create this more refined and specific query in the process of the search. Such a strategy, while similar to the linear models recounted above, is more demanding because it challenges the researcher to construct a more specific formulation of the research problem at the outset.

Changes in the information environment have produced a complicated and evolving body of information. Because of this new liquid environment, linear research models of the past are less adequate for guiding the criminal justice scholar through the multitude of resources now available. The research methods of yesterday were, in large part, determined by the nature of the body of knowledge itself (i.e., linear, classified knowledge led to a linear method of research). The authors propose that the reverse of this is now happening: new research methods are creating the format and structure of knowledge and information. Concern with how people think has resulted in nontraditional information structures. As the sheer volume and diversity of information increases, so do the access points at which researchers can employ their unique strategies.

> In the traditional information environment, the process toward publication and distribution, and the bestowing of authority, was dominated by publishers, universities, learned societies and peer review . . . [with changes in the information environment], we [are led] away from the perception that information and knowledge are relatively fixed and rigid, to an environment where information is mutable and dynamic, and its half-life is shortened. To cope with this new information environment, a new learning strategy has to be adopted; one that sufficiently couples information evaluation skills with comprehensive information retrieval skills. (Bouloukos, et al, 1995, 216–17.)

Research in criminal justice is often an interdisciplinary task that deals with ideas and models of the world from divergent sources. Because of this fact, linear, cyclical, and unidirectional models are less adequate for guiding the advanced modern researcher through the multidimensional topography of criminal justice information. Concurrently, as criminal justice has evolved into an amalgam of various social sciences, natural sciences, and humanities, so has the information environment in which it exists. The continued massive expansion of printed, electronic, and multimedia resources will make the linear approach less and less useful and maybe even impossible.

Since the movement from linearity to a new liquid information space is a complex and evolving one, the bulk of this guide retains a traditional resource format. However, much of this book will include technologically current sources for criminal justice information which tend to pull the researcher away from an unyielding information hierarchy.

REFERENCES

Bouloukos, Adam C., Dennis C. Benamati, and Graeme R. Newman. "Teaching Information Literacy in Criminal Justice: Observations from the University at Albany." *Journal of Criminal Justice Education* 6 (2): 213 (1995).

Lutzker, Marilyn, and Eleanor Ferrall. *Criminal Justice Research in Libraries*. New York: Greenwood Press, 1986.

Miksa, Francis. "Shifting Directions in LIS Classification." Richardson, Robert (ed.), In *Classification Theory in the Computer Age: Conversations Across the Disciplines, 76–88*. Albany, NY: School of Information Science and Policy and the Professional Development Program, Nelson A. Rockefeller College of Public Affairs and Policy, State University of New York at Albany, 1989.

O'Block, Robert. *Criminal Justice Research Sources.* 3d ed. Cincinnati, OH: Anderson, 1992.

Sutherland, Edwin H., and Donald R. Cressey. *Criminology.* Philadelphia: J. B. Lippincott, 1978.

Svenonious, Elaine. *The Conceptual Foundations of Descriptive Cataloging*. San Diego, CA: Academic Press, 1989.

Chapter 2

Locating Authorities and Establishing Professional Connections

A WORD ON AUTHORITIES

For the purposes of this book, an *authority* on criminal justice is an individual—government official, independent researcher, professor, librarian, or professional—or an institution—governmental or nongovernmental agency, academic institution, research organization, or professional association.

Whether personal or institutional, authorities are of two types: performative and cognitive. Performative authority grows out of the legal status of an individual or institution. Congress, representatives to Congress, courts, judges, administrative agencies, and officials

have performative authority. Individual members of institutions have performative authority when acting in their official capacity. Thus, a judge or a court has the authority to decide the outcome of a dispute. Legislators and legislatures have the authority to enact legislation, and chief executives—presidents and governors—have the authority to execute law. Performative authority is bestowed upon an individual by law. Failure to obey performative authority usually invokes some kind of legal sanction.

Cognitive authority is bestowed upon individuals and institutions by their peers because of their knowledge, their understanding of a subject, or their experiences. A college professor has cognitive authority based upon her or his knowledge of a field. A medical doctor has cognitive authority based on the number of successful operations of a particular type he or she has performed. A judge may have performative authority when speaking from the bench but only cognitive authority when speaking about law to a civic group. Cognitive authority is usually bestowed upon an individual by his or her peers, and it is more likely to be questioned and tested than performative authority. Failure to yield to cognitive authority does not result in a legal sanction.

The measure of performative authority is clear, but the measure of cognitive authority is subject to many variables—everything from simple truth to ideological conformity. The decision of how much weight to give to a cognitive authority is often a matter of determining the acceptedness of an authority's work. Such a determination—whether right or wrong—is based on factors such as the authority's *quantity* of publications and speeches, the *quality* of these publications and speeches, the *prestige* of an authority's publisher and audience, and the number of *references* made to the individual's work. Peer groups and publishers serve an important gate-keeping function in academics. Although it is not always the case, and it may not always be fair, they serve as filters through which only the most *reliable* information can seep. Thus, work that is published in the most prestigious periodicals and by the most important presses—sustained and improved over time, and accepted by associations, conferences, academic institutions, and other individual authorities—yields cognitive authority for its creator.

Caveat to Using Authorities

In this chapter we offer you a number of ways to find authorities on criminal justice. But using individuals as sources of information is a sensitive matter. Your quest might lead you to peers, professional colleagues, and faculty members at your own institution. For the most part, that is where you should begin your search. However, problems can arise when you depart from your peer group for information. Such would be the case when an undergraduate student boldly makes a telephone call to a prestigious professor at another university to ask for information that will be used in a short term paper.

It is safe to say that if you are a government official in a policy-making position, a researcher affiliated with an institution, or a graduate student conducting dissertation level research, your peer group is reasonably sophisticated. If you are an undergraduate student, keep a low profile and discuss your research question with a faculty member in your department.

MAKING INDIVIDUAL CONNECTIONS

The traditional method of finding information through printed sources in libraries is an important part of the research process, but the fact is information, and links to information, often come across the collegial *back fence*. That is, we often start the research process with peers and colleagues in our own *backyard*. Think a moment about a chain of events that can lead, often in an unconscious way, to a vast amount of information. You speak to a peer or colleague whose knowledge you trust or who has a particular insight. He or she provides you with a piece of information but also knows someone else with more information. You contact that person, who then becomes a source of information for future research as well as for your current quest. Your new contact indicates that research is being conducted at a particular institute, which you then call. You are referred to a professor who provides you with information and informs you of an upcoming conference on the subject. You decide to attend the conference where you make more connections. In that manner, a single existing personal contact has blossomed into several personal and institutional contacts, thus potentially yielding an enormous amount of information. These informally gathered authorities serve as an enormous source of information that you should not ignore.

Because information found through informal sources such as peers and colleagues takes time to acquire and verify, it is wise to begin your research with informal information gathering. Starting in this way not only provides an important first sounding board, it also allows your contacts to develop and ferment as library research progresses.

There is no tried and true progression you should follow in informal information gathering. Information seekers usually use a berrypicking approach wherein one source leads to another. The progression to the next source, or the next piece of information, is based on such variables as the location, quantity, quality, and veracity of the last. For example, if you have evaluated a piece of information gathered from one source to be good, you are likely to continue on with leads that come from that source. But if the last piece of information was bad, you might go off in another direction.

The simple matter of locating an individual who might provide information is perplexing. However, there are a number of information resources available that can reduce the frustration of finding the next berry.

For instance, if you are attempting to locate an individual whose name you already have, the shortest route is to contact associations of which he or she may be a member. The membership directories of such organizations provide addresses and phone numbers. If your colleague was able to provide you with the e-mail address of a possible information source, you can ask questions and seek advice inexpensively by sending an e-mail over the Internet. You can also gain access to a large number of people with a specific interest to address your research question, if not expertise, through discussion lists and bulletin boards.

Assessing the Authority of Internet Resources

The Internet is a widely acclaimed resource for the dissemination and acquisition of information. The researcher should be aware, however, that information available on the Internet is very much like information posted on a community bulletin board or a telephone pole at a street corner. Anyone can do it, and anyone who is so inclined, will. The problems associated with acquiring information on the Internet are similar to the problems faced with street corner postings. You don't always know its source, nor can you count on its reliability: no publisher or editorial board has judged the information to be true or to be the result of proven research methods. In addition, information is posted and altered without reference to the person or body responsible. Even if you do know the source, you are frequently left with some doubt as to its authority. You may be given the name of the person who posted it, and you may even know his or her e-mail address, but what do you know about his or her *authority*? The authors have provided resources with information that will assist you in establishing the authority of a source in various parts of this book.

For a discussion of the impact of the Internet and electronic information on criminal justice research, please refer to:

Bouloukos, Adam C., Dennis C. Benamati, and Graeme R. Newman. "Teaching Information Literacy in Criminal Justice: Observations from the University at Albany." *Journal of Criminal Justice Education.* 6(2): 213–33 (1995)

Internet Discussion Lists

Discussion lists serve several important functions to the profession and the professional. Finding an au-

thority or information is only one of them. Like a professional newsletter, they keep participants abreast of developments and trends in their disciplines and fields. Subscribing, reading, and participating in a professional discussion is also a way to stay aware of new thinking that shapes the future of the field.

A particular discussion list is usually the responsibility of the list owner, who often has an institutional tie. All discussion lists do not necessarily emanate from an institution, but institutional backing provides the technical expertise and support needed to maintain one. Although some variations do occur, individuals can access a discussion list through the following process: An individual *subscribes* to a particular *list* by sending an e-mail message to the *listserver* requesting a *subscription* (a listserver is a combination of computer software and hardware*)*. The listserver reads the message, enters a subscription for the person who sent the message, and adds their e-mail address to the list. Once an individual subscribes to the list, he or she typically receives a message indicating how to *unsubscribe*, how and where to send a message to the list, how to search the archives of the list, and how to perform other important operations. From this point on, the subscriber receives every message that is sent to the list and may also send messages to the list. To stop receiving and sending messages, the subscriber must unsubscribe.

Once you have subscribed to a list, you can send an e-mail message with your request for information to the list. You can also pose a question or make comments on other messages sent to the list. Keep in mind that whenever you send a message to the list, your request will be distributed to everyone who subscribes, and everyone who subscribes will be able to read what you wrote. The advantage of discussion lists is that people with a keen interest in a particular topic, or with information they are willing to share, will often give useful responses. Discussion lists are, therefore, an excellent way to stay on top of developments in the field of criminal justice. Students looking for a thesis or dissertation topic will find it useful to subscribe and follow the discussion because lists are sometimes the first places that new ideas appear.

When you *post*, or send, a question to a discussion list, also keep in mind that the expert with the appropriate answer may not subscribe to that particular list. By *cross-posting* your request, or sending it to a number of different but related discussion lists, you increase your question's exposure and the chances that you will reach the appropriate expert.

Network etiquette requires you to send responses to a posted question directly to the person who sent it and not to the list. This keeps network traffic down. Be sure *not* to use your e-mail *reply* command when responding to a posted question, especially if you are sending comments about a message intended only for a particular recipient. More than one scholar has been embarrassed by inadvertently sending a reply to an entire list.

Lists can become a forum for heated debate. Some lists are *moderated* by the list owner in order to keep the discussion on point, and sometimes to prevent inappropriate commentary. The list owner takes the responsibility of reading all messages sent to the list. He or she then chooses to forward messages for distribution to the list or not. This is one way a list owner can control the nature of the discussion that occurs on his or her list. *Unmoderated* lists, on the other hand, are not censored in any way. Every message you send to an unmoderated list is automatically forwarded to all the subscribers.

Most lists are also archived. An archive of a discussion list is composed of all the messages that have ever been distributed by the list. A researcher can search through the archives of a list to discover whether or not discussion has occurred on a particular topic of inquiry. These archived messages can then be retrieved and read. Archives are kept for varying periods of time and are accessed in various ways. Your listserver should provide you with instructions on how to retrieve them.

Below you will find a selection of discussion lists related to criminal justice. Our selections are an attempt to give the reader an idea of the variety of criminal justice related topics covered by the lists. Some of those that we have selected represent the most heavily trafficked lists.

ADDICT-L (Prevention of Alcohol, Tobacco & Other Drug Abuse Council). Kent State University. Not moderated. Archived daily and kept for about six months.

To subscribe, send e-mail to:
Listserv@kentvm.kent.edu

Your message should read: SUB ADDICT-L <First name> <Last name>

List owner: ddelmoni@kentvm

The ADDICT-L list was designed with the intent of providing academic and scholarly information exchange regarding addiction. Appropriate discussion includes the presentation of questions, concepts, and theories involved in the study and treatment of addictions. This list is *not* intended as a support group for addicts or recovering ad-

dicts. Subscribers searching for support with recovery issues will not find the discussion on this list helpful.

BLKCRIM (Black Criminologist Discussion List). University of Maryland at College Park. Not moderated. Archived for an unknown length of time.

To subscribe, send e-mail to:
Listserv@umdd.umd.edu

Your message should read: Subscribe BLKCRIM <First name> <Last name>

List owner: Calvin C. Johnson, c-cjohnson@bss2.umd.edu

This list is used by black criminology professors, graduate students, and administrators to transmit information of interest to the group (e.g., publication of journal articles, calls for papers for special journal issues, tenure news, and job openings). Potential subscribers to the BLKCRIM list are asked to complete a short questionnaire that must be approved before a subscriber is added to the list, thus, subscription is limited.

BULLY-L (Bullying and Victimizations in Schools). University of Nijmegen, Department of Developmental Psychology, Netherlands. Not moderated. Archived, period is yet to be determined.

To subscribe, send e-mail to:
LISTSERV@nic.SURFnet.nl

Your message should read: SUBSCRIBE BULLY-L <First name> <Last name>

List owner: Gerbert Haselager, u212230@vm.uci.kun.nl

BULLY-L is an international discussion list whose goal is to exchange information about bullying and victimization in childhood and adolescence, especially in schools. This topic is studied by social researchers in several European countries, Japan, and the United States. These studies usually report numbers of victims in school classes.

CJUST-L (Criminal Justice Discussion List). City University of New York, John Jay College of Criminal Justice, Lloyd Sealy Library. Moderated (messages may be manually edited before they are distributed to remove extraneous text, blank lines, or quoted text). Archived for an undetermined period of time.

To subscribe, send e-mail to:
LISTSERV@CUNYVM.BITNET or
LISTSERV@CUNYVM.CUNY.EDU

Your message should read: SUB CJUST-L <First name> <Last name>

List owner: Alex Rudd, ahrjj@cunyvm.cuny.edu

CJUST-L is an academic discussion list addressing numerous criminal justice issues. CJUST-L subscribers are academics, students, attorneys, police officers, court officials, judges, corrections officials, private security executives, mental health professionals, journalists, military personnel, and others who simply have an interest in the criminal justice system. There are no rules or policies regarding how issues are to be treated on the list, but it is understood that its academic nature affects what is posted. The majority of postings address the criminal justice system in the United States, but some are in regards to the criminal justice systems in Canada, Australia, and the United Kingdom The only topic that is prohibited is the right to keep and bear arms.

DRUGABUS (Drug Abuse Education Information and Research). University of Maryland at Baltimore, School of Pharmacy, Office of Substance Abuse Studies. Not moderated. Archived indefinitely.

To subscribe, send e-mail to:
Listserv@umab.edu

Your message should read: TELL listserv at umab sub drugabus

List owner: Trent Tschirgi, ttschirg@umab

The DRUGABUS list was started to give health professionals involved in drug abuse research a place to share ideas and resources. Some of its subscribers do expert witness consultations for the legal system. Legal and criminal justice professionals are also welcome to post questions to the list.

POLICE-L (Police Discussion List). City University of New York, John Jay College of Criminal Justice, Lloyd Sealy Library. Not moderated. Archived.

To subscribe, send e-mail to:
LISTSERV@CUNYVM.BITNET or
LISTSERV@CUNYVM.CUNY.EDU

Your message should read: SUB POLICE-L <First name> <Last name>

List owner: Alex Rudd,
AHRJJ@CUNYVM.BITNET

The POLICE-L list is restricted to current or former law enforcement officers and federal and state agents, including retired, reserve, and auxiliary officers, and has participants from eight countries in addition to the United States. Most discussion is focused on practical matters related to law enforcement. Criminal justice issues are discussed in the context of, and from the perspective of, law enforcement officers. No topic has been banned on POLICE-L. The list exists because of the recognition of the increasing professionalism of law enforcement in many countries around the world. The hope is that the factual and intellectual exchanges that take place on the list will further this evolution.

The listserver responds to subscription requests with further information and directions. Those requesting a subscription must send the list owner a photocopy of their identification (e.g., shield, badge, identification card) to verify their status as a law enforcement officer. Once this documentation is received, the applicant is added to the list and notified of his or her subscription. List members are encouraged upon joining to subscribe to the CJUST-L list as well.

PSRT-L (Political Science Research Teaching List). Not moderated. Archived for an indefinite period.

To subscribe, send e-mail to:
listserv@missou1.missouri.edu

Your message should read: sub psrt-l <First name> <Last name>

List owner: Gary Klass, gmklass@ilstu.edu

This academic discussion list deals with issues of interest to researchers and teachers in political science. Not intended to serve as a public forum for debate over current issues in politics.

PSYLAW-L (Psychology and Law, International Policy). Sponsored jointly by the America Psychology-Law Society, Division 41 of the American Psychological Association, and the Psychology and Law Division of the International Association for Applied Psychology. Not moderated. Archived from January, 1992.

To subscribe, send e-mail to:
listserv@utepvm.ep.utexas.edu

Your message should read: sub psylaw-l <First name> <Last name>

List owner: Roy S. Malpass, rmalpass@mail.utep.edu

The PSYLAW-L list addresses the interconnections between psychology and law. Its subjects include clinical/forensic practice, research on jury decision making, eyewitness identification, subliminal perceptions, and the ethics of recovered memory testimony.

UNCJIN-L (United Nations Crime and Justice Information Network List). Funded in part by the United States Bureau of Justice Statistics (since 1990). Other supporters are the United Nations Criminal Justice and Crime Prevention Branch in Vienna, the State University of New York at Albany, and the Research Foundation of the State University of New York. Not moderated. Archived.

To subscribe, send e-mail to:
listserv@lserv.un.or.at

Your message should read: SUBSCRIBE UNCJIN-L <First name> <Last name>

For information, contact: Adam Bouloukos, aboulouk@unov.un.or.at

The goal of the United Nations Crime and Justice Information Network (UNCJIN) (see chapter 9 for more information) is to establish a worldwide network to enhance dissemination and the exchange of information concerning criminal justice and crime prevention issues. As part of this goal, the UNCJIN maintains an electronic list, which facilitates information exchange and interlinkages among policy makers, planners, practitioners, scholars, and other experts, as well as United Nations national correspondents and research institutions. It provides gateways for the transfer of knowledge, including research results, between criminal justice documentation centers and libraries around the world in support of the establishment and expansion of computerized national and local criminal justice systems.

Finding Discussion Lists and Bulletin Boards on Your Own

Computerized discussion lists come and go, and frequently the only way to know of a particular list is through professional contacts. Reference librarians who concentrate in criminal justice are an excellent source of information about criminal justice discussion lists. Many subscribe themselves in order to stay on top of the subject, or they hear about them through librarian discussion lists. Several Internet resources are also available with information about discussion lists.

Directory of Electronic Journals, Newsletters, and Academic Discussion Lists. Washington, DC: As-

sociation of Research Libraries, Office of Scientific and Academic Publishing, 1991.

For those who want a directory of discussion lists printed on paper, the Association of Research Libraries has compiled the *Directory of Electronic Journals, Newsletters, and Academic Discussion Lists*. This directory includes Kovacs' listing of discussion groups as well as electronically published and distributed journals and newsletters. It is updated annually and includes a keyword/subject index for items of interest to the scholar. Exhibit 2-1 is the entry for the *Journal of Criminal Justice and Popular Culture*. The directory includes information on how to subscribe to the journals and discussion lists covered. Information on electronic journals includes the kinds of articles accepted and whether the journals are peer reviewed.

Kovacs, Diane. **"E-Mail Discussion Groups."** http://www.nova.edu/Inter-Links/listserv.html. gopher:arl.cni.org:70/11/scomm/edir/edir95 (February 10, 1997)

---

602 Journal of Criminal Justice and Popular Culture The Journal of Criminal Justice and Popular Culture aims to serve the criminal justice/criminological community by publishing critical review essays that take as their subject some variant of popular culture, including, but not limited to, films, documentaries, books, plays, lyrics/music, paintings, photography, and computer programs/video games. In addition, JCJPC also publishes original manuscripts that attend to the intersection of popular culture and criminal justice. Review essays are intended to explore the depiction of criminal justice issues in the various forms of popular culture, providing educators with suggestions for utilizing these mediums as pedagogical tools and others with ideas about how these forms may be gainfully employed in research efforts. Manuscripts may be theoretical or empirical, but they are expected to highlight and focus on the interplay of popular culture and criminal justice in all dimensions of society.

ISSN:	1070-8286
First issue:	05/21/93
Peer rev'd:	yes
Formats:	ASCII, HTML
Distribution:	LISTSERV, www
Frequency:	bi-monthly
URL:	http://www.scj.albany.edu:90/jcjpc/
Subs/Access:	email: listserv@UACSC2.ALBANY.EDU
	message: SUBSCRIBE CJMOVIES <firstname> <lastname>
Back issues:	http://www.scj.albany.edu:90/jcjpc/
	email: listserv@UACSC2.ALBANY.EDU
	message: SUBSCRIBE CJMOVIES <firstname> <lastname>
Contact:	Jack Reed
	University at Albany, State University of New York
	School of Criminal Justice
	Draper Hall # 209
	135 Western Avenue
	Albany, NY 12222
	Phone: 518-442-3935
	Fax: 518-442-5603
	sunycrj@uacsc2.albany.edu
Submissions:	Authors may submit review essays and manuscripts to JCJPC in two ways. First, review essays and manuscripts may be sent electronically to the editors. Submissions sent via regular mail should be stored on IBM formatted disks (3 1/2" or 5 1/4") in ASCII or Wordperfect 5.1 or lower.
Iss Agency:	University at Albany, State University of New York School of Criminal Justice
Subscriptions:	1,006

DIRECTORY OF ELECTRONIC JOURNALS, NEWSLETTERS, AND ACADEMIC DISCUSSION LISTS. WASHINGTON, DC: ASSOCIATION OF RESEARCH LIBRARIES, OFFICE OF SCIENTIFIC AND ACADEMIC PUBLISHING, 1ST ED. (JULY 1991).

EXHIBIT 2-1

Diane K. Kovacs has compiled an authoritative and classified listing of more than 1,700 scholarly discussion lists, which may be downloaded using file transfer or hypertext transfer protocol through a World Wide Web site. The Web site has a classified listing and a way to search by subject. (Try the subject headings law, criminology, and justice.) The Web page also provides the user with information about what a listserver is, how to subscribe and unsubscribe, and how to access archives. There are other sites on the World Wide Web with information about discussion lists, but if you are involved in serious research, you will want to take the extra time needed to look at the Kovacs list.

Louis-Jacques, Lyonette. **"Law Lists."** www. lib.uchicago.edu/~llou/lawlists/info.html (February 10, 1997).

If you are searching for a discussion list on a legal topic, refer to the comprehensive list of law-related groups maintained by Lyonette Louis-Jacques of the University of Chicago. Her Web site gives information on approximately 400 lists and 150 newsgroups. Subscription information is included. *Law Lists* is searchable by keyword at http://www.lib.uchicago.edu/cgi- bin/law-lists.

Motley, Lynne. *Modem USA: Low Cost and Free Online Sources for Information, the Internet, Databases, and Electronic Bulletin Boards via Personal Computer and Modem in 50 States and Washington, D.C.* 2d ed. Takoma Park, MD: Allium Press, 1994.

If you are looking for local bulletin boards to exchange information, look at Lynne Motley's *Modem USA*.

Finding an Individual's E-Mail Address

Contacting a known authority can be problematic. Using one of the biographical directories or electronic mail resources described below can be helpful and enhance your ability to access them. When faculty and researchers are on sabbatical or leave, those who have e-mail often forward their mail or simply access it using the Internet telnet function. Whether your search for an authority is time sensitive or not, e-mail offers a fast and reliable way to contact an individual. It's better than a telephone call because while experts may have a phone, they don't always have voice mail. It's better than a letter because it's faster.

"National Phone Book." http://www. switchboard.com/ (February 10, 1997).

The "National Phone Book" Web site is a free nationwide residential and business telephone directory.

"Yahoo People Search." http://www.yahoo.com/ search/people/ (February 11, 1997).

This site provides you with the address and phone number of an individual if you can indicate the city and state in which he or she resides.

WEIGHING THE AUTHORITY OF SOURCES WITH PRINTED BIOGRAPHICAL INFORMATION

When you go out on the Internet looking for information, remember that just about anyone, whether they know anything about your subject or not, can post information and respond to requests. Of course, your sources might not always come from the Internet; some could be informal referrals from colleagues. Part of the problem with informal referrals is that you might not be sure of a source's authority in the field.

A number of library resources provide information that allows you to weigh the value of an individual's input into your important research problem. Obviously the more you know about your source, the better you can judge his or her authority. You can research an individual's background and education, their place in history if applicable, and, in some instances, you can find a bibliography of their works. The authors have listed a few of the most authoritative biographical works on historical figures as well as dictionaries and directories with information on contemporary figures. Directories can also be helpful if you are looking for addresses and telephone numbers.

Remember that when you are looking into the careers of professionals such as criminologists, sociologists, and legal experts, the most complete biographical information about a person's profession can sometimes be found in nonbiographical sources. Subject-oriented encyclopedias such as *The Encyclopaedia of Crime and Justice* and *The Encyclopedia of the American Constitution* often give a good accounting of the lives of important figures. Depending on the person's stature, general encyclopedias such as the *Encyclopedia Britannica* and *Encyclopedia Americana* can also provide in-depth information. (See chapter 3, page 52, for a more detailed examination of encyclopedias and their use in criminal justice research.) Biographical information on leading figures in government is also available in several directories listed in this chapter.

Indexes to Biographical Information

Library of Congress subject headings: Biography—Bibliography; Biography—20th Century—Indexes—Periodicals

Bio-base. Detroit, MI: Gale Research, 1984–.

> *Bio-base* is an index of approximately 9,000,000 biographical sketches found in more than 275 current and historical biographical dictionaries. Gale Research, an important source in reference publishing, supplements its master cumulations, expected every five years, with annual cumulations. The indexed sources include biographical dictionaries, such as who's who dictionaries, subject encyclopedias, and literary criticism, all of which include biographical information and their own indexes. *Bio-base* does not index periodicals or books of biography of single individuals. For access to information from this type of source, try general periodical indexes and library catalogs, covered elsewhere in this book. (See *Biography Index* below and refer to chapters 4 and 5). *Bio-base* is available online through the commerical database gateway service DIALOG (see page 77 for a general description of this type of service), on CD-ROM, and is the microfiche version of the *Biography and Genealogy Master Index* listed below.

Biography and Genealogy Master Index. 2d ed. Detroit, MI: Gale Research, 1980–.

DIALOG: File 287

> *Biography and Genealogy Master Index* is a consolidated version of Bio-base. See description of Bio-base above.

Biography Index: A Cumulative Index to Biographical Material in Books and Magazines. New York: Wilson, 1947–.

> *Biography Index* is an index to biographical material appearing in periodicals. Selected additional periodicals and current books of individual and collective biography are included. This index is issued quarterly with cumulative annual volumes.

Marquis Who's Who Publications: Index to All Books. Chicago: Marquis, 1974–.

> The Marquis Company has prepared this index to all their publications to assist you in finding biographical information among its many resources described in depth in the following sections. In addition, the 49th edition (1995) of *Who's Who in America* includes helpful indexes that point to individuals by geography and profession, a retiree index, and a necrology—a listing of biographees who have recently died.

Biographical Information on Living Individuals

> Library of Congress subject headings: United States—Biography; United States—Biography—Dictionaries; College teachers—United States—Directories

Marquis Who's Who. . . . Chicago: Marquis.
> *Who's Who in America,* 1899/1900–
> *Who's Who in the East,* 1942–
> *Who's Who in the Midwest,* 1949–
> *Who's Who in the South and Southwest,* 1947–

Who's Who in the West, 1964–
Who's Who in American Law, 1977/78–
Who's Who of American Women, 1970/71–
Who's Who of Emerging Leaders in America, 1990–
Who's Who in the World, 1971/72–

> A favorite source of biographical information is *Marquis's Who's Who* series of dictionaries. These respected biographical sources are updated annually and can be relied upon for information on people from many different walks of life. Some of the resources are general in nature, covering prominent Americans from various regions in the United States, Canada, and Mexico. More specialized titles in the series provide biographical information on prominent members of the legal professions, prominent women, and "emerging leaders." Titles from this series that are most useful in criminal justice research are listed above.
>
> The biographies found in these volumes are brief but usually cover vital information such as birth date, parents' names, spouse and children, education, profession and positions held, civic affiliations, some bibliographical data, publications, and current address and phone number. See exhibit 2-2 for a key to a representative Marquis' biography. Inclusion in Who's Who titles is based on two criteria: position of responsibility and level of achievement attained during a "career of noteworthy activity." Invitations to be included are initiated by Marquis researchers and editors, but as a consumer you should be aware that all biographical information is provided by the biographees. Biographees update their entries at the request of the editors when new editions are issued. Many biographees are moved from one directory to another and may be represented in several at once.

Other sources of biographical information are directories of faculty members of universities. While there is only a small amount of biographical information in these directories, you will find addresses, telephone numbers, and current affiliations. A retrospective search can help you verify a professor's career path.

Faculty Directory of Higher Education. Detroit, MI: Gale Research, 1988–.

> This 12-volume, subject-classified directory is updated annually and provides the names, addresses, and courses taught for more than 600,000 teaching faculty at more than 3,100 U.S. colleges, universities, and community colleges, as well as 220 selected Canadian institutions.

National Faculty Directory. Detroit, MI: Gale Research, 1970–.

> The *National Faculty Directory* gives the names (in alphabetical order), departmental affiliations, and institutional addresses of more than 650,000 teaching faculty at approximately 3,600 U.S. colleges and universities, as well as 240 Canadian institutions using instructional materials primarily in English. This resource is updated and verified continuously through institutional calendars and directories supplied by individual colleges. In order for

[1] **GIBSON, OSCAR JULIUS,** [2] physician, medical educator; [3] b. Syracuse, N.Y., Aug. 31, 1937; [4] s. Paul Oliver and Elizabeth H. (Thrun) G.; [5] m. Judith S. Gonzalez, Apr. 28, 1968; [6] children: Richard Gary, Matthew Cary, Samuel Perry. [7] BA magna cum laude, U. Pa., 1960; MD, Harvard U., 1964. [8] Diplomate Am. Bd. Internal Medicine, Am. Bd. Preventive Medicine. [9] Intern Barnes Hosp., St. Louis, 1964–65, resident, 1965–66; clin. assoc. Nat. Heart Inst., NIH, Bethesda, Md., 1966–68; chief resident medicine U. Okla. Hosps., 1968–69; asst. prof. community health Okla. Med. Ctr., 1969–70, assoc. prof., 1970–74, prof., chmn. dept., 1974–80; dean U. Okla. Coll. Medicine, 1978–82; v.p. med. staff affairs Bapt. Med. Ctr., Oklahoma City, 1982–86, exec. v.p., 1986–88, chmn., 1988; [10] mem. governing bd. Ambulatory Health Care Consortium, Inc., 1979–80; mem. Okla. Bd. Medicolegal Examiners, 1985–. [11] Contrib. articles to profl. jours. [12] Bd. dirs., v.p. Okla. Arthritis Found., 1982–; trustee North Central Mental Health Ctr., 1985–. [13] Served with U.S. Army, 1955–56. [14] Recipient R. T. Chadwick award NIH, 1968; Am. Heart Assn. grantee, 1985–86, 88. [15] Fellow Assn. Tchrs. Preventive Medicine; mem. Am. Fedn. Clin. Research, Assn. Med. Colls., AAAS, AMA, Masons, Shriners, Sigma Xi. [16] Republican. [17] Roman Catholic. [18] Avocations: swimming, weight lifting, travel. [19] Home: 6060 N Ridge Ave Oklahoma City OK 73126 [20] Office: Bapt Med Ctr 1986 Cuba Hwy Oklahoma City OK 73120

KEY

[1]	Name
[2]	Occupation
[3]	Vital statistics
[4]	Parents
[5]	Marriage
[6]	Children
[7]	Education
[8]	Professional certifications
[9]	Career
[10]	Career related
[11]	Writings and creative works
[12]	Civic and political activities
[13]	Military
[14]	Awards and fellowships
[15]	Professional and association memberships, clubs and lodges
[16]	Political affiliation
[17]	Religion
[18]	Avocations
[19]	Home address
[20]	Office address

WHO'S WHO IN AMERICA. CHICAGO: MARQUIS, 1899/1900-.

EXHIBIT 2-2

faculty members to be included, their names must appear in official college publications as "teaching" faculty. Librarians and researchers who have faculty status, but no teaching load, are not included.

Biographical Information on Criminologists

Library of Congress subject headings: Criminologists

Mannheim, Hermann, ed. *Pioneers in Criminology.* 2d ed. Montclair, NJ: Patterson Smith, 1972.

Pioneers in Criminology provides brief biographical accounts of the lives of criminologists from the mid-eighteenth to the mid-twentieth century.

Martin, Randy, Robert J. Mutchnick, and Timothy W. Austin. *Criminological Thought: Pioneers Past and Present.* New York: Macmillan, 1990.

This work provides in-depth biographies of 15 pre-eminent criminologists including Robert Park, Walter Reckless, Robert Merton, Howard Becker, and Richard Quinney.

Information on Individuals Now Deceased

Library of Congress subject headings: United States—Biography—Dictionaries; Great Britain—Biography; Great Britain—Bio-Bibliography

Dictionary of American Biography. New York: Scribner's, 1928–37.

The *Dictionary of American Biography* is one of the most highly regarded biographical dictionaries and should be considered an authoritative source for information on Americans living from the earliest times to its writing in the 1920s and 1930s. It was originally published in 20 volumes with two supplements in 1944 and 1958. A later edition (1943) included information from the two supplements folded into the base set and added supplemental volumes, published from 1944 to 1988, covering the period up to 1980. A comprehensive index covers the base set and the eight supplements.

Smith, Elder. *Dictionary of National Biography.* London: Smith, Elder, 1908–09.

The *Dictionary of National Biography* is probably the most revered source for biographical information. Biographies are generally written by scholars and are considered authoritative. This resource covers all noteworthy inhabitants of Britain, Ireland, and the American colonies up to the 1900s when it was written. Supplements bring coverage up to 1985, the latest of these having been published in 1990.

Who Was Who in America. Chicago: Marquis.

Although it can be considered a complete set, *Who Was Who in America* is composed of two titles. This may be useful information when searching for it in your library catalog. The volume covering the period 1897 to 1942 was published first, then the volume covering 1607 to 1896. This later volume, referred to as the "Historical Volume," was published in 1943. Both these volumes were later revised to add new entries and cover longer periods of time. The works are also periodically referred to as "A component volume of Who's Who in American history," and "A companion biographical reference work to Who's Who in

America." The original work covers notable Americans and others who have made a substantial contribution to the history of the United States. Later volumes, covering the period up to the present, include sketches of individuals whose biographies have been removed from *Who's Who in America* following their deaths.

When All Else Fails

Even after referring to Internet and printed resources, you still may not succeed in locating information about an authority. Directories can miss individuals who may be of benefit to your research. When all else fails, don't forget that phone books are also a likely place to find people. If you at least have an idea of the state and city where they work, you may still have a chance of finding them. Many libraries keep telephone book collections of various sizes, which may include all telephone directories or just those from major metropolitan areas. Collections of telephone books are also available in microform and CD-ROM at many large libraries.

Online services, such as LEXIS-NEXIS, WESTLAW, and CompuServe, also provide access to information about people. Private investigation firms and *skip tracers* are also involved in finding individuals, and many of them exist around the United States. If you're really desperate and are willing to pay to locate someone, you can try these services.

MAKING INSTITUTIONAL CONNECTIONS

In the previous section, we covered some of the sources you can use to identify and locate an individual who can be a source of information. We also included sources that can be useful in assessing the *cognitive* authority, or value, of an individual you have used as a source of information or interpretation. Making institutional connections is just as important as making individual ones. An institution can be a wealth of information because of its individual members and employees as well as its activities, what we will call the *collective consciousness* of an organization. As a source of information, the collective consciousness of an organization resides in the work of the organization as well as in its mission, charge, history, and publications that the organization has collected or produced. These publications include such sources as conference papers, committee minutes, memoirs of officers (past and present), annual reports, library collections, archives, and various end-products. The following section lists resources you can use to connect to the institutional and collective knowledge of

universities, research organizations, associations, libraries, governments, and conferences around North America and the world.

Colleges and Universities

> Library of Congress subject headings: Universities and colleges—United States—Graduate work—Directories; Universities and colleges—*Geog.*—Directories; Universities and colleges—Directories

Educational institutions have always been considered a source of authoritative information. Simply turn on the television to a news program, a news magazine, or a serious talk show and chances are you will find an authority drawn from the faculty of an institution of higher learning. As already mentioned, as individuals, these college and university faculty members are authorities you do not want to overlook, but several of them together constitute an incredible quantity of knowledge. A group of educated colleagues, either as a faculty or as members of a scholarly society, represent a whole that is greater than the sum of its parts and as a collective, should be sought out, if only for the diversity of its views.

Because our emphasis in this work is on research, the authors have chosen to direct you to graduate faculties. Although graduate faculties are not necessarily more authoritative than undergraduate faculties, in fact there is a great deal of cross-over, they are more likely to be involved in research. Undergraduate faculties are more involved in teaching. As with all authorities, remember to be discrete and only contact them if you are involved in serious or dissertation level research.

Gourman Report: A Rating of Graduate and Professional Programs in American and International Universities. Los Angeles: National Education Standards, 1980–.

> For those who follow the ranking of programs, this guide attempts to rank graduate programs in various disciplines. The 6th edition includes a listing of criminal justice programs in the United States, although it doesn't attempt to order them except alphabetically.

Peterson's Guide to . . . Princeton, NJ: Peterson's ONLINE: "Peterson's Education Center." http://www.petersons.com (May 27, 1997).

> *Peterson's Guides* are perhaps the most familiar directories of academic institutions. The volumes covering graduate programs are updated annually and describe accredited academic programs in the United States. Programs in Canada, Mexico, Europe, and Africa are included if they are accredited by agencies from the United States. Information about these programs is presented first in capsu-

lated descriptions, grouped by discipline, which include the name, address, and telephone number of the host institution, dean or department head, entrance requirements, faculty numbers, and faculty research interests. Full descriptions, referenced at the capsulated descriptions, include program of study and other information relevant to admissions. Most helpful to the researcher trying to make a contact is the section on research facilities, which gives the names of research institutions affiliated with the program, college, or university. (See exhibit 2-3 for a sample page.) The Web site indicated above provides links to information about programs at individual institutions. Although it is not complete for all institutions, it mirrors information found in the printed publications.

Like Marquis' *Who's Who*, the source of the information for Peterson's publications is the colleges and universities themselves. You may want to view the entries you find in the guides as marketing tools or as a way for an institution to look attractive to the reading public. Although they are couched in some nicely crafted prose, you can, nevertheless, find accurate directory-type information about the programs offered.

If you need to locate a faculty outside the United States, try the *International Handbook of Universities* or *World List of Universities.*

International Association of Universities. *International Handbook of Universities.* 13th ed. Paris: International Association of Universities; New York: Stockton Press, 1993–.

This biennial publication lists alphabetically by country over 4,000 institutions in 169 countries. Institutions listed are degree-granting institutions at the university level, selected by the "appropriate higher education authorities in the countries concerned." Entries include the institution's name, faculty, colleges, departments, schools, and institutes, as well as brief descriptions of the history, structure, and cooperative agreements with institutions in other countries.

International Association of Universities. *World List of Universities.* 11th ed. Paris: International Association of Universities, 1973/74–.

A complementary volume to the *International Handbook of Universities,* the *World List of Universities* includes approximately 9,000 institutions in 158 countries and emphasizes schools and colleges within universities. Universities and "other institutions of higher education" are listed separately.

Research Centers and Institutions

Library of Congress subject headings: Research—*Geog.*—Directories; Learned institutions and societies—*Geog.*—Directories; Research institutes—Directories; Research institutes—*Geog.*—Directories; Government agencies—*Geog.*—Directories

Since World War II, the U.S. government has spent a great deal of money funding research at universities and colleges. A large amount of new knowledge has accumulated over the years as a result of this expenditure, and a number of foundations and institutions have grown from this university research. Like faculties at educational institutions, staff members at a research center are excellent sources of information and are often at the forefront of new developments in a discipline.

Although Peterson's directories can point a researcher toward host universities, the information they contain about these organizations is limited, and only passing mention is made of subordinate research centers. In addition, important research is carried on at independent, nonprofit, and government research centers.

For direct links to criminal justice research centers, try the resources listed below.

International Research Centers Directory. Detroit, MI: Gale Research, 1981–.

This work is subtitled a world guide to government, university, independent nonprofit, and commercial research and development centers, institutes, laboratories, bureaus, test facilities, experiment stations, and data collection and analysis centers, as well as foundations, councils, and other organizations which support research. It is arranged geographically with a keyword subject index.

Research Centers Directory. Detroit, MI: Gale Research, 1965–.

The various directories of research centers published by Gale Research are an important source in identifying and locating research organizations. The *Research Centers Directory* lists more than 13,400 university-related and nonprofit organizations carrying on continued research. Research is broadly defined by the directory. Centers are listed and described under 17 subject areas, including government and public affairs, behavioral and social sciences, and regional and area studies. Within these subjects, entries are arranged alphabetically by sponsoring university (if applicable) and then by center name. Entries include center names, addresses, telephone numbers, e-mail addresses, budgets, research activities, and publications.

Four indexes provide excellent access to the institutions listed: a master index includes all research centers, organizations, and parent institutions in one alphabetical listing; a personal name index lists the directors of organizations; a geographic index lists entries by location; and a subject index uses 5,000 terms and cross references. The master index also includes former names and defunct and inactive centers. Although it is published irregularly, the *Research Centers Directory* is kept up to date between issues by *New Research Centers,* first published, also by Gale Research, in 1965. Also available online through DIALOG file 115. (See exhibit 2-4 for sample entries.

UNIVERSITY AT ALBANY,
STATE UNIVERSITY OF NEW YORK

Nelson A. Rockefeller College of Public Affairs and Policy

Programs of Study

The schools that form Rockefeller College are the Graduate School of Public Affairs, the School of Criminal Justice, the School of Information Science and Policy, and the School of Social Welfare. All four offer opportunities for public affairs education, policy research, internships, and field placements. These graduate programs prepare women and men for careers as public managers, researchers, political leaders, policy analysts, educators, information specialists, and social welfare practitioners.

Rockefeller College offers doctoral degree programs in criminal justice, political science, public administration, information science, and social welfare. The doctoral programs require 60 graduate course credits plus a dissertation (except social welfare, which requires a master's degree plus 36 credits and a dissertation). Master's degree programs are offered in each of these fields and in library science and public affairs and policy. Master's programs require between 30 and 48 graduate course credits. The University requires two consecutive semesters of full-time study for all doctoral programs and the M.S.W. program.

The internship program is an important component of many of the programs at Rockefeller College. Internships provide graduate students with part-time positions, some with salary, in the public sector. The field practicum is an integral part of the programs in social welfare, giving students the opportunity to apply, integrate, and develop knowledge, skills, and attitudes while in practice.

Research Facilities

Research opportunities are available through a number of research centers and institutes. University research centers at the Rockefeller College include the Center for Policy Research, the Center for Women in Government, the Hindelang Criminal Justice Research Center, and the Ringel Institute of Gerontology. Rockefeller College also supports the Center for Legislative Development, the Institute for Traffic Safety Management and Research, the Center for Social Work Practice Research, the Film and Television Documentation Center, and the Center for Human Services Research. The College is also closely affiliated with the Nelson A. Rockefeller Institute of Government, a nationally recognized center for the study of state and local government.

The Governor Thomas E. Dewey Library for Public Affairs and Policy is located on the downtown campus and supports the curricula and research needs of the schools within Rockefeller College. The University's main library houses a large collection of books and periodicals and is a selective depository for U.S. government publications and documents of local, state, foreign, and international governmental agencies.

Financial Aid

The College offers fellowship and assistantship awards ranging from $7000 to $14,000 plus tuition scholarship. Several University-wide scholarships are also available, as are specialized scholarships and awards in each of the schools of Rockefeller College. Financial assistance may also be provided through faculty research projects or training programs. Students must apply for financial assistance when applying for admission.

Additional financial aid is available through state and federal programs, including the New York State Tuition Assistance Program (TAP), the Federal Perkins Loan and Federal Work-Study programs, and the New York Higher Education Assistance Corporation Loans (GSL, ALAS).

Cost of Study

In 1995–96, New York State resident tuition is $2550 per semester ($213 per credit for fewer than 12 credits). Out-of-state resident tuition is $4208 per semester (or $351 per credit for fewer than 12 credits). The University fee for full-time students is $12.50 per semester, and the University Graduate Student Organization fee is $15 per semester.

Living and Housing Costs

On-campus graduate housing in Freedom Quad, which has an apartment-like setting, ranges from $1649 to $2177 per semester based on the number of bedrooms in the apartment. Off-campus housing is available, and the cost varies. The cost of an on-campus cafeteria plan ranges from $163 per semester (lunches only) to $669 per semester (20 meals per week). Books and supplies cost approximately $350 per semester.

Student Group

Approximately 85 percent of the students at Rockefeller College are New York State residents. Many students enroll directly from undergraduate school, while others are studying for professional advancement. Over 20 percent of the 1,350 graduate students at Rockefeller College are doctoral students.

Location

Located in the state capital, Rockefeller College is near the legislature, the courts, and state agency headquarters. Albany has a civic center and the Empire State Plaza, which includes performing arts and convention facilities and the New York State Museum and State Library. Albany is 150 miles from New York City and 165 miles from Boston. It is near the Berkshires, the Catskills, and the Adirondacks—areas noted for their recreational and cultural opportunities.

The University and The College

The Rockefeller College is part of the University at Albany of the State University of New York. The University at Albany, founded in 1844, is the oldest state-chartered public institution of higher education in New York. The main campus of the University at Albany, which opened in 1966, occupies a 400-acre site at the western edge of Albany. Regular bus service is provided between the two campuses.

The University at Albany enrolls 17,000 students, over 30 percent of whom are graduate students. The University has eight degree-granting schools and colleges and offers 33 doctoral degree programs and 59 master's degree programs.

Applying

Applicants must hold a bachelor's degree from a recognized college or university. Applications must be made on the official application form of Rockefeller College. Specific admission requirements and application deadlines are included in application packets for each program. Generally, applications are due by March 1 for fall enrollment (except social welfare, which is February 15) and November 1 for spring enrollment (when permitted). International students must apply through the Office of Graduate Admissions, Administration Building, Room 112, 1400 Washington Avenue (telephone: 518-442-3980).

Correspondence and Information

Graduate Admissions Office
Nelson A. Rockefeller College of Public Affairs and Policy
The University at Albany
Draper Hall, Room 112
135 Western Avenue
Albany, New York 12222
Telephone: 518-442-5201

Peterson's Guide to Graduate Programs in the Humanities, Arts, and Social Sciences 1996

PETERSON'S GUIDE TO GRADUATE PROGRAMS . . . . PRINCETON, NJ : PETERSON'S GUIDES,

EXHIBIT 2-3

★10664★
McMaster University - Program for Quantitative Studies in Economics and Population
Faculty of Social Sci.   **Phone:** (905)525-9140
KTH-426   **Fax:** (905)521-8232
1280 Main St. W
Hamilton, ON, Canada L8S 4M4
Frank T. Denton, Dir.
E-mail: kalikag@mcmail.cis.mcmaster.ca
Founded: 1981. **Description:** Integral unit of Faculty of Social Sciences at McMaster University. **Staff:** 40 Faculty. **Financial Support:** Parent institution. **Research:** Broad-based studies in quantitative economics, demography, and related social science areas. **Publications:** QSEP Research Reports (30/year).

★10665★
Media Action Research Center
PO Box 320   **Phone:** (615)742-5451
Nashville, TN 37202-0320   **Fax:** (615)742-5404
Wilford Bane, Jr., Contact
Founded: 1974. **Description:** Independent, nonprofit, research and educational organization. **Financial Support:** Foundations, individual gifts. **Research:** Impact of television on viewers, including studies on sexual behavior in television programs, stereotyping of women and minorities, effects of prosocial viewing on children, Saturday morning children's programs, content messages in Saturday morning commercials, music and music videos, the influence of media on incidence of rape, and biblical values and television. **Publications:** Media and Values Magazine (quarterly). **Educational Activities:** Workshops.

★10666★
Medical University of South Carolina - Crime Victims Research and Treatment Center (CVC)
Dept. of Psychiatry & Behavioral Sci.   **Phone:** (803)792-2945
171 Ashley Ave.   **Fax:** (803)792-3388
Charleston, SC 29425-0742
Dr. Dean Kilpatrick, Dir.
E-mail: craftv@musc.edu
Home Page: http://www.musc.edu/cvc/
Founded: 1977. **Description:** Integral unit of Department of Psychiatry and Behavioral Sciences, Medical University of South Carolina. **Financial Support:** Industry, U.S. government, state government. **Research:** Psychological effects of criminal victimization, including effects of rape on married, cohabitating, and dating relationships; psychological impact of the criminal justice system on victims; characteristics of incest victims and their families; characteristics of criminal offenders; and trauma effects due to auto, industrial, or fire-related incidents, as well as natural disasters and other traumatic events. **Educational Activities:** Workshops and education programs for professionals and the public; Specialized training for clinical psychology interns, social work interns, and postdoctoral fellows on treatment of victimization-related problems. **Services:** Consults with attorneys and provides testimony in criminal and civil court cases involving rape, child molestation, and battering of women; Provides evaluation and treatment services for victims and their families; Works with solicitors' offices and police departments to prepare victims and their families for trial witnesses; Provides consultation to public policy makers on victimization-related topics.

★10667★
Meharry Medical College - I Have a Future Program
1005 D.B. Todd Blvd.   **Phone:** (615)327-6100
Campus Box A-90   **Fax:** (615)327-6992
Nashville, TN 37208
Lorraine W. Greene, Dir.
E-mail: fosterh63@ccvax.mmc.edu
Description: Research and community service organization of the Department of Obstetrics and Gynecology at Meharry Medical College, operating under an advisory committee. **Financial Support:** Foundations, industry, state government, individual gifts. **Research:** Develops models to prevent teen pregnancy, substance abuse, homicide and violence, and unemployment. Conducts annual assessments of youth between the ages of 10- and 17-years old to measure knowledge, attitudes, and behaviors related to sexuality, contraception, pregnancy, self-concept, delinquency activity, social support, family environment, and psychosocial maturity. **Educational Activities:** Parent Empowerment Program, a community-based family alternative program for

training in effective communication, group leadership, crisis intervention, and parent effectiveness skills. **Services:** Technical assistance in program planning and evaluation strategies; Operates clinics in housing projects to provide physical examinations, lifestyle assessments, pregnancy tests, screening for sexually transmitted diseases, and distribution of contraceptives.

★10668★
Memorial University of Newfoundland - Gerontology Centre
St. John's, NF, Canada A1B 3X9   **Phone:** (709)737-4381
Dr. Albert Kozma, Dir.   **Fax:** (709)737-4510
Founded: 1984. **Description:** Research, education, and community service unit of Department of Psychology at Memorial University of Newfoundland. **Research Budget:** C$30,000. **Staff:** 25 Faculty, 2 Administrative, 20 Other. **Financial Support:** Parent institution, businesses, individual gifts, fees. **Research:** Gerontology, focusing on quality of life studies, including determinants of subjective well-being in the elderly, loneliness, pursuits of the creative elderly, and adjustment after bereavement; prevention of later life illness, including longitudinal investigation of health behavior consequences; determinants and treatment of later life illness, including hypertension, immune system function, Alzheimer's disease and cognitive disorders, and medication use; aging and behavior change, including learning and memory, hearing loss, and cognitive and physical performance; and the social context of aging, including abuse and victimization of the elderly, detection of dysfunction by physicians, social networks, and resource requirements of the ill. **Educational Activities:** Colloquium and Symposium series; Educational and Community Services; Conferences, open to the public. **Services:** Contract research and expert assistance to government agencies.

★10669★
Memorial University of Newfoundland - Institute for Folklore Studies in Britain and Canada
Dept. of Folklore   **Phone:** (709)737-8402
St. John's, NF, Canada A1C 5S7   **Fax:** (709)737-4569
Dr. Paul Smith, Codir.
E-mail: ifsbac@kean.ucs.mun.ca
Description: Joint program of the Department of Folklore at Memorial University of Newfoundland and the Centre for English Cultural Tradition and Language at the University of Sheffield, Sheffield, England. **Research:** Folklore in Britain in Canada, including interdisciplinary studies in the fields of oral history, linguistics, anthropology, sociology, literature, and Canadian studies. **Educational Activities:** Courses and summer school in England, focusing on folklore aspects of the British Isles.

★10670★
Mental Research Institute
555 Middlefield Rd.   **Phone:** (415)321-3055
Palo Alto, CA 94301   **Fax:** (415)321-3785
Dianne Holzel, Off.Mgr.
Founded: 1959. **Description:** Independent, nonprofit, research, training, and clinical services organization. **Staff:** 5 Research, 20 Support, 3 Administrative. **Financial Support:** Foundations, U.S. government. **Research:** Interaction in and between families and other human behavior social systems, including multidisciplinary studies of social processes in families and larger social groups; action and interface between families and other groups or community institutions; operations of complex social systems and communication in industry and governmental systems; formal and informal education; juvenile delinquency; drug abuse; and methods for measuring differences in family behavior patterns. Provides training programs for workers in the mental health field and for persons interested in family systems and communication. **Educational Activities:** Workshops on family communication, therapy and community relations; Symposium (annually), during the summer at Stanford University. **Library Holdings:** 1,500 Volumes. **Subjects:** Social sciences.

★10671★
Mexican-American Cultural Center
3019 W. French Pl.   **Phone:** (210)732-2156
PO Box 28185   **Fax:** (210)732-9072
San Antonio, TX 78228
Sister Maria Elena Gonzalez, Contact
Founded: 1972. **Description:** Independent, nonprofit organization. **Financial Support:** Endowment income, tuition. **Also Known As:**

EXHIBIT 2-4

Note the entry for the Medical University of South Carolina's Crime Victims Research and Treatment Center Web site).

Research Services Directory. Detroit, MI: Gale Research, 1981–.

This is a directory of private sector research services available in the U.S. on a contract or fee basis. It includes firms such as information brokers and forensic investigators and is indexed by subject, firm name, contact person or chief executive, and city or state.

Santoro, Carla Masotti, ed. *World Directory of Criminological Institutes.* 6th ed. Rome: United Nations Interregional Crime and Justice Institute, 1995.

The *World Directory of Criminological Institutes* is a directory of research institutions with addresses, fax numbers, telephone numbers, and personnel listings. Summaries of projects, types of activities, and library information are also published here.

Research is not the sole purview of private and university research organizations; studies of issues affecting the U.S. are carried out by government organizations as well. However, government organizations that carry on research are often involved in administrative functions that make identifying their research arms difficult. While access to basic information about government institutions such as the National Institutes of Health and the National Institute of Justice is available through a number of government-published resources (such as the *U.S. Government Manual*), effective access by research subject is not. The following privately published resource does provide subject area access through its index.

Government Research Directory. 3d ed. Detroit, MI: Gale Research, 1985–.

Gale Research publishes this directory of approximately 3,900 U.S. and Canadian government-funded research centers. Entries include organization name, parent organization, address, telephone number, director, and a brief description of research activities and publications. (See exhibit 2-5.) Entries are arranged by U.S. agency, with a separate section on Canadian government agencies. This work provides a master index of research units and parent agencies arranged alphabetically, a subject index with 2,000 terms and cross-references, and a geographic index. Also available online in DIALOG, file 115.

Associations, Organizations, and Foundations

Library of Congress subject headings: Associations, institutions, etc.—Directories; International agencies—Directories; Associations, institutions, etc.—*Geog.*—Directories; Corporations, Nonprofit—*Geog.*—Directories; Societies—*Geog.*—Directories; Organizations—Directories; Societies—Directories; Criminal justice, administration of—*Geog.*—Directories

In addition to gathering at academic institutions, experts organize into associations intended for the advancement of their disciplines. Associations such as the International Association of Chiefs of Police, the American Society of Criminology, and the Academy of Criminal Justice Sciences are familiar to those who are involved in the field. An often-expressed goal of these organizations is the sharing of information and knowledge. Professionals, faculty, and researchers often attend association conferences, present papers, and read association journals, newsletters, and annual reports. As mentioned, attending conferences is a reliable way to identify and meet experts in an area of research and to learn some of its substance. Although you may have to pay a registration fee, contact with attendees and with the subjects discussed is an important part of professional life. Attending a traditional cocktail party may also be a good way to meet some of the more prominent members of an association, as well as a casual way to get in your research questions without being too obvious.

Perhaps the fastest way to find information on individuals within a profession is to contact directly organizations they may belong to and request a membership directory, although they may only release the directory to dues-paying members. Nearly every organization has a membership directory that can be useful in identifying and locating an authority, and through them, you will be able to get addresses and phone numbers. Other organizational publications, especially conference programs and special reports, can also help you identify authorities in the field. Another indication of cognitive authority is offices held within scholarly societies. If a body of people have elected a member to an office that represents them all, you have some indication that the officer is held in esteem by his or her colleagues. Below we have listed some criminal-justice related organizations that you may contact directly, a selection of their publications, and the name of an organization officer.

Academy of Criminal Justice Sciences (ACJS). Northern Kentucky University, 402 Nunn Hall, Highland Heights, KY 41099-5998. Founded in 1963; 2,400 members; $225,000 budget.
Telephone: 606-572-5634
Fax: 606-572-6665

Publications: *ACJS Employment Bulletin* (eight-per-year newsletter), *ACJS Today* (quarterly newsletter), *Journal of Criminal Justice Education* (semiannual journal), *Jus-*

★3039★
Department of Justice
U.S. Parole Commission
Information Systems
5550 Friendship Blvd.   Phone: (301)492-5980
Chevy Chase, MD 20815   Fax: (301)492-6694
Sheldon Adelberg, Director

Organizational Notes: *Founded:* 1972. *Former Names:* Research and Program Development Unit. *Staff:* 5.

Research Activities and Fields: Unit conducts a program of research and development on parole/sentencing and correctional research.

Publications and Services: Research results are published as research reports and journal articles.

★3040★
National Institute of Justice
Office of Crime Prevention and Criminal Justice
  Research
Crime Prevention and Enforcement Division
633 Indiana Ave., N.W., Rm. 860   Phone: (202)724-2949
Washington, DC 20531   Fax: (202)724-6394
Dr. Fred Heinzelmann, Director

Organizational Notes: *Staff:* 4 research professionals and 1 other.

Research Activities and Fields: Supports and conducts research in program areas relating to public safety and security, victims of crime, and white collar and organized crime, focusing on reducing crime and fear through the coordination of crime prevention efforts involving the police, the community and the private sector, research and evaluation to assist victims of crime, and the prevention and control of specific crimes including white collar and organized crime.

Publications and Services: Research results are published in primary journals, as research reports and proceedings, and in Research in Brief and NIJ Reports.

Drug Enforcement Administration

★3041★
Mid-Atlantic Laboratory
460 New York Ave., N.W.   Phone: (202)275-6478
Washington, DC 20532
Paul DeZan, Director

Organizational Notes: One of seven field laboratories of the Office of Forensic Sciences of the Drug Enforcement Administration.

Research Activities and Fields: Drug enforcement. Seeks to determine sources of the major drugs that are abused, such as heroin. Develops analytical procedures for new substances, including procedures for their characterization. Evaluates state of the art instrumentation. Provides technical and scientific assistance to

GOVERNMENT RESEARCH DIRECTORY. DETROIT, MI: GALE RESEARCH, 3D ED. (1985)-

EXHIBIT 2-5

tice *Quarterly* (quarterly journal), *Membership Directory* (annual directory)

American Association for Correctional Psychology (AACP). West Virginia Graduate College, P.O. Box 1003, Institute, WV 25112. Founded in 1953; 400 members.
Telephone: 304-766-1929
  Publications: *The Correctional Psychologist* (quarterly newsletter), *Criminal Justice and Behavior* (quarterly journal)

American Bar Association, Section of Criminal Justice. 1800 M Street NW, 2d Floor, S. Lobby, Washington, DC 20036. Founded in 1921; 9,700 members; 12 staff.
Telephone: 202-331-2260
Fax: 202-331-2220
Director: Laurie Robinson
  Publications: *A Practitioners Guide to the Anti Drug Abuse Act of 1988* (monograph), *ABA Criminal Justice Standards* (monograph), *ABA Policy on AIDS and the Criminal Justice System* (monograph), *Capital Case Sentencing: How to Protect Your Client* (monograph), *Criminal Justice* (quarterly periodical)

American Correctional Association (ACA). 4380 Forbes Blvd., Lanham, MD 20706-4322 Founded in 1870; 25,000 members; 109 staff.
Telephone: 301-918-1700
Toll-free: 800-222-5646
Fax: 301-918-1900
  Publications: *Corrections Today* (bimonthly journal), *On the Line* (five-per-year newsletter), *Directory of Juvenile and Adult Institutions* (annual directory), *National Jail & Adult Detention Directory* (semiannual directory), *Probation and Parole Directory* (semiannual directory), *National Juvenile Detention Directory* (semiannual directory)

American Psychological Association (APA). 750 1st Street NE, Washington, DC 20002-4242. Founded in 1892; 118,000 members; $531,000 budget.
Telephone: 202-336-5500
  Publications: *Psychological Abstracts*, *PsycLit* (online and CD-ROM version of *Psychological Abstracts*), *APA Membership Register* (periodic), membership directory, *APA Monitor* (journal)

American Society of Criminology (ASC). (Formerly: Society for the Advancement of Criminology [1956].) 1314 Kinnear Road, Suite 212, Columbus, OH 43212. Founded in 1941; 2,500 members; $350,000 budget.
Telephone: 614-292-9207
Fax: 614-292-6767
  Publications: *American Society of Criminology* (annual membership directory), *The Criminologist* (bimonthly

newsletter), *Criminology: An Interdisciplinary Journal* (quarterly journal)

American Sociological Association (ASA). (Formerly the American Sociological Society.) 1722 N Street NW, Washington, DC 20036. Founded in 1905; 12,300 members; $2,000,000 budget.

Telephone: 202-833-3410

Publications: *American Sociological Association—Annual Meeting Proceedings, American Sociological Association—Directory of Departments* (semiannual directory), *American Sociological Association—Directory of Members* (biannual membership directory), *American Sociological Review* (journal)

National Criminal Justice Association (NCJA). (Formerly National Conference of State Criminal Justice Planning Administrators [1980].) 444 N Capital Street NW, Suite 618, Washington, DC 20001. Founded in 1971; 1,100 members; 8 staff, $900,000 budget.

Telephone: 204-347-4900

Fax: 202-508-3859

Publications: *Justice Research* (bimonthly newsletter), *Juvenile Justice* (three-per-year newsletter), newsletter (title varies, monthly)

Police Foundation (PF). 1001 22nd Street NW, Suite. 200, Washington, DC 20037. Founded in 1970; nonmembership.

Telephone: 202-833-1460

Fax: 202-659-9149

Publications: Research Reports

World Criminal Justice Library Network (WCJLN). Criminal Justice/NCCD Library, Rutgers University, 15 Washington Street, 4th floor, Newark, NJ 07102. Founded in 1991; 61 member institutions.

Telephone: 973-353-5522

Fax: 973-353-1275

Attention: Phyllis Schultze,
    pschultz@andromeda.rutgers.edu

World Wide Web: http://info.rutgers.edu/newark/ WCJLEN.html

Publications: Directory of Member Institutions

While membership directories of organizations do not usually specify who is an *authority,* many organizations are divided into special interest groups or round tables by specialization, and lists of the members of these subunits can help narrow your search for an expert. Experts and interested individuals also dedicate time and effort into changing legislation and policy, and they often form independent interest groups. These independent interest groups are useful sources of information if your purpose is to find differing viewpoints on a topic. When seeking out the diverse ideas of these groups on criminal justice topics, the following directory can be useful.

Hallett, Michael A., and Dennis J. Palumbo. *U.S. Criminal Justice Interest Groups: Institutional Profiles.* Westport, CT: Greenwood Press, 1993.

U.S. *Criminal Justice Interest Groups* lists all the major interest groups in the three areas of criminal justice: law enforcement, courts, and corrections. In identifying interest groups, the authors include those attempting to pressure the government to adopt policies as well as those attempting to raise consciousness about criminal justice issues, which have been ignored in the past. Entries include the name of the organization, address, organizational history, mission statement, key policy activity or concerns, and additional sources of information. Other useful features include a statistical summary of survey results and a directory of the groups' regular publications.

As already asserted, the Internet has become a valuable source of information, including information about organizations that can add substance to your research. The information available on the Internet varies from organization to organization, but many organizations have developed their own gopher and World Wide Web sites. Access to these sites can be achieved through one of the many Web search engines or by referring to the site below.

University of Waterloo, Canada. **"Scholarly Societies Project."** http://www.lib.uwaterloo.ca/society/ overview.html (February 6, 1997).

The Scholarly Societies Project of the University of Waterloo, Canada, has attempted to keep track of the sites created by associations and organizations and has created a Web site of the same name to manage these sources of information. Their Web site provides subject access as well as a simple listing of nearly 600 sites around the world.

While you may already be familiar with the names of criminology and criminal justice organizations, finding their addresses is another matter. You may also want to contact an organization related to a particular subject, for example an organization that deals with forensics. In such cases, a directory of associations can help locate such organizations.

Encyclopedia of Associations. Detroit, MI: Gale Research, 1961–.

The *Encyclopedia of Associations* is a "comprehensive source of detailed information concerning more than 22,000 nonprofit American membership organizations of national scope." It includes eight categories of associations: national associations, nonprofit membership associations, international associations that have a direct link between the United States and another country or region, local and regional associations, nonmembership organizations if they provide information to the public, for-profit organizations if their names suggest that they are nonprofit organizations, informal organizations, defunct organizations, and untraceable associations that have no known address as of the publishing date of that particular edition. Entries are organized into broad subject headings, the most useful of which to criminal justice research is Legal, Governmental, Public Administration, and Military Organizations. In addition to addresses, you will find information about the availability of scholarships, libraries, and publications.

A keyword index is available, which also provides access to associations listed in related Gale Research publications. Also available on disk, magnetic tape in a fielded format, CD-ROM, and online through DIALOG, file 114.

Encyclopedia of Associations. Regional, State and Local Associations. Detroit, MI: Gale Research, 1988/89–.

Encyclopedia of Associations. International Organizations. Detroit, MI: Gale Research, 1989–.

For individuals seeking information about associations that are not national in scope, Gale Research has compiled these two complementary publications.

One type of organization that is particularly useful in completing criminal justice research is intergovernmental organizations, which provide a wealth of law, policy, and information. While most are covered in the *Encyclopedia of Associations*, compiling a list of them can be difficult. For more access to intergovernmental agencies and organizations, please refer to the section State Agencies, Courts Officials, and Employees.

World Guide to Scientific Associations and Learned Societies. 6th ed. Munchen and Paris: K.G. Saur, 1994–.

The *World Guide to Scientific Associations and Learned Societies* contains information on approximately 17,200 associations and societies in the fields of science, culture, and technology arranged alphabetically by country, state, and region, including name, address, phone number, telex and fax, year founded, number of members, officers, areas of activity, and periodical publications. It has a subject index and publications index as well as a German-English concordance to areas of specialization. The depth of information provided in the *World Guide* can be compared with that of the *Yearbook of International Organizations*. (See exhibit 2-6 for a sample entry.)

Yearbook of International Organizations. Brussels: Union of International Associations, 1948–.

The *Yearbook of International Organizations* is a three-volume collection of international organizations in a variety of fields. Volume 1 contains descriptions and cross-references, Volume 2 lists a country directory of secretariats and memberships, and Volume 3 contains the subject directory and index. Association names are given in English and in the official language of the organization.

Like the *Encyclopedia of Associations*, the *Yearbook of International Organizations* provides fairly detailed information.

Conferences, Conventions, and Congresses

Library of Congress subject headings: Congresses and conventions—Directories; International cooperation—Directories; Social sciences—Congresses—Directories; search also under name of conference and name of sponsoring organization or institution

Like an organization, conferences, conventions, symposia, seminars, and congresses are a source of information that should not be overlooked. These gatherings may take place on a regular basis, such as the annual meeting of a learned society; they may be unique gatherings of individuals to discuss a specific topic for the purpose of suggesting policy; or they may be meetings of individuals such as government officials or academics for the purpose of sharing information. Conference papers, reports of proceedings, summaries, or full-text transcripts of such conferences can be helpful sources of information. The texts of recommendations, resolutions, or agreements made during these meetings can be helpful sources of information as well. Congresses have also been known to spawn new organizations that focus on the topics of the original meeting, including new electronic discussion groups. Aside from published or distributed products resulting from these meetings, the potential for personal contacts and exposure to new ideas is always a draw.

You can learn about such meetings in a variety of ways: informally through personal contacts, other meetings, and discussion groups or formally through association newsletters and other publications. Some meetings, however, may go unnoticed except for the resources described below.

International Congress Calendar. Brussels: Union of International Associations, 1960/61–.

The *International Congress Calendar* is published quarterly and lists international meetings that have been held regularly for a number of years. The listings are geographical, chronological, and analytical and are based on information supplied to the organizers in response to regular questionnaires.

World Meetings: Social & Behavioral Sciences, Human Services & Management. Chestnut Hill, MA: World Meetings Information Center, 1977–.

American Society for Theatre Research (ASTR), c/o Theatre Dept, University of Rhode Island, Kingston, RI 02881-0824
T: (401) 792-2706; Fax: (401) 792-7198
Founded: 1956; Members: 700
Gen Secr: Gordon Armstrong
Focus: Perf Arts
Periodicals
Newsletter (weekly)
Theatre Survey (weekly) 14090

American Society for Therapeutic Radiology and Oncology (ASTRO), 1101 Market St, Ste 1400, Philadelphia, PA 19107
T: (215) 574-3180; Fax: (215) 928-0153
Founded: 1955; Members: 4200
Gen Secr: Frances Glica
Focus: Radiology; Cell Biol & Cancer Res
Periodicals
ASTRO Newsletter
The International Journal of Radiation Oncology, Biology and Physics 14091

American Society for the Study of Orthodontics (ASSO), 50-12 204 St, Oakland Gardens, NY 11364
T: (212) 224-8898
Founded: 1945; Members: 300
Gen Secr: Daisy N. Buchalter
Focus: Dent
Periodicals
ASSO Newsletter (weekly)
International Journal of Orthodontics (3 times annually) 14092

American Society for Training and Development (ASTD), 1640 King St, Box 1443, Alexandria, VA 22313
T: (703) 683-8100; Fax: (703) 683-8103
Founded: 1944; Members: 55000
Gen Secr: Curtis E. Plott
Focus: Educ; Econ
Periodicals
Journal (weekly)
National Report on Human Resources (weekly) 14093

American Society for Value Inquiry (ASVI), c/o Prof. Tom Regan, Dept of Philosophy, North Carolina State University, Raleigh, NC 14201
T: (716) 881-3200
Founded: 1970; Members: 200
Pres: Prof. Tom Regan
Focus: Philos
Periodicals
Journal of Value Inquiry (weekly)
Newsletter (weekly) 14094

American Society of Abdominal Surgery (ASAS), 675 Main St, Melrose, MA 02176
T: (617) 665-6102
Founded: 1959; Members: 9300
Gen Secr: Blaise F. Alfano
Focus: Surgery
Periodicals
Abdominal Surgery (weekly)
The Surgeon 14095

American Society of Addiction Medicine (ASAM), 5225 Wisconsin Av, Ste 409, Washington, DC 20015
T: (202) 244-8948; Fax: (202) 537-7252
Founded: 1954; Members: 3500
Pres: Anthony B. Radcliffe
Focus: Med
Periodicals
Journal of Addictive Diseases (weekly)

American Society of Animal Science (ASAS), c/o Carl D. Johnson, 309 W Clark St, Campaign, IL 61820
T: (217) 356-3182
Founded: 1908; Members: 4588
Gen Secr: Carl D. Johnson
Focus: Zoology
Periodicals
ASAS Handbook and Membership Directory (bi-annually)
Combined Abstracts (weekly)
Journal of Animal Science (weekly) . . 14100

American Society of Bakery Engineers (ASBE), 2 N Riverside Plaza, Rm 1733, Chicago, IL 60606
T: (312) 332-2246
Founded: 1924; Members: 2700
Pres: Robert A. Fischer
Focus: Food
Periodicals
Letter (weekly)
Proceedings (weekly) 14101

American Society of Body and Design Engineers (ASBDE), Wilshire Office Center, Ste 3031, 24634 Five Mile, Redford, MI 48239
T: (313) 532-6100
Founded: 1946; Members: 1500
Gen Secr: H. Eby
Focus: Eng
Periodicals
Body Engineering Journal (weekly)
Directory (weekly)
Newsletter (7 times annually)
Proceedings (weekly) 14102

American Society of Brewing Chemists (ASBC), 3340 Pilot Knob Rd, Saint Paul, MN 55121-2097
T: (612) 454-7250; Fax: (612) 454-0766
Founded: 1934; Members: 600
Gen Secr: Steven C. Nelson
Focus: Chem
Periodical
Journal of the ASBC (weekly) 14103

American Society of Cataract and Refractive Surgery (ASCRS), 4000 Lugato Rd, Ste 850, Fairfax, VA 22033
T: (703) 591-2220; Fax: (703) 591-0614
Founded: 1974; Members: 4500
Gen Secr: David A. Karcher
Focus: Surgery
Periodical
Journal of Cataract and Refractive Surgery (weekly) 14104

American Society of Certified Engineering Technicians (ASCET), POB 371474, El Paso, TX 79937
T: (915) 591-5115
Founded: 1964; Members: 3000
Gen Secr: Kurt H. Schuler
Focus: Eng
Periodicals
Annual Report (weekly)
Certified Engineering Technician Magazine (weekly)
President's Message (weekly) . . . 14105

American Society of Church History (ASCH), 328 Deland Av, Indialantic, FL 32903
T: (407) 768-8306
Founded: 1888; Members: 1550
Gen Secr: William B. Miller
Focus: Hist
Periodical
Church History (weekly) 14106

American Society of Civil Engineers (ASCE),

Periodicals
American Journal of Clinical Hypnosis (weekly)
Directory (weekly)
News Letter (8 times annually) 14108

American Society of Clinical Oncology (ASCO), 435 N Michigan Av, Ste 1717, Chicago, IL 60611-4067
T: (312) 644-0828; Fax: (312) 644-8557
Founded: 1964; Members: 8744
Gen Secr: James B. Gantenberg
Focus: Cell Biol & Cancer Res
Periodicals
Directory (biennial)
Journal of Clinical Oncology (weekly) . . 14109

American Society of Clinical Pathologists (ASCP), 2100 W Harrison St, Chicago, IL 60612
T: (312) 738-1336; Fax: (312) 738-1619
Founded: 1922; Members: 50000
Gen Secr: Robert C. Rock
Focus: Pathology
Periodicals
American Journal of Clinical Pathology (weekly)
Laboratory Medicine (weekly) 14110

American Society of Colon and Rectal Surgeons (ASCRS), 800 E Northwest Hwy, Ste 1080, Palatine, IL 60067
T: (708) 359-9184; Fax: (708) 359-7367
Founded: 1899; Members: 1500
Gen Secr: James R. Slawny
Focus: Surgery
Periodical
Diseases of the Colon and Rectum (weekly)
. . . . 14111

American Society of Consultant Pharmacists (ASCP), 1321 Duke St, Alexandria, VA 22314-3563
T: (703) 739-1300; Fax: (703) 739-1321
Founded: 1969; Members: 5000
Gen Secr: R. Timothy Webster
Focus: Pharmacol
Periodicals
Clinical Consult Newsletter (weekly)
The Consultant Pharmacist Journal (weekly)
Update Newsletter (weekly) 14112

American Society of Contemporary Medicine and Surgery (ASCMS), 233 E Erie St, Ste 710, Chicago, IL 60611
T: (312) 951-1400
Founded: 1968; Members: 8000
Gen Secr: John G. Bellows
Focus: Surgery; Med
Periodical
Comprehensive Therapy (weekly) 14113

American Society of Contemporary Ophthalmology (ASCO), 233 E Erie St, Ste 710, Chicago, IL 60611
T: (312) 951-1400; Fax: (800) 621-4002
Founded: 1966; Members: 6000
Gen Secr: John G. Bellows
Focus: Ophthal
Periodicals
Annals of Ophthalmology (weekly)
Glaucoma (weekly) 14114

American Society of Criminology (ASC), 1314 Kinnear Rd, Ste 212, Columbus, OH 43212
T: (614) 292-9207
Founded: 1941; Members: 2150
Gen Secr: Joseph E. Scott
Focus: Criminology
Periodicals
The Criminologist Newsletter (weekly)
Criminology (weekly) 14115

WORLD GUIDE TO SCIENTIFIC ASSOCIATIONS AND LEARNED SOCIETIES. MUNCHEN, PARIS: K.G. SAUR, 6TH ED. (1994)-

EXHIBIT 2-6

World Meetings is an extremely thorough source of information on meetings taking place around the world and is revised and updated quarterly. Entries include meeting title, location, date, name and acronym of sponsor, person or organization to contact for more information, meeting description, estimated attendance with restrictions, registration dates, abstract and paper deadlines, and the availability of abstracts, papers, and proceedings. Among the 27 categories of interest to criminologists are International Affairs; Law and Criminology; Management and Administration; Psychiatry, Psychology and Mental Health; Sociology; and Urban Affairs. *World Meetings* also includes a subject index useful when looking for a conference on a specific subject.

See exhibit 2-7 for the entry on the Annual Meeting of the Academy of Criminal Justice Sciences held in Las Vegas in March 1996, and note that information provided is clearly labeled.

Conference Proceedings

Library of Congress subject headings: Social sciences—Congresses—Bibliography; Humanities—Congresses—Bibliography; Criminal justice, administration of—Congresses—Bibliography; *Subject*—Congresses—Bibliography; search also under name of conference as author

People get together for conferences to exchange information. The *informal* exchange is as important as the *formal* exchange, but unless you have access to the lounges and luncheons, your only chance of getting information from a conference is through a transcript of its proceedings. Such documentation takes several forms: agenda documents, abstracts of sessions, papers presented, and transcripts of individual sessions and plenary sessions. Transcripts of conventions are usually prepared by the host organizations as a matter of course. They may also publish and distribute conference proceedings in organizational journals or as separate works. When an organization is not responsible for sponsoring the conference, it can be more difficult to locate proceedings, unless your library already owns them. Listed below are two references that will help you locate any proceedings that have been published.

Directory of Published Proceedings. Series SSH: Social Sciences/Humanities. Harrison, NY: InterDok, 1968–.

The *Directory of Published Proceedings* is a bibliography of preprints and published proceedings of congresses, conferences, symposia, meetings, and seminars that have taken place around the world. Citations to publications are arranged chronologically and include such important information as the date and location of the conference, conference theme, sponsoring organization, title, editor, publisher and distributor of publications, and an accession number. *Published Proceedings* is published quarterly, cumulated every four years, and includes a cumulated index in the final issue of each volume. It also includes a list of publishers with addresses, an editors index, a location index, an acronym listing, and a keyword sponsor index.

Proceedings are valuable to research but are often difficult to locate in libraries. Therefore, the InterDok Corporation has a document delivery service that can sup-

---

Exhibit: 352 exhibits

¶ **961 0246** : Ann Mtg of the Academy of **Criminal Justice Sciences**
Las Vegas (Nevada), United States: Riviera Hotel
12-16 Mar 96
Sponsor: Acad of Criminal Justice Sciences (ACJS)
Gen Info: Lee Ross, Program Chair, University of Wisconsin, School of Social Welfare, Box 786, 1133 Enderis Hall, Milwaukee, WI 53201, United States, tel: 414-229-6134, fax: 414-229-5311, e-mail: Lross@alpha1.csd.uwm.edu; Pat Delancey, ACJS
Content: Theme is *The Future of Crime and Justice*
Attendance: 1,800. RESTRICTIONS: None
  COST: US$55-$90
Paper Deadlines: 15 Oct 95 (abstracts); 1 Feb 96 (papers). LANGUAGE: Eng. RESTRICTIONS: None
Publication: ●ABSTRACTS—FORM: In program. LANGUAGE: Eng
Exhibit: 30-35

¶ **961 0247** : Pacific **Telecommunications** Conf (PTC'96)
Honolulu (Hawaii), United States: Sheraton Waikiki Hotel
14-18 Jan 96
Sponsor: Pacific Telecommunications Council (PTC)
Gen Info: PTC
Content: Main theme is the information infrastructure: users, resources and strategies; other topics: socio-economic issues; regulatory, legal and political issues; business and finance solutions; country studies; and technologies and standards (100 papers in Eng)
Attendance: 1,250. RESTRICTIONS: None
  COST: US$85-$1,200 on site
Paper Deadlines: Past
Publication: ●ABSTRACTS—FORM: Bound vol, proceedings & world-wide web (Internet). LANGUAGE: Eng. DATE: 14 Jan 96. SOURCE: Internet address - http://www.ptc.org. Proceedings included in conference registration otherwise US$250
Exhibit: 60

WORLD MEETINGS: SOCIAL & BEHAVIORAL SCIENCES, HUMAN SERVICES & MANAGEMENT. CHESTNUT HILL, MA: WORLD MEETINGS INFORMATION CENTER, 1977-

EXHIBIT 2-7

---

ply researchers with copies of the proceedings listed. (See exhibit 2-8 for a sample page from *Published Proceedings*, noting the price, order number, and number of pages and volumes listed for each reference.)

Index to Social Sciences and Humanities Proceedings. Philadelphia: Institute for Scientific Information, 1979–.

The *Index to Social Sciences and Humanities Proceedings* (*ISSHP*) indexes proceedings published in almost any form, including books, reports, preprints, and journal literature. This worldwide compilation focuses on the social sciences and humanities including criminology and penology.

Preface

The Directory of Published Proceedings is a bibliographic service citing preprints as well as published proceedings of congresses, conferences, symposia, meetings and seminars that have all taken place world-wide from 1964 to date. Series SEMT Science/Engineering/Medicine/Technology is published 10 times a year, from September to June. A cumulated annual volume is also published. A cumulated index supplement is available three times per year. Indices for annual volumes are published at 2 and 5 year intervals. *Production began in September, 1964.* Series SSH Social Sciences/Humanities provides quarterly information of proceedings in these subject areas. The 4th issue in each volume contains a cumulative index for that year. Cumulative volumes are also published at 4 year intervals. *Production began in January, 1968.* Series PCE Pollution Control/Ecology provides proceedings citations extracted from current SEMT and SSH volumes. *Production began in 1974.* Series MLS Medical/Life Sciences provides proceedings citations extracted from the current SEMT and SSH volumes. *Production began in 1990.*

Also available from InterDok...

MIND: The Meetings Index is a bi-monthly bibliographic journal providing information on *future* events world-wide. InterDok's Acquisitions Service provides customers with searching and procurement support for proceedings.

Guide

The main body of the directory is composed of citations listing published conference material. Citations are arranged chronologically by the month and year of the respective conference. To the right of the date is the citation number. Together, the date and citation number form an access number to identify the citation within the indices. Access numbers may also be used by customers when ordering through our Acquisitions Service:

Sample Citation:

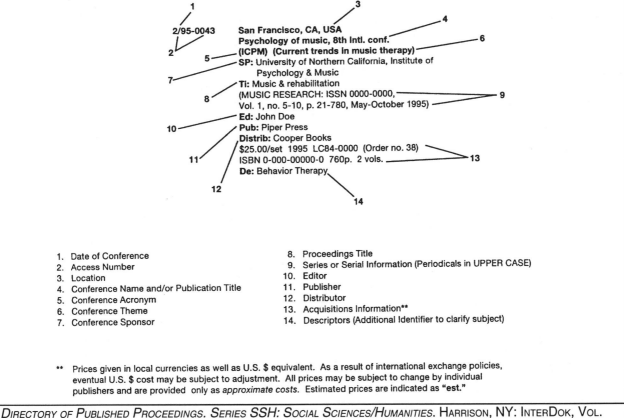

1. Date of Conference
2. Access Number
3. Location
4. Conference Name and/or Publication Title
5. Conference Acronym
6. Conference Theme
7. Conference Sponsor

8. Proceedings Title
9. Series or Serial Information (Periodicals in UPPER CASE)
10. Editor
11. Publisher
12. Distributor
13. Acquisitions Information**
14. Descriptors (Additional Identifier to clarify subject)

** Prices given in local currencies as well as U.S. $ equivalent. As a result of international exchange policies, eventual U.S. $ cost may be subject to adjustment. All prices may be subject to change by individual publishers and are provided only as *approximate costs.* Estimated prices are indicated as "est."

DIRECTORY OF PUBLISHED PROCEEDINGS. SERIES SSH: SOCIAL SCIENCES/HUMANITIES. HARRISON, NY: INTERDOK, VOL. 1(1968)-

EXHIBIT 2-8

The main section of *ISSHP* contains complete bibliographic information about proceedings, and the papers they contain are displayed in a contents-page format. Indexes comprise a category index, which enables the researcher to look for proceedings by general topic of interest; a Permuterm Subject Index, where significant words in the titles of papers are paired with every other significant word; a sponsor index, which lists alphabetically the sponsor of meetings covered in the issue; an author-editor index, which names all authors and up to nine editors for each proceeding; a meeting location index, which alphabetically arranges the location of the meeting by country, state, and city; and a corporate index, which indexes proceedings by the location of the primary author's organizational affiliation.

Libraries and Librarians

Library of Congress subject headings: Libraries— Directories; Libraries—United States—Directories; Libraries—*Geog.*—Directories; Special libraries—United States—Directories; Information services—United States—Directories

Libraries have always been regarded as repositories of knowledge. Although this metaphor has lost its usefulness in describing the institution, libraries are, nonetheless, places where you can find the knowledge that has been printed in books and journals. As repositories of knowledge, libraries have greater authority than any other institution.

In the metaphor of the library as repository of knowledge, the librarian's responsibility was, in part, to tend to the security, preservation, and organization of the collection of books. The librarian acted as a gatekeeper. But as this metaphor is changing, so too is the image of the librarian. The profession has evolved, and librarians are now responsible for facilitating access to the information in the books. Further, in a new metaphor of the library as window to information, the librarian's responsibility is to facilitate access to information in any form and at any location.

Accessing libraries and librarians is an important part of finding information. Library directories are described below, including information about libraries, collections, collections' emphases, and staffs.

American Library Directory. New York: R.R. Bowker, 1923–.

The *American Library Directory* provides fairly detailed information about libraries in the United States, Canada, and Mexico. The arrangement of libraries is alphabetical by state, region, or province; city; and name of library or parent institution. Entries for individual libraries include name, address, Internet address, key personnel, and libraries' holdings or special collections. Libraries are coded by type, for example, A=Armed Forces, C=College or University, G=Government, J=Junior College, L=Law, M=Medical, P=Public, R=Religious, or S=Special (which includes industry and company libraries as well as libraries affiliated with clubs or foundations). A personnel index lists phone numbers and addresses. Notably, the library system (online catalog) used and database search services are also listed.

The *American Library Directory* is an extremely thorough resource with information about the collections, staff, and services of specific libraries. Exhibit 2-9 shows part of the directory entry for Rutgers University Libraries.

Kathleen Piperato; Staff 4 (prof 2, nonprof 2)
Library Holdings: Bk titles 20,000; Per sub 150; Rpts 6000, Standards 1000; CD ROM titles 15; Micro — Film 900. VF 4
Subject Interests: Nuclear eng, nuclear power
Special Collections: Industry Standards; Vendor Catalogs
Automation Info: IBM mainframe in use. Terminals - 12; staff & patrons use. Cataloging - OCLC; online cat, staff searches. Online ref searches - 100 per month; staff searches. CD-ROM - 3 workstations. Online Pub Access Catalog (OPAC)
Publications: InfoConnection - Nuclear Update
Partic in Knight-Ridder Info, Inc; OCLC Online Computer Libr Ctr, Inc; Palinet & Union Libr Catalogue of Pa; S Jersey Regional Libr Coop; Westlaw

ROBINSON, ST JOHN & WAYNE, Law Library, Two Penn Plaza E, 07105. SAN 323-8334. Tel 201-491-3300. FAX 201-491-3333. *Dir* Scott L Fisher; Staff 3 (prof 1, cler 2)
Founded 1971. Staff only; ILL
Library Holdings: Bk vols 15,000

RUTGERS, THE STATE UNIVERSITY OF NEW JERSEY
Justice Henry Ackerson Law Library, Samuel I Newhouse Law Ctr, 15 Washington St, 07102-3192. SAN 351-0816. Tel 201-648-5964. FAX 201-648-1356. Elec Mail andromeda.rutgers.edu. *Librn* Carol A Roehrenbeck; *Circ & ILL* Marjorie Crawford; *Pub Servs* Steven C Perkins; *Tech Serv* Felice K Lowell; *Acq* Paul Axel-Lute; Staff 22 (prof 10, cler 12)
Founded 1946. Enrl 765
1994-95 Income $1,650,032 (incl parent inst $1,619,820, gen inc $30,212) Mats Exp $551,376, Bks $27,447, Per $96,478, Other Print Mat $320,429, Doc $9526, Presv $16,381, Micro $6248, AV Mats $5297, Machine Read Mat $10,150, Database Fees $59,420, Plt Op & Maint $89,016; Sal $1,004,479 (total prof $622,086; cler $341,904, students $40,489)
1995-96 Projected Income $1,611,967
Library Holdings: Bk titles 97,052, bk vols & bd per 263,499; Ser sub 3036; CD ROM titles 11; Micro — Cards 63,000, fiche 546,534, film 8556; AV — A-tapes 1468
Special Collections: Law Library of US Supreme Court Justice Bradley (Bradley Coll). US & State Doc Dep
Automation Info: Shared (network/utility) computer in use. Terminals - Cat 1, PAC 4, ser 6; staff & patrons use. Cataloging - Res Librs Info Network; online cat - INNOPAC, staff & patrons search. Online Pub Access Catalog (OPAC); OPAC Internet Address: law-new.rutgers.edu (login: library); Internet Home Page Address: http://www.rutgers.edu/lawschool.html
Mem of Asn of Res Librs
Partic in Knight-Ridder Info, Inc; Res Librs Group, Inc; RLIN; Westlaw
John Cotton Dana Library, 185 University Ave, 07102. SAN 351-0786. Tel 201-648-5901; Interlibrary Loan Service Tel. No.: 648-5902. FAX 201-648-1133. *Dir* Lynn S Mullins; *Head Tech Servs & Media* Judy Jeng; *Head Pub Serv* Natalie Borisovets; *Govt Doc* Open; *Serials* Andrea Lakios; *Bibliog Instr* Roberta Tipton; *On-Line Servs* Roberta Tipton; *Head Circ* Ann Watkins. Subject Specialists: *Bus* Ka neng Au; *Bus* Robert Tipton; *Criminal Justice* Phyllis Schultze; *Sci* Veronica Calderhead. Staff 38 (prof 12, nonprof 26)
Founded 1927. Enrl 10,000; Fac 500; Highest Degree: Doctorate 1994-95 Mats Exp $890,267, Bks $125,022, Per $655,070, Presv $26,961, Micro $21,882, AV Mats $9354, Machine Read Mat $7191, CD ROM $44,787; Sal $1,732,570 (admin & mgr prof $513,336; total nonprof $705,898, students $62,771)
Library Holdings: Bk vols 309,925; Ser sub (incl per) 3326; Doc bd 218,616; Bd per 105,299; CD ROM titles 212; AV — Total 15,351. VF 17,740
Subject Interests: Bus & mgt, humanities, nursing, sci-tech, soc & behav sci
Special Collections: US & State Doc Dep
Automation Info: IBM PC models in use. Terminals - Acq 2, admin 1, circ 3, ref 2; staff use, patrons use 24. Circulation - GEAC. Online ref searches - Staff searches. CD-ROM - 24 workstations. Online Pub Access Catalog (OPAC); OPAC Internet Address: Mullins@Zodiac.edu
Publications: Library Guide Series, Library News Release
Mem of Asn of Res Librs
Partic in BRS; Ctr for Res Librs; Knight-Ridder Info, Inc; Medline; NY Metrop Ref & Res Libr Agency; Res Librs Group, Inc; RLIN; SDC
Friends of Library Group
See New Brunswick entry for budget figures for the University's library system
Special Collections, Departmental and Institute Libraries
— Criminal Justice NCCD Collection, 15 Washington St, 4th flr, 07102. SAN 327-9499. Tel 201-648-5522. FAX 201-648-1275. *Info Specialist* Phyllis Schultze
1994-95 Mats Exp $27,992, Bks $18,776, Per $6751, Presv $2465; Sal $55,801 (total prof $48,058; total nonprof $7743)
Library Holdings: Bk titles 15,743; Per sub 229, vols bd 1948; Dissertations 6688; Res rpts 48,470; CD ROM titles 3; Micro Microforms 21,720. VF 5617
Automation Info: Online Pub Access Catalog (OPAC)
Publications: Acquisitions List (bi-monthly)
Mem of Asn of Res Librs

AMERICAN LIBRARY DIRECTORY. NEW YORK: R.R. BOWKER, 1923-

EXHIBIT 2-9

Near the bottom of the entry, Special Collections, Departmental and Institute Libraries are indicated, including information about the Criminal Justice/National Council on Crime and Delinquency Library at Rutgers. In larger institutions, subject-oriented libraries are often a fact of life. Keep in mind, however, that while individual entries indicate special collections, the directory has no index indicating subject area strengths for collections. If you are attempting to identify libraries with specialized collections in an area such as criminal justice, you might have trouble using this resource.

Evinger, William R. *Directory of Federal Libraries*, 3d ed. Phoenix, AZ : Oryx, 1997.

This current resource provides directory information on over 2,000 government libraries around the world. Entries also include special subjects covered and circulation and reference policies. Indexes are available by subject specialty, type of library, and geographic location.

"Yahoo Reference: Libraries." www.yahoo.com/Reference/Libraries (March 10, 1997).

Yahoo is a search tool for finding information on the World Wide Web, but the company also maintains several directories, one of which provides links to library Web pages. This Yahoo site refers to libraries by type, for example, public libraries, law libraries, and state libraries, and by geographic designation, such as Australia, Canada, and Croatia, as well as some references to specific libraries such as the National Archives and Records Administration. The links at this site generally lead to library home pages that may not always lead to directories of staffs and services.

Special libraries are libraries that are built around a collection that is limited in subject matter. They maintain more detailed collections on specific subjects or a group of closely related topics. These libraries often operate in support of a special mission or activity chosen by their sponsoring organization. Listed below are resources that can help you identify such libraries.

Directory of Special Libraries and Information Centers. Detroit, MI: Gale Research, 1963–.

The *Directory of Special Libraries and Information Centers* is a guide to more than 21,700 special libraries, research libraries, information centers, and archives. It also includes data centers maintained by government agencies, business, industry, newspapers, educational institutions, nonprofit organizations, societies in the fields of science and engineering, medicine, law, art, religion, the social sciences, and the humanities. The centers covered fall into five major categories: (1) subject divisions, departmental collections, and professional libraries maintained by colleges and universities; (2) branches, divisions, departments, and special collections in large public library systems; (3) company libraries that operate within the framework of a business or industry; (4) governmental libraries; and (5) libraries supported by nonprofit organizations, associations, and institutions.

Descriptive listings are arranged alphabetically by name of the sponsoring organization. A subject index classifies the libraries and information centers described in the main section of the book by the principal topics of their holdings. It employs more than 4,000 terms and cross-references to classify the major field of interest of each library described. Entries contain the following information: name of organization, name of library or information center, address, telephone number, head of library, subjects, special collections, automated operations, computerized information services, publications, special catalogs and indexes, and principal staff names.

Subject Collections. New York: R.R. Bowker, 1958–.

Subject Collections is a compilation of libraries, excluding college and university archives, listed alphabetically by subject. It is updated irregularly and contains nearly 66,000 entries from 5,882 institutions. Entries include the name, address, areas of expertise, and types of materials. The citations are not as complete as in the *American Library Directory*, but when used together, they provide the user with a wealth of useful information. The subject arrangement of collections makes it easier to find libraries specializing in various disciplines. (See exhibit 2-10 for a sample entry.)

Criminal justice research also involves access to government document collections, which poses a special problem for the researcher. The federal government is the most prolific publisher of information in the United States, and it employs a variety of forms of delivery—books, periodicals, CD-ROM, online, microform, sound recordings, reports, and even three-fold pamphlets. State publications are as important as federal ones, but they present an even greater problem for the criminal justice researcher because there are fewer bibliographic sources for them. Such publications—those of states and to some extent the federal government—represent a large portion of the body of materials known as *grey literature*, also referred to as *fugitive literature* by librarians.

Libraries have for many years treated government materials differently than other publications. The reasons for this approach lie in the materials themselves but also in the methods of acquiring, maintaining, and accessing them. Since these publications are generated at the public expense and offered free to many libraries, the federal government regulates their distribution and processing; for instance, they must be retained for a specific period of time, despite time-sensitivity and format. More significantly, federal publications that are supplied free to libraries must be available to the public even if the libraries themselves are closed to public access. State publications suffer

CRIMES AND MISDEMEANORS see
Criminal Law

CRIMINAL ASSAULT see Rape

CRIMINAL INVESTIGATION

DC —GEORGETOWN UNIVERSITY
LIBRARY, Special Collections Div, 37 & O
Sts NW, **Washington**, 20057. Tel 202-687-
7444. FAX 202-687-7501.
Holdings: Cat Mss Pix
Notes: Political assassinations, espec
materials pertaining to the assassinations of
John F Kennedy and Robert F Kennedy and
the investigations thereof.

†MD —INTERNATIONAL ASSOCIATION
OF CHIEFS OF POLICE, 13 Firstfield Rd,
PO Box 6010, **Gaithersburg**, 20760.
Holdings: Vols (6000) Cat Mss
Notes: Collection heavy in criminal
investigation, crime prevention, police
administration and management. Collecting
in public sector labor relations, family
violence, terrorism.

WA —SEATTLE PUBLIC LIBRARY, 1000
Fourth Ave, **Seattle**, 98104.
Holdings: Vols (18,000) Cat Mss Maps
Notes: Includes pamphlets and clippings on
municipal affairs, especially Seattle.
Emphasis on urban planning, criminal
investigation, policy analysis, finance.

CRIMINAL JUSTICE,
ADMINISTRATION OF

DC —AMERICAN INSTITUTE FOR
RESEARCH LIBRARY, 1055 Thomas
Jefferson St NW, **Washington**, 20007. Tel
202-342-5000.

†IL —NORTHWESTERN UNIVERSITY,
School of Law, Library, 357 E Chicago Ave,
Chicago, 60611.
Holdings: Cat
Notes: Comprehensive collections of Anglo-
American and foreign (especially European)
law; Roman and Canon law (selective);
international law; European Common
Market; Williams Collection of Legal
Instruments (AD 1300-1700); George W
Shaw Collection of Early European Law.
Incl 500 ms legal documents.

†IN —INDIANA LAW ENFORCEMENT
ACADEMY, David F Allen Memorial
Learning Resources Center, Rd 700 E, PO
Box 313, **Plainfield**, 46168.
Holdings: Vols (4500) Cat Slides 16mm
Films
Notes: Concentrated in the areas of police
science, criminology, and law.

MA —CONNECTICUT VALLEY
HISTORICAL MUSEUM & ARCHIVES,
194 State St, **Springfield**, 01103.
Notes: Nearly 300 vols of 150 years of jail
records containing admission records,
doctor's logs, prison industry ledgers, etc,
describing local crimes and criminals.
Recovered from the Hampden County lock-
up storage area in 1991. Describes
individuals' sentences, character of
confinement, etc.

SUBJECT COLLECTIONS. NEW YORK: R.R. BOWKER, 1ST
ED. (1958)-

EXHIBIT 2-10

from similar restrictions; however, they are not published in the same quantity or distributed as widely.

This mix of factors has led to the treatment of government publications as special materials and to the creation of the Depository Library System. See chapter 7 for a more in-depth treatment of this topic. We cover directories of government document depository libraries here because government libraries, including depository libraries, are one source of professional connections, but you will find further details in chapter 7.

Directory of Government Document Collections & Librarians. Washington, DC: Congressional Information Service, 1974–.

The *Directory of Government Document Collections & Librarians* is a valuable resource for finding federal and state publications and is endorsed by the American Library Association's Government Documents Round Table. It is a comprehensive guide to libraries, collections, and librarians involved in providing access to state and federal government publications. Section 1 provides a state-by-state, city-by-city directory to government documents libraries, with names and addresses; telephone and fax numbers; e-mail addresses; descriptions of collections, including subject specialties and the date collecting began; and finally names and titles of librarians responsible for the documents. Section 2 is a name index to the libraries listed in section 1. Section 3 is a document collections index divided into four subsections referring to the types of documents collected by the institutions surveyed: state, local, international, and foreign. State and local collections are listed under their *home* state and localities only. Depository libraries—those likely to have the most complete collections—are indicated with a star (*). Section 4 is a special collections index. Section 5 is a geographic listing of library school instructors who teach government publications courses. Section 6 lists state agencies and individuals responsible for administering their respective state documents programs. Section 7 is an alphabetical listing by state of Bureau of the Census State Data Centers and individuals responsible for providing access to Census data. Sections 8 through 10 provide a personal name index, other names to know, and association and government offices listings respectively.

Various library organizations also keep membership directories that include both libraries and individuals. Directories of organizations such as the World Criminal Justice Library Network and the American Association of Law Libraries provide access to information about the collections and staffs of libraries that collect in areas of criminal justice and law.

MAKING FEDERAL GOVERNMENT CONNECTIONS

No human organization plays a greater part in the administration of justice than government. Government agencies and personnel are important not only to writing, enforcing, and adjudicating criminal law but also to setting the standards and policies under which it operates. Access to these agencies and individuals can be gained through all the means outlined in previous sections; but, recalling the difference between performative and cognitive authority (see this chapter, "A Word on Authorities"), you are aware that there is a substantial difference between what Jimmy Carter says today and what he said as president of the United States. Government officials acting in their official capacities are speaking for their agencies or governments. Their authority to address an issue comes from their oath of office. While they may have personal opinions and impressions that are valid and authoritative outside their official capacities, the expression of those ideas is often limited to *off-the-record* conversation. The following sources will assist the researcher in identifying and locating government officials who have authority over some area of governmental activity, thus in evaluating the information you receive from them, keep in mind that they are acting in their official capacity, not expressing their personal views.

United States Federal Government

> Library of Congress subject headings: United States—Politics and government—Handbooks, manuals, etc.; Washington Metropolitan Area—Directories; Washington (D.C.)—Directories; United States—Executive departments—Handbooks, manuals, etc.; United States—Politics and government—Handbooks, manuals, etc.

Described below are two directories with information about all branches, agencies, and officials of the federal government. Succeeding sections cover directories for individual branches or agencies.

Office of the Federal Register, National Archives and Records Services, General Services Administration. *United States Government Manual.* Washington, DC: U.S. Government Printing Office, 1973–.

> The *United States Government Manual* is the "official handbook of the Federal government," providing comprehensive information on the agencies of the legislative, judicial, and executive branches of government. It includes information on quasi-official agencies, international or-

ganizations in which the U.S. participates, and boards, commissions, and committees. It is arranged by branch of government and provides organizational charts, names, addresses, telephone numbers, a description of each agency (see exhibit 2-11), a list of major office holders, sources of information, libraries, referral telephone numbers, and regional offices. Entries also give citations for the sections in the *United States Code* from which the agency receives its authority. Other agencies that are quasi-governmental or nongovernmental but that have a *presence* in government through their advocacy programs are also covered. Sometimes referred to as the *Government Organization Manual,* it also includes an agency and name index.

Washington Information Directory. Washington, DC: Congressional Quarterly, 1975/76–.

> While the *United States Government Manual*, described above, is the most authoritative resource available on the

---

Offices

Attorney General The Attorney General, as head of the Department of Justice and chief law enforcement officer of the Federal Government, represents the United States in legal matters generally and gives advice and opinions to the President and to the heads of the executive departments of the Government when so requested. The Attorney General appears in person to represent the Government before the U.S. Supreme Court in cases of exceptional gravity or importance.

Deputy Attorney General The Deputy Attorney General advises and assists the Attorney General in formulating and implementing Department policies and programs and in providing overall supervision and direction to all organizational units of the Department. The Deputy Attorney General is authorized to exercise all the power and authority of the Attorney General, except where such power or authority is prohibited by law from delegation or has been delegated to another official. In the absence of the Attorney General, the Deputy Attorney General acts as Attorney General.

Associate Attorney General The Associate Attorney General advises and assists the Attorney General and Deputy Attorney General in formulating and implementing Department policies and programs pertaining to civil matters and immigration. The Associate Attorney General exercises the power and authority vested in the Attorney General to serve as the Attorney General's designee to determine whether a handicapped person can achieve the purpose of a program without fundamental changes in its nature; and if an action would result in a fundamental alteration in the nature of a program or activity, or in undue financial and administrative burdens.

Solicitor General The Solicitor General represents the U.S. Government in cases before the Supreme Court. He decides what cases the Government should ask the Supreme Court to review and what position the Government should take in

cases before the Court. Also, he supervises the preparation of the Government's Supreme Court briefs and other legal documents and the conduct of the oral arguments in the Court. He or his staff argue most of the Government's cases in the Supreme Court. The Solicitor General's duties also include deciding whether the United States should appeal in all cases it loses before the lower courts.

Legal Counsel The Assistant Attorney General in charge of the Office of Legal Counsel assists the Attorney General in his function as legal adviser to the President and all the executive branch agencies. The Office drafts legal opinions of the Attorney General rendered in response to requests from the President and heads of the executive departments. It also provides its own written opinions and informal advice in response to requests from the various agencies of the Government as well as offices within the Department and from Presidential staff and advisers. Such requests typically deal with legal issues of particular complexity and importance about which two or more agencies are in disagreement or with pending legislation. The Office is also responsible for providing legal advice to the executive branch on all constitutional questions.

All Executive orders and proclamations proposed to be issued by the President are reviewed by the Office of Legal Counsel for form and legality, as are various other matters that require the President's formal approval.

In addition to serving as, in effect, outside counsel for the other agencies of the executive branch, the Office of Legal Counsel also functions as general counsel for the Department itself. It reviews all proposed orders of the Attorney General and all regulations requiring the Attorney General's approval.

The Office coordinates the work of the Department with respect to treaties, executive agreements, and international organizations. It performs a variety of

---

UNITED STATES GOVERNMENT MANUAL. WASHINGTON, DC: OFFICE OF THE FEDERAL REGISTER, NATIONAL ARCHIVES AND RECORDS SERVICES, GENERAL SERVICES ADMINISTRATION: FOR SALE BY THE SUPT. OF DOCS., U.S. G.P.O., 1973-

EXHIBIT 2-11

agencies and branches of the U.S. government, the *Washington Information Directory* is the more usable one. Instead of being arranged by agency, which can be daunting for the uninitiated, this Directory is organized into chapters by subject area. Each chapter gathers agencies together by related areas of interest, such as International Affairs, Social Services, Law and Justice, and Congress and Politics, and provides a detailed table of contents. Entries include address, telephone number, fax, chief official, and a brief description of the agency, organization, committee, or nongovernmental organization related to the particular subject. Other sections deal with the Executive Office of the President, executive departments, and federal agencies. Helpful features of the "Ready Reference" section are a listing of foreign embassies, directories of the current Congress, and regional Federal Information Centers arranged by agency.

Congress and Congressional Staff

Library of Congress subject headings: United States Congress—Directories; United States Congress—Biography; United States Congress—Officials and employees—Directories; United States Congress—Registers; Directories, Governmental—United States

Article 1, Section 1 of the U.S. Constitution states that "All legislative powers herein granted shall be vested in a Congress of the United States." As such, the Congress has the authority to pass all legislation necessary to the administration of justice as it pertains to federal jurisdiction. Access to representatives, senators, and the staffs that advise and facilitate the making of law can be an important part of researching a criminal justice topic. The resources given below can assist you in contacting them.

Congressional Staff Directory. Mount Vernon, VA: Staff Directories, 1959–.

The *Congressional Staff Directory* is one in the series of significant directories published by the Staff Directories company. It has been published annually since 1959 and semiannually since 1989 emphasizing information on the staffs of the members of Congress, its committees, and its subcommittees. Part 1 includes information on state delegations to Congress, complete with district facts—geographic, demographic, and voting—as well as vital statistics on the representatives themselves. Part 2 provides similar biographical information on members of the Senate. Part 3 reports information on joint committees of Congress. Part 4 covers the House of Representatives, its staffs, and officers, as well as each committee and subcommittee, including vital statistics and photographs of each representative. Part 5 is a state-by-state listing of counties, populations, and congressional districts. The directory's final section provides biographical information on congressional staff members. Name and keyword

subject indexes provide access to congressional delegations and their staffs.

Congressional Yellow Book. Washington, DC: Washington Monitor, 1976–.

The *Congressional Yellow Book* is one of about a dozen directories in the Yellow Book series. It provides basic biographical statistics on each senator and representative, including addresses for their Washington, DC, and state offices, telephone and fax numbers, committee assignments, and names and titles of key staff members. If you are seeking information on the various House, Senate, and joint committees of Congress, you will find addresses, telephone and fax numbers, and an inventory of committee members and key aides, as well as a description of the scope of the committee's charge. Section 6 is a survey of those holding leadership positions in both houses, their names, staffs, and an overview of their responsibilities. Finally, congressional support agencies, such as the Congressional Budget Office, General Accounting Office, the Government Printing Office, and the Library of Congress are covered in section 7. The *Congressional Yellow Book* also provides useful staff and organization indexes.

U.S. Congress. *Congressional Pictorial Directory*. Washington, DC: U.S. Government Printing Office.

U.S. Congress. **"Congressional Pictorial Directory."** http://www.access.gpo.gov/congress/105_pictorial/index.html (March 10, 1997).

This source, available in both print and on the Web, is composed of photographs of the members of Congress accompanied by some basic biographical information. The Web version is only for the current Congress.

U.S. Congress. *Official Congressional Directory*. Washington, DC: U.S. Government Printing Office, 1809–.

U.S. Congress. **"Congressional Directory."** http://www.access.gpo.gov/congress/cong001.html (March 10, 1997).

The *Official Congressional Directory* is one of the oldest working handbooks of the U.S. government. Published with each new session of Congress, it offers biographical sketches of members, office addresses, telephone numbers, descriptions of congressional districts, and the zip codes included in them. Also given are directories of the staffs of congressional boards and commissions, committees, cabinet level departments, diplomatic information, the executive and judicial branches, and international organizations. An interesting and useful feature is a list of members of the press that are admitted to the press gallery and their affiliations. The Web site is keyword searchable.

The World Wide Web also provides access to government, and the U.S. Congress has not been lax in making a place for itself on the Internet. The authors predict that as time passes, data about individual staffs will also be available. Two institutions, the Library of Congress (http://www.loc.gov and http://thomas.loc.gov/) and the Villanova Center for Information Law and Policy (http://www.law.vill.edu), have gathered together superior Web pages that contain links to various files about Congress, the Judiciary, the executive branch, and federal agencies. Watch the two sites given below for expanding coverage.

U.S. Library of Congress. **"Thomas: Legislative Information on the Internet."** http://thomas.loc.gov/ (March 10, 1997).

> As of this writing, "Thomas" provides links to the House and Senate. The House site is a gateway to House directories, House e-mail addresses, and information about members of the House of Representatives including biographical information. The Senate site provides directory-type information. Make a *bookmark* for this site so you can keep an eye on it. It's already very elegant and is bound to continue developing.

Villanova University. **"Villanova Center for Information Law and Policy."** http://www.law.vill.edu/ (March 10, 1997).

> Be sure to explore the "Villanova Center for Information Law and Policy" Web site, which provides links to federal government Web sites for the legislative, judicial, and executive branches, as well as cabinet-level departments. Additional classes of links cover federal independent establishments and government corporations, federal government consortia and quasi-official agencies, selected multilateral organizations and international sites, nongovernmental federally related sites, and search sites.

Federal Agencies

> Library of Congress subject headings: Administrative agencies—United States—Directories; Government agencies—United States—Directories; Executive departments—United States—Directories; United States—Officials and employees—Directories; Independent regulatory commissions—United States—Directories; Administrative procedure—United States; United States—Executive departments—Directories; Independent regulatory commissions—United States—Periodicals; Government—United States—Directories; Government agencies—United States—Directories

As U.S. society has become more complex, so has its government. Representatives to Congress would probably be the first to concede that the legislative branch simply cannot study all issues in sufficient detail to pass the laws required to govern modern social interaction. Much of what we know as law today is actually delegated legislation, that is, law made by

administrative agencies that are able to investigate the details necessary to, for example, collect taxes and assure that food is pure, measurements are honest, and flood plains are managed. As the purview of agency-generated legislation has become larger, so too has the number of agencies required to produce it. As a result, researching the administration of criminal justice may require access to information produced by dozens of agencies, not to mention the three branches of U.S. government.

In a previous section, we noted sources of general information about the agencies and branches of the federal government. These sources can provide information about key personnel and information services and can be especially helpful in determining the mission and scope of an agency's charge. But when researching government agencies, you may require more detailed information about staffs than previously provided. You will find sources for such information below.

Federal Regulatory Directory. Washington, DC: Congressional Quarterly, 1979/80–.

> Although not as comprehensive or detailed in its listing of personnel as the sources that follow, the *Federal Regulatory Directory* is more thorough in its description of agencies than the *United States Government Manual* mentioned in a previous section. The first part of the directory profiles the 13 largest regulatory agencies with an in-depth description of the agency's powers and responsibilities, history, and outlook. Information on agencies is composed of short biographies, photos of commissioners or board members, organization charts, telephone numbers, information sources and libraries, and enabling legislation and bibliographies. Part 2 covers approximately 100 important agencies, giving history, responsibilities, organizational information, telephone numbers, information sources, and regional offices. Additional information on Internet access and bulletin boards, when available, is also included. Among the indexes and appendixes are lists of relevant acts of Congress, a name index, and a subject agency index.

Federal Staff Directory. Mount Vernon, VA: Staff Directories, 1982–.

> The *Federal Staff Directory* is one of several directories in a series that reports on the federal government. It gives information on more than 38,000 key people in the executive branch, including the military, nongovernmental, and international organizations, such as names, job titles, addresses, and telecommunications information. This useful resource is divided into five sections: the Executive Office of the President; cabinet level departments, including staffs and statements of agency responsibility; independent agencies, also with staffs and statements of responsibility, as well as statutory authority; and quasi-

official agencies—both international and nongovernmental organizations. Section 5 provides biographical information on executives that is often not available elsewhere. As in the *Federal Yellow Book*, each section has its own detailed table of contents. Published twice per year, the *Directory* also includes a subject index with approximately 15,000 entries and an individual name index.

Federal Yellow Book. Washington, DC: Washington Monitor, 1976–.

The *Federal Yellow Book* is divided into four sections, covering the Executive Office of the President and the Office of the Vice President, federal departments at the cabinet level, independent agencies, and regional offices. It provides data about more than 35,000 people in the executive branch such as names, addresses, and telecommunications numbers. Biographies and photographs are provided for the heads of agencies and departments. It is updated quarterly so information about the vast resources of the federal government is kept current. A useful feature of the *Federal Yellow Book* is the extensive use of tables of contents, which are provided at the beginning of the book and each section, and the use of detailed tables to assist in navigating through information about departments and agencies. These aids can be particularly helpful when identifying agencies related to a topic of study. For even greater detail about administrative personnel, refer to the *Federal Yellow Book*'s complementary publication the *Federal Regional Yellow Book*.

Federal Courts and Court Personnel

Library of Congress subject headings: Courts—United States—Directories; Judges—United States—Directories; Judges—United States—Biography; Courts—United States—Officials and employees—Biography; Court records—United States—Information services—Directories; Public records—United States—Information services—Directories

Access to the courts and court personnel is also important to the criminal justice researcher. The courts preside over trials and sentencing of criminals, both of which are frequent subjects of research. Resources noted below can lead you in the right direction.

Judicial Staff Directory. Mount Vernon, VA: Staff Directories, 1986–.

Judicial Yellow Book. Mount Vernon, VA: Staff Directories, 1986–.

The *Judicial Staff Directory* is another of the important directories produced by Staff Directories, Ltd., again, emphasizing staff contacts. Part 1 covers the national courts, including the U.S. Supreme Court, and other federal courts of general and limited jurisdiction. Part 2 is a circuit-by-circuit directory of judges, magistrates, staffs, judges' secretaries, and law clerks. These include information regarding the court of appeals, the district courts,

bankruptcy court, U.S. attorneys, and U.S. marshals. The location where the courts sit and the counties and cities under their jurisdictions are also covered. Part 3 is dedicated to the U.S. Department of Justice, its offices, and staffs, with complete addresses and telephone numbers. Part 4 lists states, their respective counties, county populations, and circuit and judicial districts. Part 5 takes a geographic approach with maps of the judicial districts. Like other Staff Directories publications, a separate section offers biographies of judges and key court personnel. Part 6 comprises five indexes pertaining to judges, each listed respectively by (1) appointing president, (2) year of appointment, (3) alphabetically, (4) judicial statistics, and (5) judicial nominations. The *Judicial Staff Directory* is published annually and includes a name index.

The Sourcebook of Federal Courts, U.S. District and Bankruptcy: The Definitive Guide to Searching for Case Information at the Local Level within the Federal Court System. Tempe, AZ: BRB Publications, 1993.

If the information you seek is court records, the *Sourcebook of Federal Courts, U.S. District and Bankruptcy* is an extremely useful guide. This publication presents very thorough descriptions on how to access the records of district and bankruptcy courts by mail, by phone, in person, and online. It also includes descriptions of courts' record keeping systems and brief directory information on court staffs.

The *Judicial Yellow Book,* along with the above mentioned *Judicial Staff Directory,* represents the most comprehensive of the sources available to direct you to the staffs of the various federal courts. Others include

American Bar Association. *Directory of Minority Judges in the United States*. Chicago, IL: American Bar Association, 1994.

U.S. Administrative Office of the United States Courts. *United States Court Directory*. Washington, DC: U.S. Administrative Office of the United States Courts, 1978–.

Two sources that provide the same information as those above but at less depth are

BNA's Directory of State and Federal Courts, Judges, and Clerks: A State-by State and Federal Listing. 4th ed. Washington, DC: Bureau of National Affairs, 1992.

WANT Publishing. *Want's Federal-State Court Directory.* Washington, DC: WANT Publishing, 1984.

BNA's Directory of State and Federal Courts, Judges, and Clerks and *Want's Federal-State Court Directory's* descriptions of electronic access systems to information in the Federal Courts—ACES (Appeals Court Electronic Access)

and PACER (Public Access to Court Electronic Records)—are unique and particularly useful. The information available on both systems is surveyed, including instructions on how to access them.

MAKING STATE AND INTERGOVERNMENTAL CONNECTIONS

Criminal justice is not the sole purview of the federal government. Because the federal government has become increasingly concerned with crime over the past few years, there is a tendency to believe that criminal justice is primarily a federal matter. This *nationalization* of crime and the prosecution of high-profile cases in the popular media have led to this growing misconception. The fact is, however, that much more criminal law and justice is enacted and administered at the state and local level than the federal. Statistics on public expenditure demonstrate this point: In 1990, the total expenditure of the federal government in all classes of activity—police protection, judicial, legal services, public defense, corrections, and "other justice"—was approximately $10,059,000,000. State and local governments, on the other hand, spent $28,005,000,000 and $39,667,000,000, respectively (*Statistical Abstract of the United States*, 1994).

Many of the resources furnished in previous sections pertaining to the federal government also cover state governments. But there are also a number of resources that can direct you principally to the state and local levels. Some of these sources are commercially published, while others are publications of the state and municipal governments themselves.

State Agencies, Courts, Officials, and Employees

> Library of Congress subject headings: State governments—United States—Directories; State governments—United States—Officials and employees; State governments—United States—Officials and employees—Registers; Legislators—United States—States—Directories; State governments—Periodicals; State governments—United States—Handbooks, manuals, etc.—Bibliography—Periodicals; Legislative bodies—United States—States—Handbooks, manuals, etc.—Bibliography—Periodicals; *Geog.*—Politics and government—Directories; *Geog.*—Executive departments—Directories; State governments—United States—Handbooks, manuals, etc.—Bibliography

A few commercially published sources provide information on all 50 states in one binding. They are most useful when you are gathering data on a number of states or for states outside of your own. If your research is limited to your own state, official publications, such as state registers and official state telephone books, are usually your best resource. However, commercial publications' coverage of state personnel is impressive, and they often employ more effective subject classification of officers and offices than official publications do. When seeking information about state courts, also refer to the directories of federal courts described in previous sections.

The Book of the States. Lexington, KY: Council of State Governments, 1935–.
> *The Book of the States* has been published biennially by the Council of State Governments since 1935. The book is designed to provide information on the structures, administration, regulation, elections, financing, and functional activities of state governments. It covers facts about executive, legislative, and judicial branches; their intergovernmental relations; and their primary areas of public service. The current 1996/97 edition consists of 10 chapters that cover data for all 50 states and U.S. jurisdictions as well as an appendix of essays that includes critical examinations of issues before state governments. *The Book of the States* is the council's flagship publication and is supplemented by three other council directories published in one binder under the title *State Leadership Directories*. We describe *State Leadership Directories* and each of its constituent parts below.

State Leadership Directories. Lexington, KY: Council of State Governments, 1995–.
> *State Leadership Directories* is available in a loose-leaf binder format consisting of three resources with three separate identities: *State Legislative Leadership, Committees, and Staff*; *State Elective Officials and the Legislatures*; and *State Administrative Officials Classified by Function*.

State Administrative Officials Classified by Functions. Lexington, KY: Council of State Governments, 1967–1994, 1995–.
> *State Administrative Officials Classified by Functions* lists the names, titles, addresses, and telephone numbers of thousands of the highest ranking state administrators (whether elected or appointed) by the state government function for which they are responsible. Of the more than 150 separate functional categories of administrative responsibility handled by state administrative officials, more than 10 pertain to criminal justice: chief justice, corrections, court administration, criminal justice data, criminal justice planning, juvenile rehabilitation, law enforcement, parole and probation (adult), public defender, state police, victims of crime compensation, and vocational rehabilitation.
>
> This resource is especially valuable because of this functional classification system; it allows you to find just the right state official to help solve a problem or answer a

need. Unfortunately, the functional categories and accompanying definitions presented in this book do not apply to all states since state governments are organized in diverse ways. (See exhibit 2-12 for a sample page. This source is also available in microform.)

State Elective Officials and the Legislatures. Lexington, KY: Council of State Governments, 1977–1994; 1995–.

> *State Elective Officials and the Legislatures* comprises three components covering selected state executive branch officials, state court of last resort judges (whether elected or appointed), and state legislators. It includes rosters for all 50 states, the District of Columbia, and U.S. territories. Members of the courts of last resort are listed by name only. Because members of these courts are not elected by the public in all states, a two-letter code appears alongside the name of the court to indicate the method by which the judges are selected for and retained in office. The legislative rosters are organized by chamber and include the names, parties, districts, and mailing addresses of the legislatures. The information reported is primarily collected from state election administration offices, legislative service chamber research agencies, and court administration offices. This resource is also available in microform.

State Legislative Leadership, Committees, and Staff. Lexington, KY: Council of State Governments, 1979–1994; 1995–.

> The *State Legislative Leadership, Committees, and Staff* directory comprises two sections: legislative organization and legislative directory. Section 1, legislative organization, lists names, addresses, and telephone numbers by state. Under state name, you can find each state's primary office building name, capital, address, telephone number, and general office hours. Under officer and staff service, you can find, listed by chamber, the officers, staffs, public information offices, and research and policy units that serve the entire membership or just the majority and minority parties. Standing committees covers substantive standing committees, fiscal committees, and procedural committees. Legislative agencies covers agencies created by the legislature to serve both chambers.
>
> Section 2, the legislative directory, contains listings of selected legislative officers, committees, and functions, including senate presidents and house speakers; pro tempores, majority and minority, of both chambers; and the senate secretaries and house clerks. Committees are categorized by areas of interest, such as judiciary and social and human services. Also available in microform.

State Yellow Book. New York: Monitor Publishing, 1989–.

> This semiannual publication is a directory to more than 35,000 employees and officers in the executive and legislative branches of government for the 50 states, the District of Columbia, and U.S. territories. It is divided into four areas of coverage: executive branches, legislative branches, state profiles, and intergovernmental agencies. Each entry gives office name, address, telephone and fax numbers, and e-mail addresses (when available). Photographs and biographical profiles of the state governors are provided in addition to the names, titles, and telephone numbers of the top personnel of each office or agency. The state profiles section provides useful, and sometimes difficult-to-obtain information, such as how to access vital records. The *State Yellow Book* also includes a subject index and a separate personnel index, as well as a listing of intergovernmental organizations.

As mentioned above, official state publications, such as state registers and official state telephone books, are usually your best resource for identifying who to contact (and where they can be contacted) in state and local governments. State directories are referred to by various generic terms, among them are state blue books, state red books, legislative manuals, state registers, and state manuals. Finding the correct subject heading or keyword to use in a library catalog can be problematic. This is one of those instances when, having failed to find the correct subject heading or a reasonable title word to access these resources, you should ask a librarian to assist you. Bibliographic sources, such as the one listed below, can also be instrumental in finding the correct title of a specific state's register.

State Reference Publications: A Bibliographic Guide to State Blue Books, Legislative Manuals and Other General Reference Sources. Topeka, KS: Government Research Service, 1991–.

> *State Reference Publications* is a valuable bibliographic source for the often hard-to-find directories and reference materials of state governments. It furnishes references for local- and state-oriented publications including abstracts, prices, publishers' names, addresses, and telephone and fax numbers. References are categorized into several types: blue books and general reference, legislative manuals and handbooks, directories and biographies, statistical abstracts, government and politics books, and other reference sources.

Since the World Wide Web has taken a vital role in dissemination of information, states have begun to create their own home pages. As of this writing, many of these sites are solely marketing tools; as state governments catch up with technology, the amount of directory information they offer should increase dramatically.

Piper Resources. **"State and Local Government on the Net."** http://www.webcom.com/~piper/state/states.html (March 10, 1997).

> Add this Web site to your list of bookmarks or add it to your own Web page so you can visit it easily. "['State and

Law Enforcement

Conducts state-level
criminal investigations.

ALABAMA
Jeff Sessions
Attorney General
Off. of the Attorney
    General
State House
11 S. Union St., Ste. 310
Montgomery, AL 36130-
0152
Phone: (334) 242-7300
Fax: (334) 242-7458

Gene Mitchell
Director
Dept. of Public Safety
500 Dexter Ave.
Montgomery, AL 36130-
4001
Phone: (334) 242-4394
Fax: (334) 242-0512

ALASKA
Ronald L. Otte
Commissioner
Dept. of Public Safety
P.O. Box 111200
Juneau, AK 99811-1200
Phone: (907) 465-4322
Fax: (907) 465-4362

ARIZONA
Joe Albo
Director
Dept. of Public Safety
2102 W. Encanto Blvd.
Phoenix, AZ 85005-6638
Phone: (602) 223-2359

ARKANSAS
John Bailey
Director
State Police
P.O. Box 5901
Little Rock, AR 72215
Phone: (501) 221-8200
Fax: (501) 224-4722

CALIFORNIA
Daniel E. Lungren
Attorney General
1515 K St., Ste. 511
Sacramento, CA 95814
Phone: (916) 324-5437

COLORADO
Carl W. Whiteside
Director
Bur. of Investigation
Dept. of Public Safety
690 Kipling St.
Lakewood, CO 80215
Phone: (303) 239-4300
Fax: (303) 235-0568

CONNECTICUT
John M. Bailey
Chief State's Attorney
Div. of Criminal Justice
340 Quinnipiac St.
P.O. Box 5000
Wallingford, CT 06492
Phone: (203) 265-2373

DELAWARE
Alan D. Ellingsworth
Superintendent
State Police
State Police Headquarters
1441 N. DuPont Hwy.
Dover, DE 19901
Phone: (302) 739-5911
Fax: (302) 739-5966

FLORIDA
Tim Moore
Commissioner
Dept. of Law Enforcement
P.O. Box 1489
Tallahassee, FL 32302
Phone: (904) 488-8771
Fax: (904) 488-2189

GEORGIA
Milton E. Nix, Jr.
Director
Bur. of Investigtion
3121 Panthersville Rd.
Decatur, GA 30034
Phone: (404) 244-2501

HAWAII
Margery S. Bronster
Attorney General
425 Queen St.
Honolulu, HI 96813
Phone: (808) 586-1500
Fax: (808) 586-1239

IDAHO
Robert Sobba
Director
Alcoholic Beverage
    Control Div.
Dept. of Law Enforcement
P.O. Box 700
Meridian, ID 83680
Phone: (208) 884-7003

ILLINOIS
Terrence Gainer
Director
State Police
103 State Armory
Springfield, IL 62706
Phone: (217) 782-4593
Fax: (217) 785-2821

INDIANA
Lloyd R. Jennings
Superintendent
State Police
IGC-North, 3rd Fl.
Indianapolis, IN 46204
Phone: (317) 232-8241

IOWA
Darwin Chapman
Director
Div. of Criminal
    Investigation
Dept. of Public Safety
Wallace State Off. Bldg.
E. 9th & Grand Ave.
Des Moines, IA 50319
Phone: (515) 281-6203

KANSAS
Larry Welch
Director
Bur. of Investigation
1620 SW Tyler
Topeka, KS 66612-1837
Phone: (913) 296-8200
Fax: (913) 296-6781

KENTUCKY
Gary Rose
Commissioner
Dept. of State Police
Justice Cabinet
919 Versailles Rd.
Frankfort, KY 40601
Phone: (502) 695-6300
Fax: (502) 573-6615

LOUISIANA
Jannitta Antoine
Deputy Secretary
Dept. of Public Safety and
    Corrections
P.O. Box 94304
Baton Rouge, LA 70804-
9304
Phone: (504) 342-6744

MAINE
Andrew Ketterer
Attorney General
Dept. of Attorney General
6 State House Station
Augusta, ME 04333
Phone: (207) 626-8800

MARYLAND
David Mitchell
Superintendent
State Police
State Police Headquaters
1201 Reisterstown Rd.
Baltimore, MD 21208
Phone: (410) 653-4219

MASSACHUSETTS
Charles Henderson
Commissioner
Div. of State Police
Dept. of Public Safety
470 Worcester Rd.
Framingham, MA 01701
Phone: (508) 820-2350
Fax: (617) 727-6874

MICHIGAN
Mike Robinson
Director
Dept. of State Police
714 S. Harrison Rd.
E. Lansing, MI 48823
Phone: (517) 336-6157
Fax: (517) 336-6255

MINNESOTA
Nicholas V. O'Hara
Superintendent
Bur. of Criminal
    Apprehension
Dept. of Public Safety
1246 Univ. Ave.
St. Paul, MN 55104
Phone: (612) 642-0600
Fax: (612) 642-0633
Email: nicholas.o'hara@
    state.mn.us

STATE ADMINISTRATIVE OFFICIALS CLASSIFIED BY FUNCTIONS. LEXINGTON, KY: COUNCIL OF STATE GOVERNMENTS, 1967-
1994; 1995-

EXHIBIT 2-12

Local Government on the Net'] is intended to maintain and update the list of state government information services on the Internet. With few exceptions this list is confined to servers controlled and managed by state and local agencies and excludes information found on freenet and commercial services. Although the main state server is listed under the executive branch, it may contain information related to the legislative or judicial branches of state government. Local and regional government sites are included if they (1) have a domain that is obviously a city (ci) or county (co) one; (2) include specific mention of the government agency responsible for the site; or (3) have pages that include more than listings from local telephone books or brochures." In addition to links to state sites and sites that relate to the states, this site contains links to national organizations serving state and local governments and to other services related to state government.

Intergovernmental Organizations

Intergovernmental organizations, like other kinds of organizations, gather to share information and knowledge, but sometimes they exist for other reasons as well. The National Conference of Commissioners on Uniform State Laws, for example, is composed of individuals in the legal profession appointed to the conference by the states' governors. Their mission is to promote uniformity in state law on subjects where uniformity is deemed desirable and practicable. They are responsible for drafting documents such as the *Model Penal Code,* the *Uniform Controlled Substances Act,* and the *Criminal Extradition Act* to name a few. State legislatures, in turn, adopt these acts at their discretion via the usual legislative processes. Another such organization is the Council of State Governments. The council is considered a joint agency of all state governments that, through its various programs, works to strengthen individual states as well as their interactions with each other. Several of the council's publications, such as the *Book of the States* listed above, are useful tools for identifying and contacting state government officials who may respond to your research interests. The authors have also listed the intergovernmental organizations most pertinent to criminal justice research.

American Judges Association
  National Center for State Courts
  300 Newport Avenue
  Williamsburg, VA 23187
  Telephone: 804-253-2000
  Fax: 804-229-7899

Association of State Correctional Administrators
  Spring Hill West
  South Salem, NY 10590
  Telephone: 914-533-2562
  Fax: 914-533-2105

Conference of State Court Administrators
  National Center for State Courts
  300 Newport Avenue
  Williamsburg, VA 23187
  Telephone: 804-253-2000
  Fax: 804-229-7899

Council of State Governments
  3560 Iron Works Pike
  P.O. Box 11910
  Lexington, KY 40578
  Telephone: 606-244-8000
  World Wide Web: http://www.csg.org/

International Association of Chiefs of Police
  515 N. Washington Street
  Alexandria, VA 22314
  Telephone: 703-836-6767
  Fax: 703-836-4543
  World Wide Web: http://www.amdahl.com/ext/iacp/

International Association of Correctional Officers
  1033 W. Van Bern, Suite 500
  Chicago, IL 60607
  Telephone: 312-996-5401
  Fax: 312-413-0458

National Association of Attorneys General
  444 N. Capitol Street, NW, Suite 339
  Washington, DC 20001
  Telephone: 202-434-8000
  Fax: 202-434-8008

National Center for State Courts
  300 Newport Avenue
  Williamsburg, VA 23187
  Telephone: 804-253-2000
  Fax: 804-229-7899
  World Wide Web: http://www.ncsc.dni.us/

National Conference of Commissioners on Uniform State Laws
  676 N. Saint Clair Street, Suite 1700
  Chicago, IL 60611
  Telephone: 313-915-0195
  Fax: 312-915-0187

National Criminal Justice Association
  444 N. Capitol Street, NW, Suite 618
  Washington, DC 20001
  Telephone: 202-347-4900
  Fax: 202-508-3859

Chapter 3
Sources of Basic Information

Guides to the Literature
- Criminal Justice
- Sociology
- Psychology
- Law and Legal Research
- General Guides to the Literature

General Reference Materials
- Dictionaries
- Criminal Justice Dictionaries
- Sociology Dictionaries
- Psychology Dictionaries
- Law Dictionaries

- Foreign Language Dictionaries in Criminal Justice and Law
- Slang Dictionaries
- Thesauri
- Encyclopedias and Handbooks
- Criminal Justice Encyclopedias
- Sociology Encyclopedias
- Psychology Encyclopedias
- Law Encyclopedias

Annual Reviews of the Literature

Book Reviews

Two important elements of effective research are (1) building a vocabulary in the subject of your inquiry so that you can connect to information about it, and (2) understanding how information and concepts in your subject are arranged so that you can combine them in a meaningful way.

In some instances, you will have enough of a vocabulary in your subject to begin gathering books and periodical articles, searching databases, and talking to authorities almost immediately. There will be times, however, when the subject is new to you. Your inability to describe it can hamper your research because you don't have sufficient knowledge of the jargon. Likewise, if you don't know the information terrain, how the subject is organized, how it relates to the larger topic of criminal justice, or where it connects to subtopics of the discipline, you may not be able to adequately connect essential and relevant concepts. In chapter 1, we described the whole of criminal justice and how it evolved from other disciplines. This basic information is useful, but it is not enough to begin research on the complicated issues such as criminal recidivism. Thus, although your vocabulary lesson on the subject has begun with your reading of chapter 1, you may need additional, but still basic, information.

In this chapter we have collected tools that will help you acquire a basic vocabulary and a knowledge of the arrangement of information in criminal justice. Thus, you will find a collection of relevant dictionaries and encyclopedias. These are the tools you can use to begin to build your vocabulary and knowledge of the subject. We have also included guides to and reviews of the literature as sources for understanding how information in criminal justice is arranged.

As your research progresses from the most basic sources to the more scholarly ones, your vocabulary and understanding of it will increase. You will find that by the time you have completed your work, the coverage you found initially in an encyclopedia will seem elementary.

GUIDES TO THE LITERATURE

As with any research project, the user must develop a strategy for selecting material. Most researchers want to locate the best and most appropriate sources. Therefore, the researcher must develop a search strategy and know, as precisely as possible, the kind of data necessary and where they can be found. The evaluative nature of guides to the literature is instrumental in this process.

Guides to the literature are designed to introduce the researcher to significant works in a specific field in a systematic way. Beginning with a guide to the literature is often an ideal way to begin a research project. Guides provide an overview of the most significant sources of information and assist the user by describing specific tools and ways to use them. Guides generally make use of such specialized reference tools as periodical indexing and abstracting services, encyclopedias, dictionaries, handbooks, online services, bibliographies, and government publications. Those that evaluate, describe, and compare the various works are especially useful. In brief, they teach the reader how to study the subject and provide a map of the vast amount of literature that exists in any given discipline.

Generally, some of the sources listed in a guide will not be available. However, guides can lead you to a significant amount of material available in your library and at least make you aware of the existence of other materials that may be of use. You can then decide whether to search out the titles unavailable at your local library, either by interlibrary loan or by visiting a nearby library.

No discipline exists in a vacuum. Although criminology is generally considered a subdiscipline of sociology and you may tend to rely on sources from this discipline, you should also consult guides for other disciplines because they could prove useful for a given research project. You cannot write a research paper on white-collar crime, for example, without consulting literature guides on business information and law. In short, researchers should always develop an interdisciplinary approach when searching the literature.

The guides described below focus on criminal justice and those areas of study most closely related to criminal justice: sociology, psychology, and law. The sources listed were chosen for their usefulness and should be available in most large library collections. Although the current listing is limited to these disciplines, similar guides exist for political science, business, anthropology, economics, education, and other general subject areas.

Additionally, many guides to researching narrow areas or time-sensitive subjects may appear in the periodical literature. Articles in journals such as *Law Library Journal* will provide useful guides to researching topics such as Islamic Criminal Law. To access guides published in periodicals, see chapter 5 on periodical indexes.

Criminal Justice Guides to the Literature

Library of Congress subject headings: Criminal justice, administration of—Bibliography; Reference books—Bibliography; Reference books—Criminal justice

Lutzker, Marilyn, and Eleanor Ferrall. *Criminal Justice Research in Libraries: Strategies and Resources.* New York: Greenwood Press, 1986.

Although somewhat dated, *Criminal Justice Research in Libraries* is an excellent book for locating criminal justice reference sources. It has particularly good sections on efficiency in research and historical research with primary sources.

O'Block, Robert L. *Criminal Justice Research Sources.* 3d ed. Cincinnati: Anderson, 1992.

Criminal Justice Research Sources is designed to lead students through the process of criminal justice research with a wide range of available sources. There are many sources listed here, but evaluative annotations are somewhat limited. This resource has no index, which proves frustrating when looking for a specific title or author.

Wright, Martin, ed. *Use of Criminology Literature.* London: Butterworth; Hamden, CT: Shoe String, 1974.

Major criminological literature of the United Kingdom and the United States is discussed in this book. After a brief discussion on how to conduct a literature search, various experts discuss the most important literature in their particular area of interest. This title is particularly useful for its evaluative comments of some of the earlier literature of the field.

Some guides on specific criminal justice topics have begun to appear, such as the three listed below from ABC-CLIO.

Atkins, Stephen E. *Terrorism: A Reference Handbook.* Santa Barbara, CA: ABC-CLIO, 1992.

Kruschke, Earl R. *Gun Control: A Reference Handbook.* Santa Barbara, CA: ABC-CLIO, 1995.

Ryan, Patrick J. *Organized Crime: A Reference Handbook.* Santa Barbara, CA: ABC-CLIO, 1995.

All three of these resources have a similar format, which includes a general introduction to the subject discussed, a chronology of events, biographical sketches, legislation and statistical data, a directory of organizations, and selected print and nonprint resources. These could prove very helpful to the undergraduate student or as a general introduction to the selected topic. Watch for more guides of this type from a variety of publishers.

Sociology Guides to the Literature

Library of Congress subject headings: Reference books—Sociology—Bibliography; Sociology—Bibliography; Social sciences—Bibliography; Social sciences—Bibliography; Sociology—Outlines, syllabi, etc.; Sociology—Study and teaching

Aby, Stephen H. *Sociology: A Guide to Reference and Information Sources.* Littleton, CO: Libraries Unlimited, 1987.

This guide exposes the reader to more than 600 major reference sources within the social sciences. Contained within are descriptions of indexes, bibliographies, dictionaries, and other reference works published between 1970 and early 1986. Materials published before 1970 are listed if they are considered classics in the field. Author, title, and subject indexes are also included.

Bart, Pauline, and Linda Frankel. *The Student Sociologist's Handbook.* 4th ed. New York: Random House, 1986.

This do-it-yourself guide is an excellent resource on the mechanics of writing a sociology paper and the primary library research materials in the discipline. There are chapters on periodical literature, abstracting and indexing services, bibliographies, bibliographic aids, and governmental and nongovernmental sources of statistical data. An epilogue discusses career opportunities for sociologists. Appendixes contain outlines of the Dewey and Library of Congress classification systems. This is a particularly useful source for undergraduates.

Day, Alan, and Joan M. Harvey, with Marilyn Mullay, eds. *Walford's Guide to Reference Material.* Vol. 2, *Social and Historical Sciences, Philosophy and Religion.* 5th ed. London: Library Association, 1991, 1992; distributed in the U.S. by UNIPUB.

Walford's standard reference guide is international in scope but emphasizes English-language materials, especially British ones. Each social science discipline is addressed in a separate chapter and entries are arranged by subject in each chapter. Annotations generally contain quotations from reviewing sources and occasionally refer the user to related works. It has a combined author-title-subject index.

Herron, Nancy L., ed. *The Social Sciences: A Cross-Disciplinary Guide to Selected Sources.* Englewood, CO: Libraries Unlimited, 1989.

The Social Sciences is a collection of essays and bibliographies on the social sciences in general and on the specific areas of anthropology, communications, economics and business, education, geography, history, law and legal issues, political science, psychology, sociology, and statistics and demographics. It is selective, citing only the most important references and periodicals in a given area. Of particular interest to the criminal justice researcher are the chapters on law and legal issues and sociology. Remaining chapters offer general introductions to the literature of related subjects. Author, title, and subject indexes are included.

Hoselitz, Berthod F. *A Reader's Guide to the Social Sciences.* Rev. ed. New York: Free Press, 1970.

This collection of essays is useful as a general introduction to the literature of the social sciences. The essays cover the various social science disciplines, each including a selective list of books, journals, and bibliographies.

Li, Tze-Chung. *Social Science Reference Sources: A Practical Guide.* 2d ed. Westport, CT: Greenwood Press, 1990.

Some 2,200 basic reference sources in the social sciences are discussed in the second edition of *Social Sciences Reference Sources.* This guide inventories materials on the social sciences in general, as well as the subdisciplines of cultural anthropology, business, economics, education, geography, history, law, political science, psychology, and sociology.

Webb, William H., Alan R. Beals, and Carl Milton. *Sources of Information in the Social Sciences.* 3d ed. Chicago: American Library Association, 1986.

Considered an indispensable bibliographic resource for the social sciences, *Sources of Information* is particularly noted for its comprehensiveness and authoritative annotations. Chapter 1 covers general titles and is followed by chapters on history, geography, economics and business administration, sociology, anthropology, psychology, education, and political science. Each chapter lists citations to the standard reference titles in the given area. Also furnished is a brief essay on the origin and development of the discipline and a description of its major subdisciplines.

Psychology Guides to the Literature

Library of Congress subject headings: Reference books—Psychology—Bibliography; Psychology—Bibliography; Psychology—Research

Baxter, Pam M. *Psychology: A Guide to Reference and Information Sources.* Englewood, CO: Libraries Unlimited, 1993.

Psychology provides approximately 600 sources in psychology, focusing on materials published after 1970. Sections address general social science and reference works, specific social science materials, general psychology reference sources, and special topics in psychology. Works are listed alphabetically, and entries contain full bibliographical data and an evaluative comment. Emphasis is placed on quality electronic resources.

Borchardt, D. H., and R. D. Francis. *How to Find Out in Psychology: A Guide to the Literature and Methods of Research.* New York: Pergamon Press, 1984.

Written for the advanced student, chapters furnish an overview of the discipline, an excellent discussion of research methods, a description of the major bibliographic aids in the field, and information on the profession, including details on education, training, careers, and organizations in psychology. Author and subject indexes are included.

McGinnis, Raymond G. *Research Guide for Psychology.* Westport, CT: Greenwood Press, 1982.

Although the *Research Guide for Psychology* may be a bit dated, it is still considered an excellent guide to psychology and related disciplines. Seventeen bibliographic essays provide lengthy discussions of over 1,200 information sources, with entries arranged according to the classification system of *Psychological Abstracts* (see chapter 5, page 106). The first chapter covers general references sources in psychology and is followed by chapters addressing additional major topics and many more subtopics. Under each heading, works are arranged into four sections: "Research Guides," "Substantive Information Sources," "Substantive Bibliographic Sources," and "Bibliographic Information Sources." Of particular interest to the criminal justice researcher are sections on social issues such as psychological disorders, including antisocial behavior, and treatment and prevention, including behavior modification, rehabilitation, and penology. Complete bibliographic citations are given in a separate section at the end of the book for all works mentioned in the chapters. A combined author-title-subject index is provided.

Reed, Jeffrey G., and Pam M. Baxter. *Library Use: A Handbook for Psychology.* 2d ed. Washington, DC: American Psychological Association, 1992.

Library Use is a good introductory guide designed with the college student in mind. Chapters show the student how to start a research paper, how to locate books, the use of indexes, doing citation searching, locating and using government publications, computer searching, and the use of psychological tests and measurements. Two particularly useful sections are those on citation searching using the *Social Sciences Citation Index* (see chapter 5, page 97) and searching *Psychological Abstracts* (see chapter 5, page 106). This guide is well illustrated and is designed to cover sources typically found in a college library.

Law and Legal Research Guides to the Literature

Library of Congress subject headings: Legal research—United States

Cohen, Morris L., Robert C. Berring, and Kent C. Olson. *How to Find the Law.* 9th ed. St. Paul, MN: West Publishing Co., 1989.

This legal research guide is a standard source for those interested in learning to use the primary and secondary sources of American law. Additional chapters cover international law, English and Commonwealth legal materials, foreign and comparative law and research strategies.

Jacobstein, J. Myron, Roy M. Mersky, and Donald J. Dunn. *Fundamentals of Legal Research.* 6th ed. Westbury, NY: Foundation Press, 1994.

Now in its sixth edition, *Fundamentals of Legal Research* is considered a standard guide for students. Although its primary focus is American law, separate chapters are devoted to international law and English legal research. Initial chapters on how the law works through legislation, administrative regulations, and court decisions precede a description of how to use the publications available. Also included are a glossary, a table of legal abbreviations, a bibliography of state guides to legal research, a discussion of legal research in U.S. territories, information on the national reporter system, a listing of specialized report services by subject, and an index.

Price, Miles O., Harry Bitner, and Shirley Raissi Bysiewicz. *Effective Legal Research.* 4th ed. Boston : Little, Brown and Co., 1979.

Although this guide has not been revised in several years, it is considered a classic in the field. Earlier editions are particularly useful to law librarians because they provide comprehensive inventories of printed legal literature.

Reams, Bernard D., Jr., James M. Murray, and Margaret H. McDermott. *American Legal Literature: A Guide to Selected Legal Resources.* Littleton, CO: Libraries Unlimited, 1985.

American Legal Literature annotates over 550 legal resources in three sections: "Current Primary Legal Materials," "Selected Legal Reference Sources," and "Subject Bibliography of Law-Related Monographs." Of particular note is the listing of monographs in section three, which includes brief annotations of over 200 alphabetically arranged topics.

See chapter 8, page 157 for other guides to the legal literature.

General Guides to the Literature

The library guide listed below is more general in nature than the specific ones listed above. Balay's *Guide to Reference Books*, found in virtually every library, is an excellent source for a general overview of reference materials.

Balay, Robert, ed. *Guide to Reference Books.* 11th ed. Chicago: American Library Association, 1996.

This excellent multidisciplinary guide provides brief, critical annotations on over 15,500 reference books (generally defined). Arrangement is by broad category: general reference works, humanities, social and behavioral sciences, history and area studies, science and technology, and medicine. The researcher should find the section "Social and Behavioral Sciences" of primary interest, but the other categories can be consulted for references on related disciplines. An index provides author, title, and subject access to materials covered. Since criminal justice is extremely interdisciplinary, Balay's work is helpful in identifying guides, bibliographies, indexes, encyclopedias, and other reference works in related areas with which the researcher may not be familiar. Exhibit 3-1 displays parts of the section on criminology.

CRIMINOLOGY

Guides

Lutzker, Marilyn. Criminal justice research in libraries : strategies and resources / Marilyn Lutzker and Eleanor Ferrall. N.Y. : Greenwood, 1986. 167 p.   **CK242**
     Useful for both experienced and novice researchers. Includes a discussion of the organization of information in criminal justice, research design and control, and bibliographic searching, including computer database searching. Presents suggested research sources, special areas of research, and lists of subject headings and directories.
                                                        Z5703.4.C73L87

Bibliography

Beirne, Piers. Comparative criminology : an annotated bibliography / compiled by Piers Beirne and Joan Hill. N.Y. : Greenwood, 1991. 144 p. (Research and bibliographical guides in criminal justice, no. 3).   **CK243**
     Lists articles, books and book chapters dealing with cross-national study of crime. 500 entries, listed alphabetically within 11 chapters. Author and subject indexes.   Z5703.B44

Berens, John F. Criminal justice documents : a selective, annotated bibliography of U.S. government publications since 1975. N.Y. : Greenwood, 1987. 236 p. (Bibliographies and indexes in law and political science, no. 7).   **CK244**

Indexes; Abstract journals

Criminal justice abstracts. v. 9 (Mar. 1977)– . Monsey, N.Y. [etc.] : Willow Tree Pr. [etc.], 1977– . Quarterly.
                                                        CK248
     Earlier titles: *Information review on crime and delinquency* and *Selected highlights of crime and delinquency literature,* 1968–69; *Crime and delinquency literature,* 1970–76. Publ. 1968–83 by the National Council on Crime and Delinquency.
     Abstracts of books, journal articles, dissertations and reports, arranged alphabetically by author in six broad sections (Crime, the offender, and the victim; Juvenile justice and delinquency; Police; Courts and the legal process; Adult corrections; Crime prevention and control strategies). Some issues include specialized bibliographies or literature reviews. Subject and geographical index; author index. A cumulative index covering 1968–85 was published in 1989.   HV6001.C67

Criminal justice periodical index. 1975– . [Ann Arbor, Mich.] : Indexing Services, Univ. Microfilms, 1975– . 3 issues per year, including annual bound cumulation.   **CK249**
     Indexes by author and subject more than 100 U.S., British and Canadian journals in the fields of corrections, criminal law, criminology, drug abuse, family law, juvenile justice, police studies, prison ad-

BALAY, ROBERT, ED. *GUIDE TO REFERENCE BOOKS.* 11TH ED. CHICAGO: AMERICAN LIBRARY ASSOCIATION, 1996.

EXHIBIT 3-1

GENERAL REFERENCE MATERIALS

Dictionaries

The dictionary has long been the traditional source to which we have turned for vocabulary needs. It gives us an alphabetical listing of words, along with the pronunciation, spelling, and a precise definition of a given term or concept. It may also give the origin of a word, its part of speech, related terms, equivalent words in foreign languages, and examples of its use. A dictionary sets an authoritative standard. When researching or writing a research paper, you often find it necessary to consult a wide range of dictionaries.

Most of us are familiar with the college-type dictionary, and often this is all we need to satisfy our vocabulary needs. But, for fuller treatment of the more specialized words used in subject areas, you may need to reach beyond the abridged college dictionary traditionally found on the student's desk. A good, general unabridged dictionary is an excellent first choice in many instances. It offers good coverage of most social science terms and, in addition to definitions, includes information on the etymology, syllabification, and pronunciation of words. In fact, definitions in general dictionaries may be more extensive than those found in more specialized dictionaries. Two excellent dictionaries of this type are *Webster's Third New World Dictionary of the English Language* and the *Random House Unabridged Dictionary,* which is known for its inclusion of more contemporary terminology.

These are but two examples of some of the excellent unabridged dictionaries that you should consult. However, because all fields of study have their own unique language and special vocabulary—and criminal justice is no exception— it is often necessary to consult a subject dictionary to obtain a more precise definition of a term, to clarify the meaning of a special or technical term, or to locate synonyms that more clearly demonstrate a term's relationship to words of similar meaning within the subject area. Subject dictionaries may include new words, current biographical sketches of noted individuals in the discipline, describe agencies in the field, report landmark legal cases, or note important reports and studies. A specialized subject dictionary can also be an important source of terms for computer or CD-ROM searches. However, specialized dictionaries are often not concerned with etymology, syllabification, or pronunciation. If criminal justice dictionaries are unavailable at your local library, remember that most criminal justice textbooks have a limited dictionary (or glossary) and the *Encyclopedia of Crime and Justice* (see page 55) has an extensive one.

Another type of dictionary included here and in chapter 3 is the biographical dictionary. These generally give brief accounts of noted individuals or those associated with noteworthy criminal events. Some of these dictionaries have special features, including summaries of important Supreme Court cases and listings of relevant agencies.

Criminal Justice Dictionaries

Library of Congress subject headings: Crime and criminals—Biography—Dictionaries; Crime and criminals—Dictionaries; Criminal justice, administration of—Dictionaries; Law enforcement—Dictionaries; Corrections—Dictionaries

Beckman, Erik, comp. *The Criminal Justice Dictionary.* 2d ed. Ann Arbor, MI: Pierian Press, 1983.

Notice in exhibit 3-2 the brevity of the definitions given by Beckman of the approximately 3,000 terms from the fields of law (L), police administration (PA), corrections (Cor), criminology (Cr'y) and criminalistics (Cr's). Since definitions are short, other sources should be consulted when a fuller discussion of a term is needed.

Champion, Dean J. *The Roxbury Dictionary of Criminal Justice: Key Terms and Major Court Cases.* Los Angeles, CA: Roxbury, 1997.

This extensive, interdisciplinary-oriented dictionary is divided into two sections. The first provides definitions of criminal justice terms—many of which are accompanied by examples from the research literature—and listings of leading criminological theorists. The second section is an alphabetized and indexed listing of significant U.S. Supreme Court cases relevant to the criminal justice system.

DeSola, Ralph. *Crime Dictionary.* Rev. ed. New York: Facts on File, 1988.

The highly regarded *Crime Dictionary* provides over 10,000 definitions of terms relating to all aspects of crime—from the vocabulary of criminals to that of law enforcement officials. The revised edition includes over 1,500 entries encompassing the latest terminology on topics such as legal terms, law enforcement language, medical and psychiatric terms relating to crime and drug addiction, relevant abbreviations, weapons, prison nicknames, terms relating to white-collar crime, names of criminal gangs and terrorist groups, government crime-fighting agencies, criminal slang, and historical references. Appendixes include a section of terms and phrases relating to crime from various foreign languages, place-name nicknames used in the underworld and upperworld, and selected sources of print fiction, nonfiction, and other media sources relating to crime.

ABANDON (L)
  To give up one's interest in property.
ABANDUN (ABANDUM) (L)
  Any thing abandoned, surrendered, or confiscated.
ABATE (L)
  To put an end to.
ABANDONMENT (L)
  Relinquishment of a claim or privilege.
ABDUCTION (L)
  The crime or forcibly, fraudulently or by criminal persuasion, taking away a person; kidnapping.
      See also: Kidnapping.
ABET (L)
  To aid, encourage, or incite another to commit a criminal offense.
ABEYANCE (L)
  In expectation; the condition of a right when there is no person presently entitled to it; a legal delay or holding period.
ABIDE (L)
  To submit to or conform to something, i.e., an order of court or a legal decision.
ABJUDICATE (L)
  To give away or transfer by force of law.
ABJURE (L)
  To renounce.
ABNORMAL BEHAVIOR (Cr'y)
  Deviation from socially accepted patterns of behavior, in different historical periods, and in different social situations.
ABORTICIDE (Cr'y, L)
  The removal of the fetus from the uterus.
ABORTION (Cr'y, L)
  The termination of pregnancy before the fetus reaches a point viability or capability of life outside the womb. May be a miscarriage or a premature expulsion of the fetus.
ABORTIVE TRIAL (L)
  A trial terminated without reaching a verdict, a mistrial.
ABROGATE (L)
  To annul or repeal a former law by the passage of a new one.
ABSCOND (L)
  To leave one's usual residence; to conceal oneself in order to avoid legal proceedings; to disappear, sometimes with the property of others.
ABSENCE (L)
  Nonappearance; being away from one's domicile. When continued for seven years, without the person being heard from, a

BECKMAN, ERIK, COMP. *THE CRIMINAL JUSTICE DICTIONARY.* 2D ED. ANN ARBOR, MI: PIERIAN PRESS, 1983.

EXHIBIT 3-2

Fay, John J. *The Alcohol/Drug Abuse Dictionary and Encyclopedia.* Springfield, IL: Charles C. Thomas, 1988.

The *Alcohol/Drug Abuse Dictionary and Encyclopedia* defines over 1,400 terms, phrases, and concepts related to drug and alcohol abuse. Entries cover the broad spectrum from the coarse language of the drug subculture to the professional language of law and medicine. Appendixes cover listings of jargon peculiar to drug users, state agencies for alcohol and drug abuse control, drug poison information centers, and drug and alcohol abuse resource agencies, as well as an index of generic names of commonly abused substances cross-referenced with brand names.

Fay, John J. *Butterworth's Security Dictionary: Terms and Concepts.* Boston: Butterworth, 1987.

Intended for both the security professional and the practitioner, this book presents short, concise definitions of the language of the security field. Separate sections list abbreviations commonly used, procedural concepts, legal concepts, and organizational concepts. Useful appendixes include a list of terrorist groups, electronic security system symbols; metric conversion tables; and measurement tables. A brief bibliography of sources is included.

Fay, John J. *The Police Dictionary and Encyclopedia.* Springfield, IL: Charles C. Thomas, 1988.

This specialized dictionary defines clearly approximately 5,000 terms, phrases, and concepts in law enforcement. Of particular note is the inclusion of slang terms that are used by individuals with whom the police may come in contact. Summaries of Supreme Court decisions of special interest to police officers are included.

Kohn, George C. *Dictionary of Culprits and Criminals.* Scarecrow, 1986.

The *Dictionary of Culprits and Criminals* contains concise sketches of more than 1,100 assassins, murderers, spies, traitors, terrorists, kidnappers, poisoners, rapists, gangsters, racketeers, swindlers, con artists, impostors, forgers, counterfeiters, pirates, thieves, burglars, gunfighters, Western outlaws, and other unsavory characters. Entries include the full name of the individual, including well-known nicknames, date of birth and death, a career outline, and how the individual died. Cross-references are indicated by capital letters within entries. *See also* references direct the reader to other individuals linked to the criminal. American figures predominate, but European and other individuals well known to Americans are also included. One subject index lists individuals by type of crime (e.g. assassin, spy, murderer, poisoner, racketeer); a second index lists names and book titles.

Martin, Julian A., and Nicholas A. Astone. *Criminal Justice Vocabulary.* Springfield, IL: Charles C. Thomas, 1980.

Criminal Justice Vocabulary provides short definitions for criminal justice terms, including slang, legal terminology, technical jargon, brand names, abbreviations, organizations, and other words and phrases. Pronunciation is provided where the author deemed necessary. This dictionary is good for slang definitions, but for general terms, a more general dictionary should be consulted.

Nash, Jay Robert. *Dictionary of Crime: Criminal Justice, Criminology, & Law Enforcement.* New York: Paragon House, 1992.

The *Dictionary of Crime* gives brief entries of slang, drug lingo, law enforcement terminology, and legal terms.

Rush, George E. *Dictionary of Criminal Justice: With Summaries of Supreme Court Cases Affecting Criminal Justice.* 4th ed. Guilford, CT: Dushkin, 1994.

Now in its fourth edition, the now standard *Dictionary of Criminal Justice* provides over 3,600 definitions of terms specific to the study of criminal justice. Interdisciplinary in nature, it includes medical, legal, forensic, sociological, anthropological, psychological, and management terms commonly used in criminal justice. Summaries of more than 800 important Supreme Court cases affecting criminal justice are included, as well as descriptions and addresses of many criminal justice-related agencies. The dictionary also has an index of court cases cited, appendixes of doctoral programs in criminal justice, a listing of forensic agencies and organizations, an annotated listing of health and consumer toll-free hotlines, and a list of juried referred journals in criminal justice, including affiliation and publishing data.

SEARCH Group. *Dictionary of Criminal Justice Data Terminology: Terms and Definitions Proposed for Interstate and National Data Collection and Exchange.* 2d ed. Washington, DC: U.S. Department of Justice, 1981.

This *Dictionary* is useful for finding definitions of terms used in criminal justice statistics. Although mainly intended for system developers or managers, data originators, and statistical data users, these clearly written definitions should also be of use to researchers, academics, and criminal justice professionals. See exhibit 3-3 for a sample page from the dictionary demonstrating the use of *see* and *see also* references. Annotations provide depth and context to the definitions.

Walsh, Dermot, and Adrian Poole, eds. *A Dictionary of Criminology.* Boston: Routledge & Kegan Paul, 1983.

Definitions vary in length in this selective dictionary. Accompanying each definition are usage, cross-references, and further references.

Williams, Vergil L. *Dictionary of American Penology: An Introductory Guide.* Westport, CT: Greenwood Press, 1979.

This updated encyclopedic dictionary presents information on a wide variety of topics related to the American correctional system in the mid-1990s. Alphabetically arranged entries describe various aspects of the prison system, including profiles of each state prison system and major components of the federal system. Each entry concludes with relevant references for further information. Appendixes include a listing of prison reform organizations, prison system addresses, and U.S. government statistics pertaining to correctional activities. A useful bibliography and subject/name index are included.

Sociology Dictionaries

Library of Congress subject headings: Social Sciences—Dictionaries; Social sciences—Methodology—Dictionaries; Sociology—Dictionaries

Since criminal justice is closely related to sociology, dictionaries in sociology are also extremely valuable. When deciding which source to use, try to determine whether a concise definition will do or if a lengthy

runaway—(juveniles) UCR 29   In Uniform Crime Reports terminology, the name of the UCR offense category used to record and report apprehensions of juvenile runaways for protective custody, as defined by local statute.

annotation

The *UCR Handbook* states: "For purposes of the Uniform Crime Reporting program, report in this category apprehensions for protective custody as defined by your local statute. Count arrests made by other jurisdictions of runaways from your jurisdiction. Do not include protective custody actions with respect to runaways you take for other jurisdictions."

See also **delinquency**.

search   see **illegal search and seizure**

search warrant   *recommended statistical terminology*   A document issued by a judicial officer which directs a law enforcement officer to conduct a search at a specific location, for specified property or persons relating to a crime(s), to seize the property or persons if found, and to account for the results of the search to the issuing judicial officer.

annotation

A search warrant can be issued only if a judicial officer is satisfied that there is **probable cause** (see entry) to believe that the person(s) or object(s) being sought will be found at the location indicated. See also **illegal search and seizure**.

security   The restriction of inmate movement within a correctional facility, usually divided into maximum, medium and minimum levels.

annotation

Security level is not solely a physical characteristic of correctional facilities but a type of physical custodial status of inmates, relating both to restrictive architectural features of buildings or areas and to human regulation of inmate movement within the facility.

No standard definition of security levels is offered in this terminology because the defining physical and behavioral restrictive features vary greatly among jurisdictions. The proposed correctional facility terminology distinguishes between confinement facilities and residential facilities, according to the inmates' daily access, or lack of daily access, to external community activities and resources, and not according to internal restrictiveness. See **correctional facility (adult)**.

Data publications concerning security classifications should provide the definitions of security and security levels used in the reporting jurisdiction.

seizure   see **illegal search and seizure**

self-defense   The protection of oneself or one's property from unlawful injury or the immediate risk of unlawful injury; the justification for an act which would otherwise constitute an offense, that the person who committed it reasonably believed that the act was necessary to protect self or property from immediate danger.

DICTIONARY OF CRIMINAL JUSTICE DATA TERMINOLOGY: TERMS AND DEFINITIONS PROPOSED FOR INTERSTATE AND NATIONAL DATA COLLECTION AND EXCHANGE. 2D ED. BY SEARCH GROUP, INC.

EXHIBIT 3-3

discussion of a term is necessary. While most dictionaries give adequate clarification of terms, an encyclopedic dictionary, or even an encyclopedia, may be the best resource for in-depth explanations. Listed below are several sociology dictionaries that will serve you well. Note that some of the very fine dictionaries included are of British origin. Sometimes this perspective will be beneficial, but be aware that differences do occur.

Abercombie, Nicholas, Stephen Hill, and Bryan S. Turner. *The Penguin Dictionary of Sociology*. 3d ed. London; New York: Penguin Books, 1994.

> *The Penguin Dictionary of Sociology*, written by British sociologists, contains clear and precise definitions and the researcher is frequently referred to related terms defined elsewhere. Also included are biographies of major sociologists and an appendix of significant books and articles referred to in the definitions.

Gould, Julius, and William L. Kolb, eds. *A Dictionary of the Social Sciences*. New York: Free Press, 1964.

> Some 270 scholars from the United States and Great Britain produced this highly regarded dictionary, which contains lengthy definitions of over 1,000 terms. Using A to D sections under each term, the editors define each term, provide background for divergent usages, present short bibliographies, and make extensive use of cross-references. (See exhibit 3-4 for the definition of criminology.) As you read this example, keep in mind that the dictionary was published in 1964 and the definitions of words evolve with time. You will find that the discipline has evolved a bit since this work was published.

Jary, David, and Julia Jary. *The HarperCollins Dictionary of Sociology*. New York: Harper-Perennial/ HarperCollins, 1991.

> *The HarperCollins Dictionary of Sociology* presents short definitions of sociological terms, a number of short biographical entries, and definitions of statistical terms (with illustrative tables) used by social scientists. Cross-references are generously provided along with a bibliography.

Johnson, Allan G. *The Blackwell Dictionary of Sociology: A User's Guide to Sociological Language*. Cambridge, MA: Blackwell Reference, 1995.

> Published in 1995, *The Blackwell Dictionary of Sociology* presents lengthy definitions of sociological terms and biographical sketches of major sociological figures. There are numerous *see* and *see also* references, some illustrations, and many suggestions for further reference. Although a limited number of criminal justice terms are defined, this is a good source for definitions of general sociological terms.

Lachmann, Richard, ed. *The Encyclopedic Dictionary of Sociology*. 4th ed. Guilford, CT: Dushkin, 1991.

> *The Encyclopedic Dictionary of Sociology* offers good, succinct entries of more that 1,350 terms prepared by 120 authorities. It provides easy access to the terminology, institutions, and practices of modern sociology. Longer articles are signed, and liberal use is made of *see* and *see also* references.

Marshall, Gordon, ed. *The Concise Oxford Dictionary of Sociology*. Oxford; New York: Oxford University Press, 1994.

This source is intended for researchers without extensive knowledge of the discipline. Written by a distinguished team of sociologists from the University of Essex (UK), the *Oxford Dictionary* contains lengthy articles and gives references to key works in the subject area and biographical sketches of notable deceased individuals. *See* references and asterisks lead the user to related entries. The dictionary provides fairly good coverage of criminal justice concepts.

Miller, P. McC., and M. J. Wilson. *A Dictionary of Social Science Methods*. New York: Wiley, 1983.

> This dictionary is useful for anyone involved in quantitative research. The 1,000 alphabetically arranged definitions of terms and techniques used in empirical research methods in the social sciences are concise and clearly written. Numerous cross-references to related terms are provided.

Psychology Dictionaries

> Library of Congress subject headings: Psychiatry—Dictionaries; Psychology—Dictionaries; Psychology, Physiological—Dictionaries

Listed below are some useful dictionaries in psychology. As you approach subjects that are interdisciplinary, constant attention should be paid to the available resources in other disciplines. While the lists here are limited to some of the more closely related disciplines, remember to check similar sources in other disciplines, namely anthropology, political science, and economics, using general guides to the literature such as Balay's *Guide to Reference Books*. (See page 42.)

Harre, Rom, and Roger Lamb, eds. *The Encyclopedic Dictionary of Psychology*. Cambridge, MA: MIT Press, 1983.

> More than 300 academic scholars from the United States and abroad contributed to this excellent source. Signed entries vary from a single paragraph to more than a page in length and contain brief bibliographies. Biographies are included. *See* references are amply provided as well as a combined name-subject index.

Goldenson, Robert M., ed. *Longman Dictionary of Psychology and Psychiatry*. New York: Longman, 1984.

> This general psychological dictionary gives excellent coverage to the vocabulary of psychology, psychiatry, and related fields. There are 21,000 definitions of terms and phrases and more than 1,000 biographical entries.

Pettijohn, Terry F., ed. *The Encyclopedic Dictionary of Psychology*. 4th ed. Guilford, CT: Dushkin, 1991.

> *The Encyclopedic Dictionary of Psychology* presents concise definitions of psychological terms, ample cross-references, illustrations, topic guides, subject maps, and

enjoy a comprehensive criminal code whereas the U.K. does not.

It is however possible to detect certain underlying unities in the notion of offences against the criminal law. (a) Such conduct is usually socially harmful and morally blameworthy. (b) Such conduct is also sufficiently serious for it to merit state intervention; it is not simply left to the individuals who may have been wronged to seek redress by way of civil action in the courts.

It should, however, be noted that: (a) By no means all antisocial conduct is criminal; (b) The test of moral wrong is not infallible, for many acts which are highly immoral may be quite outside criminal law. (c) It has been strongly suggested that some acts which are at present regarded as criminal offences should no longer be so treated, e.g. homosexual behaviour between consenting adult males, and attempted suicide. The Wolfenden Report contends that there must be a realm of private morality and immorality which is not the law's concern because crime and sin cannot be equated (ibid., p. 24).

C. Some criminologists have sought to widen the definition of crime so as to include types of socially deviant behaviour which are not punishable as offences in the courts but which are regarded as sociologically significant. For example, E. Sutherland, in his book on *White Collar Crime* (New York: The Dryden Press, 1949) writes about forms of business or commercial activity which are essentially dishonest or socially harmful, but may not *legally* constitute a criminal offence. This approach may be valuable in revealing the shortcomings of the criminal law or the true nature of deviant behaviour. However, it would be wise for criminologists not to stray too far from the consideration of behaviour legally defined as criminal (see J. Hall, *General Principles of Criminal Law*, Indianapolis: Bobbs-Merrill, 1947, pp. 10–11; D. R. Taft, *Criminology*, New York: The Macmillan Co., 1956, pp. 15–16).

J. E. Hall Williams

See also: CRIMINOLOGY

Criminology (Also Penology)

A. *Criminology* and *penology* are those subfields of sociology in which the investigator attempts to formulate and test theories as to why criminal law becomes law, why people break such laws, why societies do what they do to those who break such laws, and what the effects of varying modes of law enforcement are. Thus it is apparent that the two disciplines are concerned with the enforcement, by means of formal sanctions, of conformity to social norms, and with the conditions which produce nonconformity; and being so concerned are logically a part of the general field of social control (q.v.).

B. Contemporary criminology and penology give attention mostly to 'civilized' societies with formalized government. In such a context the criminologist has been forced to define crime as the violation of any law interpreted as protecting the public welfare, violation of which results in the charging of the state's law enforcement agencies with the responsibility of apprehension and punishment of the offender. Such a definition is necessary, even though many of these laws have never been the result of consensus (q.v.). Despite the heterogeneity of the laws which may be defined as criminal laws, and of the acts which may be defined as crimes, there is considerable unanimity among criminologists as to the major areas of investigation. These are: (a) statistical data on crimes and criminals; (b) police systems for apprehending violators; (c) court systems for trying the accused; (d) systems for treating or punishing the convicted; (e) systematic analysis of social conditions predictive of criminal behaviour and possibilities of rehabilitation.

C. By virtue of the nature of their subject matter, criminology and penology are applied sciences. The whole law enforcement machinery of society is an effort to prevent law violation. Thus the development of a body of theory concerning the causes of crime and the possibilities of modifying these causes is an integral part of the task of the criminologist. Similarly, the penologist is confronted with the task of evaluating and perhaps inventing systems of punishment and treatment.

Harlan W. Gilmore

See also: CRIME (also CRIMINAL LAW)
SOCIAL CONTROL
SOCIAL DISORGANIZATION

Cross-Cousins

A. In modern English a cousin is a cognate of the same generation as the person in reference. A first cousin is the child of a sibling (i.e. brother or sister) of a parent. A *cross-cousin* is a first cousin who is the child of a father's sister

GOULD, JULIUS, AND WILLIAM L. KOLB, EDS. *A DICTIONARY OF THE SOCIAL SCIENCES*. NEW YORK: FREE PRESS, 1964.

EXHIBIT 3-4

subject directories. Longer entries are signed, and all entries are prepared by experts in the field.

Law Dictionaries

Library of Congress subject headings: Law—Dictionaries; Law—United States—Dictionaries; Law—United States—Terminology

While the authors furnish the context for using the leading law dictionaries more fully in chapter 8, brief descriptions are also provided below.

Anderson, William S. *Ballentine's Law Dictionary, with Pronunciations*. San Francisco: Bancroft-Whitney, 1969.

One of the standard dictionaries in law, *Ballentine's* offers precise definitions of legal terms, along with their correct pronunciations. Definitions are based on court decisions, with case citations provided.

Black, Henry Campbell. *Black's Law Dictionary: Definitions of the Terms and Phrases of American and English Jurisprudence, Ancient and Modern.* 6th ed. St. Paul, MN: West Publishing, 1990.

> *Black's* is another standard legal authority for precise definitions and correct pronunciation of terms, phrases, and maxims used in all areas of American and English jurisprudence. Citations to court decisions and other legal authorities are included when a term has been affected by legislation, court rules, or court decisions. Numerous cross-references are used, and there is a separate list of legal abbreviations. This dictionary is available online through WESTLAW.

Burton, William C. *Legal Thesaurus.* 2d ed. New York: Macmillan, 1992.

> The *Legal Thesaurus* is designed to provide the legal researcher with terms that are not contained in a general thesaurus. Entries include the part of speech, a definition if multiple meanings exist, associated legal concepts, related foreign phrases and concepts, and related words and terms. This work includes an extensive index to assist the user in locating synonyms and is extremely useful in formulating WESTLAW and LEXIS-NEXIS keyword searches.

Gifis, Steven H. *Law Dictionary.* 3d ed. Hauppauge, NY: Barron's Educational Series, 1991.

> This resource is another excellent law dictionary designed for the law student and other legal professionals. Be sure to consult the "Key to Effective Use of This Dictionary." Useful appendixes present the U.S. Constitution, the American Bar Association model codes and rules of professional responsibility and professional conduct, a listing of the federal judicial circuits and system, and a listing of U.S. Supreme Court justices, 1989–1990.

Oran, Daniel. *Oran's Dictionary of the Law.* 2d ed. St. Paul, MN: West Publishing, 1991.

> *Oran's Dictionary* provides concise, contemporary definitions.

Foreign Language Dictionaries in Criminal Justice and Law

> Library of Congress subject headings: Criminal law—United States—Dictionaries—Spanish; Law—Dictionaries—Polyglot

With the ever-increasing interest in international criminal justice issues and the vast amount of scholarly criminal justice literature that exists in French, German, Dutch, Spanish, and Russian, for example, researchers can become frustrated unless they have at least a minimal proficiency in a given foreign language. Frequently, the researcher turns either to someone who has a working knowledge of the language or to an English-language abstract. But even the most resourceful or fluent researcher occasionally needs to consult a foreign language dictionary for help. Although any good bilingual or multilingual dictionary can be helpful, specialized criminal justice and law dictionaries, like the ones listed below, give particular emphasis to the words of the criminal justice field.

Adler, J. A., ed. *Elsevier's Dictionary of Criminal Science in Eight Languages: English/American—French—Italian—Spanish—Portuguese—Dutch—Swedish—German.* Amsterdam; New York: Elsevier, 1960.

> This multilanguage glossary covers criminal law, criminology, criminalistics, and auxiliary sciences through 10,930 numbered English and American terms, each accompanied by one-world equivalents in seven other languages.

Benmaman, Virginia, Norma C. Connolly, and Robert Scott. *Bilingual Dictionary of Criminal Justice Terms (English/Spanish).* 2d ed. Binghamton, NY: Gould, 1991.

> The *Bilingual Dictionary of Criminal Justice Terms* is designed to meet the needs of those working in the U.S. court system, where a knowledge of Spanish terminology in criminal procedure of the U.S. common-law system is appropriate. Approximately 900 frequently used English-language terms are listed alphabetically, followed by the Spanish equivalent. (See exhibit 3-5.) Concise definitions are provided in nontechnical language and are frequently followed by explanatory notes and *see also* references. The dictionary also contains a flowchart of the procedural steps from arrest to disposition of a case, penal offense charts, a list of reference works used in compiling the book, and a Spanish index designed to enable the user to locate the English term when a Spanish term is known. With a large Spanish-speaking population in the U.S., this is a good source for English-Spanish translation within the field.

Egbert, Lawrence Deems, and Fernando Morales-Macedo. *Multilingual Law Dictionary: English — Français — Español — Deutsch.* Dobbs Ferry, NY: Oceana: 1978.

> This dictionary is a listing of equivalent legal terms in English, French, German, and Spanish.

Ingleton, Roy. *Elsevier's Dictionary of Police and Criminal Law: English—French and French—English.* Amsterdam; New York: Elsevier, 1992.

> This bilingual dictionary, consisting of separate listings for English and French, is designed to assist police officers, lawyers, and others interested in the translation of

•**Criminal Sexual Contact
(New Jersey, New Mexico)**
The intentional touching by the perpetrator of the victim's private parts directly or through clothing, or causing the victim to touch the private parts of the perpetrator by forcible compulsion or restraint, or if the victim is incapable of consent by reason of age or physical incapacity.

Syn **Sexual abuse
(Arizona, New York)
Sexual Battery
(California)**

•**Criminal sexual contact of a minor (New Mexico)**
The intentional touching by the perpetrator of the victim's private parts directly or through clothing, or causing the victim to touch the private parts of the perpetrator.

Syn **Indecency with a Child
(Texas)
Indecent acts with
children
(Washington, DC)
Molestation of a child
(Arizona)**

Note: Age of child may vary according to jurisdiction.

•**Criminal sexual penetration
(New Mexico)**
The unlawful oral, anal or vaginal penetration or union with the sexual organ of another, or the genital or anal penetration by any object. Seriousness of this offense is conditioned by the age of the victim, the use of force with or without a deadly weapon or the presence of more than one perpetrator.

Abuso deshonesto

Actos corporales externos, impúdicos para la sociedad, realizados abusando de la situación de la víctima, sea mediante coacción o constreñimiento, o por su edad o incapacidad física.

**Abuso deshonesto de un
menor impúber**
Actos corporales externos, impúdicos para la sociedad, realizados abusando de un menor impúber.

Acceso carnal violento

Penetración ilegal por vía oral, vaginal o anal, del miembro viril, o de otro objeto por vía vaginal o anal. La gravedad del delito depende de la edad de la víctima; de que se haya usado o no fuerza, con arma mortífera o sin ella; o de la presencia de más de un agresor.

BENMAMAN, VIRGINIA, NORMA C. CONNOLLY, AND ROBERT SCOTT. *BILINGUAL DICTIONARY OF CRIMINAL JUSTICE TERMS (ENGLISH/SPANISH).* 2D ED. BINGHAMTON, NY: GOULD, 1991.

EXHIBIT 3-5

specialized words and phrases used by the police forces of the United Kingdom and France. Equivalent definitions are given for many of the terms used in criminal law, policing, drugs, and terrorism. Slang and jargon terms used both by the police and criminals are included and relevant acronyms are furnished after the alphabetical entries.

Slang Dictionaries

Library of Congress subject headings: Cant—Dictionaries; Crime and criminals—Language (New words, slang, etc.); English language—Dictionaries—Slang; Police—United States—Language (New words, slang, etc.); Prisoners—United States—Language (New words, slang, etc.)

The colorful language of prisoners, criminals, drug addicts, the underworld, and police has been studied extensively and captured in several slang dictionaries. The classic *Dictionary of American Slang* (Crowell, 1960), compiled by Harold Flexner and Stuart Berg, is useful, but for the criminal justice researcher, slang dictionaries specific to criminal justice are more valuable. In these works, referenced below, you will find definitions for such terms as *double saw* (a $20 dollar bill) and *wing-ding* (a feigned fit or spasm).

Bentley, William K., and James M. Corbett. *Prison Slang: Words and Expressions Depicting Life Behind Bars.* Jefferson, NC: McFarland, 1992.

> Written by ex-inmates, this highly specialized dictionary of the slang terminology of prisoners is arranged alphabetically in categories relating to various aspects of prison life.

Goldin, Hyman E., Frank O'Leary, and Marris Lipsius. *Dictionary of American Underworld Lingo.* Boston: Twayne, 1950.

> The *Dictionary of American Underworld Lingo,* written by two inmates and a prison chaplain, comprises 5,000 entries of the vocabulary of crime. The work is divided into two sections: the first, "Underworld—English," is the larger of the two and includes definitions, while the second section, "English—Underworld," serves as an index to the first.

Maurer, David M. *Language of the Underworld.* Compiled and edited by Allan W. Futrell and Charles B. Wordell. Lexington, KY: University Press of Kentucky, 1981.

> Maurer studied subcultures by investigating the speech patterns of their members. This collection of Maurer's writings drawn from more than 200 books, monographs, articles, and professional papers is arranged in chronological order according to publication date. Selections of particular interest to criminal justice researchers include "The Argot of the Underworld," "Prostitutes and Criminal Argots," "Place Names in the Underworld," "The Argot of Pickpockets," and "The Argot of Confidence Men." The work also offers general and keyword indexes.

Partridge, Eric. *A Dictionary of the Underworld.* 3d ed. London: Routledge & Kegan Paul, 1968.

> This historical and classic dictionary of American and British underworld slang presents short concise listings of the vocabularies of crooks, criminals, racketeers, beggars, tramps, convicts, and petty crooks, as well as the commercial underworld, the drug trade, and the white slave trade. Each definition gives the source of the given meaning and the date of its first known use. Where else can you find a definition for *bucker* (a taxicab driver whose meter is fixed to mark to high) or a *high tober gloak* (a well-dressed and mounted highwayman). In addition to slang terminology, initialisms and place names are also included.

Philbin, Tom. *Cop Speak: The Lingo of Law Enforcement and Crime.* New York: Wiley, 1996.

> *Cop Speak* covers the lingo of police officers and criminals, as well as terms and phrases that reflect all aspects of police work. In addition to brief definitions, many entries also include a brief discussion—sometimes with information on the origin of the term. Cross-references point to related terms.

Thesauri

A thesaurus can be used to identify synonymous words and as a source of controlled vocabulary, that is, words and phrases with specific meanings authorized for use in subject searching. Notably, the three large databases often consulted by criminal justice researchers for bibliographic searching—*National Criminal Justice Reference Service, Sociological Abstracts,* and *Psychological Abstracts*—each have printed thesauri for use with their databases. You should consult such a thesaurus before beginning a search using either printed or online sources. To do so, you must first determine which subject terms will be productive for a given search. A thesaurus can assist in expanding or narrowing your research focus by providing major subject headings for a given term, hierarchical subdivisions, and cross-references to broader, narrower, and related terms. Listed below are a few such thesauri intended for use with specific materials or databases.

In addition to the printed thesauri noted here, you should also consult the *Library of Congress Subject Headings* (see page 69), generally available near the library catalog, before using either a card catalog or an online version of an institution's catalog.

Booth, Barbara, and Michael Blair. *Thesaurus of Sociological Indexing Terms.* 2d ed. La Jolla, CA: Sociological Abstracts, 1989.

> The *Thesaurus of Sociological Indexing Terms* comprises the controlled vocabulary for use with *Sociological Abstracts* (see page 108) and consists of (1) an alphabetical listing of terms, with cross-references from "unacceptable" terms and suggested related terms, and (2) a "rotated" list of terms, which arranges the acceptable terms by "significant" words.

National Criminal Justice Reference Service. *National Criminal Justice Thesaurus: Descriptors for Indexing Law Enforcement and Criminal Justice Information.* Washington, DC: National Criminal Justice Reference Services, 1992.

> The *National Criminal Justice Thesaurus* is intended for use with the National Criminal Justice Reference Service (NCJRS) database but is a handy guide for indexing terms in criminal justice for other applications as well. Descriptors are arranged into four major sections: "Substantive Descriptors," "Organizational Descriptors," "Geographic Descriptors," and "KWOC [Keyword-out-of-Context] Descriptors." This printed work can be an effective aid in

searches of bibliographic databases in criminology, as well in developing a list of search terms for library catalogs or periodical indexes and abstracts.

See exhibit 3-6 for an example page from the *Thesaurus*: bolded terms are *terms of art* used by the NCJRS for indexing. The terms that follow each heading are grouped and labeled as BT (broader term), NT (narrower term). or RT (related term). Thesauri like this one are extremely effective tools for acquiring a vocabulary in a discipline before searching through the literature.

Walker, Alvin. *Thesaurus of Psychological Index Terms.* 7th ed. Washington, DC: American Psychological Association, 1994.

> The *Thesaurus of Psychological Index Terms* is an inventory of the descriptors used for indexing and searching *Psychological Abstracts* and the PsycLit database. (See page 106.)

Encyclopedias and Handbooks

Encyclopedias are highly revered reference works that present us with an overview of knowledge on important subjects. Typically, they contain articles describing concepts, people, events, and places. Often they are accompanied by illustrations, photographs, diagrams, maps, charts, bibliographies, or glossaries. Today many of them are available on CD-ROM. Although encyclopedias are usually arranged alphabetically, they may be arranged by theme or topic. Usually written for the layperson, they are designed to make difficult subjects intelligible. Extensive indexes and generous use of *see* and *see also* references are indispensable tools that make the knowledge contained in encyclopedias accessible to the user.

Traditionally, researchers have turned to multivolume, multidiscipline encyclopedias such as the *Encyclopaedia Britannica* and *Encyclopedia Americana* for general descriptions and as a starting point for research. For research on broad criminal justice issues, such as prisons, delinquency, or police, general encyclopedias are still important as a beginning point. In fact the latest edition of the *Encyclopaedia Britannica* contains lengthy articles on many broad topics in criminal justice. The article on police is 16 pages in length, contains a good bibliography, and is written by an expert in the field. Similar articles in other general encyclopedias tend to be a bit shorter but still present a general overview of the subjects covered. However, general encyclopedias by their very nature and scope are necessarily limited. Therefore, you should consult specific subject encyclopedias when available.

Many highly specialized encyclopedias exist in the field of criminal justice. With increased interest in many of the more popular aspects of the discipline, encyclopedias on the mafia, policing, serial killers, and noted murderers, for example, are an integral part of the literature. Although usually not considered the most scholarly source for information, they do present interesting facts, figures, and brief sketches that can prove helpful or just plain entertaining.

The best place to start is the *Encyclopedia of Crime and Justice* (see Kadish, 1983 below)—an excellent subject encyclopedia that presents the researcher with good background articles on many subjects within the field. Articles are lengthy, signed, and contain bibliographies for further reading. Remember that the *Encyclopedia* was published in 1983 and is now somewhat dated. Regard it as a synthesis of knowledge at the time it was written and make sure to supplement it with more current research, either by a more contemporary review article, a more recently published handbook, or research published in a scholarly book.

In addition to the *Encyclopedia of Crime and Justice*, several excellent encyclopedias in sociology, psychology, and law contain articles that are scholarly, lengthy summaries of existing knowledge in the field written by experts. Older, highly regarded encyclopedias such as the *Encyclopedia of the Social Sciences* (1959, see page 60) and its successor, the *International Encyclopedia of the Social Sciences* (1968, see page 62), are important sources for scholarly, historical perspectives on social science issues. Remember, however, that encyclopedias are starting points and are not intended to be a substitute for in-depth study of a subject area. Also bear in mind that many of them are somewhat dated, and current sources must be used to bring the information up-to-date. In the words of George Sarton, "It is wise to refer to encyclopedias for first guidance; it is priggish to disregard them; [and] it is foolish to depend too much on them" (*Guide to the History of Science*).

The authors have decided to include handbooks in the following section as well because whereas encyclopedias have been thought to give comprehensive coverage to a broad subject area, many reference books now contain the word *handbook* in the title. For the most part, the handbooks listed below are similar to encyclopedias but cover a narrower subject area, offer a more current perspective, and generally contain a collection of essays written by experts.

08515		**Felony courts**
	SN	(Hear cases involving major crimes, such as murder, rape or arson)
08784	RT	Courts/
04613		Criminal investigation/
11149		Night courts
00018		Offense classification
05244		Penalty severity rating
08628		**Felony murder**
	SN	(Homicide committed during another crime, such as armed robbery or burglary but not premeditated)
00472	BT	Homicide
04603		Murder
00027	RT	Adult felony system
03639		Manslaughter
00018		Offense classification
05244		Penalty severity rating
10114		**Felony probation**
04045	BT	Probation
10187	RT	Fleeing felons
10128		Probation costs
08579		Probation evaluation
00319		Probation or parole decisionmaking
		Felony system (adult)
		USE Adult felony system
10076		**Female attorneys**
04852	BT	Attorneys
04215		Females
04894	RT	Equal opportunity employment
09028		**Female correctional guards**
05317	BT	Correctional guards
04658		Correctional personnel
08337	RT	Burnout syndrome
08703		Corrections occupational stress
08974		Corrections personnel selection
11071		Corrections staff gender differences
09078		Female recruitment
08372		Peer assessment
04410		Personnel evaluation
		Female crime causes
		USE Female deviance
08845		**Female crime patterns**
	SN	(Examinations of the nature of offenses by women)
04814	BT	Crime patterns
04541	RT	Behavior typologies
04287		Criminal methods
09871		Female deviance
04818		Future trends
06713		Genetic influences on behavior
08895		Male female offender comparisons
04536		Role perception
09871		**Female deviance**
	UF	Female crime causes
04540	BT	Deviance
08845	RT	Female crime patterns
04532		Socially handicapped
09920		Terrorism causes
		Female guerrillas
		USE Female revolutionaries
05072		**Female inmates**
00411	BT	Female offenders
04215		Females
03919		Inmates
00715		Offenders
10124	NT	Pregnant inmates
05067	RT	Children of inmates
04360		Imprisonment
09835		Prison nurseries
05221		Womens correctional institutions
09273		**Female judges**
04350	BT	Court personnel
04215		Females
00549		Judges
04894	RT	Equal opportunity employment
08349		Feminism
01715		Judge selection

05119		**Female juvenile delinquents**
04215	BT	Females
09504		Juvenile delinquents
03990		Juveniles
10227	RT	Adolescent females
00411		Female offenders
05175		Female status offenders
09503		Juvenile delinquency
09505		Juvenile offenders
05397		Juvenile prostitution
00952		Prostitution
11181		**Female murderers**
00411	BT	Female offenders
04215		Females
00715		Offenders
08325	RT	Abused women
09108		Female victims
10125		Premenstrual syndrome (PMS)
08671		Violent women
00411		**Female offenders**
04215	BT	Females
00715		Offenders
05072	NT	Female inmates
11181		Female murderers
10437		Female sex offenders
05175		Female status offenders
10124		Pregnant inmates
10381		Pregnant offenders
05067	RT	Children of inmates
04761		Coeducational corrections facilities
05119		Female juvenile delinquents
08895		Male female offender comparisons
03671		Male offenders
05352		Nonbehavioral correlates of crime
10125		Premenstrual syndrome (PMS)
08513		Women offender apprenticeship prgs
		Female police officers
		USE Policewomen
09777		**Female police recruits**
04106	BT	Police recruits
04894	RT	Equal opportunity employment
09078		Female recruitment
10442		Gender issues
05125		Male female police performance comp
04362		Police personnel
09550		Police recruit training
09805		Police staff recruitment
09587		**Female police training**
09708	RT	Minority police training
00851		Police responsibilities
05312		Police spouses
08739		Police team training
00860		Police training/
09078		**Female recruitment**
04134	BT	Recruitment
11071	RT	Corrections staff gender differences
09060		Criminal justice careers
09028		Female correctional guards
09777		Female police recruits
05125		Male female police performance comp
04079		Personnel retention
08242		**Female revolutionaries**
	UF	Female guerrillas
		Female terrorists
08119	RT	Counter-terrorist tactics
04526		Political offenders
02206		Revolutionary or terrorist groups
09920		Terrorism causes
04298		Terrorism/
08391		Terrorist profiles
02339		Urban guerrilla warfare
10437		**Female sex offenders**
	SN	(Female perpetrators of sexual abuse)
00411	BT	Female offenders
04215		Females
00715		Offenders
08339	RT	Child sexual abuse
01299		Indecency
10369		Male sexual abuse victims
08935		Sex offense investigations

NATIONAL CRIMINAL JUSTICE THESAURUS: DESCRIPTORS FOR INDEXING LAW ENFORCEMENT AND CRIMINAL JUSTICE INFORMATION. WASHINGTON, DC: NATIONAL CRIMINAL JUSTICE REFERENCE SERVICE.

EXHIBIT 3-6

Criminal Justice Encyclopedias

Library of Congress subject headings: Crime and criminals—Encyclopedias; Criminal justice, administration of—Encyclopedias; Police—United States—Encyclopedias; *Subject*— Encyclopedias

Andrade, John. *World Police & Paramilitary Forces.* New York: Stockton Press, 1985.

World Police & Paramilitary Forces is a survey of police and internal security forces for 177 countries, including the history of each force, its organization and strength, its role in maintaining internal security, and some brief background on the country in which it presides. A selective bibliography provides relevant books available in most large libraries and an appendix lists special equipment available for security duties.

Bailey, William G., ed. *The Encyclopedia of Police Science.* 2d ed. New York: Garland, 1995.

This updated version of *The Encyclopedia of Police Science* contains over 200 entries on various aspects of policing and criminal justice issues. Lengthy, alphabetically arranged articles are well written, signed by police scholars and practitioners from the United States, and conclude with good bibliographies. While most articles deal with the American policing scene, a few are international. Biographies of noted individuals are included. Be sure to use the subject index and appendixes entitled "Bibliography of Police History" and "Index to Legal Cases."

Becker, Harold K., and Donna Lee Becker. *Handbook of the World's Police.* Metuchen, NJ: Scarecrow, 1986.

Entries in the *World's Police* are divided into seven major geographic areas: Africa, Caribbean, Europe, Far East, Middle East, North America, and South America. For each of 160 countries, there is an outline map, information on the history, government, population, language, religion, capital, and police force. The omission of an index makes it difficult to locate individual countries.

Brodsky, Stanley L., and H. O'Neal Smitherman. *Handbook of Scales for Research in Crime and Delinquency.* New York: Plenum Press, 1983.

This unique reference guide provides information on the use of scales in criminal justice research. After introductory chapters on the topic in general, selection criteria, and some how-to-use-this-book information, there are eight chapters entitled "Minnesota Multiphasic Personality Inventory and California Psychological Inventory," "Law Enforcement and Police," "Courts and the Law," "Corrections," "Delinquency," "Offenders," "Crime and Criminality," and "General Scales." Each entry includes a list of references. A bibliography and a subject–scale title index conclude the volume.

Burgess, Ann Wolbert, ed. *Rape and Sexual Assault III: A Research Handbook.* New York: Garland, 1991.

This volume is the third in a series on rape and sexual assault. Earlier volumes were published in 1985 and 1988 and can still be consulted. Titles of sample articles are "The Aftermath of Rape and Sexual Assault," "Victim Populations," "Care Providers," "Aggressors," "The Rape of Street Prostitutes," and "Responding to Rape Victims' Needs."

Cohen, Daniel. *Encyclopedia of Unsolved Crimes.* New York: Dodd, Mead, 1989.

This specialized encyclopedia involves famous cases that attracted public attention but are still considered "unsolved." Articles are arranged into six sections: "Whodunit," "Historic Mysteries," "Was It a Crime?," "Motive Unknown," "Whatever Happened to . . . ?," and "Getting Away with It." The author offers a possible answer to each mystery, but does not draw any conclusions. Cases include the Black Dahlia, Zodiac Killer, Jack the Ripper, Lizzie Borden, Jimmy Hoffa, Dr. Sam Sheppard, and 62 others.

Cyriax, Oliver. *Crime: An Encyclopedia.* London: Andre Deutsch, 1993.

Crime comprises brief essays that describe persons, places, and terminology associated with noted crimes. While it has a decidedly British bent, notable American events are covered as well. A selective bibliography is included, and the index is essential since many of the entries are not under an expected heading.

Davis, Nanette J. *Prostitution: An International Handbook on Trends, Problems, and Policies.* Westport, CT: Greenwood Press, 1993.

This handbook addresses prostitution in multicultural terms using a comparative approach. Articles on prostitution cover 16 countries: Australia, Brazil, Canada, China, England and Wales, Italy, Japan, the Netherlands, Norway, Portugal, Singapore, Taiwan, the United States, Vietnam, West Germany, and Yugoslavia. In each of the 16 country-titled chapters, there is a discussion of (1) social and legal definitions of prostitution, (2) history and trends, (3) theories of prostitution, (4) contemporary status, (5) prostitution and the law, (6) intervention with prostitutes, (7) and social policy concerning prostitution. It has a selective bibliography and separate name and subject indexes.

DiCanio, Margaret. *The Encyclopedia of Violence: Origins, Attitudes, Consequences.* New York: Facts on File, 1993.

Written by a single author, this book aims to present an overview of all aspects of violence, including the social and psychological origins of violent behavior, the cultural and social attitudes that sustain it, the varieties of violence, and its consequences. Appendixes include resources in areas such as the prevention of violence, children, domestic violence, substance abuse, and civil and human rights.

Fay, John J., ed. *Encyclopedia of Security Management: Techniques and Technology.* Boston: Butterworth-Heinemann, 1993.

Although designed for security managers, this alphabetically arranged encyclopedia may be of use when researching issues of security management. It encompasses topics in security administration, specialized security functions, and technology. Articles are a few pages in length, signed, and citation sources listed. A subject index is also included.

Fennelly, Lawrence J., ed. *Handbook of Loss Prevention and Crime Prevention*. 3d ed. Boston: Butterworth's, 1995.

Over 40 security and crime prevention professionals address the methods (e.g., environmental design, security surveys, fire and safety), operations and equipment (e.g., locks, physical barriers, closed circuit television), applications (e.g., security needs of the retail industry, transportation, banks), and management issues of loss prevention and crime prevention.

Gaute, J. H. H., and Robin Odell. *Lady Killers*. Bath, United Kingdom: Firecrest Books, 1981.

Gaute, J. H. H., and Robin Odell. *Lady Killers II*. Bath, United Kingdom: Firecrest Books, 1982.

Both *Lady Killers* and *Lady Killers II* deal with true crimes in which women were the murderers.

Gaute, J. H. H., and Robin Odell. *Murder "Whatdunit": An Illustrated Account of the Methods of Murder*. New York: St. Martin's, 1982.

Murder "Whatdunit" presents concepts and working details of the forensic aspects of murder investigation, thereby giving the reader information on the tools and methods of crime investigation. This resource is also intended to be a reference for professional criminologists.

Gaute, J. H. H., and Robin Odell. *The New Murderer's Who's Who*. London: Harrap, 1989.

The New Murderer's Who's Who is an updated version of a classic reference on notorious murderers who made headlines in their day. Alphabetically arranged entries give a full outline of each case. While coverage is predominately focused on the U.S. and Britain, Europe and the other continents are adequately represented. The book is well illustrated, and an extensive bibliography guides the reader to books of further interest.

Glaser, Daniel, ed. *Handbook of Criminology*. Chicago: Rand McNally, 1974.

The *Handbook of Criminology* presents lengthy essays on all aspects of criminology. Thirty-one articles are grouped into four sections: "Explanations for Crime and Delinquency," "Law Enforcement and Adjudication," "Corrections," and "Prevention of Crime and Delinquency."

Inciardi, James A., ed. *Handbook of Drug Control in the United States*. New York: Greenwood Press, 1990.

The *Handbook of Drug Control* is a reference volume on drug control in the United States with both a historical and contemporary perspective. The *Handbook* is divided into four sections: Part 1 provides the reader with a history of the drug problem, the roots of the current policy effort, the use of drug treatment as a means of demand reduction, and an examination of the correlation between drug use and crime. Part 2 details contemporary efforts at supply and demand reduction, and part 3 discusses problematic sectors and controversies in current drug control efforts, such as foreign policy, drug testing and the constitution, and the legalization of drugs. Part 4 includes appendixes on drug scheduling, drug paraphernalia laws, extradition and drug trafficking, a summary of the 1990 National Drug Control Strategy, federal and state controlled substances acts, and sources of information on drug abuse. The volume concludes with a selective bibliography and name and subject indexes.

Ingleton, Roy D. *Police of the World*. New York: Scribner's, 1979.

Alphabetically arranged by country, entries include general background, and then information on the origins, organization, uniforms, weapons, chief of police, and police authority for each country listed. This source is well illustrated with tables and photographs.

Johnson, Elmer H., ed. *Handbook on Crime and Delinquency Prevention*. Westport, CT: Greenwood Press, 1987.

This anthology of 14 essays examines the diverse issue of crime prevention. After an introductory chapter entitled "The What, How, Who, and Where of Prevention," subsequent chapters cover diverse topics as indicated by such titles as "Environmental Design As a Rationale for Prevention," "Schooling and Delinquency," "Dealing with Crime on the Streets," and "Prevention in Business and Industry."

Johnson, Elmer H., ed. *International Handbook of Contemporary Developments in Criminology*. 2 vols. Westport, CT: Greenwood Press, 1983.

The first volume in this set addresses general issues, such as the International Society of Criminology, the United Nations, developing countries, women and international criminology, and radical criminology. Volume 2 presents profiles on countries such as Argentina, Brazil, Canada, Chile, Costa Rica, Mexico, and the United States.

Kadish, Sanford H., ed. *Encyclopedia of Crime and Justice*. 4 vols. New York: Free Press, 1983.

This four-volume set of 286 essays authored by noted American scholars is an excellent source of background information for both professionals and laypersons on most topics of interest in criminal justice. Entries are lengthy, signed, and each has a short bibliography of additional sources. Volume 4 has a glossary, an index of cases, an index of legal documents, and a general subject-name index. Students and researchers alike are fortunate to have such a fine subject encyclopedia on criminal justice issues available. The encyclopedia is an excellent place to start on topics of interest in criminal justice. Information can be updated by current, state-of-the art reviews. See exhibit 3-7 for an example of the concluding signature, cross-references, and bibliography of a particular article,

ceedings, the system of appeals in criminal matters, the organization of defense services, the possibility of restitution in the criminal process, and the conflict between the integrity of court proceedings and the rights of the press.

THOMAS WEIGEND

See also ADVERSARY SYSTEM; COMPARATIVE CRIMINAL LAW AND ENFORCEMENT, *articles on* CHINA *and* SOVIET UNION; CRIMINAL LAW REFORM; CRIMINAL PROCEDURE: CONSTITUTIONAL ASPECTS; MILITARY JUSTICE: COMPARATIVE ASPECTS; PROSECUTION: COMPARATIVE ASPECTS.

BIBLIOGRAPHY

ABE, HARUO. "Police Interrogation Privileges and Limitations under Foreign Law: An International Symposium—Japan." *Journal of Criminal Law, Criminology, and Police Science* 52 (1961): 67–72.

BAYLEY, DAVID H. *Forces of Order: Police Behavior in Japan and the United States.* Berkeley and Los Angeles: University of California Press, 1976.

CASPER, GERHARD, and ZEISEL, HANS. "Lay Judges in the German Criminal Courts." *Journal of Legal Studies* 1 (1972): 135–191.

Code de procédure pénale. 21st ed. Petits Codes Dalloz. Paris: Dalloz, 1979–1980. Translated as *The French Code of Criminal Procedure.* Translated by Gerald L. Koch. American Series of Foreign Penal Codes 7. South Hackensack, N.J.: Rothman, 1964.

Code of Criminal Procedure of Japan. Rev. ed. EHS Law Bulletin Series. Tokyo: Eibun-Horei-Sha, 1975.

DAMAŠKA, MIRJAN. "Evidentiary Barriers to Conviction and Two Models of Criminal Procedure: A Comparative Study." *University of Pennsylvania Law Review* 121 (1973): 506–589.

———. "Structures of Authority and Comparative Criminal Procedure." *Yale Law Journal* 84 (1975): 480–544.

DANDO, SHIGEMITSU. *The Japanese Law of Criminal Procedure.* Translated by B. J. George, Jr. South Hackensack, N.J.: Rothman, 1965.

DAVIS, KENNETH C.; BUSCK, LARS et al. *Discretionary Justice in Europe and America.* Urbana: University of Illinois Press, 1976.

FELSTINER, WILLIAM L. F. "Plea Contracts in West Germany." *Law and Society Review* 13 (1979): 309–325.

GOLDSTEIN, ABRAHAM S., and MARCUS, MARTIN. "The Myth of Judicial Supervision in Three 'Inquisitorial' Systems: France, Italy, and Germany." *Yale Law Journal* 87 (1977): 240–283.

GREBING, GERHARDT. "Staatsanwaltschaft und Strafverfolgungspraxis in Frankreich." *Funktion und Tätigkeit der Anklagebehörde im ausländischen Recht.* Edited by Hans-Heinrich Jescheck and Rudolf Leibinger, with the assistance of J. Driendl et al. Baden-Baden, Federal Republic of Germany: Nomos, 1979, pp. 13–81.

HERRMANN, JOACHIM. *Die Reform der deutschen Hauptverhandlung nach dem Vorbild des anglo-amerikanischen Strafverfahrens.*

Bonn, Federal Republic of Germany: Röhrscheid, 1971.

KÜHNE, HANS-HEINER. "Opportunität und quasi-richterliche Tätigkeit des japanischen Staatsanwalts." *Zeitschrift für die gesamte Strafrechtswissenschaft* 85 (1973): 1079–1101.

LANGBEIN, JOHN H. *Comparative Criminal Procedure: Germany.* St. Paul: West, 1977.

———. "Mixed Court and Jury Court: Could the Continental Alternative Fill the American Need?" *American Bar Foundation Research Journal* (1981): 195–219.

MERLE, ROGER, and VITU, ANDRÉ. *Procédure pénale.* Traité de droit criminel, vol. 2. 3d ed. Paris: Editions Cujas, 1979.

STÉFANI, GASTON; LEVASSEUR, GEORGES; and BOULOC, BERNARD. *Procédure pénale.* 11th ed. Paris: Dalloz, 1980.

VOLKMANN-SCHLUCK, THOMAS. *Der spanische Strafprozess zwischen Inquisitions- und Parteiverfahren.* Baden-Baden, Federal Republic of Germany: Nomos, 1979.

WEIGEND, THOMAS. "Continental Cures for American Ailments: European Criminal Procedure as a Model for Law Reform." *Crime and Justice: An Annual Review of Research,* vol. 2. Edited by Norval Morris and Michael Tonry. University of Chicago Press, 1980, pp. 381–428.

WEINREB, LLOYD L. *Denial of Justice: Criminal Process in the United States.* New York: Free Press, 1977.

ZIPF, HEINZ. *Kriminalpolitik.* 2d ed. Heidelberg and Karlsruhe, Federal Republic of Germany: C. F. Müller, 1980.

CRIMINAL SUBCULTURES

See CRIME CAUSATION: SOCIOLOGICAL THEORIES; DELINQUENT AND CRIMINAL SUBCULTURES; PRISONS: PRISON SUBCULTURE.

CRIMINAL SYNDICALISM

See SEDITION.

CRIMINOLOGY

The study of crime has probably existed almost as long as lawbreaking. It is traced from prehistoric to modern times in INTELLECTUAL HISTORY, *which has an international perspective. The article* MODERN CONTROVERSIES *discusses in detail current issues in criminology, with special focus on the English-speaking world. The third article,* RESEARCH METHODS, *analyzes a series of strategies for studying crime, each method designed to minimize some types of errors but also having limitations in coping with other types of errors, either in feasibility or in the ethical problems that it creates.*

1. INTELLECTUAL HISTORY	Israel Drapkin
2. MODERN CONTROVERSIES	James F. Short, Jr.
3. RESEARCH METHODS	Alden D. Miller

KADISH, SANFORD H., ED. *ENCYCLOPEDIA OF CRIME AND JUSTICE.* NEW YORK: FREE PRESS, 1983. 4 VOLS.

EXHIBIT 3-7

as well as the *scope note* and outline beginning the next—all useful features when focusing on a topic.

Kagehiro, Dorothy, and William Laufer, eds. *Handbook of Psychology and Law.* New York: Springer-Verlag, 1992.

Intended for the professional seeking information in the fields of law, psychology, and psychology and law, the *Handbook of Psychology* has the following sections for the criminal justice user: "Legal Procedure," "Law of Evidence," "Criminal Law," "Juvenile and Family Law," and "Mental Health Law."

Kelly, Robert J., Ko-Lin Chin, and Rufus Schatzberg, eds. *Handbook of Organized Crime in the United States.* Westport, CT: Greenwood Press, 1994.

This anthology includes 21 reviews and studies that provide a comprehensive overview of organized crime in the U.S. The articles are arranged into the following sections: "Background Issues," "Perspectives on Organized Crime: Theory and Research," "Organized Crime Groups and Operations," and "Control and Containment: Law Enforcement Strategies." An epilogue considers research methods for the study of organized crime, and a biographical essay lists specialized readings.

Klein, Malcolm W., and Katherine S. Teilmann, eds. *Handbook of Criminal Justice Evaluation.* Beverly Hills, CA: Sage, 1980.

Divided into five sections, the *Handbook of Criminal Justice Evaluation* examines the state-of-the-art in criminal justice evaluation, provides descriptions of several approaches to the evaluation process, explores unique features of criminal justice evaluation, addresses the issue of measurement of outcome, and looks at specific fields in criminal justice evaluation (i.e., evaluation changes in female criminality, widening the net in diversion, evaluating correctional systems, evaluating criminal justice legislation, and evaluating the use of evaluations).

Krivacska, James J., and John Money, eds. *The Handbook of Forensic Sexology: Biomedical and Criminological Perspectives.* Amherst, NY: Prometheus Books, 1994.

This anthology presents 24 essays on the science of sexology from the perspective of social policy and legal systems. The range of sexual behaviors such as pedophilia, incest, rape, exhibitionism and voyeurism, prostitution, and sexual harassment are examined in part 1. Part 2 addresses such issues as the case management of sex offenses, Satanism, and adult offenders.

Kurian, George T. *World Encyclopedia of Police Forces and Penal Systems.* New York: Facts on File, 1989.

This *World Encyclopedia* presents information on the history, organization, and education of police forces in 183 countries, including short descriptions of the penal system for each country. Includes a bibliography of 34 sources for additional information, appendixes on Interpol and world police systems, and an index.

Lane, Brian, and Wilfred Gregg. *The Book of Execution: An Encyclopedia of Methods of Judicial Execution.* London: Headline, 1994.

Lane, Brian, and Wilfred Gregg. *The Encyclopedia of Cruel and Unusual Punishment.* London: True Crime, 1993.

Lane, Brian, and Wilfred Gregg. *The Encyclopedia of Mass Murder.* London: Headline, 1994.

Published in England, these titles are of the true crime genre; however, they provide useful information on the specific crime topics covered. Due to the public's fascination with popular crime, you can look for more titles of this nature in the future.

Lane, Brian, and Wilfred Gregg. *The New Encyclopedia of Serial Killers.* London: Headline, 1996.

A popular crime encyclopedia, *Serial Killers* presents brief entries on an array of international serial killers. Includes a select bibliography, general reference works to consult for further information, and alphabetical and geographic indexes.

Lentz, Harris M., III. *Assassinations and Executions: An Encyclopedia of Political Violence.* Jefferson, NC: McFarland, 1977.

Assassinations and Executions' approximately 4,700 entries present a worldwide overview of political assassinations and executions, unsuccessful attempts against major world figures, and violent political events and their victims. For each entry, details include the manner, the motive, the assailant (if known), brief biographical information on the victims, the immediate effects on the political climate of the day, and, in some cases, the fate of the assassins.

MacDonald, Scott B., and Bruce Zagaris, eds. *International Handbook on Drug Control.* Westport, CT: Greenwood Press, 1992.

Essays in this handbook address the drug trade in 21 countries: the United States, Canada, Bolivia, Brazil, Caribbean offshore, Colombia, Mexico, Panama, Peru, the Southern Cone, Western Europe, the Netherlands, Sweden, the United Kingdom, the former Soviet Union, Afghanistan, Iran, Pakistan, Turkey, India, the Golden Triangle, and Singapore.

Maguire, Mike, Rod Morgan, and Robert Reiner, eds. *Oxford Handbook of Criminology.* Oxford, UK: Clarendon Press, 1994.

This collection of 25 essays aims to present a "comprehensive, state-of-the-art map of criminological analysis, research, and debate in Britain today." This volume, the first in what is intended to be a continuing series, is divided into four parts: "Theoretical and Historical Perspectives," "Crime and Causation," "Crime Control and Criminal Justice," and "Social Dimensions of Crime and Justice."

Marley, David F. *Pirates and Privateers of the Americas.* Santa Barbara, CA: ABC-CLIO, 1994.

Using an *A–Z* format, *Pirates and Privateers* profiles the individuals, battles, weapons, ships, and fleets of pirates and privateers from the buccaneer days of the mid-seventeenth to early eighteenth centuries. This encyclopedia includes a select bibliography for further reading and a subject index.

Marshall, W. L., D. R. Laws, and H. E. Barbaree, eds. *Handbook of Sexual Assault: Issues, Theories, and Treatment of the Offender.* New York: Plenum Press, 1990.

The *Handbook of Sexual Assault* examines the assessment and treatment of sex offenders as well as theories concerning the development and maintenance of such crimes.

McShane, Marilyn D., and Frank P. Williams, eds. *Encyclopedia of American Prisons.* New York: Garland, 1995.

Over 160 signed articles address the issue of incarceration in America. Articles ranging from 1,000 to 5,000 words in length address a wide range of issues, including religion in prison, handling convicts with AIDS, juveniles behind bars, boot camps, life without parole, racial conflict in prisons, and sexual exploitation. Each entry includes a selective bibliography, and the work has a comprehensive name and subject index and a chronology of important events in prison history.

Nash, Jay Robert. *Bloodletters and Badmen: A Narrative Encyclopedia of American Criminals from the Pilgrims to the Present.* New York: M. Evans, 1973.

Written by American true crime writer Jay Robert Nash, *Bloodletters and Badmen* consists of biographical entries describing outlaws, thieves, brothel keepers, syndicate gangsters, arsonists, rapists, kidnappers, murderers, forgers, embezzlers, bombers, assassins, bank robbers, and hijackers from America's criminal past.

Nash, Jay Robert. *Encyclopedia of World Crime.* 6 vols. Wilmette, IL, Crime Books; North Bellmore, NY: Marshall Cavendish, 1990.

The *Encyclopedia of World Crime* is a good source for biographical information on crime figures and proves both entertaining and informative. This popular encyclopedia is really a biographical encyclopedia primarily of crime figures, the majority of them from the U.S. Also included are criminal cases, places, events, and important persons in criminal justice, the judiciary, and penology. Three and one-half of the volumes are devoted to biographical entries; the second half of Volume 4 includes supplements consisting of chronologies of specific crimes (from arson to Western outlaws and gunmen), definitions, and directory information). Volume 5 is a dictionary of current criminal justice terminology, including slang and law enforcement terms. Volume 6 is an unclassified bibliography, a subject index, and a proper name index. Unfortunately, since the bibliography is so lengthy (over 25,000 entries) and also unclassified, it is difficult to use. The set is well illustrated with over 4,000 photographs and illustrations.

Four separate volumes, all published by Paragon House in 1992, organized along topic lines, and all extractions from the larger six-volume set, are also available: *Dictionary of Crime: Criminal Justice, Criminology, and Law Enforcement, Encyclopedia of Western Lawmen and Outlaws, World Encyclopedia of Organized Crime,* and *World Encyclopedia of 20th Century Crime.* Again, these are not scholarly volumes, but they do represent good true crime journalism.

Nash, Jay Robert. *Jay Robert Nash's Crime Chronology: A Worldwide Record, 1900–1983.* New York: Facts on File, 1984.

Nash chronologically lists selected crimes perpetrated during the twentieth century up to the year of publication. Entries fall under five main headings: "Murder," "Robbery," "Organized Crime," "White-Collar Crime," and "Miscellaneous." Brief paragraphs detail each crime, and good use is made of photographs. An extensive name index is helpful for locating a specific case.

Nash, Jay Robert. *Look for the Woman: A Narrative Encyclopedia of Female Poisoners, Swindlers, and Spies from Elizabethan Times to the Present.* New York: M. Evans, 1981.

Over 300 infamous female criminals from Elizabethan times to the 1980s are profiled in this alphabetically arranged encyclopedia, recording the activities of female poisoners, kidnappers, thieves, extortionists, terrorists, murderers, swindlers, and spies.

Newton, Michael. *Hunting Humans: An Encyclopedia of Modern Serial Killers.* Port Townsend, WA: Loompanics, 1990.

Descriptive entries give information on 544 twentieth-century serial murder cases.

Newton, Michael, and Judy Ann Newton. *The FBI Most Wanted: An Encyclopedia.* New York: Garland, 1989.

The Ten Most Wanted Fugitives program was begun by FBI director J. Edgar Hoover on March 14, 1950. Arranged chronologically, biographical sketches of each fugitive include known background, offenses, prison time, cohorts, and life in crime. The encyclopedia is well illustrated with appropriate mug shots, and an appendix gives additional data on each individual.

Newton, Michael, and Judy Ann Newton. *Racial and Religious Violence in America: A Chronology.* New York: Garland, 1991.

Events are listed chronologically beginning in the year 1500 and ending in 1989. There is a bibliography and an index by type of act with subdivisions by geographical area.

Patterson, Richard. *The Train Robbery Era: An Encyclopedia History.* Boulder, CO: Pruett, 1991.

Encyclopedic treatment is given to the history of the train robbery era. Well-written entries document the outlaws, gangs, places, and railway lines involved during this period. Entries include source notation and are well illustrated; cross-references connect related entries. A selective bibliography is provided for further study.

Quay, Herbert C., ed. *Handbook of Juvenile Delinquency*. New York: Wiley, 1987.

The *Handbook of Juvenile Delinquency* discusses the origin and treatment of the delinquent in psychological terms, including epidemiology, psychological correlates, family contributions to delinquency, patterns of delinquent behavior, prediction, prevention, treatment, and research issues.

Saferstein, Richard. *Forensic Science Handbook*. Vol. 3. Englewood Cliffs, NJ: Prentice Hall, 1993.

This is the third volume in a three-part series on forensic science. Earlier volumes were published in 1982 and 1988. Each consists of essays on the practice of criminalistics.

Scott, Harold R., ed. *The Concise Encyclopedia of Crime and Criminals*. New York: Hawthorn Books, 1961.

Although somewhat dated, this source comprises handy biographies of major criminals, criminologists, lawyers, judges, and detectives, as well as useful articles covering the important issues of the time.

Shoemaker, Donald J., ed. *International Handbook on Juvenile Justice*. Westport, CT: Greenwood Press, 1996.

This handbook compares the current systems of juvenile justice in 19 countries. Each chapter depicts one country analyzing the history, formal and informal policies, current issues and problems, and trends and future prospects of its juvenile justice system. The countries represented are Brazil, Canada, China, Egypt, England, France, Germany, Greece, Hong Kong, India, Japan, Mexico, Nigeria, the Philippines, Poland, South Africa, and the United States.

Sifakis, Carl. *The Encyclopedia of American Crime*. New York: Facts on File, 1982.

The *Encyclopedia of American Crime* lists more than 1,500 entries consisting of biographies of people involved with crime or criminal justice; detailed descriptions of various types of crime; explanations of con games and swindles; histories of law enforcement agencies; profiles of famous weapons; histories of infamous neighborhoods and vice districts; definitions of terms of underworld and police slang and legal concepts; and stories of infamous crimes, trials, and hoaxes. The encyclopedia is well illustrated with drawings and photographs. A subject-geographic index is also included.

Sifakis, Carl. *Encyclopedia of Assassinations*. New York: Facts on File, 1991.

The *Encyclopedia of Assassinations* is an international look at intended or actual victims and their assassins from 500 B.C. to the 1990s. Entries are listed alphabetically by victim, and an appendix lists the victim by nationality and place of assassination. A selective bibliography and an alphabetical index are included. This work falls into the category of popular reading but still gives brief, fairly beneficial information on the topic.

Sifakis, Carl. *Hoaxes and Scams: A Compendium of Deceptions, Ruses and Swindles*. New York: Facts on File, 1993.

Another in the true crime genre, this compendium details the origins and methods of numerous scams and gives biographical information on a number of famous con artists and swindlers. The book is well illustrated and includes a selective bibliography, an index of personalities, and an index of subjects.

Sifakis, Carl. *The Mafia Encyclopedia*. New York: Facts on File, 1987.

The *Mafia Encyclopedia* presents a compelling look at the mafia, tracing its development in America from the late nineteenth century through Prohibition, its rise to power in organized crime in the 1930s and 1940s, and its operations to the late 1980s. This work is a quick reference source for information on mafia-related issues, but the serious researcher will need to consult other materials as well.

Thachrah, John Richard. *Encyclopedia of Terrorism and Political Violence*. London; New York: Routledge & Kegan Paul, 1987.

The *Encyclopedia of Terrorism and Political Violence* covers leading figures and organizations associated with political violence and reviews terrorist activities in individual countries. Theories and concepts connected with terrorism, major terrorist incidents, and new trends are explored and discussed. Entries are listed alphabetically, and there is a subject-name index.

Torres, Donald A. *Handbook of Federal Police and Investigative Agencies*. Westport, CT: Greenwood Press, 1985.

This handbook presents profiles of 61 U.S. federal police and investigative agencies. Information is provided on each agency's history, organization, authority and jurisdiction, qualifications and training, and branch officers.

Torres, Donald A. *Handbook of State Police, Highway Patrols, and Investigative Agencies*. New York: Greenwood Press, 1987.

This work presents data on state police, highway patrols, and investigative agencies, covering organizational structure, primary duties, jurisdiction, and educational and training qualifications of sworn personnel.

Tullis, LaMond. *Handbook of Research on the Illicit Drug Trade*. Westport, CT: Greenwood Press, 1991.

The *Handbook of Research on the Illicit Drug Trade* explores the social and economic consequences of the production, trafficking, and use of cocaine, heroin, and cannabis. This work includes a survey of the published literature and an extensive annotated bibliography of some 2,000 published sources.

Vandome, Nick. *Crime and Criminals*. New York: Chambers Kingfisher Graham, 1992.

Some 200 entries cover a range of criminals including assassins, pirates, famous murderers, and serial killers, as well as cases such as those of Lizzie Borden, Jack the Ripper, and Charles Manson. This is a popular encyclopedia and good entertainment, but it is not a definitive reference work.

Van Hasselt, Vincent B., ed. *Handbook of Family Violence*. New York: Plenum Press, 1988.

Nineteen essays by noted scholars and clinicians assess what is known about family violence. Part 1 presents an overview of the field, part 2 is entitled "Theoretical Models," part 3 "Forms of Family Violence," and part 4 explores such special topics as violence among intimates, prevention of wife abuse, the role of neurological factors and alcoholism, the treatment of domestic abuse in the legal system, and cross-cultural perspectives.

Weiner, Irving B., and Allen K. Hess, eds. *Handbook of Forensic Psychology*. New York: Wiley, 1987.

Essays provide background in forensic psychology as a professional field, illustrating civil and criminal justice proceedings as areas of professional practice.

Wilson, Colin, and Patricia Pitman. *Encyclopedia of Murder*. New York: G. P. Putnam's Sons, 1962.

In entries from "Assassinations" to "Without a Body Murders," this popular crime encyclopedia presents a worldwide array of murder cases with articles on fingerprints and the death penalty, for example. The encyclopedia concludes with a selected bibliography and subject and general indexes (mostly individual names).

Wilson, Colin, and Donald Seaman. *Encyclopedia of Modern Murder, 1962–82*. New York: G. P. Putnam's Sons, 1985.

This work supplements Wilson and Pitman's earlier *Encyclopedia of Murder* (1962, listed above) with over 100 noted murderers, assassins, and terrorist groups active during the period between 1962 and 1982. This well-illustrated book has a popular orientation but can be useful for brief sketches of criminals. Entries do not include bibliographical references, but there is a short list of recommended readings and a name index at the end.

Sociology Encyclopedias

Library of Congress subject headings: Social sciences—Encyclopedias; Sociology—Encyclopedias

Borgatta, Edgar F., ed. *Encyclopedia of Sociology*. 4 vols. New York: Macmillan, 1992.

Approximately 400 lengthy, signed articles provide excellent summaries of sociological concepts and theories. Intended for a broad range of users, entries are written by noted scholars, principally from the United States and Canada. Articles are arranged alphabetically; are indexed by terms, individuals, and book titles; and include extensive bibliographies and *see* and *see also* references to guide the user to related items. Entries that address criminal justice issues are "Court Systems of the United States," "Crime Rates," "Criminology," "Family Violence," "Ju-

venile Delinquency and Juvenile Crime," "Prostitution," "Sexual Violence and Abuse," and "White-Collar Crime." As expected, criminal justice is approached from a sociological perspective. However, when a criminologist must access or assess sociologically related topics, the *Encyclopedia of Sociology* provides a grounding in the discipline's vocabulary.

Kuper, Adam, and Jessica Kuper, eds. *The Social Science Encyclopedia*. Rev. ed. Boston: Routledge & Kegan Paul, 1989.

Over 500 scholars give overviews of the social sciences, addressing issues in political science, sociology, economics, anthropology, psychology, law, history, and education. Most articles are less than a page, and about 10 percent of the entries are biographies. Cross-references are numerous, articles are signed and conclude with a bibliography.

Magill, Frank N., ed. *Survey of the Social Sciences*. 5 vols. Pasadena, CA; Englewood Cliffs, NJ: Salem Press, 1994.

This excellent encyclopedia is written with the general reader in mind. Three hundred and thirty-eight lengthy articles address topics from 15 subfields of sociology such as aging and ageism, collective behavior and social movements, culture, deviance and social control, origins and definitions of sociology, population studies or demography, racial and ethnic relations, sex and gender, social change, social institutions, social stratification, social structure, socialization and social interaction, sociological research, and urban and rural life. Articles of particular interest to criminal justice researchers are "Anomie and Deviance," "Capital Punishment," "Child Abuse and Neglect," "Courts," "Criminal Justice System," "Gangs," "Police," and "Prison and Recidivism." The text of articles is divided into three sections: "Overview," "Applications," and "Context." An annotated bibliography follows each section and cross-references list related articles in other volumes of the set. Volume 5 has a short glossary.

Mann, Michael, ed. *The International Encyclopedia of Sociology*. New York: Continuum, 1984.

An excellent source for brief discussions, this single-volume encyclopedia contains 750 concise entries on the basic terms, phrases, concepts, and theories of sociology. Included are biographical sketches of noted sociologists. Numerous cross-references to related terms are given, and the user is often referred to important sources of additional information.

Seligman, E.R.A., and A. Johnson, eds. *Encyclopaedia of the Social Sciences*. 15 vols. 1930–35. Reprint (15 vols. in 5), New York: Macmillan, 1951.

An excellent survey of the social sciences as of the 1930s, this reference source is still valuable for a historical perspective on sociological issues. Signed articles cover important concepts and advances in political science, economics, law, anthropology, sociology, penology, social work, and the social aspects of cognate subjects. Approximately one-half of the entries are brief biographies and all contain ample cross-references. Unfortunately, this series lacks an index.

Exhibit 3-8 shows the beginning and end of the article entitled "Criminology." As with the use of dictionaries, the use of a dated encyclopedia can cause some problems. The subject that follows "Criminology," for example, is "Cripples." The words used to describe topics change from generation to generation.

Sills, David, ed. *International Encyclopedia of the Social Sciences.* 19 vols. New York: Macmillan; Free Press, 1968.

This standard encyclopedia and its articles are of lasting significance. It is an update to the authoritative *Encyclopedia of the Social Sciences* covering the social sciences of the 1960s. It consists of approximately 1,900 lengthy, original articles authored by some 1,500 prominent social scientists from 30 countries and represents the disciplines of anthropology, economics, geography, history, law, political science, psychiatry, psychology, sociology, and statistics. Articles are arranged alphabetically and include bibliographies. There are numerous cross-references and a detailed index is provided in a separate volume. A biographical supplement was published in 1979 (Volume 18) as was a dictionary of quotations (Volume 19) in 1991.

Psychology Encyclopedias

Library of Congress subject headings: Psychiatry—Encyclopedias; Psychology—Encyclopedias

Colman, Andrew M., ed. *Companion Encyclopedia of Psychology.* 2 vols. New York; Routledge, Chapman & Hall, 1994.

This two-volume work contains well-written, succinct articles on all branches of psychological research and professional practice. Volume 1 contains the following sections: an introduction, "Biological Aspects of Behavior," "Sensation and Perception," "Cognition," "Learning and Skills," "Emotion and Motivation," and "Individual Differences and Personality." Volume 2 contains sections on "Developmental Psychology," "Social Psychology," "Abnormal Psychology," "Special Topics," "Research Methods and Statistics," and the "Professions of Psychology." There are subject and author indexes.

Corsini, Raymond J., ed. *Encyclopedia of Psychology.* 4 vols. 2d ed. New York: Wiley, 1994.

This highly regarded compilation contains scholarly articles on all aspects of psychology. Over 500 contributors authored the 2,000 entries covering all major areas of interest in this diverse field. The articles are clearly written and include references to additional materials to assist the reader. The fourth volume contains biographies, a bibliography, separate name and subject indexes, and an appendix. Articles of relevance to the criminal justice researcher are "Deviance," "Juvenile Delinquency," "Rape," "Sexual Abuse," and "Violence and Sexuality in the Mass Media." This more advanced work is best-suited

for researchers with some previous knowledge of psychology.

Eysenck, H. J., ed. *Encyclopedia of Psychology.* 3 vols. 1972. New York: Herder. Reprint, (3 vols. in 1), New York: Seabury Press, 1979.

The *Encyclopedia of Psychology* presents an authoritative, general treatment of important terms and concepts in the field for both the specialist and the layperson. Articles are alphabetically arranged and contributed by over 300 experts. Most articles are signed, and often they are accompanied by a brief bibliography. There is a list of abbreviations, a key to contributors' initials, and a list of main articles; however, the work has no index and few illustrations.

Magill, Frank N., ed. *Survey of Social Science: Psychology Series.* 6 vols. Pasadena, CA: Salem Press, 1993.

This six-volume set is an excellent place to begin for an introduction to psychological issues. Four hundred and ten signed articles give lengthy descriptions in 18 areas of psychology: "Biological Bases of Behavior," "Cognition," "Consciousness," "Developmental Psychology," "Emotion," "Intelligence and Intelligence Testing," "Language," Learning," "Memory," "Motivation," "Origin and Definition of Psychology," "Personality," "Psychological Methodologies," "Psychopathology," "Psychotherapy," "Sensation and Perception," "Social Psychology," and "Stress." Articles are signed and indicate the type of psychology, subfield of study, a brief summary, and principle terms, which are then followed by the main entry divided into three sections: "Overview," Applications," and "Context." Volume 6 has a glossary and an index to the complete set, but biographies are not included.

Manstead, Antony, S. R., and Miles Hewstone. *The Blackwell Encyclopedia of Social Psychology.* London: Blackwell Reference, 1995.

Written by a team of international scholars, this single-volume encyclopedia presents helpful articles on all aspects of social psychology. Entries range from very brief to some of more than 3,000 words. Bibliographies of important sources are included, and there are cross-references and a subject index.

Ramachandran, V. S., ed. *Encyclopedia of Human Behavior.* 4 vols. San Diego: Academic Press, 1994.

The *Encyclopedia of Human Behavior,* intended for students and professionals, contains scholarly, signed articles that address issues of human behavior. Articles of interest to the criminal justice researcher include "Aggression," "Child Abuse," "Eyewitness Testimony," "Forensic Psychology," "Jury Psychology," and "Pornography." Each article contains an outline, a glossary, cross-references, and a bibliography. Volume 4 is an index to the set.

Wolman, Benjamin B., ed. *International Encyclopedia of Psychiatry, Psychology, Psychoanalysis, and Neurology.* 12 vols. New York: Van Nostrand

CRIMINOLOGY deals particularly with the criminal himself, giving special emphasis to the problem of the causation of crime. Scientific interest in the study of the criminal came late because the criminal was classed with the sinner as a theological problem. Both were considered perverse free moral agents who had deliberately violated the will of God. The criminal had also defied the law of the land, and savage punishment was therefore believed to be thoroughly deserved. The full responsibility of the criminal for his own conduct was assumed, and the persons who prescribed and executed punishment were believed to be serving God as well as man. Hence there was little basis for restraint in punishment or little incentive to look into the problem from a naturalistic or human point of view. The rise of scientific criminology had to wait upon the development of a new intellectual perspective and the accumulation of scientific knowledge which would undermine the ancient theological approach to the criminal and his treatment. Criminology is therefore distinctly a product of the nineteenth century although its foundations run back into the first half of the eighteenth.

The origins of a scientific interest in the nature of the criminal were derived from biology and physiology. Aristotle in his treatise on physiognomy anticipated the criminal anthropologists to some extent, and by the time of Grataroli and Della Porta physiognomics had reached a fairly high state of development. With Lavater (1741–1801) and Gall (1758–1828) scientific criminology begins. There is a real filiation of doctrine running through the physiognomists to Gall, Morel and Lombroso. These men drew upon the early physical anthropologists and physiologists and tried as far as possible to use scientific methods in clearing up the mysteries of human behavior. To this group rather than to the criminal law reformers must be assigned the credit for establishing scientific criminology.

Another impetus to criminology and the improved treatment of the criminal was derived from criminal jurisprudence, which strove to abolish torture and to eliminate the barbarous punishments that characterized European procedure. Montesquieu in his *Lettres persanes* (1721) in the form of satire and irony ridiculed the prevalent barbarism in the treatment of criminals. The abuses also attracted the stinging criticism of Voltaire. But the most influential work of the eighteenth century was that of Cesare Bonesana, Marchese di Beccaria. Beccaria's essential doctrines were: the criterion for all reform must be the greatest happiness for the greatest number; the seriousness of a crime must

States. It has had translated into English and published nine of the most important European criminology classics. Law and medicine in relation to crime have been drawn together in the American Society of Medical Jurisprudence. Psychiatrists interested particularly in the social applications of mental hygiene have founded the American Ortho-psychiatric Society, which is especially devoted to the problems of crime and probably does more to advance modern methods in the treatment of crimes than any other American organization. The National Society for Mental Hygiene, founded in 1909, has taken a real interest in the problems of crime, especially in crime prevention. The Commonwealth Fund, a foundation interested especially in mental hygiene, has contributed liberally to research in the borderland between psychiatry and criminology. Organizations such as the federal Children's Bureau have done much to introduce modern methods in juvenile courts and probation. More effective work is being done by these specialized organizations than by the older official organizations in criminology and penology.

HARRY E. BARNES

See: CRIME; JUVENILE DELINQUENCY; CRIMINAL LAW; PUNISHMENT; CORPORAL PUNISHMENT; PENAL INSTITUTIONS; DEGENERATION; PSYCHIATRY. See also biographies of important criminologists.

Consult: WORKS OF HISTORIC INTEREST: Beccaria, Cesare Bonesana, *Dei delitti e delle pene* (Monaco 1764), tr. as *Essay on Crimes and Punishments* (London 1769); Antonini, Giuseppe, *I precursori di C. Lombroso*, Piccola Biblioteca di Scienze Moderne, no. xxii (Turin 1900); Lombroso, Cesare, *Crime, causes et remèdes* (2nd ed. Paris 1906), tr. by H. P. Horton (Boston 1911); Ferri, Enrico, *I nuovi orizzonti del diritto e della procedura penale* (5th ed. with title *Sociologia criminale*, 2 vols., Turin 1929–30), tr. by J. Kelly (Boston 1917), and *Socialismo e scienza positiva* (Rome 1894); Garofalo, Raffaelle, *Criminologia* (2nd ed. Turin 1891), tr. by R. W. Millar (Boston 1914); Benedikt, M., *Die Seelenkunde des Menschen als reine Erfahrungswissenschaft* (Leipsic 1895); Colajanni, N., *La sociologia criminale*, 2 vols. (Catania 1889); Ferrero, G. L., *Criminal Man According to the Classification of Cesare Lombroso* (New York 1911); Féré, C., *Dégénérescence et criminalité* (2nd ed. Paris 1895); Corre, A., *L'ethnographie criminelle* (Paris 1914); Bonfigli, C., *La storia naturale del delitto* (Milan 1893); Kovalevsky, P., *La psychologie criminelle* (Paris 1903); Maudsley, H., *Responsibility in Mental Disease* (London 1874); Bleuler, E., *Der geborene Verbrecher* (Munich 1896); Tarde, Gabriel, *La criminalité comparée* (Paris 1924), and *La philosophie pénale* (5th ed. Paris 1900), tr. by R. Howell (Boston 1912); Vaccaro, M. A., *Saggi critici di sociologia e di criminologia* (Turin 1903); Aubert, A., *La médio-social* (Paris 1902); Loria, A., *Le basi eco-*

SELIGMAN, E.R.A., EDITOR-IN-CHIEF; ASSOCIATE EDITOR, A. JOHNSON. *ENCYCLOPEDIA OF THE SOCIAL SCIENCES.* NEW YORK: MACMILLAN, 1930-35. 15 VOLS. (REPRINTED 1951 IN 5 VOLS.)

EXHIBIT 3-8

Reinhold, 1977 (Produced for Aesculapius Publishers by Van Nostrand Reinhold.). Progress volume, 1983.

> This excellent encyclopedia contains lengthy, well-documented articles in the fields of psychiatry, psychology, psychoanalysis, neurology, and related disciplines. Written by 1,500 specialists, articles are signed, and most include a selected bibliography. Volume 12 has a complete list of articles and name and subject indexes.

Law Encyclopedias

> Library of Congress subject headings: Law—
> United States—Dictionaries

These sources and their use in legal research are covered in greater depth in chapter 8.

American Jurisprudence. 2d ed. Rochester, NY: Lawyers Co-op, 1962–.

> This multivolume encyclopedia provides a subject-oriented approach to legal information with over 400 alphabetically arranged topics covering federal and state laws in the U.S. Extensive footnotes provide citations to legal authorities. Each volume contains its own index, and there is a separate index for the whole set. A tables volume provides access to those topics that treat specific acts such as the Model Penal Code. Annual cumulative pocket supplements update this work.

Corpus Juris Secundum. St. Paul, MN: West Publishing, 1936–.

> *Corpus Juris Secundum* is a standard subject encyclopedia for the legal profession. This work compares and contrasts the legal practices of the federal and state governments. Each article is supported by complete citations to all cases in point. Some volumes contain their own indexes, and there is a separate complete index to the entire set. Although there is no table of cases, the legal abbreviations used are printed in each volume. Annual cumulative pocket parts update this encyclopedia.

The Guide to American Law: Everyone's Legal Encyclopedia. 12 vols. St. Paul, MN: West Publishing, 1983–.

> This concise legal encyclopedia examines over 5,000 major theories, concepts, and personalities of American jurisprudence in terms "everyone" can understand. Entries describe legal principles and concepts, landmark documents and important acts, famous trials, and historical movements and events. Included are biographies of important individuals, descriptions of legal organizations, and information on regulatory agencies and departments. Articles vary in size, from concise, single-sentence entries to articles of several pages. Updated by an annual yearbook.

ANNUAL REVIEWS OF THE LITERATURE

> Library of Congress subject headings: Crime and criminals—Periodicals; Criminal justice, administration of—Periodicals; Subject—Periodicals

Review articles are similar to encyclopedic articles in that they attempt to present an overview of a subject; however, they are generally written for the specialist rather than the layperson. Review articles aim to present a state-of-the-art essay by synthesizing significant research into a concise summary. Since most reviews are comprehensive, critical summaries on a given topic, they offer an excellent way to become familiar with seminal research literature. The Annual Review company's excellent set of annual reviews is particularly noteworthy; the most beneficial titles in this series to criminal justice researchers are *Annual Review of Anthropology, Annual Review of Psychology,* and *Annual Review of Sociology.*

In addition, some scholarly journals, such as the *Psychological Bulletin,* regularly publish review articles. These articles can usually be located with periodical indexes or through indexing and abstracting databases such as *Criminal Justice Abstracts* or *Criminology, Penology, and Police Science Abstracts.* (See chapter 5 for listings of these resources.) Some databases allow you to retrieve review articles separately from others through the use of a *document-type* feature. Another good source of review information is academic dissertations, because often the first chapter of a dissertation is a review of the literature. (See chapter 4, page 90 for a discussion on finding dissertations.)

The serial publications listed below consist entirely of reviews of the literature in criminal justice.

Advances in Criminological Theory. New Brunswick, NJ: Transaction, 1989–.

> The *Advances in Criminological Theory* series focuses on original articles on criminological theory. Certain volumes have focused on a particular theme, such as *Facts, Frameworks, and Forecasts* (Volume 3), *New Directions in Criminological Theory* (Volume 4), *Routine Activity and Rational Choice* (Volume 5), and *The Legacy of Anomie Theory* (Volume 6).

Crime and Justice: An Annual Review of Research. Chicago: University of Chicago Press, 1979–.

> *Crime and Justice* is a highly regarded series that addresses the latest international developments in criminal justice research. Commissioned essays written by experts in their field of study address topics on core areas of research in crime and justice, including legal, psychological, biological, sociological, historical, and ethical issues. Although most volumes address a wide range of topics of current interest, several thematic ones have been published, namely *Modern Policing, Drugs and Crime, Family Violence,* and *Building a Safer Society.*

Criminal Justice History: An International Annual. Westport, CT: Meckler, 1980–.

> This annual presents a wide array of articles on the historical aspects of crime and criminal justice. Authors represent a wide of range disciplines, including history, law, anthropology, sociology, political science, and criminal justice.
>
> In addition to scholarly essays, each volume contains several book reviews of titles with historical interest to the field.

Criminal Law Review. New York: Clark Boardman, 1979–.

> Each volume in the *Criminal Law Review* series includes previously published articles considered to be at the cutting edge of current thinking on important criminal law issues.

BOOK REVIEWS

> Library of Congress subject headings: Books—Reviews—Indexes; Books—Reviews—Periodicals

As part of your research, you may wish to consider how an author's treatment of a subject has been viewed by his or her peers. While a publisher may consider a book worthy of publication, there may be individuals in the field who disagree with the author's conclusions, research methods, or even the thesis of their work. Thus an important part of evaluating information that you are about to use is to seek out others' evaluations of it. Book reviews are a major source of evaluative information.

Combined Retrospective Index to Book Reviews in Scholarly Journals, 1886-1974. Arlington, VA: Carrollton Press, 1979. 15 vols.

> A very useful guide to some one million book reviews published in approximately 500 journals from 1886–1974.

Book Review Digest. New York: H. W. Wilson, 1906–. (Monthly, with quarterly and annual cumulations.)

> This title is particularly useful as it includes excerpts as well as the source from published reviews of the titles covered. However, the number of sources from which reviews are taken is relatively small, and the list often does not include scholarly journals.

Book Review Index. Detroit: Gale, 1965–. (Monthly, with quarterly and annual cumulations.) Available in CD-ROM, diskette/magnetic tape, and online via Dialog, file 137.

> *Book Review Index* (BRI) currently indexes reviews to over 85,000 titles. No excerpts are included, but this source includes many more titles than *Book Review Digest.* Sources of the reviews indexed represent a wide range of popular, academic, and professional interests. BRI's definition of a review is very broad and can include critical comment or simply a description of a book's contents.

Contemporary Sociology: A Journal of Reviews. Washington, DC: American Sociological Association, 1972–. (Bimonthly.)

> Contains reviews and review essays of important new titles in the social sciences. Relevant entries are under the section entitled "Criminology, Deviance, Law."

Index to Legal Periodicals. New York: H. W. Wilson, 1909–.

> See chapter 5 for a complete description of this index. Its significance here is as a source of books reviews on legal subjects.

Rzepecki, Arnold M; and Paul Guenther, eds. *Book Review Index to Social Science Periodicals.* Ann Arbor, MI: Pierian Press, 1978–1981. 4 vols.

> Volumes in the set are arranged chronologically with coverage from 1964 to March 1974. Covers scholarly reviews of books in economics and management, education, history, anthropology, area and ethnic studies, political science, and sociology.

Social Pathology: A Journal of Reviews. Albany, NY: Harrow and Heston, 1995– .

> Covering the areas of criminology, justice studies, social control, social problems, and deviance, this journal offers literature reviews and in-depth book reviews of current literature in the field. The featured review essays average 10–20 pages in length, and the book reviews are approximately 5 pages in length. This source is good for keeping current with major new book titles, particularly because of the evaluative nature of the review and the emphasis on placing a particular work within the existing literature in an area.

Social Sciences Index. New York: H. W. Wilson, 1907–. (Quarterly, with annual cumulations.)

> Besides being a major index to articles in the social sciences, this index also includes entries for books reviewed in the journals covered by the index. These are listed by both author and title at the end of each issue under the heading "Book Reviews."

Chapter 4
Tools for Identifying, Locating, and Retrieving Books, Documents, and Other Information Sources

---

Among the tools that assist the researcher in gathering references to books, documents, and other sources of information is that genre of resources referred to as *bibliographic databases.* Bibliographic databases comprise a wide range of formats: electronic, print, and union catalogs as used by libraries; directories of databases available through gateway services; search engines to the World Wide Web; and printed bibliographies. This chapter covers the limitations and effective use of such tools and provides references for many of the best examples available. Although the authors discuss similar resources later in other chapters—chapter 5 covers indexes and abstracts to periodicals, and chapter 6, indexes to statistical sources—this chapter provides the reader with a general foundation in the research of varied topics, including resources and approaches specific to the field of criminal justice.

While all bibliographic databases provide a record of the existence of information sources, some also provide a means to locate and therefore retrieve the information. For instance, when you use a library catalog, you are given a call number, that is, the address of the item on the shelf. Likewise, union catalogs identify the library or libraries that own an item and frequently give you the call number as well.

The authors would like you to consider, perhaps for the first time, the notion that search engines to the World Wide Web are also bibliographic databases: tools used to identify, locate, and retrieve information. When you move from a catalog terminal to the shelf location of a book, you move through *physical space;* when you select a link on a Web page that connects to the text of a document, you move through *cyberspace.* Both catalogs and search engines are examples of tools that allow you to identify as well as locate and retrieve information.

Included in this discussion of bibliographic databases are suggestions to make the most of their use, ways to avoid pitfalls, and an analysis of their limitations. We talk about their limitations because, as we proceed with *how* to use them, you'll have a clearer idea of where you can go wrong.

Finally, the authors often refer in the text of this chapter to bibliographic databases as *catalogs;* however, in most instances, we are referring to any kind of database, print or online, that provides access to the literature.

DETERMINING THE SCOPE OF YOUR RESEARCH

Before beginning a research project and a literature search, you need to determine the scope of your research. To begin, consider what kind of literature you need to find and ask yourself the questions listed below. The answers should guide you toward the resources, indexes, and databases needed to find them. This process is important to your final product and instrumental to the efficiency of your work. After completing this process, you will have a better idea of the context within which you will be using the tools described in this chapter, and, if your project is to be comprehensive, you will be able to select the right array of tools to use.

How broad is the topic you are researching and can the topic be reasonably narrowed or broadened? The fact of the matter is you won't always know if your topic is too broad or narrow until you have some familiarity with it. That's why faculty, colleagues, librarians, and mentors are important to the initial stages of research. If you ask several people who know something about the subject or its literature, they will not only give you information about it, but they will also give you some indication of its breadth. At this initial stage, you should also consider reading encyclopedic and general works on your sub-

ject to understand its scope. Such works are treated in chapter 3.

What kind of treatment will you be giving the subject? Will your treatment be comprehensive or narrowly defined? Will it be popular or scholarly? Will it be a historical treatment? Will it be theoretical, policy oriented, or practical? Do you intend a complete treatment of the subject or are you only going to suggest that your subject needs complete treatment?

Are you looking for primary or secondary sources, or both? To what extent will you need to find *primary sources,* such as government reports, laws, and statistics? To what extent will you need to find analyses of primary sources or *secondary sources?* To what extent do you need to find both? To the novice, the difference between primary and secondary sources can be confusing. Primary sources are original documentation or *evidence* of the existence of some phenomenon; secondary sources or analyses refer to and synthesize primary sources, talking *about* a phenomenon. Ordinary research often requires both.

What role does timeliness play in your subject? Is it an old subject or a new one? Is your approach to it new or old? If your subject or approach is new, how new? If your research deals with some event or phenomenon, did it occur within the last two weeks, the last month, the last year, the last decade, or longer?

How much information is available on your subject? A preliminary literature search will help you answer this last question. Read the next two sections—"The Limitations of Bibliographic Databases" and "Conducting Searches"—then access some of the bibliographic resources indicated in this chapter to answer this question.

SELECTING THE RIGHT TOOL FOR THE JOB

As with any project that requires the use of tools, it is important to understand the limitations of the tools in the context of the job you are to perform. For example, the rechargeable electric screwdrivers you can buy for $19.95 are great for small jobs around the house. However, if you make your living installing drywall with drywall screws, this kind of screwdriver just won't hold up—it has its limitations. The same is true of the tools we cover in this chapter. For the most part, catalogs and bibliographic resources are equal to the job; but if your search for information sources is to be exhaustive, it is important to understand that they have limitations. This chapter will help you find ways around these obstacles; for instance, you might select a number of resources that, when used together, provide as complete a coverage as you need.

Limitations in Scope

The scope of a catalog or bibliographic database can be limited by any number of variables including the age of the library and its collection, the mission of the library, subjects covered, period of time covered, journals indexed, types of books or journals included (scholarly or general literature), or the forms of materials included (books, periodicals, government publications, or microforms). For example, a library catalog might be limited in scope to the monographic and journal holdings of just that one library. To expand the results of your literature search, you might have to visit other libraries to see if they hold any additional information. But visiting other libraries can be an expensive proposition unless you live in a metropolitan area or you have access to the Internet. The catalog you are using might also be limited to the literature that appears in books, meaning that periodicals are not included. Some indexes, such as the *Readers' Guide,* are limited to popular literature; the *National Criminal Justice Reference Service* does not include "scholarly periodical literature" before a certain date; and *Criminal Justice Abstracts* does not include newsletters. Some periodical indexes, because of the date they began publishing, are not useful for historical research.

Limitations in Item Descriptions

A bibliographic database often provides only a description of a *physical* item and relatively little description of the subject content of the book or periodical. For example, a library catalog in the traditional sense is a description of the physical characteristics of the package in which information is stored—a sequence of pages, bound together with a cover, of a specific size and length—known to us as a book, a periodical, or either reproduced on microform.

In the catalog entry below you will see relatively little information about the subject content of the book it describes.

Looking at the elements of this catalog entry, you first see the title and its editor. You know it was copyrighted in 1980 and published in Beverly Hills by Sage Publications. It comprises 335 pages and is 23 centimeters tall. It is Volume 4 of the Sage Annual Reviews of Studies in Deviance series. Most of these elements constitute a *physical* description of the work. The only indication we have of its subject content are the two subject headings, "crime and criminals" and "deviant behavior," and its call number, HV6028 .C72. These elements are intended to give you an idea of the entirety of the subject of this item. But if you look at its table of contents, you will likely find that it deals with much more than is indicated here.

Limitations in Subject Analysis

We've already seen how catalog entries provide relatively scant information on the subject content of a work. What's even more challenging to the researcher is that what little is available is also rife with limitations.

The subject analysis provided by a catalog or database of books, articles, or government reports is, by its nature, derivative. Catalogers, for example, who are responsible for assigning subject headings, gener-

TITLE:	Crime and deviance: a comparative perspective / edited by Graeme R. Newman.
PUBLISHED:	Beverly Hills: Sage Publications, c1980.
DESCRIPTION:	335 p.; graphs ; 23 cm.
SUBJECT HEADINGS:	Crime and criminals. Deviant behavior.
OTHER ACCESS POINTS:	Newman, Graeme R.
SERIES:	Sage annual reviews of studies in deviance ; v. 4
NOTES:	Includes bibliographies.
CALL NUMBER:	HV6028 .C72

ally refer only to the title page, table of contents, and preface or introduction of the work to gather an idea of the book's subject content; they do not read the entire work. Indexers and abstracters for periodicals typically do not read the entire article and rely instead on the author's abstract, the headings used within the article, and the introduction. Yet, they assign subject headings to books and periodical articles that you count on to find materials.

Further, for a person to reliably access resources by subject in a catalog or index, he or she must use an authorized list of subject headings or topics. Such authorized subject headings are referred to as a *controlled vocabulary*. A controlled vocabulary, which can be found in thesauri, creates uniformity in the language or terms applied to books, articles, and documents dealing with the same subject. (See pages 51–52 and below for a list of thesauri typically used in catalogs and indexes.) Therefore, a researcher can rely on finding all works on a subject gathered together under a consistent term. However, there are limitations that the serious researcher—even those who are well versed in the use of thesauri, indexes, and catalogs—should be aware of. These limitations result from the nature of thesauri, the application of subject terms, and rules for their application.

One such limitation is that the appropriate application of subject terms is a function of the subject expertise of the person applying them. For the most part, those who apply subject headings are competent, but anomalies do occur. An example is if a cataloger were to apply the subject heading "Antitrust" to a book dealing with "Trusts and estates." Another is if an indexer were to apply a general term when a more specific term is available and more suitable.

Another limitation is related to the policies of the library or index publisher used in assigning subject headings. One policy that affects the quality of the subject analysis is the number of headings to be applied to an item. The rule for library catalogs, for instance, has traditionally been to apply no more than three or four subject headings, even though the work may deal with a much greater number. This old rule stems from the days when catalogers had to type, on a typewriter, each card that went into the catalog; adding more subject headings meant typing more cards. In an online environment, this rule is no longer applicable. Although the reason for its existence has long been forgotten by many, the rule lives on in some libraries. Similarly, publishers of indexes may have rules regarding the number of subject headings to be applied.

A second policy deals with the specificity of the headings applied. For example, the Library of Congress, which performs about 80 percent of the cataloging used by libraries, has established a policy of assigning only the *most specific* headings to a work. Thus, if you are doing research on some broad area of criminal justice and have searched for that subject in the catalog, you would find only general books on the subject. To research a topic's component parts, you would have to look up each part separately.

A third consideration is policies that deal with the subdivision of headings. Headings can be subdivided many different ways. This is done geographically, as in *"Subject—Slovenia,"* or by form of material, such as *"Subject—Law and legislation."* The decision to begin subdividing a subject often occurs long after the first heading has been entered into the index or catalog. Indexers and catalogers usually make a decision to begin subdividing *after* a specified number of entries have been placed in the catalog or index.

The nature of language, as it relates to the culture of the person assigning the headings, and the era in which the headings are assigned, also impact subject analysis. For example, current research on the topic of female offenders yields a number of titles, but the subject term "Female offenders" is relatively new, first appearing in *Library of Congress Subject Headings* (the major thesaurus used for cataloging books) in the 1980s. A historical treatment would require you to use the term "Delinquent women" as well, since it was the term used prior to the 1980s. As another example, consider how you would do historical research on the topic of homelessness. If you were looking in a variety of sources or the same source over a period of time, you might need to search under the terms "Bag ladies," "Hobos," and "Indigents" in addition to "Homeless." Language changes, and with it, the words we use to describe concepts. Catalogs do not always change with the times; thus, you might have to find additional terms to describe your topic, especially if your treatment is historical. Even when subject headings do change with the times, they are often slow to do so. Consequently, new terms of art, may not be reflected in thesauri, even as cross-references, until they are established as valid and useful headings.

SEARCHING BIBLIOGRAPHIC DATABASES

Printed catalogs and indexes provide you with a limited number of ways to access books and articles. Traditionally you would have to look up an item by author, title, or subject. Very few, if any, printed indexes allow you to find a book or article by the publisher, the city in which it was published, the table of contents or index, or the date published. None allow you to look up a work by size or color. Likewise, you cannot find an article by the title of the journal in which it was published.

Electronic databases, however, usually offer a wide range of search capabilities. Such databases are generally *structured databases,* which means that information about each resource is stored in *fields.* All the fields that relate to a particular item comprise a *record.* Each field is usually named to help users recognize its contents; for example, the title field contains the title, the author field contains the name of the author, and the subject field contains the subject headings assigned. Although you might not be able to find a book by its publisher or the title of an article by the journal in which it was published, in an electronic environment, much more of a bibliographic record is accessible than in a print environment. The extent of field accessibility depends upon whether the software allows you to search particular fields and whether the producer of the database permits such searches as a matter of policy.

Just the same, structured databases generally offer access to more information than printed ones simply because they are computerized. Most structured databases provide access to more fields of information than just the author, subject, and title. You can limit your search by date, language, and other information within a record. Libraries are also beginning to introduce into their catalogs—and to make searchable—the tables of contents of books and indexes to periodical literature. Thus, electronic indexes and catalogs offer many more access points to information than do those in print form.

Most online databases also allow libraries and index publishers to compensate for some of the shortcomings of catalogs and indexes we discussed earlier. The ability to make global changes provides the opportunity, for example, to change all subject headings to the current form. Thus, all records with the subject heading "Delinquent Women" can, conceivably, be converted to the heading "Female Offenders" instead. However, you should be aware that these global changes do not always occur with 100 percent reliability.

Author and Title Searches

Because a search for an author or title is usually straightforward and requires no explanation, this section will not deal with the topic in depth. Quite simply, if you know the title or author of a work, search for it in the catalog or index; if it's there, you'll find it. The authors' only word of caution is to consult a librarian when searching for items by *corporate author.* Such works are considered to be the product of an organization and can be a problem. Refer to the section below on keyword searching for advice on what to do if you don't know the precise name of an author or the exact title of a work.

Subject Searches

A thesaurus is an authorized list of subject headings that provides consistency in the words or terms used to describe a subject. One, and only one, term or phrase from a thesaurus represents a certain concept within the catalog or index to which it applies. When you search an electronic database by *subject,* you are searching only the *subject field.*

Library of Congress Subject Headings. Washington, DC: Cataloging Distribution Service, Library of Congress.

> *Library of Congress Subject Headings (LCSH),* now published annually, is the most widely used set of subject headings for library catalogs. Knowing how to use this resource is essential for detailed and comprehensive research.

Another important thesaurus is the *National Criminal Justice Thesaurus,*

National Criminal Justice Thesaurus. Rockville, MD: U.S. Department of Justice, National Institute of Justice, National Criminal Justice Reference Service (NCJRS), 1978–.

> The *National Criminal Justice Thesaurus* contains listings of descriptors, or terms, used to index literature in the National Institute of Justice/NCJRS document database. (See chapter 5.) It is published annually and provides subject headings for the books, articles, government publications, and other documents indexed by the NCJRS.

In subject searching, the use of a thesaurus is important. For example, if you were searching for books on women criminals, you would first look in *Library of Congress Subject Headings (LCSH)* under that term. (Although the authors use *LCSH* in the following examples, the principles used are the same for any thesaurus.) There you would find the following entry:

Women criminals
  USE   Female offenders

In this case, the thesaurus is telling you that any catalog that uses *Library of Congress Subject Headings* will not use the term "Women criminals" but, instead, the term "Female offenders." Thus, you have identified the term that the catalog uses for all materials that deal with the subject of women criminals. When you search for this term you will find all the materials that deal with this topic gathered together for you. If the catalog has successfully automated the thesaurus into the system, a search for "Women criminals" in the catalog would automatically yield a message to use "Female offenders."

In addition to helping you identify which term to use with a particular catalog, index, or database, a thesaurus can also assist you in the analysis of your topic for searching purposes. In a previous section of this chapter, the authors suggested that you determine the scope of your topic by considering how it could be reasonably narrowed or broadened. (See page 66.) Keep this in mind as you look at the information found under the topic "Female offenders" listed below. This entry is taken from the *Library of Congress Subject Headings*.

> **Female offenders** (*May Subd Geog*)
> UF   Delinquent women
>   *[Former heading]*
>   Offenders, female
>   Women—Crime
>   Women criminals
>   Women offenders
> BT   Criminals
> NT   Delinquent girls
>   Procuresses
>   Women murderers
>   Women narcotics dealers
>   Women outlaws

The subject "Female offenders" is in boldface type indicating that it is a subject heading used in the catalog. The list of subjects following the designation "UF" (used for) are those referring you to "Female offenders"—notice "Women criminals" on the list. The term "[former heading]" inserted after the term "Delinquent women" indicates that "Delinquent women" was formerly used as the main term for this subject. For your research to be thorough, you should search that subject heading in the catalog as well. Although you may not find anything, it could be worth the effort.

"BT" (broader terms) indicates terms, in this case "Criminals," that are broader than the main one. The list of terms following "NT" (narrower terms) are

more narrow. In this way, the thesaurus indicates that some broader and narrower terms are used by the catalog or database. Reference to these listings is a minor but nonetheless valid way to broaden or narrow the topic of your research as well as your search for information.

Going back to the beginning of the entry, "(May Subd Geog)" (which applies more to library catalogs than indexes) indicates that the subject may be subdivided geographically in the catalog. In other words, if a book deals with female offenders in a geographical area, it may be listed as such in the catalog: for example, "Female offenders—South Carolina." Therefore, limiting your search by geographic area is another way you can limit the topic of your research or your search for information, especially if you find too much on female offenders generally.

However a word of caution is needed here, too. As mentioned in a previous section, the decision to begin subdividing a subject often occurs long after the first headings have been entered into a catalog. Catalogers usually make the decision to begin subdividing after a specified number of entries have been placed in the catalog under the more general heading. This means that if you find just a few items under a subdivided subject when you expect to find a lot, you should also look at the more general subject heading without the subdivision. It is possible that the catalog just recently began to subdivide the topic, and you'll find more resources by looking at the more general subject heading.

In the example shown below, notice some additional notations found in the thesaurus entry for "Criminology."

> **Criminology** (*May Subd Geog*)
> *[HV6001-HV6030]*
> Here are entered works on the discipline that studies the causes, detection, and prevention of crime, and the treatment or punishment of criminals. Works on the occurrence of crime are entered under Crime. Works on the criminal justice system are entered under Criminal justice, administration of.
> UF   Crime—Study and teaching
> BT   Social sciences
> RT   Crime
>   Criminals

Following the heading "Criminology" and the notation indicating geographical subdivision (discussed earlier) is a range of *call numbers:* [HV6001-HV6030].

These call numbers—which you will find listed in *LCSH* entries from time to time—represent a range of call numbers under which books on the subject of criminology are classified. In this case, "classified" means the books are physically located next to each other on the shelf. Although formal how-to guides such as this one usually don't mention the value of browsing around library shelves, the authors believe that you should take advantage of any opportunity to serendipitously discover an important work just by looking around a bit—especially because catalog and index searching can be imprecise.

Following the call numbers in this entry is a *scope note,* which defines how the term is used in the catalog. This particular scope note indicates that sources on the occurrence of crime are entered under the subject "Crime" and that if your research really deals with the criminal justice system, you should research the topic "Criminal justice, administration of." These scope notes help direct you to the right subject headings if direction is needed. Also, following the designation "RT"(related terms) are two headings you should check if your search for books dealing with criminology fails.

Approaching a catalog or index through a thesaurus is one way to find information on a subject, but it is not the only one. Another approach, which is indirect but still legitimate, is to search for the subjects listed in the catalog record for a book that you already know is on your topic. This search should yield a list of books that deal with the same topic(s).

Despite the benefits of searching structured databases by subject, keep in mind that you only have access to the subject field, and within that field, you are limited to the terms used by that catalog or index's thesaurus. As already mentioned, subject headings used by thesauri often lag behind the language of a discipline. Words that more accurately describe a subject may not be found in thesauri until they have been established as valid and useful headings. In addition, as you can see from the above example for "Female offenders," a subject can be described by many different terms. Sometimes descriptive terms appear in the titles of books and periodical articles as well as other parts of a bibliographic record, even though they are not yet authorized headings.

Keyword Searches

Keyword searching is a feature of many electronic databases that allows you to break away from the controlled vocabulary of thesauri. Using keyword searching, you can access terms in many fields of a structured database, and you can even find specified words in full-text sources. For some full-text databases, like the *LEXIS* computer-assisted legal research database, keyword searching is the only way you can carry out a search—there is no controlled vocabulary.

Searching by keyword is productive because it places fewer limitations on vocabulary and increases the amount of text that can be searched. It is especially useful when you are searching for a document that you know exists but for which you have only partial information. Typical situations that fall into this category are when you know just a few words of a title or just the author's last name; when you know an article deals with a specific phenomenon, such as recidivism; or when you know an article is published in a particular journal.

An effective keyword search must use words that actually appear in searchable fields of the record. Searchable fields are usually author, title, subject, and certain additional fields that a vendor or library have made available. These additional fields often contain the full text of documents, abstracts, journal titles, dates of publication, tables of contents, and sometimes even document indexes.

Because the keyword you enter must appear within the record, you need to ask yourself, "What words would the author have used in the title or text?" "What words would the abstractor have used to write the abstract?" and "What subject headings would have been applied to the document?" In order to perform keyword searching, you also need to have a reasonable grounding in the vocabulary of your topic of research, acquired through some preliminary reading. Reference works such as encyclopedias, handbooks, and annual literature reviews can provide you with such a vocabulary. (See chapter 3 for more information.)

Despite your best efforts, however, such a grounding might be difficult to achieve. To help you increase the effectiveness of your search, therefore, most keyword searchable databases also allow you to search for synonyms along with your keyword. This broadens your search to include words that might have been used instead of, or in addition to, the words that you initially considered. To use keywords in your search, you need to use *Boolean operators,* sometimes called

Boolean connectors. The most common operators are *AND, OR,* and *NOT,* but occasionally *BUT NOT* is also available. (Most databases also provide other search features such as *root expansion,* which makes keyword searching extremely powerful.) Because Boolean operators and root expansion features are commonly available with most databases, the authors do not delve into specifics here; however, the rules regarding their use do vary, and we recommend that you ask a librarian, read the handouts that most libraries prepare, or take one of the many tutorials that are offered with database products.

However, there are problems with keyword searching that arise primarily when using comprehensive databases, such as library catalogs that deal with many different subjects. The issue goes back to language: different disciplines often use the same word to describe totally different concepts. One such word is *evidence.* This word is used in anthropology, law, logic, psychology, biology, and astronomy, just to name a few. It is also used in many different ways within disciplines, such as in law. If you perform a keyword search for "evidence" on a library catalog, you will get a list of sources that deal with many different subjects, only some of which speak to the issues you are addressing. In this case, conducting a keyword search overbroadens your scope to include too many areas of study or knowledge. When you get too many *hits,* you should limit your search of the literature by combining it with a search of a specific field. In the example of *evidence,* you could also do a subject search using controlled vocabulary from a thesaurus to help narrow your search.

With a full text-database that employs subject analysis, such as WESTLAW, a combination of keywords and subject headings can be especially helpful. For example, in order to research judges' application of public policy in the disposition of criminal cases, you would do a keyword search for *policy,* but you would compare it with a subject search for the appropriate subject heading, in this case "Criminal Law." This use of subject headings would restrict your search to criminal matters and eliminate policy-oriented subjects such as "Environmental law" and "Employment at-will," not to mention "Insurance."

Reading the Entire Record

Finally, using a catalog or database can lead to more than just the identification of a book or article. The authors suggest that you learn to read all the information in catalog records because imbedded within them,

in fields that may not be searchable, is a true wealth of knowledge.

If your objective in doing a database search is to find literature, watch for an indication that the book, report, or journal article includes a bibliography. If the result of your search was pertinent to your research, then many of the items listed in its bibliography could be useful too. Also look for other authors that list people who are in some way associated with the intellectual content of the work. If you're looking for experts and authorities, it may be worth your while to follow up on these as well.

Finally, if a book has proven to be valuable to your research and a *series note* indicates that it is part of a series, look for the other books in the series; they may be helpful too. An example of a series note is shown in the catalog record earlier in this chapter on page 67. This record shows that the work is Volume 4 in the series "Sage Annual Reviews of Studies in Deviance." If you do a title search for "Sage Annual Reviews of Studies in Deviance," the catalog will list all books in the series owned by the library.

SEARCHING LIBRARY CATALOGS

Union Catalogs

> Library of Congress subject headings: Catalogs, Subject; Catalogs, Union—United States—periodicals; Moving-pictures—Catalogs; Filmstrips—Catalogs; Audio-visual materials—Catalogs; Manuscripts—United States—Catalogs; Libraries, Depository—United States; United States—Government publications—Bibliography—Union lists

When you search a particular library's card or online catalog, you have access to all the materials owned by that library. That means that your research is limited to the contents of that library and it alone. This restriction is acceptable if your library has all the materials that has been published on your topic, but even the biggest library collections are not as complete as they have been in the past.

As the amount of published information grew and library budgets remained relatively stagnant, libraries were not able to acquire as many resources as they had previously. To offset the impact of economics, libraries began to cooperate with each other in a variety of ways. One of those ways was to initiate interlibrary loan systems, which made library collections available to other libraries. Thus, books and periodicals from one library were made available to users of many others. In part to facilitate this activity, libraries also made their catalogs available to each other through the advent of the *union catalog*—one catalog containing the holdings of many libraries.

While many of the same limitations apply to the use of union catalogs as to local catalogs, the scope of union catalogs is much broader. The value of union catalogs goes beyond finding the location of a publication that you have already identified. They also act as a bibliography of works held by libraries included in the catalog, and like subject bibliographies, they expand your pool of resources. Using a union catalog is a vital part of a literature review conducted in advance of writing a thesis or dissertation.

Listed below are some of the most well-known and well-regarded union catalogs available.

The National Union Catalog [microfiche]. Washington, DC: Library of Congress, 1942–1946 [and supplements].

> *The National Union Catalog* (NUC) comprises works cataloged by the Library of Congress and contributing libraries. It is a research and reference tool for the world's most significant books that are acquired and cataloged by the Library of Congress. It was available in book form until 1983 but is now issued only in microfiche. The NUC contains currently issued Library of Congress printed card entries for books, atlases, periodicals, and other serials in practically all languages. Excluded from the NUC is Library of Congress entries for music, musical sound recordings, motion pictures, and filmstrips. The NUC is arranged alphabetically by author or by title. The order of arrangement of titles under authors is alphabetical.
>
> The NUC has gone through many changes and reincarnations and can be extremely difficult to use. While the book form reproduced catalog cards photographically, the more recent microfiche entries are even more confusing. The authors encourage you to seek the assistance of a librarian instead of trying to use this resource on your own.

OCLC Online Union Catalog [electronic database]. Dublin, OH: Online Computer Library Center (OCLC).

> "The OCLC Online Union Catalog (OLUC) is the world's largest and most comprehensive database of bibliographic information." As of this writing it contained more than 28 million records of books, periodicals, manuscripts, and audiovisual materials from libraries all over the world. Participating libraries include the Library of Congress, the National Library of Medicine, the U.S. Government Printing Office, and national libraries such as the British Library, the National Library of Canada, and the National Library of Australia. OLUC grows by nearly 2 million records each year. Although some of these records are duplicates, OCLC company policies attempt to keep duplication to a minimum.
>
> OLUC is offered as a searchable database through OCLC's EPIC database gateway service and as the *WorldCat* database on the FirstSearch service. As available through FirstSearch and EPIC, every word in the bibliographic records is indexed and searchable, and the records include the names of the holding libraries. Both versions of OLUC also allow the use of Boolean operators by subject, keyword, title and author, and a number of other possibilities. *WorldCat* is by far the simpler of the two to use, however, and requires no special training to search.

Research Libraries Information Network [electronic database]. Stanford, CA: Research Libraries Group.

> The Research Libraries Information Network (RLIN) database currently contains approximately 20 million records. What it lacks in quantity it makes up for in quality of holdings. Contributing libraries include some of the largest academic libraries in the United States, and a large proportion of them are law libraries such as Columbia, Harvard, Yale, and Cornell. The Library of Congress contributes its cataloging to the RLIN system as well.
>
> Up until the initiation of new search capabilities through the EPIC and FirstSearch services, the RLIN was easier to search than OCLC's product (see above). Because it was the only "bibliographic utility" to allow subject searching, it was preferred for literature searches. Today, it seems somewhat archaic because users require some training to search and retrieve information. Boolean operators are permitted for searching the author, title, and subject fields of the records.

Other union catalogs important to completing a thorough identification of literature on your topic of research are the *Western Library Network* (*WLN*) and Australia's *CINCH* database.

Internet Accessible Catalogs

Some of the first and most useful databases available on the Internet were library catalogs. Catalogs were originally available over the Internet only through *telnet,* a software application that allowed users to *login* to remote computers. However, there were two problems with this method: first, you had to know the *Internet Protocol (IP) address* (a series of numbers that identify the machine being addressed, for example 129.252.86.180) of the catalog; and second, you had to be familiar enough with the library's online system and unique search routine to be able to use it.

This latter issue was, and still is, only a minor concern. While different library systems look and feel different, most are quite intuitive and usually provide enough onscreen guidance to make them easy to learn. However, when you access a library catalog for the first time, be sure to read all the instructions and take the time to think about the onscreen guides—before you get frustrated. If you browse catalogs on the Internet quite often, you will begin to recognize Innovative Interfaces, NOTIS, Geac Advance, Dynix, and other common library systems.

The former problem, knowing the IP address of the library you want to search, has been overcome by the advent of *gopher*. Gopher is the name of a software *client;* but the term *gopher site* is also used to refer to a gopher-accessible Internet site that uses a *menu system* to help you find documents without knowing their IP addresses. To make library catalogs easily available, gopher site managers collect the IP addresses of electronically available catalogs, create text menus with the names of the sites, then create automatic connections or *links* to them. In other words, when you connect to a gopher site with your gopher client and click on a menu item, you are automatically connected to the corresponding Internet site.

For example, if you connect to a gopher site and select a menu option that reads, "Library Catalogs from around the World," you might be connected to another menu that lists the continents. If you choose, for example, "North America," you might be connected to still another menu listing of all the countries in North America. From that menu, you might choose "United States," and a menu listing all the states would appear. Choose a state and then the name of an institution within the state and you would be automatically connected to that institution. Thus, you only need to know the geographic location of the library you want to "visit" in order to make a connection to its catalog. While this sounds like a lengthy process by today's superhighway standards, it was and continues to be an enormous service.

With the expansion of the World Wide Web, many library catalogs are available at Web sites. Be certain, however, that your browser, Netscape for example, is configured to launch supporting applications that make access to the library catalogs possible. These applications are software packages that emulate certain terminal types, such as TN3270 and VT100. When you click on the catalog link, the browser invokes the terminal emulation software and keeps it open throughout the search session, then closes it when you sign off the catalog.

Searching the catalogs of individual libraries using gopher or the World Wide Web offers many advantages over using union catalog microfiche and databases. First of all, you do not have to pay to access individual libraries—both OCLC's database and RLIN require payment (if not by you, then by the library). These databases are also usually accessed as a service through your library and therefore are only available

during its hours of operation. Using the Internet, you can access these catalogs at any time of the day or night. Finally, Internet-accessible catalogs are eminently portable—that is, they are accessible from any location that has an Internet connection.

Although using gopher and the Web is still not as efficient as searching a union catalog, searching the catalogs of individual libraries using a *browser* yields many advantages over both of these approaches. (See pages 79–80 for a discussion of the World Wide Web and Web search engines.) For example, most World Wide Web sites accessible through browsers offer more than just library catalogs. If you are planning to visit an academic institution and want to take advantage of its resources while there, you can do some searching on the Web ahead of time and save your onsite time for the intellectual content of your work. There are a host of other advantages that can be gained from accessing catalogs via a browser, but perhaps the most important is that the user-friendly browser gives you the opportunity to find materials in some of the largest and best criminal justice libraries in the country and around the world without leaving home. Your literature search can be thorough, and you can still gain insight into the location of materials you need.

Try a few of the libraries listed below using telnet or a gopher client, or a World Wide Web browser.

Rutgers University Library. *(Includes the collection of the Rutgers Criminal Justice/National Council on Crime and Delinquency Library)*
Telnet or Gopher: 128.6.54.7 *or* info.rutgers.edu
Browser: http://www.rutgers.edu/rulib/

University of Pennsylvania
Telnet or Gopher: 165.123.33.31 *or* gopher.library.upenn.edu
Browser: http://www.library.upenn.edu/

Michigan State University
Telnet or Gopher: 35.8.2.99 *or* magic.lib.msu.edu
Browser: http://web.msu.edu/library

University of Arizona
Telnet or Gopher: 128.196.252.3 *or* idx.telcom.arizona.edu
Browser: http://www.library.arizona.edu/

University at Albany, State University of New York
Telnet or Gopher: 128.204.1.120 *or* library.albany.edu
Browser: http://www.albany.edu/library/

University of South Florida
Browser: http://www.lib.usf.edu

If you are attempting to find a library that isn't listed here, try one of the two sites given below for listings or direct connections.

Berkeley Digital Library

Browser: http://sunsite.berkeley.edu/Libweb/

Yale University Gopher

Browser: gopher: //libgopher.yale.edu:70/11/

Once you have connected to a remote library catalog and feel comfortable using it, remember to apply the information about library catalogs described above to make the most of your visit.

Using the Internet to access library catalogs is an excellent way to expand your search for literature; the only drawback is that you have to search each catalog individually. Union catalogs, though expensive to use, still provide you with access to a number of libraries in one database. Since they include the holdings of a number of libraries, you are likely to identify resources that are not held in your local library, but also resources that are held in libraries you didn't think of visiting on the Internet.

Printed Library Catalogs

Some of the more prestigious institutions have published their library catalogs in book form for distribution and sale. The two works listed below represent significant printed criminal justice catalogs.

Cambridge University Institute of Criminology. *The Catalogue of the Radzinowicz Library.* 6 vols. Boston: G. K. Hall, 1979.

> These six volumes, representing the holdings of the Radzinowicz Library, consist of an author catalog, a periodical catalog, a classified catalog, and a subject index to the classified catalog. This work provides international coverage of over 19,000 monographs, approximately 9,500 pamphlets and reports, 192 periodicals, and many suspended titles.

Los Angeles Public Library Municipal Reference Library. *Catalog of the Police Library of the Los Angeles Public Library.* 2 vols. Boston: G. K. Hall, 1972.

> Similar to the Radzinowicz catalog, this catalog includes reports, pamphlets, and periodical articles from the Police Library of the Los Angeles Public Library. A supplement was published in 1980 also consisting of 2 volumes.

However, the publication and distribution of book catalogs has faded in significance since the advent of electronic access to library catalogs and other bibliographic databases.

FINDING ONLINE INFORMATION

> Library of Congress subject headings: Internet (Computer network)—Directories; BITNET (Computer network)—Directories; Information services—Directories; Information services—United States—Directories; Databases—Directories; Databases—United States—Directories; Computer bulletin boards—Directories; Information storage and retrieval systems—Directories; Information storage and retrieval systems—Criminal justice, administration of—United States; Information storage and retrieval systems—*Subject*—United States; Machine-readable bibliographic data—Directories; Periodicals—Databases—Directories; Data libraries; Bibliography—Databases—Directories; CD-ROM—Directories; search also under name of system, e.g., LEXIS (Information retrieval system)

When you go to a library looking for information, you often already know what you want to find: perhaps you have a reference to a book, or perhaps you have used a thesaurus to find subject headings appropriate to your topic. Either way, you access the online catalog, then do a keyword search for the book or a subject search for your topic. To your dismay, you do not find your book nor much on your subject. What should you do next? Don't give up.

Library catalogs are a record of what a library *owns*; they tell you what is shelved in the stacks and reference collections. They contain records of materials in a variety of forms—microfiche, video, audio, photographs—all of which can be, and are, owned and cataloged by the library.

However, there is another kind of resource that cannot be purchased or stored on library shelves or even in special cabinets—it is electronic information. In fact, information in electronic form is most often not owned at all by libraries. Since libraries don't own it, they frequently do not catalog it either (although this practice is changing). So, the next time you need information and can't find it, even in the catalog of the largest library in your state or province, ask a librarian if it is available on a *database*.

Although library catalogs are also databases, they are primarily bibliographic—meaning they contain bibliographic data about sources of information—and they cover only the holdings of a particular library or libraries. The databases described below are different from catalogs in that they contain either (1) specialized bibliographic data, indexes, or abstracts of the literature by subject; (2) full text of articles and other materials; or (3) data files. These databases are stored or published either on CD-ROM, floppy disk, magnetic tape, other electronic media, or are available online via a *terminal* (or a computer acting as a terminal) connected to a *network*.

Initially such databases were used by corporations, governments, and professionals to provide fast access to vast amounts of information. They came into more common use in the 1960s and 1970s to maintain and access indexes to a growing amount of periodical literature. Databases also offered libraries a way to reduce costs, manage library catalogs, and control an increasing number of books, reports, and periodicals.

Many changes and technological advances have occurred in the last 20 years. The number of database records has grown from about 52 million in 1975 to more than 6 billion in 1994. Due in part to the demands of the professions, most notably the legal profession, for computerized access to the text of information sources such as court cases, the kind of information available on databases has evolved dramatically from simple indexes to full-text resources. More powerful computers and sophisticated software have made searching for information much less daunting; and in the age of the Internet the cost of telecommunications has been reduced to a fraction of what it once was. As a result of all of these changes, databases have become more commonly available to the public. Although there is a cost associated with using some of them, searching an electronic database is a common component of modern research.

To cover all electronic databases you need to search the one source that provides comprehensive coverage of online and CD-ROM databases—the *Gale Directory of Databases*.

Gale Directory of Databases. Vol. 1, Online Databases. Detroit, MI: Gale Research, 1993.

Gale Directory of Databases. Vol. 2, CD-ROM, Diskette, Magnetic Tape, Handheld, and Batch Access Database Products. Detroit, MI: Gale Research, 1993–.

> This two-volume publication was formed by the merger of two earlier directories: Gale's *Computer-Readable Databases* and Quadra-Gale's *Directory of Online Databases*. The resulting *Directory of Databases* provides descriptions of 9,075 databases including reference and purchasing information, such as address and fax, toll and toll-free telephone numbers for publishers, online gateway services, vendors, and distributors. Volume 1 entries describe content, subject coverage, language, geographic coverage, time span, frequency updated, availability, and alternative electronic formats such as CD-ROM and magnetic tape. Volume 2 descriptions are arranged by format and include computer system requirements, software

source, and price information. The directory also includes a geographic index, subject index, and master index of all product and organization names. (See exhibit 4-1 for an example of four criminal justice databases.) This resource is available in a variety of formats including paper, CD-ROM, online and magnetic tape.

• 1502 • Criminal

• 1502 • Criminal Justice Abstracts

Willow Tree Press, Inc.   Phone: (914)362-8376
124 Willow Tree Rd.   Fax: (914)362-8376
Monsey, NY 10952

Contact: Phyllis Schultze.

Type: Bibliographic.

Content: Contains citations, with abstracts, to journals, reports, books, dissertations, magazines, and newspapers covering criminal justice topics. Includes reviews of literature, bibliographies, and highlights of selected abstracts. Corresponds to *Criminal Justice Abstracts* (formerly *Crime and Delinquency Literature*).

Subject Coverage: Criminal justice.

Language: English.

Geographic Coverage: International.

Time Span: 1968 to date.

Updating: Quarterly.

Online Availability: *WESTLAW* (CJ-CJA).

Alternate Electronic Formats: *CD-ROM* (Criminal Justice Abstracts).

• 1503 • Criminal Justice Periodical Index (CJPI)

UMI   Phone: (313)761-4700
300 N. Zeeb Rd.   800-521-0600
Ann Arbor, MI 48106   Fax: (313)973-9145

Type: Bibliographic.

Content: Contains more than 183,000 citations to articles in 120 magazines, journals, newsletters, and law reporting publications on the administration of justice and law enforcement. Corresponds to *Criminal Justice Periodical Index*.

Subject Coverage: Criminal justice and law enforcement, including crime against people and property, environmental and industrial crime, political and social crime, drug abuse, juvenile delinquency, the justice system, penology, criminal law, security systems, police, corrections, criminology, drug abuse, family law, juvenile justice, prison administration, and victimization studies.

Language: English.

Geographic Coverage: United States, Canada, and United Kingdom.

Time Span: 1975 to date.

Updating: 1000 records a month.

Online Availability: *DIALOG* (171: $60/connect hour, 40 cents/full record online, 40 cents/full record offline).

• 1504 • Criminal Law Defenses   ★

West Publishing   Phone: (612)687-7000
620 Opperman Dr.   800-328-9352
Eagan, MN 55123   Fax: (612)687-7302

Type: Full-text.

Content: Contains the complete text of *Criminal Law Defenses* by Paul H. Robinson. Provides a conceptual framework within which all criminal defenses can be considered, along with separate sections for each criminal law defense. Presents practical points collateral to the substantive law of criminal defenses.

Subject Coverage: Criminal law.

Language: English.

Time Span: Current through 1993.

Online Availability: *WESTLAW*.

Also Online As Part Of: WESTLAW®.

• 1505 • Criminology and Penal Jurisdiction

Institute of Criminology at the Faculty of   Phone: 61 331820
    Law
Trg osvoboditve 11
61001 Ljubljana, Slovenia

Type: Bibliographic.

Content: Contains bibliographic information on articles, books, congress and other materials from the field of criminology. Each record includes author, title, language of document, publication place and year, publisher/journal title, and number of pages.

Subject Coverage: Primarily criminology and penal jurisdiction. Also criminal and procedural law, criminal judiciary, criminal policy, criminal prevention, social supervision, juvenile delinquency, juvenile judiciary, criminology and police, human rights, sociology, psychology, psychiatry, social work, and education.

GALE DIRECTORY OF DATABASES. VOLUME 1: ONLINE DATABASES. DETROIT, MI: GALE RESEARCH, 1993-

EXHIBIT 4-1

Gateway Service Directories

As the volume and scope of database information has increased, companies—called *gateway services*—have emerged to provide online access to collections of otherwise separate databases. A gateway service manages customer online access to their collection of databases by offering single-search methods, consolidating payment, providing training services, and publishing directories of the databases they make available. Some of the oldest commercial gateway services are companies such as DIALOG, LEXIS-NEXIS, BRS (now OVID), and WESTLAW. Others newer to the industry are WILSONLINE and OCLC Epic, along with hundreds more. The most advantageous aspect of accessing databases through these vendors is that they have developed a single-search method for all, or nearly all, the databases they offer.

Since all vendors provide access to a large number of databases, researching their holdings is the key to comparing services and knowing whether a certain service allows you to access the full text of the *New York Times,* for instance. Each service provides a directory of databases available through their service, also called product guides, catalogs, and database lists, as well as newsletters that keep users up to date on newly available databases. Because most libraries consider databases to be *working tools*, finding them in the library catalog might be tricky—they may not be there. Therefore, you need to ask a librarian if any online services or database directories are available at the library. Bibliographies, indexes, and directories are also available to help you identify electronic databases valuable to criminal justice research.

The authors have covered a few of the most popular directories below.

Knight-Ridder Information Database Catalogue. Mountain View, CA: Knight-Ridder Information, 1996.

"Knight-Ridder Information." http://www.krinfo.com (January 3, 1996).

> The *Knight-Ridder Information Database Catalogue* inventories the online databases available through the DIALOG and DataStar services which include both indexes to the literature and full-text online sources such as newspapers and news services. The catalog includes a subject guide that categorizes the databases into 22 broad topics. The descriptions section is an alphabetical listing of databases with the file number, time coverage, frequency updated, the type of information provided, the source of the database, and a brief description of its contents. A separate pricing guide is available. The World Wide Web version of the *Database Catalog* is exactly the same as the paper version except that it also offers keyword searching of the databases.

NEXIS Product Guide. Dayton, OH: Reed Elsevier, 1992–.

LEXIS Product Guide. Dayton, OH: Reed Elsevier, 1992–.

Directory of Online Services. Dayton, OH: Reed Elsevier.

"LEXIS-NEXIS Communication Center." http://www. LEXIS-NEXIS.com (January 6, 1997).

> The *LEXIS-NEXIS Product Guides* list the online electronic databases furnished with each service, the names of the libraries and files, and the dates of coverage. Each guide provides overviews of the files and descriptions of the combinations of files that can be searched and descriptions of the databases; also indicated is whether they are full text, abstracts, or indexes. The section on pricing is an important feature to review. The *Directory of Online Services* is a compact and considerably more portable version of the product guides. A listing of libraries and databases is also available on the World Wide Web.

OVID. *OVID Online.* New York: OVID Technologies

> OVID's catalog of online databases is very thorough in its descriptions. Detailed information is provided covering scope, coverage, record structure, and examples of records. A price list is available. (Formerly *CDP Online*, formerly *BRS*.)

WESTLAW Database List. Eagan, MN: West Publishing.

> Don't be fooled by the name. WESTLAW now provides access to more than just law-related online databases. It is also a gateway to DIALOG and other information services. Its Database List is published at regular intervals and provides classified and alphabetical listings as well as a key to its pricing structure (although prices are not given in dollars). WESTLAW also provides an online version of its directory and provides scope information within the database.

The above references can assist you in identifying databases to use in your research; however, remember that they are restricted to the online databases provided by the individual services. If you sat down with several of these commercial catalogs you would still miss many databases available on CD-ROM (although CD-ROM databases are often duplicated online).

CD-ROM Database Directories

In the last half of the 1980s, advances in *laser disc* technology moved library holdings into another realm. Collections, that is the materials that libraries acquire and place at their patrons' disposal, now include more than books, periodicals, and microfiche and film. The authors want to distinguish library *collections* from the information you access online, which is not part of library collections but a resource that libraries can access when you need it. While online databases are not part of library collections, CD-ROM databases may be. Although they are not treated in all the same ways as books and periodicals, CD-ROMs are sometimes purchased and do become part of library collections. Some publishers provide CD-ROM databases as a subscription service, sometimes meaning that the laser discs have to be returned when and if the subscription is canceled. This situation is unfortunate and indicates that libraries are moving away from being able to provide the kind of archival service they once did when most knowledge was passed on with the printed word.

Databases published on CD-ROM are also sold individually as software for personal or networked computers and, in some instances, are also available online through a dial up. For the most part only librarians are interested in locating CD-ROM titles, therefore, the authors don't delve too deeply into the resources that provide information on CD-ROM products. We do, however, provide you with the two listed below.

Ensor, Pat. *CD-ROM Research Collections: An Evaluative Guide to Bibliographic and Full-Text CD-ROM Databases.* Westport, CT: Meckler, 1991.

Business & Legal CD-ROMs in Print. Westport, CT: Mecklermedia, 1993–.

Full-Text Database Directories

As mentioned above, electronic databases—online, CD-ROM, and other formats—are of three types: indexes or abstracts of the literature, full-text databases of articles and other materials, and data files. Gale's *Directory of Databases* describes all three types. Indexes and abstracts, whether in book or electronic form, however, only indicate the existence of a particular resource. If using one or both of these, you still have to rely on your local library for the full text. Many libraries do not own the journals and other materials you need for your research. On such occasions, libraries should offer to request the item on interlibrary loan. Items usually take 10 or more days to arrive, so if time is of the essence you should try to get the full text of the material online instead.

If you can't find the *Gale Directory of Databases* in your local library, see if the library has access to *Fulltext Sources Online,* which lists only full-text sources.

Fulltext Sources Online. Needham, MA: BiblioData, 1989–.

This directory of full-text databases, published twice a year in January and July, lists periodicals, newspapers, newsletters, newswires, and television and radio program transcripts on topics in science, technology, medicine, law, finance, business, industry, and the popular press. Entries are arranged alphabetically, listing title of database or file, provider, frequency updated, and time span. Entries also indicate if the online service carries all the articles from the periodical or just selected ones. Make sure to read the informative front matter—which explains "how 'full' is fulltext," and the currency of the periodicals—before going online. Issues of *Fulltext Sources Online* are cumulative and provide subject geographic indexes and a list of database vendors with names, addresses, and telephone numbers.

SEARCHING THE INTERNET: FULL-TEXT AND BIBLIOGRAPHIC DATABASES FOR THE 1990s

If you are looking for information, keep in mind that it comes in many different packages. These include books, periodicals, conference proceedings and papers, policy statements, laws, and court decisions. All these materials fall under one broad generic term—*documents.* We are accustomed to referring to these documents as having been "published," meaning that they have been accepted by a publisher, printed on paper, bound into a book, and then distributed. But due to the arrival of the Internet, this concept of publishing has changed. While the traditional information environment required information to be packaged into a physical object so that it could be distributed and read, packaging is no longer a requirement.

Although the authors still need to qualify this discussion of Internet-accessible documents with a warning to consider their origin, and therefore their authority, they remain a source of documentary information. If you are attuned to finding ways to verify their authority, they are no less a source of information than anything you find in a printed book or periodical article. As with any and all resources, you should consider the scope, coverage, timeliness, source, and content of information found at Web sites.

Throughout this work, we provide you with resources that assist in evaluating the sources of information. Those that provide information about "authorities" and "experts," covered in part in chapter 2, give the researcher a window into the individual who produced the information or commentary. Other sources, such as those that evaluate the information itself, or which critique the conclusions that authorities have drawn, are provided by such sources as *book reviews*, covered in chapter 3, and *citators*, such as *Social Science Citation Index* (chapter 5) and *Shepard's Citations* (chapter 8).

The methods of identifying and locating documentation that resides in books and periodicals are time tested and can be very sophisticated. We often learn them in primary school, and such processes are reinforced and expanded as we proceed through high school, college, and often into graduate school. The methods of finding information on the Internet are a new and completely different matter. They require new education and new ways of looking at the process of finding information.

Documents available on the Internet come in the form of text, graphics, or other files. Many reside in publicly accessible directories of computer systems connected to the Internet. Others are available to the public but are protected in some way. You may, for instance, need to know and enter a password to access them. In fact, there is a growing body of literature and law enforcement measures to protect computer files from unauthorized access. Suffice it to say that if you are prohibited from accessing a particular computer drive or directory, then you should not attempt to access it.

The tools for identifying and finding Internet documents have developed over time and when compared to the library catalog, are at once both primitive and sophisticated. They are primitive because they cannot provide the same level of "bibliographic control," or subject access. On the other hand, they are sophisticated because, unlike a library catalog, they provide immediate access to documents no matter where the document (or the researcher) is located.

As with any venture into "cyberspace," you would do well to have some depth of knowledge of how to get around. Because the purpose of the current work is not to give instruction in how to use the Internet generally, please refer to any one of the many Internet guidebooks available.

The World Wide Web

The World Wide Web is a collection of *HTML* (hypertext markup language) documents available on the Internet (at Web sites) via a software application called a browser. The Web offers an easy-to-use interface consisting of graphics, advanced formatting, and *hypertext links,* which connect the user to documents of various formats and other Web sites. We won't get into the complexities of browser software or the HTML documents that make the Web such an intuitive system to use. What is important, however, is that anyone can use it with relative ease.

The Web is a rich information environment. Because it is so simple to create Web pages and make documents available on the Web, you will find much more there today than was found on gopher sites just a few years ago. What is more, the Web melds the "older" technologies of telnet, gopher, and FTP: using your browser you still have access to non-HTML resources like telnet, gopher, and FTP, as well as e-mail. This access is especially useful because a number of valuable "gophered" documents and links continue to be maintained, although some are being moved into the more friendly Web environment.

Web Search Engines: Indexes and Hierarchical Lists

Conducting searches for information on the World Wide Web is accomplished using search engines, of which there are two types: indexes and hierarchical lists. Indexes, provided through services such as Lycos and Open Text, provide access to the Web as a whole and should be used to figure out if any Internet resources are available on a particular topic. Indexes frequently search for a word or words within documents and are useful for finding specific addresses or resources.

Hierarchical lists, like the one provided by the Yahoo! service, provide both subject analysis and access to resources. Companies that manage hierarchical lists employ people to look at individual sites and classify the resources located there by subject; therefore, these search engines are most useful for subject searches. Keep in mind that the limitations of subject analysis as discussed on pages 67–68 still apply here. In addition, the level of expertise of the employees who assign subject headings for many of these search tools has been criticized.

Listed below are a few Web indexes to try.

Alta Vista. http://altavista.digital.com/
Deja News Research Service. http://www.dejanews.com/
Lycos. http://www.lycos.com
NlightN. http://www.nlightn.com/
Open Text Index. http://www.opentext.com/omw/f-omw.html

Savvy Search. http://www.cs.colostate.edu/ ~dreiling/smartform.html
WhoWhere? PeopleSearch. http:// www.whowhere.com/
World Wide Web Worm (WWWW). http:// wwww.cs.colorado.edu/wwww

Below are some hierarchical lists to try.

Excite. http://www.excite.com/
Global Network Navigator (GNN). http:// gnn.com/gnn/GNNhome.html
Infoseek Guide. http://guide.infoseek.com/
Magellan. http://www.mckinley.com
WebCrawler. http://www.webcrawler.com
Yahoo! http://www.yahoo.com

Another type of search engine, not classified here, is listed below.

Galaxy EINet. http://galaxy.einet.net

When you conduct a search using either an index or a hierarchical list, the number of resources found, or *hits,* varies from only a few to many depending on which engine you use. Some search engines offer you the option of searching through the text of documents or just the titles of documents; others offer no choice. Some are self-contained searchers, that is, they conduct independent searches of the Web; others, like Savvy Search, actually send your search to all the others, which actually provides you with the most comprehensive list. However, such searches often take quite a bit of time to produce results, which sometimes consist of a very long list of sites. The authors suggest that you read available documentation on these search engines to become familiar with their features.

As with searching any kind of database, we suggest trying several. The following represents a summary of the results of a search for the word *prison* in several popular search engines. Notice the wide variation in the number of hits between services.

Search Engine Service	# of Hits for Prison
Excite	167,180
Infoseek	11,024
Yahoo!	160
Magellan	6,591
Web Crawler	3,139
Lycos	11,536
Alta Vista	80,000

While the authors do not delve into the specifics of how to use the many Web indexes available, an excellent discussion of the issues to consider can be found in *The World Wide Web Unleashed.* (SAMS Publishing, 1994.)

Web Sites with Criminal Justice Links

Like browsing around library collections, the authors also suggest that you browse around some of the Web sites listed below to become familiar with the information they contain. It is a good idea to visit these sites periodically because information is constantly being added to them. You can create *bookmarks* for these sites using your browser, which help you keep track of the location of the sites.

If you are ambitious, you can develop your own Web page with links to criminal justice sites. See, for example, Cecil Greek's home page listed below, probably the mother of all personal criminal justice pages. (Professor Greek has kept on top of developments in online access to information in criminal justice and has developed an exhaustive group of links to relevant Web sites.)

"California State University—Stanislaus Criminal Justice Page." http://cjwww.csustan.edu/cj/ links.html (March 12, 1997).
"Cecil Greek's Criminal Justice Links Homepage." http://www.fsu.edu/~crimdo/ cj.html (March 12, 1997).
"Department of Justice, Drug Enforcement Administration." http://www.usdoj.gov/dea/ deahome.htm (March 12, 1997).
"Department of the Treasury, Alcohol Tobacco and Firearms." http://www.atf.treas.gov/ (March 12, 1997).
"Department of the Treasury, Financial Crimes Enforcement Network." http:// www.ustreas.gov/treasury/bureaus/fincen/ (March 12, 1997).
"National Criminal Justice Reference Service." http://www.ncjrs.org/ncjhome.htm (March 12, 1997).
"National Institute of Justice." http:// www.ncjrs.org/nijhome.htm (March 12, 1997).
"NCJRS, Justice Information Center." http:// www.ncjrs.org/ (March 12, 1997).
"Police Resource List." http://police.sas.ab.ca/prl/ index.html (March 12, 1997).
"United States Department of Justice." gopher:// gopher.usdoj.gov/ (March 12, 1997).

"United States Department of Justice Web Page." http://justice2.usdoj.gov/ (March 12, 1997).

"United Nations Crime and Justice Information Network." http://www.ifs.univie.ac.at/~uncjin/uncjin.html (March 12, 1997).

"World Criminal Justice Library Electronic Network." http://info.rutgers.edu/newark/WCJLEN.html(March 12, 1997).

SEARCHING PRINTED BIBLIOGRAPHIES

We've gone the gamut on tools for finding information using all types of electronic bibliographic databases. However, it is sometimes more efficient to use a printed bibliography to locate all that has been written on a subject. Subject bibliographies are extremely useful because they focus your search to a specific field or subfield. Some subject bibliographies cite only information printed in books, but many include citations to periodical literature as well. (For a more detailed treatment of finding periodical literature using indexes and abstracts, see chapter 5.) The most useful bibliographies are those that classify books and other information sources by subject and that give brief annotations or synopses of the works listed. Those that classify books by subject are extremely valuable because they tend to supply more detailed subject analyses than library catalogs. Annotated bibliographies help streamline your research by giving you the opportunity to evaluate the usefulness of a source to your research, before going to the trouble of getting it from the shelf. In addition, most bibliographies are compiled by librarians or scholars in a field and can provide a more critical view of the source, thus saving you even more time.

Later in this work, when we deal with periodical indexes (chapter 5), we ask you to look at the scope of your source. In this chapter, we suggest that you observe the use of words like "selected" in the titles of bibliographies. Whenever the word "selected" is used in the title of a bibliography, it always means that the compilor of the bibliography has limited the number of sources listed in the bibliography based on some criterion. It is important that you read the preface of the bibliography to determine how its scope has been limited. In that way, you can further judge the usefulness of the bibliography to your research.

Bibliographies of Bibliographies

A "bibliography of bibliographies" is a collection of bibliographies. In other words, it represents a gathering of books that gather books. They tend to be very broad in their scope, perhaps covering bibliographies of all the social sciences or—when much has been written on a subject—a somewhat narrower topic within the social sciences. Such works are a useful starting point for a literature search for a master's thesis or doctoral dissertation.

Some general bibliography of bibliographies are listed below.

General

Besterman, Theodore. *A World Bibliography of Bibliographies and Bibliographical Catalogues, Calendars, Abstracts, Digests, Indexes and the Like.* 4th ed. 5 vols. Lausanne: Societas Bibliographica, 1965–66.
> Brief annotations are given of 117,187 bibliographies. Volume 5 is an alphabetical index of authors, editors, translators, and titles.

Bibliographic Index: A Cumulative Bibliography of Bibliographies. New York: W. H. Wilson, 1938–.
> This source provides good international coverage of bibliographies that have been published separately, as parts of books, or as articles.

Toomey, Alice F. *World Bibliography of Bibliographies, 1964–1974: A List of Works Represented by Library of Congress Printed Catalog Cards; A Decennial Supplement to Theodore Besterman, A World Bibliography of Bibliographies.* 2 vols. Totowa, NJ: Rowman & Littlefield, 1977.

Criminal Justice

Davis, Bruce L. *Criminological Bibliographies: Uniform Citations to Bibliographies, Indexes, and Review Articles of the Literature of Crime Study in the United States.* Westport, CT: Greenwood Press, 1978.

Klein, Carol, and David M. Horton, comps. *Bibliographies in Criminal Justice: A Selected Bibliography.* Washington, DC: U.S. National Criminal Justice Reference Services, 1979.

(See page 75 for printed versions of criminal justice library catalogs.)

Social Science Bibliographies

International Bibliography of the Social Sciences: International Bibliography of Sociology. London: Tavistock; Chicago: Aldine, 1952–. Annual.

London School of Economics. *London Bibliography of the Social Sciences.* London: London School of Economics, 1931–.

   Published every five years with annual supplements.

Classic Criminal Justice Bibliographies

The place to start for a historical bibliography devoted to criminal justice is with *A Guide to Material on Crime and Criminal Justice* by Augustus Frederick Kuhlman. It is limited to material on crime and criminals in the United States, published or in manuscript, prior to 1927.

   Continue your research with a very useful series of bibliographies compiled by Dorothy Campbell Culver for the Institute of Governmental Studies of the University of California. This series continues the excellent bibliographic standards established by the Kuhlman work. The first volume in this series covers the literature from 1927–1931, and is updated by volumes covering the years from 1932–1956. Continuing this work are a number of more specialized bibliographies, namely *The Offender* (1963), *Probation Since World War II* (1964), *Juvenile Gangs* (1966), *White-Collar Crime* (1967), *Sentencing the Offender (1971),* and *The Prison and the Prisoner* (1972).

   The following bibliographies include citations to books, periodical articles, pamphlets, videos, recordings, newspaper articles, and government documents.

Culver, Dorothy Campbell. *Bibliography of Crime and Criminal Justice, 1927–1931.* Reprint, Montclair, NJ: Patterson Smith, 1969.

Culver, Dorothy Campbell. *Bibliography of Crime and Criminal Justice, 1932–1937.* Reprint, Montclair, NJ: Patterson Smith, 1969.

Culver, Dorothy Campbell. *Administration of Justice, 1949–1956.* Reprint, Montclair, NJ: Patterson Smith, 1970.

   The first volume by Culver provides international coverage for materials published before 1927. The volume begins with a classification outline and the classified, numbered entries are listed alphabetically under the appropriate heading. When necessary to correctly identify the contents of a publication, a short annotation is included. There is a combined author, subject, and geographic index.

This excellent series is continued with the following publications by the same compiler: *Bibliography of Crime and Criminal Justice, 1927–1931.* (New York: H.W. Wilson, 1934); *Bibliography of Crime and Criminal Justice, 1932–1937* (New York: H.W. Wilson, 1939); *Sources for the Study of the Administration of Criminal Justice, 1938–1948: A Selected Bibliography.* (Sacramento, CA: Special Crime Study Commissions and California State Board of Corrections, 1949); *Administration of Justice, 1949–1956: A Selected Bibliography.* (Sacramento, CA: California State Board of Corrections, California Special Study Commission on Correctional Facilities and Services, 1956). As with the first volume, this entire series has been reprinted by Patterson Smith.

Cuming, Sir John. *Contribution towards a Bibliography Dealing with Crime and Cognate Subjects.* 3rd ed. 1935. Reprint, Montclair, NJ: Patterson Smith, 1970.

   Bibliographic entries are arranged by a detailed classification of subject headings with a subject/geographic index and an author index. Provides international coverage, but concentrates on British literature. Consists mainly of books, but some important periodical articles are included.

Klein, Fannie J. *Administration of Justice in the Courts.* 2 vols. Dobbs Ferry, NJ: Oceana, 1976.

Kuhlman, Augustus F. *Guide to Material on Crime and Criminal Justice.* 1929. Reprint, Montclair, NJ: Patterson Smith, 1969.

   Covers books, pamphlets, and articles published in Great Britain and the U.S. before 1927. Entries are classified and arranged alphabetically. When necessary to determine the contents of a source, a brief annotation if given. There is a brief subject index.

Radzinowicz, Sir Leon, and Roger G. Hood. *Criminology and the Administration of Criminal Justice: A Bibliography.* Westport, CT: Greenwood Press, 1976.

Wolfgang, Marvin E., Robert M. Figlio, and Terence P. Thornberry. *Criminology Index.* New York: Elsevier, 1975.

   This reference tool cites more than 3,000 articles and approximately 550 books and reports dealing with the etiology of crime and delinquency published from 1945 to 1972. Arranged according to three indexes (source document, paired-word subject, and criminology citation), this source is difficult to use, but it should be consulted for the work of this period. (See exhibits 4-2, 4-3, and 4-4 for sample pages.) The "Criminology Citation Index" (exhibit 4-4) is of particular value when attempting to evaluate the authority of a work or author because it points to works that cite others. When a work is cited in a subsequent article or book, it is generally used to support or refute a proposition, or the cited work may be treated in some way, perhaps criticized or explained. This is a valuable way to

KEY TO THE ELEMENTS OF THE SOURCE DOCUMENT INDEX

This collection is an alphabetical listing of articles and books by author's last name. It is a reproduction of a computer printout and can be read as follows for articles:

(author) ──────────→ GORING CB

(journal name)
(numerical code)
(PUBLICATION) J MENT SCI 03522 ◄── (type code)*

(year, volume, pages) ──→ 1918 V64, PG 129 146 TYPE J, 37R

(number of references made to other work)

(author's affiliation, if available) ──→ U LONDON

(article title) ──────→ THE ETIOLOGY OF CRIME

For books, the following items appear:

(author)
(abbreviated title) ─── GORING CB

(numerical code)
(PUBLICATION) ENG CON STAT STUDY 93522 ── (type code)*

(year, pages) ──→ 1913 PG 1 525 TYPE N, 115 R

(number of references made to other work)

(author's affiliation, if available) ──→ U LONDON

(full title) ──→ THE ENGLISH CONVICT A STATISTICAL STUDY

(publisher, place) ──→ HIS MAJESTYS STATIONERY OFFICE LONDON

---

*Type code entries are as follows:

J or Blank,	Journal
N or<,	Non Journal (includes books, meetings, reports, etc.)
D,	Dissertation
P,	Newspaper
I,	Indirect Citation
C,	Chapter Author or Contributor
L,	Law or Legal Case
K,	Unpublished

WOLFGANG, MARVIN E., ROBERT M. FIGLIO, AND TERENCE P. THORNBERRY. *CRIMINOLOGY INDEX.* NEW YORK: ELSEVIER, 1975.

EXHIBIT 4-2

see how other researchers have viewed a work which you may be mentioning in your research. (Refer also to chapter 5, page 97, for a discussion of the *Social Science Citation Index.*)

Current Criminal Justice Bibliographies

Abel, Ernest. *Homicide: A Bibliography.* New York: Greenwood Press, 1987.

Sources published prior to 1985 on homicide are included in this bibliography listing 1,919 sources. Entries are arranged alphabetically by author; items are numbered consecutively and are referred to by number in the subject index. This source is not annotated.

Aday, Ron H. *Crime and the Elderly: An Annotated Bibliography.* New York: Greenwood Press, 1988.

Entries cover elderly crime victims and offenders in this annotated bibliography of relevant literature published since 1980. Also included are listings of state agencies and private organization in the U.S. that are concerned with elderly victims and offenders.

Alali, A. Odasuo, and Gary W. Byrd. *Terrorism and the News Media: A Selected, Annotated Bibliography.* Jefferson, NC: McFarland, 1994.

More than 600 entries on the media treatment of terrorism are included in this annotated bibliography. Sources in-

KEY TO THE ELEMENTS OF THE SUBJECT INDEX

The Subject Index is composed of the pairing of each key word in a title with each of the remaining key words in that title. Words that are meaningless for subject classification, such as articles and prepositions, are not printed. Words which are too general or nonspecific to aid in classification are called half-stop words and do not appear as main headings but only as secondary headings. Because the decision to "half-stop" a title word must be made arbitrarily, a conservative stance has been taken by so designating as few words as possible. Thus, the statement "see half-stop words" appears infrequently in the Subject Index.

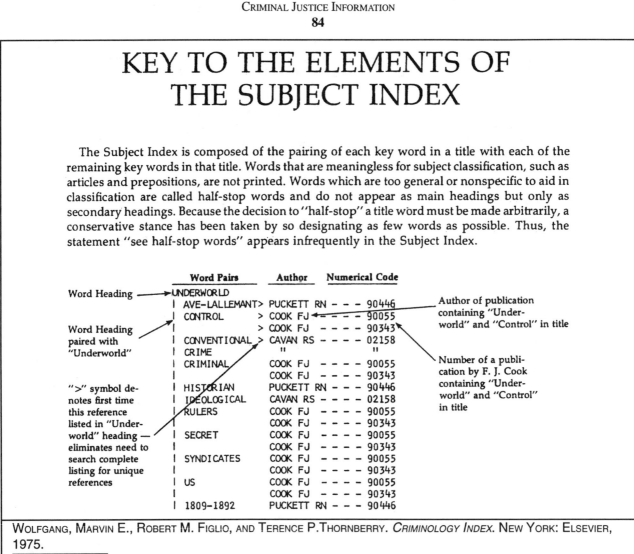

WOLFGANG, MARVIN E., ROBERT M. FIGLIO, AND TERENCE P. THORNBERRY. *CRIMINOLOGY INDEX.* NEW YORK: ELSEVIER, 1975.

EXHIBIT 4-3

---

clude scholarly journals, books, and articles. There are author, title, and subject indexes.

Bailey, William G., comp. *Police Science, 1964–1984: A Selected, Annotated Bibliography.* New York: Garland, 1986.

Entries are arranged according to topics such as general studies, police history, police administration, education and training, personality constructs, field operations, criminal and traffic investigation, and forensic science. Included are dissertations, law review articles, government documents, and other police-specific materials.

Beirne, Piers, and Joan Hill, comps. *Comparative Criminology: An Annotated Bibliography.* Westport, CT: Greenwood Press, 1991.

Describes 500 studies on crime, law, and social control in two or more cultures. Entries are arranged according to the following topics: meaning and measurement in comparative criminology, cross-national crime rates, and social control and criminal justice. The following appendices are included: lists of countries in cross-national data sets, lists of United Nations interregional crime and justice re-

search institutions' publications and staff papers, addresses of United Nations regional institutes for crime prevention, and miscellaneous research aids. There are author and subject indexes.

Berens, John F., comp. *Criminal Justice Documents: A Selective, Annotated Bibliography of U.S. Government Publications since 1975.* New York: Greenwood Press, 1987.

Some 1,094 entries detail the publications produced by government agencies between 1975 and October 1986 on criminal justice. Entries are classified into eight broad subject areas: criminal justice system, crime and criminals, police and law enforcement, law and the courts, corrections, juvenile justice and delinquency, security, and special criminal justice resources. Within each chapter, entries are broken down further by more specific subject headings. The format for each entry includes author, title, place of publication, agency, year, number of pages, and the Superintendent of Documents number. Indexes include author, subject, geographic location, and association/organization.

KEY TO THE ELEMENTS OF THE GENERAL CRIMINOLOGY CITATION INDEX

The General Criminology Citation Index is an alphabetical listing, by author, of cited work and its associated citing work, also by author. A sample of the computer printout is reproduced below and can be read as follows:

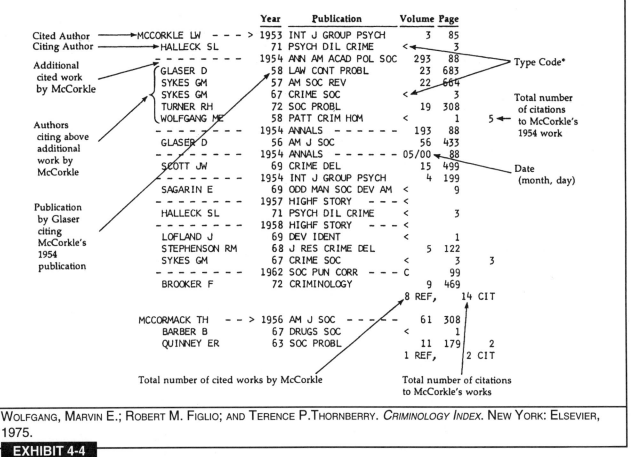

WOLFGANG, MARVIN E.; ROBERT M. FIGLIO; AND TERENCE P. THORNBERRY. *CRIMINOLOGY INDEX.* NEW YORK: ELSEVIER, 1975.

EXHIBIT 4-4

Best, Reba A., and D. Cheryn Picquet. *Computer Law and Software Protection: A Bibliography of Crime, Liability, Abuse and Security, 1984 through 1992.* Jefferson, NC: McFarland, 1993.

Over 3,000 entries on various aspects of computer crime liability and abuse and security are included in this bibliography. Topics include privacy, patents, copyright, and antitrust and trade practices. This work updates an earlier bibliography of the same title, which covered the literature from 1970 to 1984.

Beyleveld, Deryck. *A Bibliography on General Deterrence.* Farnborough, UK: Saxon House, 1980. Distributed by Lexington Books, Lexington, MA.

This extensive bibliography of books, book chapters, dissertations, and articles gives lengthy annotations on sources written between 1946 and 1979 on deterrence research. Subject access is provided through a detailed table of contents and a subject index.

Chappell, Duncan, and Rhonda D. Moore. *The Use of Criminal Penalties for Pollution of the Environment: A Selective and Annotated Bibliography of the Literature.* Ontario, Canada: Canada Department of Justice, 1988.

This interdisciplinary bibliography includes approximately 185 entries published in the fields of criminology, jurisprudence, social psychology, and industry and regulation on the issue of criminal penalties for environmental pollution. The work is subdivided into three parts: Canada, the U.S., and other jurisdictions.

Cordasco, F., and D. N. Alloway. *Crime in America: Historical Patterns and Contemporary Realities.* New York: Garland, 1985.

The 1,879 annotated sources of literature in criminology published since 1975 included in this bibliography are arranged into 17 subject categories.

Denno, Deborah W., and Ruth M. Schwarz. *Biological, Psychological, and Environmental Factors in Delinquency and Mental Disorder: An Interdisciplinary Bibliography.* Westport, CT: Greenwood Press, 1985.

This interdisciplinary bibliography includes 2,207 references for biological, psychological, and environmental explanations of child development; brain functions and central nervous system disorders; and mental disorder and crime. Arranged in three major sections, the first is a bibliography of 2,000 entries. Each is identified by a number and followed by a series of topic codes denoting the primary subject matter for that entry. The second section is a hierarchical listing of the subject headings used in section one, and the third section is the index, which links subject headings in the hierarchical listing to the entries in the bibliography.

deYoung, Mary, comp. *Child Molestation: An Annotated Bibliography.* Jefferson, NC: McFarland, 1987.

Drawing from the social science, medical, and legal literature, this annotated bibliography cites hundreds of references on the subject of child molestation. Includes separate author, title, and subject indexes.

Duguid, Stephen, and Terry A. Fowler. *Of Books and Bars: An Annotated Bibliography on Prison Education.* Burnaby, BC: Institute for the Humanities, Simon Fraser University, 1988.

Some 527 entries address a variety of issues on prison education, including literacy, administration, adult education, community links, peer teaching, program evaluation and rehabilitation, and other topics.

Engeldinger, Eugene A., comp. *Spouse Abuse: An Annotated Bibliography of Violence Between Mates.* Metuchen, NJ: Scarecrow Press, 1986.

Some 1,780 entries on spouse abuse include books, articles, master's theses and doctoral dissertations, government reports, handbooks, guides, bibliographies, and conference papers written through 1983. Entries are arranged alphabetically by author. Name and subject indexes are included.

Frasier, David K. *Murder Cases of the Twentieth Century: Biographies and Bibliographies of 280 Convicted and Accused Killers.* Jefferson, NC: McFarland, 1996.

Drawing on the "true crime" literature of the twentieth century, this presents biographical sketches of 280 famous convicted or accused murderers that are considered of historical significance. Political assassins and gangsters are excluded, and murder cases are limited to those which occurred before 1993. Entries are arranged alphabetically, and each concludes with a very useful bibliography of relevant works. There is an appendix which groups the entries by the type of crime, and a general index of authors and titles noted in the bibliographies and geographical and place names associated with the individual cases.

Friedmann, Robert R., comp. *Criminal Justice in Israel: An Annotated Bibliography of English Language Publications, 1948–1993.* Westport, CT: Greenwood Press, 1995.

This bibliographical source includes over 820 materials written on Israeli criminal justice until 1993. Entries are annotated, and there is an index of authors' names, periodicals, and subjects.

Hartz, Fred R., Michael B. Krimmel, and Emilie K. Hartz, comps. *Prison Librarianship: A Selective, Annotated, Classified Bibliography 1945–1985.* Jefferson, NC: McFarland, 1987.

Citations in this selective bibliography cover the literature on correctional librarianship from 1945 through 1987. Entries are arranged under the following categories: administration, bibliotherapy, censorship, funding, history, materials selection, service, prerelease-reentry services, and standards/guidelines.

Hewitt, John D., Eric D. Poole, and Robert M. Regoli. *Criminal Justice in America 1959–1984: An Annotated Bibliography.* New York: Garland, 1985.

This selective, annotated bibliography covers the literature on law enforcement, courts, and corrections in the U.S. from 1959 through 1985. Each of the three main sections ("Law Enforcement," "Courts," and "Corrections") are further divided into "History," "Organization," "Process," and "Issues." There are separate name and subject indexes and a list of sources.

Jerath, Bal K., and Rajinder Jerath. *Homicide: A Bibliography.* 2d ed. Boca Raton, FL: CRC Press, 1993.

This unannotated bibliography lists sources according to the following chapter topics: "Statistics"; "The Murderer"; "The Victim"; "Murder Modes"; "Causes"; "Investigation"; "Case Reports"; "Homicide, Suicide and Accidents"; "Legal Aspects"; "Assassination"; and "Prevention and Control." Includes an extensive subject index and a separate author index.

Johnson, Tanya F., James G. O'Brien, and Margaret F. Hudson, eds. *Elder Neglect and Abuse: An Annotated Bibliography.* Westport, CT: Greenwood Press, 1985.

Literature published since 1975 on the subject of elder abuse is covered in this bibliography. The 144 annotated references include books, journal articles, reports from investigative committees, hearings, conference proceedings, and research reports. The nine disciplines covered are journalism, law, medicine, nursing, psychiatry, psychology, public health, social work, and sociology. The second part of this bibliography is a directory of organizations that provide services to older adults.

Lakos, Amos. *International Terrorism: A Bibliography.* Boulder, CO: Westview Press, 1986.

This source is not annotated, but it does provide an extensive listing of English-language sources on international terrorism, including books, journal articles, reports, and government documents. After an opening chapter on reference sources, chapters are grouped under broad geographic sections (i.e., "Latin America") and then by specific countries. Entries are then subdivided by books, journal articles, and documents and reports.

Lakos, Amos. *Terrorism, 1980–1990: A Bibliography.* Boulder, CO: Westview Press, 1991.

This volume updates the author's previous work *International Terrorism*, which covers the literature on terrorism from 1965–1985. Included are books, journal articles, and other documents. Entries are not annotated and are arranged into eight chapters. There are separate subject and author indexes.

Lomax, Denise, comp, and Ronnie Mills, ed. *Expanding Knowledge in Criminal Justice: A Comprehensive Bibliography.* Washington, DC: U.S. National Institute of Justice, 1984.

This is an excellent source for identifying the many documents published by the U.S. National Institute of Justice from 1978 to 1982. Part 1 is the bibliography of publications, and part 2 identifies the various series or specialized publications, such as program models, test designs, and exemplary projects. There are separate subject and author indexes, as well as information on obtaining the documents listed.

Matthews, Catherine J. *Accountability in the Administration of Criminal Justice: A Selective Annotated Bibliography.* Toronto: Centre of Criminology, University of Toronto, 1993.

This selective bibliography includes some 250 sources on accountability, control, and responsibility in the administration of criminal justice from 1965 to 1991. Emphasis is on English-language sources from Canada, the U.S., Great Britain, Australia, and New Zealand. Section 2 addresses police complaints and civilian review of police, and section 3 considers accountability issues in the context of government and the criminal justice system. This is but one of many fine bibliographies produced by the Centre of Criminology of the University of Toronto. Not all are included here, but they are indexed and abstracted in *Criminal Justice Abstracts* (see page 102), as well as other databases; therefore the user can use databases and general indexes to bibliographies to locate others in this series.

Mickolus, Edward F. *Terrorism, 1988–1991: A Chronology of Events, and a Selectively Annotated Bibliography.* Westport, CT: Greenwood Press, 1993.

Based primarily on newspaper and periodical accounts, a selective chronology and bibliography trace international terrorist activities between 1988 and 1991. There is no index.

Mickolus, Edward F., and Peter A. Flemming. *Terrorism, 1980–1987: A Selectively Annotated Bibliography.* New York: Greenwood Press, 1988.

This update to the 1980 edition covers books, articles, and reports on terrorism published between 1980 and 1987. Categories include tactics, philosophical approaches, terrorist infrastructures, geographic areas suffering from terrorism, responses to it, the media's reaction and involvement with the groups, psychological and medical approaches to the phenomena, and fiction.

Nash, Stanley D. *Prostitution in Great Britain 1485–1902: An Annotated Bibliography.* Metuchen, NJ: Scarecrow Press, 1994.

This historical bibliography traces the rise of prostitution in Great Britain from 1485 to 1902. The 390 entries include such sources as broadsides, sermons, pamphlets, books, diaries, personal journals, travel writings, periodical accounts, newspaper articles, parliamentary documents, accounts of institutions or organizations, court records, and fiction. Entries are arranged into primary and secondary sources and then alphabetically according to three time periods (1485–1700, 1700–1800, and 1800–1902). An index to names, concepts, subjects, and titles conclude this source.

Newton, Michael. *Mass Murder: An Annotated Bibliography.* New York: Garland, 1988.

Some 620 entries cover the literature on homicide involving multiple victims. Entries are arranged in three chapters: general and encyclopedic works, specialized/psychological works, and case histories. There is a subject index.

Newton, Michael, and Judy Ann Newton. *Racial and Religious Violence in America: A Chronology.* New York: Garland, 1991.

This is a chronological listing of violent racial and religious incidents in the United States. It includes a subject bibliography and an extensive subject index that is further divided by state.

Newton, Michael, and Judy Ann Newton. *Terrorism in the United States and Europe: An Annotated Bibliography.* New York: Garland, 1988.

Covering the literature of terrorism in Europe and the United States from 1800 to 1959, this partially annotated bibliography is limited to books and periodicals. After an opening chapter on general works, entries are arranged by country. The section on terrorism in the United States includes sections on anarchism, assassination, economic violence, the Ku Klux Klan, lynching, political violence, racial violence, and social violence. There is a subject index.

Nutter, Richard W., Joe Hudson, and Burt Galaway. *Monetary Restitution and Victim/Offender Contact: An Annotated and Cross-Referenced Bibliography.* Washington, DC: U.S. National Institute of Corrections; Ottawa, Canada: Solicitor General Canada, 1989.

Annotated entries on 940 English-language sources are included in this bibliography on the use of monetary restitution and community service work orders as sanctions for offenders.

Ontiveros, Suzanne Robitaille, ed. *Global Terrorism: A Historical Bibliography.* Santa Barbara, CA: ABC-CLIO, 1986.

Sources are limited to journal articles covering over 2,000 periodicals published in some 90 countries. Entries are arranged alphabetically by author within geographic chapters.

Palmegiano, E. M. *Crime in Victorian Britain: An Annotated Bibliography from Nineteenth-Century British Magazines.* Westport, CT: Greenwood, 1993.

This annotated bibliography includes 1,614 articles published in 45 journals between 1824 and 1900 of crime in ninteteenth-century Britain. The checklist is arranged alphabetically by serial. There are separate author, select personnel (noted individuals), and subject indexes.

Pruncken, Henry W., Jr. *Special Access Required: A Practitioner's Guide to Law Enforcement Intelligence Literature.* Metuchen, NJ: Scarecrow, 1990.

This annotated bibliography of law enforcement intelligence lists approximately 1,600 monographs published from 1868 to 1990 in Australia, Canada, China, France, Germany, Holland, Ireland, the United Kingdom, and the U.S. A special section reviews computer software used to develop or upgrade an agency's intelligence capability. Additional features include a list of relevant journals, a directory of intelligence libraries, and a list of intelligence associations. Includes separate subject and author indexes.

Radelet, Michael L., and Margaret Vandiver. *Capital Punishment in America: An Annotated Bibliography.* New York: Garland, 1988.

An annotated bibliography on capital punishment includes 1,011 sources published since 1972. Some classic studies published before this date are included.

Rosen, Nathan Aaron. *Battered Wives: A Comprehensive Annotated Bibliography of Articles, Books and Statutes in the United States of America.* New York: National Center for Women and Family Law, 1988.

More than 600 books and articles concerning battered women in the U.S. are included in this annotated bibliography. A state-by-state listing of domestic violence statutes is also included.

Schlacter, Gail, ed. *Crime and Punishment in America: A Historical Bibliography.* Santa Barbara, CA: ABC-CLIO, 1984.

Some 1,396 abstracts of articles on crime in America published from 1973 to 1983 are covered in this bibliography. Entries are arranged according to eight chapter titles: "Crime and Criminality in American Life"; "Crimes of Violence"; "Crimes against Property"; "Riots, Disturbances, and Civil Disobedience"; "Political Crimes and Corruption"; "Victimless Crimes"; "Law Enforcement, Criminal Law, and the Courts"; and "Punishment, Rehabilitation, and the Prisons."

Schlesinger, Benjamin, and Rachel Schlesinger, eds. *Abuse of the Elderly: Issues and Annotated Bibliography.* Toronto: University of Toronto Press, 1988.

This source is both an anthology of 10 essays by nurses, psychiatrists, lawyers, sociologists, social workers, and social scientist on the issue of elderly abuse and an annotated bibliography of 260 items published in Canada and the U.S. from 1979 to 1987.

Schmalleger, Frank, and Robert McKenrick, eds. *Criminal Justice Ethics: Annotated Bibliography and Guide to Sources.* Westport, CT: Greenwood Press, 1991.

Ethical issues in criminal justice policy and law, police, courts, corrections, and victims' rights are addressed in this annotated bibliography of 231 entries.

Shea, Kathleen A., and Beverly R. Fletcher, comps. *Female Offenders: An Annotated Bibliography.* Westport, CT: Greenwood Press, 1997.

Entries include brief annotations to English language materials dealing with female offenders arranged according to the following chapter headings: "Criminology"; "Crimes"; "Arrest, Prosecution, Sentencing"; "Female Juveniles"; "Corrections"; "Probation and Parole"; "Political Prisoners"; and "Bibliographies." Indexes include a subject/geographic index and a separate author index.

Signorielli, Nanch, and George Gerbner. *Violence and Terror in the Mass Media: An Annotated Bibliography.* New York: Greenwood Press, 1988.

Focusing on research and scholarly works relating to violence and terror, this bibliography examines four areas: violence and mass media content, violence and mass media effects, terrorism and the mass media, and pornography. Entries consist of a bibliographic citation and a short abstract describing the results.

Smandych, Russell C., Catherine J. Matthews, and Sandra J. Cox. *Canadian Criminal Justice History: An Annotated Bibliography.* Toronto: University of Toronto Press, 1987.

Some 1,100 published and unpublished scholarly works on Canadian criminal justice written in English and French between 1867 and 1984 are covered in this annotated bibliography. Sections cover topics such as "Crime, Deviance, and Delinquency"; Courts and Administration of Criminal Justice"; and "Prisons and Social Welfare Institutions."

Theoharis, Athan. *The FBI: An Annotated Bibliography and Research Guide.* New York: Garland, 1994.

> This serves as both a research guide for the study of the U.S. Federal Bureau of Investigation (FBI) and a bibliography of information on the FBI, J. Edgar Hoover, and federal surveillance. The first section includes a manual on using the Freedom of Information Act to obtain relevant FBI records. The second section lists publications of interest to those studying the FBI, and the last section is a bibliography of 1,041 relevant books and articles.

United Nations. Interregional Crime and Justice Research Institute. *International Bibliography on Alternatives to Imprisonment 1980–1989.* Rome: 1990.

> An international bibliography of alternatives to imprisonment includes published references from 1980 to 1989. Entries are arranged alphabetically by author, with a detailed subject index. Issues addressed include probation and parole, community-based treatment programs, community service restitution programs, jail overcrowding, programs for alcohol and abuse offenders, the use of fines, and supervision.

Wright, A. J., comp. *Criminal Activity in the Deep South, 1790–1930: An Annotated Bibliography.* Westport, CT: Greenwood Press, 1989.

> Over 1,200 entries give brief, descriptive annotations of the literature on crime in the deep South from 1790 to 1930. Crime for the purposes of this bibliography is defined as "illegal activity associated with economic gain, revenge or preservation of individual or community honor." Following a 13-page chronology of crimes, entries are arranged by region and then state by state. Entries are further separated by monographs, dissertations, theses, journal articles, miscellaneous, and newspaper articles.

In addition to the useful bibliographies listed above, which tend to focus on the academic subjects of criminal justice, Vance Bibliographies and the Council of Planning Librarians produce bibliographies in series. These series focus on public policy generally and include, from time to time, bibliographies that may be of interest to criminal justice professionals and scholars. *Current Contents: Social and Behavioral Sciences* is a periodical often treated as an index in libraries. It collects and reprints the tables of contents from current issues of social science periodicals.

Books in Print, Publishers' Catalogs, and Other Sources

A large part of being up to date in a discipline is keeping up with the literature. Bibliographies are excellent sources for compiling a list of books on a subject. But bibliographies suffer one major shortcoming: they take time to publish. While bibliographies are in press, new titles on your subject are being issued. So even the most current bibliography might not cover *all* the literature. Library catalogs and union catalogs likewise take time to compile. There is always a time lag.

In order to stay on top of new publications, many scholars get on mailing lists with publishers that specialize in criminal justice subjects. In this way they receive notice of new and forthcoming titles. Another way to keep current is to read "books received" lists that are often prepared and published in journals.

Other sources, like those we list below, are useful in filling in possible gaps in literature searches. They also provide a way to verify publication information on books. These can be useful when a colleague, article, or symposium speaker makes only passing reference to a work and you have gotten only part of the title or only the author's name. Sources that verify periodical information are covered in chapter 5.

Books in Print. New York: R. R. Bowker, 1948–.

> *Books in Print* provides a comprehensive listing of books currently available from more than 30,000 publishers. Although limited to books published in the U.S., books published in foreign countries are included if they are available through a U.S. distributor. Each entry includes author, title, publisher, ISBN number, price, format, number of pages, and series. The subject guide to this set rearranges the nonfiction titles under subject headings according to Library of Congress subject headings. A directory volume provides publisher information, and a separate volume lists out-of-print titles. Related publications from this publisher include *Paperbound Books in Print* (semiannual) and *Forthcoming Books* (bimonthly). A CD-ROM version of all these titles is available as *Books in Print Plus*. They are available online through DIALOG, file 470, and OVID (BBIP).

The British National Bibliography. London: British Library, Bibliographic Services Division, 1912–.

> This is a bibliography of books deposited in the British Library for copyright purposes. It is published weekly with irregular cumulations and provides a comprehensive listing of new titles published in the United Kingdom.

Canadian Books in Print. Toronto: Univ. of Toronto Press, 1976–.

Canadian Books in Print includes books published in English by Canadian publishers and those published in French by predominantly English language publishers. *Canadian Books in Print* provides author and title access and a companion subject listing.

Cumulative Book Index. New York: Wilson, 1898–.

Cumulative Book Index (CBI) is a comprehensive catalog of books published in English since 1898. Each volume lists books under author, title, and subject and is extremely useful if your research requires historical treatment.

Whitaker's Books in Print. London: J. Whitaker & Sons, 1988–.

Whitaker's is useful in your search for British publications if you need to use a subject approach. Since 1971, Whitaker's is a computer-generated listing of publications by author, title, and keywords.

Dissertations

The dissertation is considered the culmination of the preparation for the Ph.D. degree. The dissertation process varies from institution to institution, but for the most part, it represents an exhaustive coverage of a subject. Dissertations are not only thoroughly researched works, but they also provide complete reviews of the literature in the field. Thus, they can be a good source not only of analysis of the subject, but the accompanying bibliography is extremely useful in your initial stages of research. Admittedly, the author of a dissertation has not yet been conferred the degree of doctor, but the dissertation itself has been subjected to serious scrutiny by a committee of scholars. Therefore, you have some assurance that the work has been evaluated.

Libraries treat dissertations differently. Some have only dissertations from their parent institution, others may not have any. Dissertations can be acquired either through interlibrary loan or purchase. The library catalog might contain dissertations if the library maintains a copy in its holdings, or you can identify them by using the source listed below.

Dissertation Abstracts International. Ann Arbor, MI: University Microfilms International, 1981–.

This source was first published in 1938 and has undergone several changes in title and scope since then. Currently, it is published in three parts: part A covers the humanities and social sciences, part B the sciences and engineering, and part C, which is published under the title "European Abstracts," covers foreign dissertations. Dissertations are listed under broad subject headings and then by subareas. Updated monthly.

Bibliographies and Indexes of Videos

Library of Congress subject headings: Motion pictures—Bibliography; Motion pictures—Reviews—Indexes; Video recordings—Catalogs; Video recordings—Catalogs—Periodicals

Videos can also be useful to your research, depending on the subject. You might try one of the print resources listed below to identify useful video titles.

American Film and Video Association. *American Film and Video Association Evaluations.* Fort Atkinson, WI: Highsmith Press, 1988–.

Listings are by title, giving length of program, price, and distributor. Entries include a synopsis of content, jury comments, audience level, and uses.

Bowker's Complete Video Directory. 3 vols. New York: R. R. Bowker, 1993–.

Published in 3 volumes, this annual resource is updated by supplement at midyear.

Media Review Digest: The Only Complete Guide to Review of Non-Print Media. Ann Arbor, MI: Pierian Press, 1973/74–.

Titles are arranged according to the following sections: film and video, filmstrips, audio, and miscellaneous. There is a brief summary for each entry, as well as the usual information on format, time, price, publisher, Library of Congress subject headings, and where the title has been reviewed (with excerpts).

Video Source Book: A Guide to Programs Currently Available on Video. Detroit, MI: Gale Research, 1979–.

Entries are arranged by title, and each includes a brief description, length of video, appropriate age level, and availability. Many relevant titles can be found under the heading "Crime and Criminals." This annual title has a subject index.

Chapter 5
Periodicals, News Sources, Indexes, and Abstracts

As you do research on a topic, you will find books particularly useful because of their depth of analysis and breadth of treatment. Authors of books tend to spend a good deal of time researching their subject and giving it the kind of consideration necessary. But there is another kind of literature that you should always consider when doing a research project—*periodical* literature.

Periodicals comprise a number of different types of publications; for example, journals, serials, magazines, newsletters, and newspapers are all periodicals. Each approaches its subject in a different way and for different purposes, for instance, to report, to mold opinion, to express opinion, to elicit a response, to give a specific ideological or professional slant, to analyze, to propose, to probe, or to keep its readers current. Each has a distinct policy as to what subjects will be covered, what kind of writing will be included, how important timeliness is, and what opinions or positions are acceptable. Despite these differences, they have one thing in common: They are all issued in successive parts—each part bearing a numerical or chronological designation—and they are all intended to continue being published indefinitely. To be considered a periodical, a publication must be issued at least once a year.

THE VARIETY OF PERIODICAL LITERATURE

Peer-reviewed journals. Peer-reviewed journals provide the same kind of authoritative, in-depth treatment of a subject as a book, but usually for a much narrower topic. In order for an article to appear in such a periodical, it must be read and reviewed by editors and by individuals who are considered knowledgeable in the field. These reviewers evaluate the article for its content and information and determine whether it is worthy of publication in the journal. Peer-reviewed journals are often those published by universities and learned societies, but they are published by commercial publishers as well.

Non–peer-reviewed journals. For an article to appear in a non–peer-reviewed journal, it is usually read by an editor or editorial board and evaluated for its suitability for publication. Although not always considered as authoritative as a peer-reviewed journal, these journals can contain high-quality information and analysis—especially if the editorial standards of the journal are high. Such journals are most often commercial publications.

Newsletters. Newsletters are typically intended to keep readers aware of current events and are published more frequently than other kinds of periodicals. Some newsletters are published by associations to keep their members current on association business and activities. Although *not always* considered a citable source of information, they can be a valuable resource for tracking recent developments in a field. Some provide current information in fields such as law where currency is critical. Newsletters and newsletter-type publications, such as the *Criminal Law Reporter* and *U.S. Law Week* are substantive, authoritative, and essential for staying aware of developments in criminal law. Some of this latter type may provide analysis but are usually confined to primary source information.

The popular press. For purposes here, the *popular press* covers a broad spectrum of periodicals from general news or commentary magazines to underground periodicals. Some in this category, such as *Popular Psychology*, take a *popular* approach to what might otherwise be considered a subject of scholarly literature. Such periodicals tend to be published more frequently than peer- and non–peer-reviewed journals and are less dependable as sources of *scholarly* information. What is important about these publications is that they present the researcher with the average person's perspective or at least an alternative view of an issue. The authors neither praise nor condemn them as sources of information or analysis—they have a place. The researcher should be aware, however, that there is a difference between popular magazines and scholarly literature. This difference should be weighed when using popular press periodicals as sources for research.

Printed news. Printed news sources are among the most frequently distributed sources of information. They usually include commentary of some sort and can be an important resource for in-depth coverage of the facts of an event.

Online and broadcast news. It might be difficult to think of an online service or broadcasted information as a periodical. But if you were to think of the evening edition of the television news as the evening edition of a newspaper, the stretch is not as dramatic. This electronic media does not respond any faster to an event than the print media—its value is in its

ability to disseminate the information faster. A qualitative difference can be noted between printed and online sources of the news. While both may offer commentary, the opportunity to provide it is more restricted for online and broadcast news because of its immediacy. Both print and online news, unlike other sources discussed here, are able to respond quickly to events and report facts. But to the press, the importance of one event fades quickly as other events take on relatively greater or more immediate significance. For research purposes, the importance of the press lies in its time sensitivity. If interest in an event lingers, then it becomes a topic for the popular press. Finally, if deemed of long-term significance, it will be given scholarly treatment, the results of which may be published in academic journals.

INTRODUCTION TO INDEXES AND ABSTRACTS

In this chapter, we are discussing a group of tools known as indexes and abstracts. The advantage of using a periodicals index or abstract lies in part in your ability to identify periodical articles by author, title, and subject. An often unrecognized benefit to using a published index or abstracting tool is in the convenience of being able to find articles published in a large number of periodicals rather than by browsing through issues of individual journals.

Indexes to individual periodicals. Many periodicals publish their own indexes. These may be printed within individual issues of the periodical or separately. When trying to find information located in periodical articles, it is important to recognize that some periodicals simply are not indexed by standard tools such as those we describe below. When this is the case, you will have to resort to the index compiled by the periodical publisher and find articles published in that journal only.

Indexes. An index—in addition to being a list of subjects covered in a book with corresponding page numbers—can also be a list of references to published articles. Printed indexes are most frequently used to find articles in periodicals. Like catalogs, they provide author, title, and subject access to the literature. However, not all indexes limit themselves to providing access to articles published in periodicals. Their reach may extend to information in books, chapters of books, and government reports. This arrangement is especially true of the criminal justice indexes and others whose subject scope is very narrow. Further, while we are accustomed to thinking of an index as a way to find periodical articles *by subject*, indexes may provide access to articles in other ways. Later in this chapter we mention the *Index to Legal Periodicals,* which provides access to articles on legal topics by subject, but which also provides access to articles by the names of court cases which they analyze. Other indexes, such as *the Congressional Information Service Index* (see chapter 7), provide access to congressional documents *by bill or report number*.

When using an index, it is good practice to read the introductory matter first. Indexing practices vary from publisher to publisher, and unless you are familiar with a source, you can waste valuable time. Because not all journals are indexed, always check the front matter of an index for the list of periodicals covered. If you are aware of a periodical that covers your research topic, be sure it is included in the index you are using. If the title is not indexed, you will have to refer to its own index to access articles. If you are conducting a retrospective search for periodical literature, you may also have to look through several volumes and issues of a particular tool.

Abstracts. Another resource used to locate articles are collections of references and corresponding abstracts, often referred to as *abstracting tools*. Abstracting tools provide the same author-title-subject access to articles as indexes, but they also provide summaries of the articles. These summaries, referred to as *abstracts*, help you assess the value of an article to your research and can save you the time of retrieving and reading articles that add nothing to your project. Printed indexes and abstracts, like most of the sources they cover, are published periodically.

When using an abstract for the first time, browse through it and note its arrangement. Some abstracting tools provide subject indexes that are separate from the body of the abstracts and accompanying bibliographic information. You may have to look your subjects up in one part of the tool, and then, by using reference numbers, find the abstracts and citations to the articles in another section.

Nonprint indexes and abstracts. Like other printed resources, indexes and abstracts are available in a variety of formats, including microform, CD-ROM, and online. Electronic versions, including CD-ROM and online, furnish not only author-title-subject access to articles but often keyword searching capabilities for various fields in each record as well. Electronic versions of abstracting tools, in particular, are especially helpful since the text of the abstract or summary can also be accessed through keyword searching. Another advantage to electronic indexing tools is the

time that can be saved. In print form, each volume of an index has to be searched. Electronic versions, however, tend to be cumulative. Thus one search covers all the years included in the scope of the electronic version. In addition, more and more libraries are loading electronic versions of indexing and abstracting tools into their public catalogs. One advantage of this new service is that indexes and abstracts can often be searched using the same familiar command language as used for the catalog itself.

Remember that the electronic versions of print indexes and abstracts may not cover the same time period as their paper counterparts. In some instances, even the content is different. Therefore, you should be careful to read the scope of both paper and electronic versions before contenting yourself that your search will be comprehensive. (See chapter 4 for a discussion of electronic searching tools and for a discussion of how to locate online versions of indexes and abstracts.)

Full-text access. As the full-text versions of more and more periodicals are available online, periodicals can also be located using full-text searching. (See page 78 for a discussion of "full-text" resources and page 71 for "full-text searching.") Database services such as LEXIS-NEXIS and WESTLAW provide this kind of access to law review articles.

SELECTION OF PERIODICALS, INDEXES, AND ABSTRACTS FOR RESEARCH

As stated in chapter 4, the authors suggest that you determine the scope of your research by asking yourself the following questions: What kind of treatment will you be giving the subject? Are you looking for primary or secondary sources, or both? and What part does timeliness play on your subject? Your responses to these questions help guide you in deciding which resources to use in your research.

Periodicals approach subjects in different ways and for different purposes. Each has its own policy as to which subjects will be covered, what kind of writing will be included, how important timeliness is, and which opinions or positions are acceptable. As a critical thinker, and when incorporating information into a research paper, it is essential to consider these attributes of periodicals. For example, it would be important to reflect upon the appropriateness of including information gathered from a politically strident work in a scholarly study of a criminological topic.

Indexes and abstracts are like periodicals in that an editorial decision is made about the kinds of literature indexed. The editors select periodicals for indexing and abstracting based on certain criteria. Your decision of which indexes and abstracts to use is as critical to your research as the selection of sources for content. If an index covers only popular literature, then the information you retrieve will have a popular slant.

Likewise, indexes may not provide access to all the "articles" printed in a journal. Thus you may not find letters to the editor of a journal by using an index that covers it. Journal articles, books, chapters of books, annual surveys of the literature, book reviews, short book reviews, "books received" columns, commentary, student comments, editorials, letters to the editor, program announcements, calls for papers, proceedings of association meetings, research in progress, working papers, biographies, obituaries, and advertising are all the kinds of information that may, or may not, be indexed by a specific tool.

Given the variety of literature that may be of value, the authors suggest that you select more than one indexing or abstracting tool for your literature search. Balay's *Guide to Reference Books* (see chapter 3, page 42, for a complete reference and annotation) is an extremely valuable tool for identifying reference materials of all types, including indexes and abstracts. Exhibit 5-1 shows entries from Balay's *Guide* for several criminal justice periodical indexes. Several such sources are also listed below, indexes first, by subject, then abstracts by subject.

INDEXES

Below you will find indexes listed by subject: criminal justice, law, and social science. As criminal justice is an interdisciplinary field, your research may also require you to investigate the literature of sociology, public policy, or politics. In this case, you should locate indexes and abstracts that are broader in scope than those listed below. (Use Balay's *Guide* cited above.)

Abstracting of periodicals is a very common practice when the resource covers a limited topic such as criminal justice. Indexes are usually compiled when the scope of the resource is broader. There are, however, several sources that index criminal justice literature specifically.

Criminal Justice Indexes

Library of Congress subject headings: Criminal justice, administration of—Periodicals; Criminal justice, administration of—Indexes; Criminal justice, administration of—Indexes—Periodicals; Crime—Indexes; Crime and criminals—Periodicals

Criminal Justice Periodical Index. Ann Arbor, MI: University Microfilms International, 1975–.
Online: DIALOG, file 171
> *Criminal Justice Periodical Index (CJPI)* is an important source for articles appearing in 120 U.S., British, and Canadian journals, periodicals, book reviews, and newsletters. Book reviews are arranged alphabetically by title under the corresponding subject heading "Book Reviews." Most titles indexed are available in microform from University Microfilms International (UMI). A document delivery service is also available from UMI, which may speed access to some material. Compare exhibit 5-2, a sample page from *CJPI,* an indexing tool, with exhibit 5-7, a sample page from *Criminal Justice Abstracts,* an abstracting tool.

Law Enforcement and Criminal Justice Information Database [electronic database]. Eagan, MN: International Research and Evaluation, 1954–.
CD-ROM: International Research and Evaluation.
Online: International Research and Evaluation.
> This database of bibliographic data, with some abstracts, is available in electronic form only. Its emphasis is on identifying projects, dissertations, evaluation reports, and research in law enforcement and criminal justice. Some indexing of the literature is also provided.

CINCH: The Australian Criminology Database [electronic database]. Canberra, Australia: Australian Institute of Criminology, 1968–.
CD-ROM: part of *AUSTROM* [CD-ROM], published by the Royal Melbourne Institute of Technology
Online: OZLINE: Australian Information Network
> The *CINCH* database is available in electronic form only. Its focus is on Australian criminology, but international literature from books, research reports, periodical articles, theses, and government publications can be located through this source as well. There are approximately 25,000 citations, some with abstracts.

Law Indexes

Library of Congress subject headings: Law—Periodicals—Indexes; Periodicals—Law—Indexes; Periodicals—Law—United States—Indexes

Current Index to Legal Periodicals. Seattle, WA: Gallagher Law Library, 1909–.

Lists more than 1,000 hearings, reports and other government documents in a detailed topical arrangement. Author, subject, geographic, and association/organization indexes.   Z5703.4.C73B47

Farson, Anthony Stuart. Criminal intelligence and security intelligence : a selective bibliography / comp. by A. Stuart Farson and Catherine J. Matthews. Toronto : Centre of Criminology, Univ. of Toronto, 1990. 77 p.   **CK245**

Compiled to help "scholars who want to draw distinctions between security and criminal intelligence work and to understand the context in which security intelligence work developed."—*Introd.* Focuses primarily on English-language materials about Canadian intelligence in the 1970s and 1980s. In two sections of unannotated entries, arranged alphabetically by author. The first section contains citations to books, articles, conference papers, theses, and dissertations; the second is comprised of citations to Australian, Canadian, British, and U.S. government documents. Appendix lists sources searched. Lack of index or subject arrangement hampers access.   Z5703.4.C728F37

Jerath, Bal K. Homicide : a bibliography / Bal K. Jerath, Rajinder Jerath. 2nd ed. Boca Raton, Fla. : CRC Pr., c1993. 788 p.   **CK246**

1st. ed., 1982.

An extensive interdisciplinary bibliography in 12 chapters (e.g., statistics, causes of murder, prevention and control), further subdivided by subject. Each unannotated item is assigned a brief keyword heading, which also serves as its only entry in the unsatisfactory subject index. Author index.

§ Ernest Abel, *Homicide : a bibliography* (Westport, Conn. : Greenwood, 1987) is a shorter, unannotated listing of articles and books by author, with a brief subject index. Michael Newton, *Mass murder : an annotated bibliography* (N.Y. : Garland, 1988) provides both a descriptive list of general works and case histories of over 600 murderers, with references to books, articles, and encyclopedia entries.   Z5703.4.M87J47

Ross, John M. Trials in collections : an index to famous trials throughout the world. Metuchen, N.J. : Scarecrow, 1983. 204 p.   **CK247**

An index to more than 300 compilations of trials, limited to English-language publications. Useful for finding trials that are not the subjects of separate volumes. Sources are listed by main entry and indexed by defendant or popular name and by criminal offense or other subject. The title index indicates the place and date for each trial.   K546.R67

Indexes; Abstract journals

Criminal justice abstracts. v. 9 (Mar. 1977)– . Monsey, N.Y. [etc.] : Willow Tree Pr. [etc.], 1977– . Quarterly.   **CK248**

Earlier titles: *Information review on crime and delinquency* and *Selected highlights of crime and delinquency literature,* 1968–69; *Crime and delinquency literature,* 1970–76. Publ. 1968–83 by the National Council on Crime and Delinquency.

Abstracts of books, journal articles, dissertations and reports, arranged alphabetically by author in six broad sections (Crime, the offender, and the victim; Juvenile justice and delinquency; Police; Courts and the legal process; Adult corrections; Crime prevention and control strategies). Some issues include specialized bibliographies or literature reviews. Subject and geographical index; author index. A cumulative index covering 1968–85 was published in 1989.   HV6001.C67

Criminal justice periodical index. 1975– . [Ann Arbor, Mich.] : Indexing Services, Univ. Microfilms, 1975– . 3 issues per year, including annual bound cumulation.   **CK249**

Indexes by author and subject more than 100 U.S., British and Canadian journals in the fields of corrections, criminal law, criminology, drug abuse, family law, juvenile justice, police studies, prison ad-

ministration, rehabilitation, and security systems. Includes extensive coverage of trade bulletins and newsletters as well as academic journals.

In machine-readable form as: *Criminal justice periodical index (CJPI)* [database] (Ann Arbor, Mich. : Univ. Microfilms Internat., 1975–). Available online, updated monthly.   Z5118.C9C74

Criminology, penology, and police science abstracts. Vol. 32, no. 1 (Jan./Feb. 1992)– . Amsterdam ; N.Y. : Kugler Publications, 1992– . Bimonthly.   **CK250**

Subtitle: An international abstracting service covering the etiology of crime and juvenile delinquency, the control and treatment of offenders, criminal procedure, the administration of justice, and police science.

Formed by the union of *Criminology & penology abstracts* (1980–91; former titles: *Excerpta criminologica,* 1961–68; *Abstracts on criminology and penology,* 1969–79) and *Police science abstracts* (1980–91); continues the volume numbering of the former.

English-language abstracts of books and articles in more than 200 journals, arranged by nine broad subject sections. Classified arrangement of 13 broad subjects with extensive subdivisions. Subject and author indexes.   HV6001.C74

Encyclopedias

Encyclopedia of crime and justice / Sanford H. Kadish, ed. in chief. N.Y. : Free Pr., c1983. 4 v. (1790 p.).   **CK251**

An impressive interdisciplinary survey of the nature and causes of criminal behavior, crime prevention, and the many components of the criminal justice system. American in emphasis, with international comparisons. 286 alphabetically arranged articles vary in length from 1 to 20 pages; each includes a short bibliography. A helpful "Guide to legal citations" in v. 1 not only defines abbreviations but explains both the formats of case and statutory citations and the legal significance of cited works. Glossary; legal index (tables of cases and other legal documents); general index.   HV6017.E52

The encyclopedia of police science / ed., William G. Bailey. N.Y. : Garland, 1989. [734 p.] (Garland reference library of social science, v. 413.).   **CK252**

Contains 143 signed articles on methods and issues in criminology, major historical figures, and selected institutions. Articles, ranging in length from two to 12 pages, are arranged alphabetically and include bibliographies. Appendixes provide a bibliography of police history and a bibliography of bibliographies. General index and index of legal cases.   HV7901.E53

Encyclopedia of security management : techniques & technology / ed. by John J. Fay. Boston : Butterworth-Heinemann, c1993. 792 p. : ill.   **CK253**

Covers all aspects of the security business, including issues such as access control, executive protection, fire safety, lighting, and surveillance. Signed articles by more than 70 contributors, generally two to three pages in length, are arranged alphabetically and include bibliographic references. Index.   HV8290.S365

Encyclopedia of world crime : criminal justice, criminology, and law enforcement dictionary / [ed. in chief] Jay Robert Nash. Wilmette, Ill. : CrimeBooks, 1989–90. 6 v.   **CK254**

Contents: v. 1–4, A–Z and suppl.; v. 5, Dictionary; v. 6, Index.

Contains more than 50,000 articles on all aspects of crime and law enforcement, many with illustrations and bibliographic references. Vol. 4 contains more than two dozen supplements, including chronologies of major crimes such as assassinations and bombings; descriptions of methods of capital punishment; photographs of organized crime figures; and lists of western lawmen and outlaws. The dictionary volume covers 20,000 terms, indicating sources for definitions, and contains supplements listing acronyms, landmark court cases, and major crime legislation. Vol. 6 includes a 328-page bibliography and indexes by subject and name.

BALAY, ROBERT, ED. *GUIDE TO REFERENCE BOOKS*, 11TH ED. CHICAGO: AMERICAN LIBRARY ASSOCIATION, 1996.

EXHIBIT 5-1

Presumption Of Legitimacy Didn't Justify Denying Husband's Motion For Blood Testing. *The Family Law Reporter: Court Opinions.* 22:10. (1/16/95). p1113-1114.

Roseby, Vivienne, author. Uses Of Psychological Testing In A Child-Focused Approach To Child Custody Evaluations. *Family Law Quarterly.* 29:1. (Spring/95). p97-110. +.

Selick, Karen, author. Children: The New Excuse For Everything. *Canadian Lawyer.* 20:1. (1/96). p46. Illus. +*.

Visitation—Sibling Rights—Mother's Standing To Raise Issue—Parental Rights Termination. *The Family Law Reporter: Court Opinions.* 22:13. (2/6/96). p1156.

CHILDREN
see also Day Care Centers
Inhalant Abuse Starts As Early As Six, Pediatricians Warn. *Substance Abuse Report.* 27:7. (4/1/96). p7.

Muscle Rigidity Of Cocaine-Exposed Infants Found To Resolve By Age 2. *Substance Abuse Report.* 27:3. (2/1/96). p3. Charts.

NHTSA Reports Air Bag Danger To Children. *The Police Chief.* 62:12. (12/95). p85. +*.

CHILDREN—EDUCATION
New Character Education Program Promotes Positive Behaviors And Attitudes In Children. *Juvenile Justice Digest.* 24:2. (1/18/96). p5. +*.

CHILDREN—LEGAL STATUS, LAWS, ETC.
ABA Approves Standards On Representing Abused Children. *The Family Law Reporter: Court Opinions.* 22:18. (3/12/96). p1216.

Adang, Stephen R., author. The Use Of The Polygraph With Children. *Polygraph.* 24:4. (12/95). p259-274. Charts. +*.

Attorney Should Have Been Appointed For Children In Protection Proceeding. *The Family Law Reporter: Court Opinions.* 22:9. (1/9/95). p1104-1105.

Child Abuse & Neglect—Federal Abuse Prevention Statute—Abused Child's Rights—42 USC 1983. *The Family Law Reporter: Court Opinions.* 22:8. (1/2/96). p1093-1094.

Child Support—URESA Proceeding—Uniform Paternity Act—Joinder Of Child. *The Family Law Reporter: Court Opinions.* 22:21. (4/9/96). p1254.

Custody—Tender Years Doctrine—Emotional Ties Between Parent And Child. *The Family Law Reporter: Court Opinions.* 22:6. (12/12/95). p1072.

Gardner, Chadwick N., author. Don't Come Cryin' To Daddy *Emancipation Of Minors: When Is A Parent 'Free At Last' From The Obligation Of Child Support? University Of Louisville Journal Of Family Law.* 33:4. (Fall/95). p927-948. +.

Hall, Jonathan, author. Can Children Consent To Indecent Assault? *The Criminal Law Review.* 1996:3. (3/96). p184-188. +*.

Paternity—Child's Suit Against Mother's Ex-Husband—Prior Termination Order. *The Family Law Reporter: Court Opinions.* 22:15. (2/20/96). p1179.

Paternity—Res Judicata—Alleged Father's Settlement With Mother—Child's Subsequent Suit. *The Family Law Reporter: Court Opinions.* 22:9. (1/9/95). p1106-1107.

Raeder, Myrna S., author. President's Message. *Women Lawyers Journal.* 82:1. (12/95). p4. Illus. +*.

CHOCTAW (OK). POLICE DEPARTMENT
Whetsel, John T., author. Home In The Heartland—Choctaw, Oklahoma. *The Police Chief.* 62:9. (9/95). p7. Illus. +*.

CHROMATOGRAPHY
see also Forensic Chemistry; Forensic Science
Bramble, Simon Kenneth, author. Separation Of Latent Fingermark Residue By Thin-Layer Chromatography. *Journal Of Forensic Sciences.* 40:6. (11/95). p969-975. Illus. +*.

Dasgupta, Amitava and Cynthia Gardner, authors. Distinguishing Amphetamine And Methamphetamine From Other Interfering Sympathomimetic Amines After Various Fluoro Derivatization And Analysis By Gas Chromatography-Chemical Ionization Mass Spectrometry. *Journal Of Forensic Sciences.* 40:6. (11/95). p1077-1081. +*.

Liu, Ray H., Garon Foster, Edward J. Cone and Shiv D. Kumar, authors. Selecting An Appropriate Isotopic Internal Standard For Gas Chromatography/Mass Spectrometry Analysis Of Drugs Of Abuse—Pentobarbital Example. *Journal Of Forensic Sciences.* 40:6. (11/95). p983-989. Charts and Graphs; Illus. +*.

Morello, David R. and Richard P. Meyers, authors. Qualitative And Quantitative Determination Of Residual Solvents In Illicit Cocaine HCl And Heroin HCl. *Journal Of Forensic Sciences.* 40:6. (11/95). p957-963. Charts and Graphs. +*.

CHURCH-STATE RELATIONS
see also Freedom Of Religion
Khan, Anwar N., author. Daily Collective Worship And Religious Education In British Schools. *Journal Of Law & Education.* 24:4. (Fall/95). p601-612. +.

Recent Developments In The Law: Universities And Other Institutions Of Higher Education: Constitutional Claims—Civil Rights. *Journal Of Law & Education.* 24:4. (Fall/95). p653-659. +.

Wasby, Stephen, author. Religion In The Court. *The Justice System Journal.* 18:2. (3/95). p201-202. +*.

CIGARETTE SMOKING
see Smoking
CINCINNATI (OH). POLICE DEPARTMENT
Cincy PD Faces Tidal Wave Of Retirements. *Law Enforcement News.* 22:442. (3/31/96). p5. +*.

CIRCUIT COURTS
see Courts
CITIZEN COMPLAINTS AGAINST POLICE
see Complaints Against Police
CITIZEN INVOLVEMENT IN CRIME PREVENTION
see also Civilians In Police Work; Crime Prevention
DiMascio, William, author. Report From The State Centered Program. *Overcrowded Times.* 7:1. (2/96). p19.

International News: New Zealand: Citizens Report Bad Driving. *Law And Order.* 44:4. (4/96). p6. +*.

Involving Citizens In Fighting Crime Challenges Police: NIJ Evaluation Of Community Policing Implementation Describes Problems. *Drug Policy Report.* 3:3. (3/96). p12.

Residents Say Enough. *Community Policing Digest.* 2:1. (1/11/96). p10. +*.

Small Town Residents Fight Crime In A Big Way. *Community Policing Digest.* 2:3. (2/8/96). p2-3. +*.

The Use Of Students For Protection Services At The University Of Ottawa. *Campus Law Enforcement Journal.* 26:2. (3-4/96). p15-16. +*.

Woman Fights Violence With Love To Save Her Neighborhood. *Community Policing Digest.* 2:6. (3/28/96). p9-10. +*.

Young People Talk, Clash At Crime Prevention Conference. *Juvenile Justice Digest.* 24:7. (4/4/96). p6-7. +*.

1996 National Night Out Kickoff Set For Aug. 6. *Narcotics Enforcement & Prevention Digest.* 2:6. (2/8/96). p9. +*.

CITIZENS AGAINST DRUG IMPAIRED DRIVING
A CANDID Look At Drug-Impaired Driving. *Traffic Safety.* 95:5. (9-10/95). p15. +*.

CITY TRAFFIC
see Mass Transit; Traffic Engineering
CIVIL DISOBEDIENCE
Allgeyer, Gary A., author. Social Protests In The 1990s: Planning A Response. *FBI Law Enforcement Bulletin.* 65:1. (1/96). p1-7. Illus. +*.

CIVIL PROCEDURE
see also Admissions (Law); Appellate Procedure; Attachment And Garnishment; Defense (Civil Procedure); Divorce And Divorce Settlements; Federal Rules Of Civil Procedure; Jury; Probate Law And Practice; Trial Practice
Failure To Prosecute Dismissal Reversed. *Prison Legal News.* 7:1. (1/96). p27.

Forfeiture—Drug Proceeds—Statutory Exemption For Personal Property. *The Criminal Law Reporter: Court Decisions.* 58:18. (2/7/96). p1413.

Jury Demand Must Be Timely. *Prison Legal News.* 6:12. (12/95). p20.

N.J. Governor Kills Frivolous Lawsuit Bill. *Corrections Digest.* 27:3. (1/19/96). p1,5&. +*.

Recent Developments In The Law: Universities And Other Institutions Of Higher Education: Governing Boards And Administration. *Journal Of Law & Education.* 24:4. (Fall/95). p641. +.

Reuben, Richard C., author. Re-Tailoring Jury Trial Rights: Dry-Cleaning Patent Case Raises Larger Seventh Amendment Issues. *ABA Journal.* 82:2. (2/96). p42. Illus. +*.

Yarnold, Barbara M., author. Do Courts Respond To The Political Clout Of Groups Or To Their Superior Litigation Resources/"Repeat Player" Status? *The Justice System Journal.* 18:1. (1/95). p29-42. Charts. +*.

7th Circuit Clarifies "Frivolous" And Safety Standard. *Prison Legal News.* 7:1. (1/96). p11-12.

CIVIL RIGHTS
see also Due Process Of Law; Equal Protection Of The Laws; Freedom Of Information; Freedom Of Religion; Freedom Of Speech; Freedom Of The Press; Habeas Corpus; Hispanic Americans—Civil Rights; Juveniles—Civil Rights; Mentally Handicapped—Civil Rights; Right To Counsel; Searches And Seizures; Speedy Trial; Student Rights; Women—Civil Rights
Anderson, Teresa, author. Congressional Update: Domestic Terrorism. *Security Management.* 40:1. (1/96). p77. +*.

Civil Rights Actions—Abstention—Suit For Damages Based On Allegedly Unconstitutional Arrest And Search. *The Criminal Law Reporter: Court Decisions.* 58:14. (1/10/95). p1315.

Federal Court Refuses To Apply State Limit On Decedent's Damages To Section 1983 Suit. *The Criminal Law Reporter: Court Decisions.* 58:20. (2/21/96). p1462-1463.

Felon's Civil Rights Can Be 'Restored' By Laws Of General Applicability. *The Criminal Law Reporter: Court Decisions.* 58:23. (3/13/96). p1518-1519.

The King Of The Gun Permit: Small-Town California Chief Hailed By Gun Owners. *Law Enforcement News.* 22:439. (2/14/96). p4. +*.

O'Neill, Mark, author. Naughty Little Sisters. *Canadian Lawyer.* 20:2. (2/96). p16-17&. Illus. +*.

Opinion Of The U.S. Supreme Court: Civil Rights Actions. *The Criminal Law Reporter: Extra Edition No. 1: Text No. 8.* 58:20. (2/21/96). p2045-2053.

Podgers, James, author. ABA Work At Tribunals Has Personal Touch. *ABA Journal.* 82:4. (4/96). p61. Illus. +*.

— Tribunal Staff Displays Ultimate In Diversity. *ABA Journal.* 82:4. (4/96). p57. Illus. +*.

Pressure Needed On House GOP Leadership To Move Stalled Anti-Terrorism Bill. *Security Director's Digest.* 2:3. (1/17/96). p1-2. +*.

State Statutory Limit On Decedents' Damages Applies To Federal Civil Rights Actions. *The Criminal Law Reporter: Court Decisions.* 58:19. (2/14/96). p1435-1437.

CIVIL RIGHTS—ARGENTINA
Osiel, Mark J., author. Dialogue With Dictators: Judicial Resistance In Argentina And Brazil. *Law & Social Inquiry.* 20:2. (Spring/95). p481-560. +*.

CIVIL RIGHTS—BOSNIA
Hengstler, Gary A., author. Out Of The Rubble: With Training From U.S. Lawyers, Justices On A New Constitutional Court Will Try To Establish The Rule Of Law In War-Torn Bosnia. *ABA Journal.* 82:3. (3/96). p52-58. Illus. +*.

Podgers, James, author. The World Cries For Justice. *ABA Journal.* 82:4. (4/96). p52-58&. Illus.; Charts. +*.

Prelude To Justice. *ABA Journal.* 82:3. (3/96). p52-58. +*.

Stein, Robert A., author. Lending Freedom A Hand: CEELI Brings American Legal Know-How To Bosnia-Herzegovina. *ABA Journal.* 82:4. (4/96). p101. Illus. +*.

Will 'Law Of Guns' End?: Justice Minister Says New Court Can Ease Tensions. *ABA Journal.* 82:3. (3/96). p59. Illus. +*.

CIVIL RIGHTS—BRAZIL
Osiel, Mark J., author. Dialogue With Dictators: Judicial Resistance In Argentina And Brazil. *Law & Social Inquiry.* 20:2. (Spring/95). p481-560. +*.

CIVIL RIGHTS—CANADA
Court Says Denying Prisoners Vote Is Unconstitutional. *Corrections Digest.* 27:2. (1/12/96). p1. +*.

Hacker, Bert, author. Legal Aid, 24 Hours A Day. *Canadian Lawyer.* 20:1. (1/96). p8. +*.

CIVIL RIGHTS—ETHIOPIA
Jalata, Asafa, author. The Emergence Of Oromo Nationalism And Ethiopian Reaction. *Social Justice.* 22:3. (Fall/95). p165-189. +*.

CIVIL RIGHTS—GERMANY
Weber, Joern, author. Fighting Hate Crime In Germany: Police Are Making Sure There Is No Chance For A Nazi Resurgence. *Law And Order.* 44:4. (4/96). p24-27. Illus. +*.

CIVIL RIGHTS—GREAT BRITAIN
Ashworth, Andrew, author. Crime, Community And Creeping Consequentialism. *The Criminal Law Review.* 1996:4. (4/96). p220-230. +*.

Dockley, Anita, author. Disquiet Over A Quiet Life. *Criminal Justice: Magazine Of The Howard League.* 13:4. (11/95). p9. +*.

This index is very useful as a current awareness service. It is published each week and provides a subject analysis of journal articles published during the previous week.

Current Law Index. Los Altos, CA: Information Access, 1980–.

Current Law Index (CLI) provides access to 700 law journals from the United States, Canada, Great Britain, Ireland, Australia, and New Zealand. Titles covered include academic reviews, bar association journals, specialty journals, and selected journals treating allied disciplines such as criminology. In addition to a subject index, *CLI* provides an index to articles that concern cases and statutes. See *Legal Resource Index* for electronic version.

Index to Canadian Legal Literature. Toronto: Carswell, 1981–.

Online: Info Globe Online; QL Systems Limited; Canadian Law Online.

If your research requires access to Canadian legal literature, this will be an important tool. It provides access to *Canadian Law Reviews* as well as to some books by author, title, subject, case name, and statutes. It also includes a book review index.

Index to Foreign Legal Periodicals. London: Institute for Advanced Legal Studies, 1960–.

CD-ROM: Silver Platter (coverage begins in 1985).

Online: CitaDel Service (coverage begins in 1985).

Indexes articles and essays on the topics of international and comparative law as well as domestic law of countries other than the U.S. and common law countries.

Index to Legal Periodicals. New York : H. W. Wilson, 1908–.

CD-ROM: as part of *WILSONDISC* (coverage begins in 1981).

Online: WILSONLINE, as *Index to Legal Periodicals and Books* (coverage begins in 1981); OVID: *WILP;* OCLC Epic; and OCLC FirstSearch Catalog.

The *Index to Legal Periodicals* is the longest-running index to legal periodical literature published in the United States. The bulk of the materials indexed are scholarly treatments of legal topics published in the United States, Canada, Great Britain, Ireland, Australia, and New Zealand. It is primarily a subject index: the location of journal articles by author is a two-step process for all volumes up to 1981. The online version includes indexing of approximately 2,000 books annually.

Legal Resource Index [microform]. Los Altos, CA: Information Access, 1980–.

CD-ROM: *LegalTrac* (coverage begins in 1980).

Online: LEXIS-NEXIS as Library: *LAWREV;* File: *LGLIND;* WESTLAW as *LRI.*

Legal Resource Index is the title for the microform, CD-ROM, and certain online versions of the *Current Law Index* (see above).

Social Science Indexes

Library of Congress subject headings: Social sciences—Indexes; Social sciences—Indexes—Periodicals; Social sciences—Periodicals—Indexes—Periodicals; Social sciences—Bibliography—Periodicals; Social sciences—Bibliography; Periodicals—Indexes

Social Sciences Citation Index. Philadelphia: Institute for Scientific Information, 1973–.

CD-ROM: Institute for Scientific Information.

Online: DataStar as *SSCI;* DIALOG, file 7.

Social Sciences Citation Index (*SSCI*) is an immensely valuable resource for research in any of the social sciences. It is especially valuable in determining how ideas, as published in the scholarly literature, have been treated by subsequent authors. It can also be used to build bibliographies based on those compiled by authors of articles published in research journals. Using *SSCI* can seem a bit daunting the first few times, but the amount of information you can gain access to is well worth the effort. It is invaluable for sophisticated social research, including criminal justice and criminology. We recommend its use in all levels of research where the authority of the information used is critical.

SSCI is composed of four indexes—each with a different function—that relate in some way to each of the others. The four indexes are the "Citation Index," "Corporate Index," "Source Index" and "Permuterm Subject Index." If you are considering using information from a journal article covered in *SSCI*, first check the "Citation Index" for the author ("cited author") of the article you will be using. Under the author's name you will find a list of citations of other articles written by him or her ("cited reference"). Locate the citation corresponding to the article you wish to use in your research. Following the citation will be a list of authors ("source [citing] author") and articles that have cited your source. Since these articles have cited your source, they could be worth reading for additional information on your subject. They might also have criticized or explained the article you wish to use ("codes indicating type of source item") and thus provide you with additional insights into your source. Exhibit 5-3 is the key that explains the components of the "Citation Index."

If you turn to the "Source Index" (see exhibit 5-4) and look for the author of an article that cited your source ("first source author"), you will find a bibliography ("listed references from the bibliography . . .") of sources used in the citing article. In this list, you should find your source article as well as complete bibliographic information on the citing article. This bibliography may be helpful in finding more information on your topic. Likewise, if you look up the author of your source, you will find a bibliography of articles used in the source document. In this way you can build a bibliography through one good article on your topic. You can obtain information on how other scholars have viewed your source.

SSCI also provides a keyword index to articles. The "Permuterm Subject Index" (see exhibit 5-5) comprises citations to articles that have used significant words in combination with other significant words in their titles. The "Permuterm Index" is an extremely complex but very satisfying means of finding information.

Citation Index

To use the *Citation Index*, look up the name of the first author of a work which you know to be relevant to your topic. Any of the author's works cited during the period covered by this issue of the *SSCI®* will appear in this index. You can use the names of the citing authors to enter the *Source Index* for descriptions of citing works. When the same reference has been cited by more than one source item, the source citations are arranged alphabetically by first author. Though only first authors are given in the *Citation Index*, all authors will be listed in the *Source Index*.

Sample Display

cited author ───────────	**RENOUX G** ───────────			
	73 B WORLD HEALTH ORGAN	⌐48 661⌐		
	THELIN A SC J S MED	1980 1 94		reference volume and page
cited reference year and ─────	**74 MED MAL INF** 4 159			
journal	CHANTAL J REV MED VET	132 35 94		source journal
	76 PUBLIC POLICY MARKET 53			
	WESTBROO. RA J RETAILING	⌐57 68 94⌐		volume, page, and year of source (citing) item
	RENZULLI J ───────────			
undated item ──────────	** UNPUBLISHED			
	BALDWIN AY EXCEPT CHIL	47 326 94		Codes indicating type of source item:
	77 ENRICHMENT TRIAD MOD			
source (citing) author ────────	CASSIDY J READ TEACH	35 17 94		Blank articles, reports, technical papers, etc.
	FOSTER W GIFT CHILD	25 17 94		B book reviews
E.G. RERRICK's 1972 article	ROGERS VR "	25 175 94		C corrections, errata, etc.
in the Journal of Mental Deficiency was cited by D.	**RERRICK EG** ───────────			D discussions, conference items
PITCHER in an article published in CRC Critical Reviews in Clinical Laboratory	72 J MENTAL DEFICIENCY 16 84			E editorials, editorial-like items
Sciences in 1994.	PITCHER D CRC C R LAB	13 241 94		I items about individuals (tributes, obituaries, etc.)
	REVELMACDONALD N ────────			
	75 HOMME ANIMAL 317			K chronology—a list of events in sequence.
G.A. OBUKHOV cites	78 ASEMI 9 243			L letters, communications, etc.
three publications by N. REVELMACDONALD.	78 PALAWAN PHONOLOGIE C			M meeting abstracts
	SEE SCI FOR 1 ADDITIONAL CITATION			N technical notes
	OBUKHOV GA SOC SCI INF	19 971 94 D		R reviews
additional citing item				RP reprint
indicator				W computer reviews (hardware reviews, software reviews, database reviews)
	REVILLE ───────────			
	1802 REV HIST 50 1			
reference year earlier	GOHN JB GEORGET LAW	70 943 94		
than 1900				

A complete description of each source item code appears in the Conventions Used In The Citation Index section of the instructional material.

SOCIAL SCIENCES CITATION INDEX. PHILADELPHIA: INSTITUTE FOR SCIENTIFIC INFORMATION, 1974–.

EXHIBIT 5-3

For a thorough explanation of how to use *SSCI*, refer to: Garfield, Eugene. "The Citation Index as a Search Tool." In *Social Sciences Citation Index, Guide and Lists of Source Publications*. Philadelphia: Institute for Scientific Information, 1979–.

PAIS International. New York: Public Affairs Information Service, 1991–.

CD-ROM: New York, PAIS, 1972–.

Online: DataStar, file PAIS; DIALOG, file 49; CompuServe Knowledge Index, file SOCS2; OCLC FirstSearch Catalog; OCLC EPIC; Research Libraries Information Network, file PAIS. The *Public Affairs Information Service (PAIS)* International is a selective index of the latest books, periodical articles, government documents, pamphlets, microfiche, and reports of public and private agencies relating to business, economic and social conditions, public policy and administration, and international relations and published in English, French, German, Italian, Portuguese, and Spanish throughout the world. *PAIS* aims to identify the most beneficial public affairs and public policy information to legislators, administrators, the business and financial community, policy researchers, and students. It includes bibliographic entries and, in most instances, a short abstract. See exhibit 5-6 for a sample page. Each bibliographic entry can appear under one to six subject or geographic headings. The material as it relates to criminal justice is not comprehensive, but for policy-oriented research, it is extremely valuable.

Social Sciences Index. New York: H. W. Wilson, 1974/75–.

CD-ROM: as *Social Sciences Index-CD* (coverage begins in 1983).

Source Index

To locate a full description of a source item, look up the first author. Under a given name, publications of primary authorship are described first. Items of secondary authorship follow, cross-referenced to the first author by a SEE reference.

Sample Display

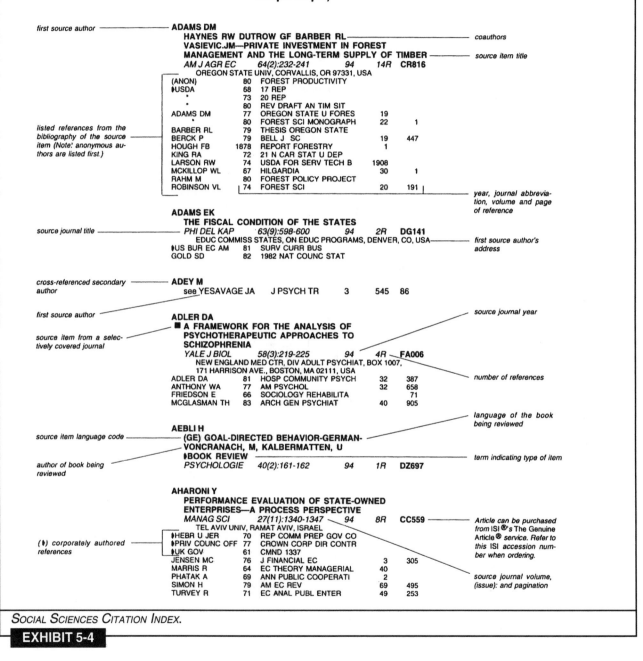

SOCIAL SCIENCES CITATION INDEX.

EXHIBIT 5-4

Permuterm® Subject Index

To find articles on a specific topic:

1. Locate any one of the words (Primary Terms) that describes the topic. If you want every unique title that includes that primary term, select only the articles marked with an arrow (◊). This eliminates repetitive examination of the same title.

2. To narrow selection, use any of the other words (Co-Terms) listed below that Primary Term. When using co-terms always disregard arrows.

3. Using authors' names consult the *Source Index* for the full titles and bibliographic data.

Sample Display

PRIMARY TERM
This word appeared in the title of one or more articles

AGEING
see AGING ——— **Cross Reference** ("SEE" other Primary Term)

Cross Reference ("sa" means "see also")

AGING
sa AGE
sa AGED
sa AGES
sa CURING
sa GERIATRIC

This mark (◊) indicates the first appearance of the source item, as represented by its author.

ACCELERATED............ ◊ WILKINSO.A
ADULTHOOD .... ◊ GEORGE LK +

Co-Term identical to Co-Term "ADULTHOOD" above

The "+" sign indicates that the source item is a critical review. A more detailed description of the review indicating whether it is a book review, database review, hardware review, or software review will appear with the source item in the Source Index.

.... ◊ STREIB F
AVERAGED.................... ◊ SMITH DBD ∅
BIOLOGY....................... ◊ LINDNER J
.... ◊ MCBROOM MJ +
FICTION......................... ◊ GERONTOL. ■

Truncated Co-Term (full word "HUMAN-POPULATION")

HUMAN-POPU. .... STREIB F
.... WILKINSO. A

To find articles concerning "AGING" and "SOCIETY" check all entries under co-term "SOCIETY".

SOCIETY .... ◊ ATCHELEY RC
.... SMITH DBD ∅
.... WILKINSO. A
.... ◊ WREN AR

The "∅" sign indicates that each of these authors has written more than one article with the relevant primary and co-terms in their titles.

SWITZERLAND............. ◊ POPULATION + ■
WOMENS..................... ◊ GAULT U
YEARS.......................... ◊ ROSSI AS
ZURICH........................ POPULATION + ■

Square block indicates that journal title is used in place of author's name when the article is anonymous

STOP-WORD
This word is on the "semi-stop" list and will appear as a co-term only.

AHEAD
see stop lists

AIDE
CASE .... ◊ FREEMAN VH
COURSE........................
MARKETINGS............... ◊ JACKSON DW
NEWEST........................

CO-TERMS
These words also appear with the word "AIDE" in article titles.

PARTNER..................... ◊ KEEFE SD
TRAINING..................... FREEMAN VH
VOLUNTEER.................

Author identical to item above

AIR-POLLUTION
sa AIR-QUALITY
sa ATMOSPHERIC-POLLUT
APPLICATION............... ◊ THAYER JM
CONTROL .... ◊ KLICIUS R
.... THAYER JM
DRAGS .... ◊ MARWICK C
FORMS.........................
HAZARDOUS .... ◊ THAYER JM

SOCIAL SCIENCES CITATION INDEX.

EXHIBIT 5-5

Nat. Bur. of Econ. Research. *Why is there more crime in cities?* Glaeser, Edward L. and Bruce Sacerdote. Ja 1996 42+[23]p bibl(s) table(s) chart(s) (NBER working pa. 5430) pa U.S. $5; elsewhere $5 plus $10 per order postage and handling; payment with order Nat Bur Econ Research

Effect of higher pecuniary benefits, lower arrest probabilities, lower probability of recognition, and characteristics that reflect tastes, social influences, and family structure; based on victimization data; US.

Wisconsin

United States. Senate. Com. on the Judiciary. Subcom. on Juvenile Justice. *Juvenile crime in Wisconsin: hearings, May 31-August 31, 1994, on determining strategies to combat juvenile violence and crime in the state of Wisconsin.* 1995 iv+86p (103d Cong., 2d sess.) (Serial no. J-103-71) (S. hearing 103-1071) (SD cat. no. Y 4.J 89/2:S.hrg.103-1071) (ISBN 0-16-052161-0) pa Supt Docs

Focuses on increase in drugs, guns, and violence; examines proposal to fund a pilot program that would use the community service model to work with nonviolent juvenile offenders and expand role of law enforcement.

CRIME PREVENTION
See also
　Security guards
　Vigilance committees

Economic aspects

Nat. Bur. of Econ. Research. *Why do so many young American men commit crimes and what might we do about it?* Freeman, Richard B. F 1996 33p bibl(s) table(s) chart(s) (NBER working pa. 5451) U.S. $5; elsewhere $5 plus $10 per order postage and handling; payment with order Nat Bur Econ Research

Effect of depressed labor market for unskilled workers on continued high level of crime by male high school dropouts; 1980s and 1990s.

United States

United States. Senate. Com. on Governmental Affairs. *Interstate identification index: is it an effective weapon in the war against violent crime? is it interstate, does it identify, and is it an index? hearing, December 6, 1994.* 1995 iii+87p chart(s) (103d Cong., 2d sess.) (S. hearing 103-1052) (SD cat. no. Y 4.G 74/9:S.hrg.103-1052) (ISBN 0-16-047548-1) pa Supt Docs

Evaluates effectiveness of computerized system of criminal records established by the National Crime Information Center.

CRIMES AGAINST HUMANITY
See also
　Atrocities
　Genocide

Social suffering. il(s) table(s) *Daedalus* 125:1-283 Winter 1996

Interdisciplinary and multicultural examination of the human experience of pain and suffering which results from the misuse of power, oppression, political violence, and atrocity; 12 articles.

United States. House. Com. on Internat. Relations. Subcom. on Internat. Operations and Human Rights. *The United Nations: management, finance, and reform: hearing, October 26, 1995.* 1996 iii+140p il(s) table(s) chart(s) (104th Cong., 1st sess.) (SD cat. no. Y 4.In 8/16:M 31/2) (ISBN 0-16-052189-0) pa Supt Docs

Examines the UN's administrative and financial problems, the referendum in the Western Sahara, and the War Crimes Tribunals for the former Yugoslavia and for Rwanda.

CRIMINAL INVESTIGATION
See also
　Electronics in criminal investigation, espionage, etc.
　Police questioning
　Undercover operations

United States

Burnham, David. *Above the law: secret deals, political fixes and other misadventures of the U.S. Department of Justice.* 1996 444p bibl(s) table(s) chart(s) index(es) (Lisa Drew bk.) (LC 95-34544) (ISBN 0-684-80699-1) U.S. $27.50; Can. $37 Simon

Argues that the Justice Department is unpoliced and often abuses its power; surveillance of citizens, ineffectiveness of war on drugs, Waco incident, and other issues. Published by Scribner.

Texas

Ethridge, Philip A. and Raul Gonzalez. *Combatting vehicle theft along the Texas border.* il(s) *FBI (Federal Bur Investigation) Law Enforcement Bul* 65:10-13 Ja 1996

Describes criminal investigation work by a multijurisdictional task force encompassing four counties and innovative funding and prosecution agreements, which have reduced the automobile theft rate in south Texas.

CRIMINAL JURISDICTION
United States

Meese, Edwin, III and Rhett DeHart. *How Washington subverts your local sheriff.* il(s) *Policy R* p 48-53 Ja/F 1996

Examines federal jurisdiction in formerly local law enforcement responsibilities, including police work, judicial proceedings, prison operation, and criminalization of environmental and regulatory laws; US.

CRIMINAL JUSTICE
See also
　Juvenile justice
　Sentences (law)

Pease, Ken and Andromachi Tseloni. *Juvenile-adult differences in criminal justice: evidence from the United Nations crime survey.* table(s) *Howard J Criminal Justice* 35:40-60 F 1996

Examines country differences in treatment of juveniles, and distinctions between male and female juveniles; based on 1975, 1980, and 1986 data.

Information services

United States. Senate. Com. on Governmental Affairs. *Interstate identification index: is it an effective weapon in the war against violent crime? is it interstate, does it identify, and is it an index? hearing, December 6, 1994.* 1995 iii+87p chart(s) (103d Cong., 2d sess.) (S. hearing 103-1052) (SD cat. no. Y 4.G 74/9:S.hrg.103-1052) (ISBN 0-16-047548-1) pa Supt Docs

Evaluates effectiveness of computerized system of criminal records established by the National Crime Information Center.

Italy

Bolzoni, Attilio and Giuseppe D'Avanzo. *La giustizia è cosa nostra: il caso Carnevale tra delitti e impunità.* 1995 204p bibl(s) index(es) (Colln. Frecce) (ISBN 88-04-38547-2) 28,000 lire Mondadori

Popular account of the criminal justice system, organized crime, and political corruption in the 1980s and 1990s; focus on role of judges and magistrates, including Corrado Carnevale.

United States

Bernat, Frances P., ed. *Women's culture and the criminal justice system.* bibl(s) table(s) *Women and Criminal Justice* 7:1-102 no 1 1995

Focus on problems faced by Black, Indian, and Mexican women; 5 articles.

Falk, Patricia J. *Novel theories of criminal defense based upon the toxicity of the social environment: urban psychosis, television intoxication, and Black rage.* *N C Law R* 74:731-811 Mr 1996

Whether or not "social toxins" such as violence, racism, and television can induce a person to commit violent crimes; US.

O'Connor, R. Daniel. *Defining the strike zone: an analysis of the classification of prior convictions under the federal "three-strikes and you're out" scheme.* *Boston Col Law R* 36:847-88 Jl 1995

Examines how state courts are likely to count previous convictions under the federal mandatory sentencing law for three felony convictions; drug offenses, age of the offender, and other issues; US.

California

Culver, John H. and Kimberly Thiesen. *The impact of "3 strikes" in California.* *Comparative State Pol* 16:14-18 D 1995

Examines effect of mandatory sentencing for persons convicted of three felonies on costs and prison crowding.

Georgia

Stalans, Loretta J. *Family harmony or individual protection? public recommendations about how police can handle domestic violence situations.* bibl(s) table(s) *Am Behavioral Scientist* 39:433-48 F 1996

Examines public attitudes toward responses to domestic violence by police and courts; based on a survey of 157 adults, Fulton county, Georgia.

Statistics

United States. Bur. of Justice Statis. *Capital punishment, 1994.* Stephan, James J. and Tracy L. Snell. F 1996 15p table(s) chart(s) (NCJ-158023) Single copies free Bureau of Justice Statistics Clearinghouse, Department BJS-236, P.O. Box 179, Annapolis Junction, MD 20701-0179

Executions, prisoners held under sentence of death, statutory changes, and other data; includes comparative statistics for various years;

United States. Bur. of Justice Statis. *Indigent defense.* Smith, Steven K. and Carol J. DeFrances. F 1996 4p table(s) (BJS selected findings. NCJ-158909) Single copies free Bureau of Justice Statistics Clearinghouse, Department BJS-236, P.O. Box 179, Annapolis Junction, MD 20701-0179

Court-appointed legal representation for indigent criminal defendants; federal, state, and local statistics; US.

Texas

Ethridge, Philip A. and Raul Gonzalez. *Combatting vehicle theft along the Texas border.* il(s) *FBI (Federal Bur Investigation) Law Enforcement Bul* 65:10-13 Ja 1996

Describes criminal investigation work by a multijurisdictional task force encompassing four counties and innovative funding and prosecution agreements, which have reduced the automobile theft rate in south Texas.

CRIMINAL LAW
See also
　Criminal procedure

CRIMINAL LAW, INTERNATIONAL
See
　International law, Private

CRIMINAL PROCEDURE
See also
　Actions and defenses
　Confession (law)
　Defense (criminal procedure)
　Trials

United States

Lemov, Penelope. *Long life on death row: most states now have a death sentence; but in many of them, a lot more criminals are entering death row than leaving it.* il(s) table(s) *Governing* 9:30-2+ Mr 1996

Reviews the situation in several states in which a long and complex appeals process postpones implementation of sentences, and efforts to shorten that process; US.

PAIS INTERNATIONAL. NEW YORK, NY: PUBLIC AFFAIRS INFORMATION SERVICE, 1991-

EXHIBIT 5-6

Online: WILSONLINE, file SSI; OVID; OCLC EPIC;OCLC FirstSearch; Ameritech Library Services.

The *Social Sciences Index* is an author-subject index, providing indexing of 415 key international English-language periodicals. In addition to feature articles in journals, it also covers review articles, scholarly replies to the literature, interviews, obituaries, and biographies. As its title implies, it also covers the gamut of the social sciences, including sociology, criminology, and political science. Periodicals related to criminal justice are *Corrections Today*, *Criminal Justice and Behavior*, *Criminal Justice Ethics*, *Crime and Delinquency*, and *Criminology*. This current title was first published in 1974/75; for indexing prior to this date, see the *International Index* and the *Social Science and Humanities Index* (cited below).

International Index. Vol. 1–Vol. 18. New York: H. W. Wilson, 1907/15–1964/65. (Title varies slightly.)

Social Science and Humanities Index. Vol. 19–Vol. 27. New York: H. W. Wilson, 1965/66–1973/74.

In your search for periodical sources, remember that the published proceedings of meetings are also a reliable source of authoritative information. See chapter 2 for directories of published proceedings.

ABSTRACTS

Criminal Justice Abstracts

Library of Congress subject headings: Criminal justice, administration of—Periodicals; Criminal justice, administration of—Abstracts; Criminal justice, administration of—Abstracts—Periodicals; Criminal justice, administration of—Abstracts—Databases; Crime—Abstracts; Crime and criminals—Abstracts; Crime and criminals—Periodicals

Criminal Justice Abstracts. Vol. 9. Monsey, NY: Willow Tree Press, 1977–.

CD-ROM: Norwood, MA: SilverPlatter Information (coverage begins in 1968).

Online: WESTLAW as *CJ-CJA* (coverage begins with 1968).

Criminal Justice Abstracts (*CJA*) publishes quality, in-depth abstracts of scholarly criminology and criminal justice literature, international in scope. Abstracts go beyond simply listing the contents of a particular document—an evaluative approach is employed wherein the main findings of the source and the methodology used to support the findings are summarized and a brief conclusion of the facts is given.

CJA is published four times each year: in March, June, September, and December. Each issue contains hundreds of abstracts of current books, journal articles, dissertations, and reports published worldwide. A listing of all periodicals with abstracts is not available in each individual issue, but a cumulative listing is provided in each year's December issue. *CJA* utilizes information from the extensive holdings of the Criminal Justice/National Council on Crime and Delinquency (NCCD) collection at Rutgers University.

The format of *CJA* is easily understandable, with the abstracts numbered consecutively as they appear in each volume. Abstracts are grouped into six major categories: "Crime, the Offender, and the Victim"; "Juvenile Justice and Delinquency"; "Police"; "Courts and the Legal Process"; "Adult Corrections"; and "Crime Prevention and Control Strategies." Indexes at the back of each volume cover authors and subject-geography. Some issues of *CJA* also include a review or bibliography that combines the research on a subject with current importance. See exhibit 5-7 for a sample entry from *CJA*; notice the depth of coverage of the entry under the category "Crime, the Offender, and the Victim."

The coverage of *CJA* is not completely retrospective. Its current form began in 1977. For a historical treatment of a topic, the researcher must use *CJA*'s predecessor titles: *Information Review on Crime and Delinquency*, *Crime and Delinquency Literature*, Vol. 1(1968–69), and *Crime and Delinquency Literature*, Vol. 2–Vol. 8 (1970–1976). (*Crime and Delinquency Literature* was formed by the merger of *Selected Highlights of Crime and Delinquency Literature*, Vol. 1 [1968–69], and *Information Review on Crime and Delinquency*, Vol. 1 [1968–69].)

The CD-ROM version of *CJA* varies slightly in content and form from the printed version: reviews and bibliographies are not included, some abstracts that were previously unpublished are included, and the researcher can take better advantage of *CJA*'s classification scheme using keyword searching. For instance, searching first by one of the major categories can effectively narrow the scope of your search at the outset. The CD-ROM version, although slightly more difficult to search than the online version described below, is much less expensive, and searching it is likely to be more familiar to the average user.

The online version available through WESTLAW also includes some abstracts that were previously unpublished; however, these abstracts are still only a subset of the printed or CD-ROM database. The strength of WESTLAW's keyword and field searching is an advantage to the user. Both the CD-ROM and online versions are retrospective to 1968. Thus they include coverage of all its various manifestations.

CJA is an excellent abstract resource for scholarly literature on criminal justice topics. Frequently, however, your research calls for other kinds of information and analysis.

The National Criminal Justice Reference Service (NCJRS) was created in 1972 by the National Institute of Justice (NIJ)—the research arm of the United States Department of Justice—to provide information

Crime, the Offender, and the Victim

0001-28 United Nations Asia and Far East Institute for the Prevention of Crime and Treatment of Offenders; Australian Institute of Criminology. *Crime trends in Asia and the Pacific.* Tokyo, Japan: 1995. 42p. [R 65768]

A report summarizes results in the Asia and the Pacific region of the Fourth United Nations Survey of Crime Trends and Operations of Criminal Justice covering the years 1986-1990. Findings are compared to results of the three earlier UN surveys in 1970-1975, 1980-1986 and 1986-1990.

Countries can be divided into 4 categories according to overall reported crime rate. Australia was in the "very high" category. Fiji, Maldives, Japan, Vanuatu, Singapore and Tonga were in the "high" category. Thailand, the Philippines, Sri Lanka, Malaysia and South Korea were in the "low" category. Nepal and India were in the "very low" category. Three of the 4 highly industrialized countries in the survey (Japan, Australia and Singapore) had high or very high levels of crime, but relatively low levels of violence. The remaining industrialized country, South Korea, had a low level of crime and a low level of violence. Three of the 5 countries with low crime rates—Thailand, Sri Lanka and the Philippines—had high levels of violence. Thus, industrialized countries recorded relatively high levels of overall crime, but an overwhelming majority of these were property offenses. Less industrialized countries recorded proportionately higher levels of violent crime.

Trends in specific offenses were as follows: *homicide* increased 23% since the preceding survey, primarily concentrated in less well-off countries; *assault* declined 12%; *rape* increased 12%, mainly due to a significant increase in less well-off countries; *robbery* increased 7%; *theft* rates decreased, with a drop of more than half in less well-off countries; and *fraud* declined 15%.

0002-28 Tittle, Charles R. *Control balance: toward a general theory of deviance.* Boulder, CO: Westview Press, 1995. 321p. [R 65021] Crime & Society series.

An essay argues that, while simple theories of crime and deviance are defensible in their own terms, they are incomplete, limited in applicability, have little explanatory power, leave questions unaddressed, and fail to fully and logically connect variables. Overall, these theories are inadequate to explain or predict criminal behavior.

These theoretical deficiencies are overcome by the development of control balance theory. The main premise of this integrated theory is that the probability of deviance, and the probability of a particular form of deviance, is largely influenced by the interplay of deviant motivation with constraint. Both motivation and constraint are functions of control: the

CRIMINAL JUSTICE ABSTRACTS. MONSEY, NY: WILLOW TREE PRESS, 1977–.

EXHIBIT 5-7

resources for the NIJ's research activities. Its mission is to "communicate information and distribute publications and materials, resulting from Institute-sponsored research, development, and evaluation studies." To fulfill this mission, NCJRS functions as a national and international clearinghouse of practical and theoretical information about criminal justice and law enforcement. Since the main function of any clearinghouse is to collect documents, NCJRS gathers documents from various sources and makes them available to subscribers through its document service, which reproduces noncopyright-protected documents on microfiche and then sends that microfiche to the subscriber.

All documents available through this service are indexed with abstracts. This published index is available in several different formats, including print, microfiche, CD-ROM, and online. Even if your library does not subscribe to the NCJRS document service, you can at least use the index to identify periodicals or other documents for your research.

National Criminal Justice Reference Service [index with abstracts].Washington, DC: National Criminal Justice Reference Service, 1972–.
CD-ROM: Washington, DC: G.P.O., 1972–.
Online: DIALOG, file 21 (coverage begins with 1972).
Gopher: ftp://ncjrs.org/pub/ncjrs/
World Wide Web: http://www.ncjrs.org/ncjhome.htm
> The *NCJRS* index, a database of bibliographic information with abstracts, is a rich source of information about the *NCJRS* document collection. Originally published on microfiche (as the *Document Retrieval Index*), the *NCJRS* index covers more than 127,000 references to government documents, private research, books, chapters in books, articles, and reports. Much of the material described is considered *grey literature* or *fugitive literature,* materials that are inaccessible through standard means such as library catalogs, indexes, and bibliographies.

The documents listed in this index are available through the NCJRS document service, which reproduces documents and distributes them on microfiche.

National Criminal Justice Reference Service [document collection on microfiche]. Washington, DC: U.S. Department of Justice, Law Enforcement Assistance Administration, National Criminal Justice Reference Service, 1980–1996.
> The *NCJRS* document collection, stored on microfiche, comprises published and unpublished books, dissertations, theoretical and empirical studies, handbooks and standards, journal articles, and audiovisual materials. Documents are collected retrospectively back to the 1970s. Materials collected and not protected by copyright are distributed to requesting subscribers on microfiche.
>
> The NCJRS service is an important resource for finding all kinds of literature and should not be overlooked, especially in research involving comparative policy research. The document service is invaluable for building a comprehensive collection of criminal justice materials. Some libraries catalog the documents they order through the service, making them all the more accessible through interlibrary loan. Their microfiche format makes them eminently transportable.
>
> The NCJRS microfiche services ceased publication in 1996 due to increased costs and decreasing subscriptions. Current documents, 90 percent of which are agency publications, are available on the NCJRS Web site. The site, at http://www.ncjrs.org/topics.htm (April 7, 1997),

categorizes documents by subject: "Corrections," "Courts," "Crime Prevention," "Criminal Justice Statistics," "Drugs and Crime," "International," "Justice Grants," "Juvenile Justice," "Law Enforcement," "Other Criminal Justice Resources," "Research and Evaluation," and "Victims." Documents under each category are available for downloading in ASCII text and Adobe Acrobat formats.

Another source of abstracts for the literature of criminal justice is published outside the United States:

Criminology, Penology and Police Science Abstracts. Amsterdam: Kugler Publications, 1992–.
> *Criminology, Penology and Police Science Abstracts*, published six times a year, provides brief, readable abstracts of international sources, as prepared by the Criminologica Foundation in cooperation with the University of Leiden, Research and Documentation Centre and Crime Prevention Unit of the Netherlands Ministry of Justice; the Police Study Centre, Warnsveld, and the Detective Training School, Zutphen, all in the Netherlands. Abstracts are in English, but the work also covers articles published in Dutch, French, and other languages. Exhibit 5-8 demonstrates the readability and clear citation style of these abstracts. There are nine broad headings under which the abstracts are classified: "Criminology," "Offenses/Deviant Behavior," "Victims," "Juvenile Justice and Delinquency," "Criminal Law," "Crime Policy," "Police," and "Courts and Corrections." The headings are placed on the inside front cover in a manner that specifies the corresponding pages of those subjects.
>
> It was first published in 1992, volume 32, as a merger of *Criminology and Penology Abstracts,* Vol. 20–Vol. 31 (1980–1991), and *Police Science Abstracts,* Vol. 8–Vol. 19 (1980–1991) (cited below). (From 1979–92, a more specific title area was introduced into the table of contents on the inside cover. There were 13 headings and many subheadings, making it easier to find information than the current 9-heading approach.) *Criminology and Penology Abstracts* and its predecessors (cited below), *Excerpta Criminologica*, Vol. 1–Vol. 8 (1961–1968), and *Abstracts on Criminology and Penology,* Vol. 9–Vol. 19 (1969–1979), provide continuous coverage of the literature since 1961.

The predecessors to *Criminology, Penology and Police Science Abstracts* are as follows:

Abstracts on Criminology and Penology. Vol. 9–Vol. 19. Deventer, Netherlands: Kluwer, 1969–1979.

Excerpta Criminologica. Vol. 1–Vol. 8. Amsterdam: Excerpta Criminologica Foundation, 1961–1968.
> Very little substantive change occurred in these sources between 1961 and 1979—only minor variations. They were a cooperative effort of the Excerpta Criminologica Foundation, the U.S. National Council on Crime and Delinquency, the Institute of State and Law of the Academy of Sciences of the USSR, and the National Bureau for Child Protection in the Hague. Thus, the scope of these publications is international.

used to address how slave women accommodated and resisted these multiple forms of oppression. The findings presented here indicate that as blacks, both sexes experienced the harsh and inhumane consequences of racism and economic exploitation. In response to their exploitation, there was a significant convergence in male and female involvement in such forms of "criminal" resistance, such as murder, assault, theft and arson. These actions were employed to improve the slaves' lot in life and to express opposition to the slave system. Criminal resistance therefore set the stage for black women's participation in the criminal activities characteristic of today. Findings also suggest that in response to sexual exploitation, gender specific forms of accommodation (e.g., acting as breeders and sex workers) were utilized in order to make slave women's lives bearable. The article concludes that the various forms of accommodation served as a preface to black women's vulnerability to sex-oriented crimes within the context of the 20th century American society.

[CTH000089]

62 Child sexual abuse and the Mexican American family: developing a cultural perspective

Lavitt, M. and Alemán, S.
Soc. Work Progr., Arizona State Univ., Phoenix, AZ

Women and Criminal Justice 1995, 7/1 (81-102) ISSN 0897-4454

Child sexual abuse research has, for the most part, neglected cultural issues. As a result, assessment, intervention and prevention strategies, devised for members of the majority culture, have not always translated well into other cultures. The authors describe the construction of a framework that integrates research on sexual abuse with the work on Mexican American family functioning.

[CTH000091]

63 Cognitive impulsivity, verbal intelligence and locus of control in violent and nonviolent mentally disordered offenders

Nussbaum, D., Choudhry, R. and Martin-Doto, C.
Dept. of Psychiat., Toronto Univ., Toronto

American Journal of Forensic Psychology 1996, 14/1 (5-30) ISSN 0733-1290

The literature on violence contains selected references to impulsivity, external locus of control and below average verbal intelligence as contributory factors to violent offending. However, conflicting reports remain unresolved regarding whether these factors might be associated with offending in general, or more specifically, violent offending. This study provides additional empirical evidence demonstrating that these variables do not readily distinguish between groups of violent and non-violent mentally disordered offenders. Additional analyses of relationships between these variables suggest that measures of cognitive impulsivity are strongly, though negatively, related to measures of verbal intelligence. Locus of control scores, divided into three ranges (internal, intermediate and external) revealed that both ex-

treme groups scored similarly on estimates of verbal IQ and number of errors on the cognitive impulsivity task, but that both internals and externals differed from intermediates on these measures. Limitations of the current study and suggestions for future work are discussed.

[CTH000098]

64 An economic analysis of the crime rate in England and Wales, 1857-92

Wong, Y.-C.R.
Hong Kong Univ., Hong Kong

Economica 1995, 62/246 (235-246) ISSN 0013-0427

This is an economic analysis of the determinants of the crime rate in England and Wales 1857-1892. In this period the overall crime rate first rose and subsequently fell. Various analysts have interpreted this to imply that criminal behavior in this period cannot be explained by economic incentives. The present study finds that the overall crime rate responded to incentives for pursuing legal and illegal activities. Growing economic prosperity and rising educational standards contributed to the overall decline in the crime rate during the second half of the 19th century. Cyclical economic fluctuations as proxied by the unemployment rate were also a significant determinant of the crime rate.

[CTH000102]

65 Influences upon managerial moral decision making: nature of the harm and magnitude of consequences

Weber, J.
A.J. Palumbo Sch. of Business Administrat., Duquesne Univ., Pittsburgh, PA

Human Relations 1996, 49/1 (1-22) ISSN 0018-7267

Business ethics research typically emphasizes the influence of personal and organizational forces upon ethical decision-making. While accepting these forces as important, D. Collins (Organizational harm, legal condemnation and stakeholder retaliation: a typology, research agenda and application *Journal of Business Ethics* 1989, *8*: 1-13) and T.M. Jones (Ethical decision making by individuals in organizations: an issue-contingent model *Academy of Management Review* 1991, *16/2*: 366-395) suggest that the moral issue and its intensity may also influence individuals' resolution of an ethical dilemma. Utilizing a sample of 259 managers and a modified Moral Judgment Interview survey, this research reports that the type of harm (i.e., the nature or kind of harm), and the magnitude of the consequences (i.e., the degree or extent of the harm affecting the victim) influence the moral reasoning criteria evoked to resolve dilemmas, as predicted by Collins and Jones. This finding has significant theoretical, empirical, and practical implications, as discussed in this paper.

[CTH000112]

EXHIBIT 5-8

Abstracts on Police Science. Vol. 1–Vol. 7. Deventer, Netherlands: Kluwer, 1973–1979.

Police Science Abstracts. Vol. 8–Vol. 19. Amsterdam: Kugler Publications, 1980–1991.

> The other contributor to the creation of *Criminology, Penology and Police Science Abstracts* (cited above), *Police Science Abstracts* traces its lineage to *Abstracts on Police Science,* first published in 1973. Both publications are international in scope and pull together literature focusing on police science, forensic science, and forensic medicine. Abstracts are printed in many languages.

Social Science Abstracts

Abstracts in Social Gerontology: Current Literature on Aging. Newbury Park, CA: Sage, 1990–.

> First published in 1990 as Volume 33, *Abstracts in Social Gerontology* is the continuation of the *Current Literature on Aging* series, which was published from 1963 to 1989. Each issue contains 250 abstracts and related bibliographic citations of recent literature. Coverage includes books, periodicals, and government publications, as well as other sources. This abstracting tool is valuable for criminal justice research into areas relating to senior citizens, such as fear of crime by the elderly, crimes committed against the elderly, and members of the community who are experiencing age-related diminished mental ability.

American Psychological Association. *Psychological Abstracts*. Washington, DC: American Psychological Association, 1927–.

CD-ROM: as *PsycLIT*. Wellesley, MA: SilverPlatter Software International (coverage begins with 1974).

Online: OVID; DataStar, file PSYC; DIALOG, file 11; CompuServe Knowledge Index, file PSYC1; OCLC EPIC; OCLC FirstSearch Catalog.

> *Psychological Abstracts*, published monthly, contains author, title, and subject indexes, and an expanded and integrated index is published twice a year. It covers nearly 1,000 journals, technical reports, monographs, and other documents. In addition, books and book chapters are covered back to 1992. Contents are divided into 22 major categories, including subchapters relevant to criminal justice studies such as "Criminal Rehabilitation and Penology" and "Forensic Psychology and Legal Issues." This work covers scholarly literature primarily and should be common fare in research dealing with psychological aspects of criminal behavior. Exhibit 5-9 is a sample page from the "Forensic Psychology and Legal Issues" subchapter.

Applied Social Sciences Index and Abstracts: ASSIA. London: Library Association Publishing, 1987–.

CD-ROM: as *ASSIA Plus*.

Online: DataStar as *ASSI*.

> *ASSIA* is composed of four sections: "Abstract Sequence," "Subject Index," "Author Index," and "Source Index"—

the "Abstract Sequence" being the main index and hub of the work. The scope of *ASSIA* is social services, economics, politics, employment, race relations, health and education, penal services, and other areas relevant to students, practitioners, and researchers who seek to serve people. The index covers professional journals, general interest periodicals, and weeklies. *ASSIA* also abstracts a number of scholarly journals in criminal justice such as *British Journal of Criminology, Canadian Journal of Criminology, Child Abuse and Neglect, Crime and Delinquency, Criminal Behaviour and Mental Health, Criminal Law Review, Howard Journal of Criminal Justice, International Journal of Offender Therapy and Comparative Criminology, Journal of Child Sexual Abuse, Journal of Criminal Law, Journal of Research in Crime and Delinquency, Police Review, Policing, Prison Service Journal*, and *Probation Journal*.

Expanded Academic Index. Foster City, CA: Information Access, 1991–.

Online: InfoTrac.

> The *Expanded Academic Index* is only available online as part of the InfoTrac suite of databases. Coverage of periodicals in the social sciences begins in 1989. A subject guide allows you to browse listings of subjects, personal names, and companies by keyword—combinations of words or phrases from titles, authors, or subjects.

Human Relations Area Files (HRAF). New Haven, CT: Human Relations Area Files.

CD-ROM: as *Cross-Cultural CD* (covering 1800 to the present).

Online: as *Electronic HRAF (EHRAF)*.

> This resource is available in various formats including microfiche. It is a collection of data and full-text resources on non-Western cultures and is an excellent source of cross-cultural information.

Human Resources Abstracts. Newbury Park, CA: Sage, 1975–.

> *Human Resources Abstracts (HRA)* continues the work of *Poverty and Human Resources Abstracts*, Vol. 1–Vol. 9 (1966–1974). Two hundred and fifty abstracts and related bibliographic citations are offered in each issue. The table of contents is divided by subject headings, and each issue contains a subject index and an author index, which are cumulated annually. Criminal justice researchers seeking information regarding education, training, hiring, and personnel issues will find it here. In addition, there are abstracts pertaining to immigration and racial and ethnic issues.

International Political Science Abstracts. Paris: International Political Science Association, 1951–.

> *International Political Science Abstracts* covers more than 800 journals from around the globe. Each issue provides a list of periodicals for which abstracts have been written in recent years. The table of contents is divided by subject areas. A subject index is included in each issue. Articles that were originally printed in English are abstracted in English; articles originally printed in other languages are

FORENSIC PSYCHOLOGY & LEGAL ISSUES   83: 29099–29105

tions in sentencing • Part VI • Stalking • Conclusion • References • Index • About the authors
[from the cover] "Domestic Violence: The Criminal Justice Response" . . . features [an] examination of this complex issue. Noting that domestic violence remains the subject of intense controversy and debate, the authors delve into the rapidly evolving nature of the criminal justice system's response to domestic violence. After providing a brief theoretical overview of the causes of domestic violence and its prevalence in our society, [the authors] examine classic models of response by individual criminal justice institutions, as well as the opportunities for and limitations of emerging approaches.

29100. Young, Alison. (U Melbourne, Dept of Criminology, Melbourne, VICT, Australia). **Imagining crime: Textual outlaws and criminal conversations.** Sage Publications, Inc: London, England, 1996. viii, 230 pp. ISBN 0-8039-8622-X (hardcover); 0-8039-8623-8 (paperback).
TABLE OF CONTENTS
Acknowledgements • Textual outlaws and criminal conversations • Criminology and the question of feminism • The universal victim and the body in crisis • The scene of the crime: Reading the justice of detective fiction • The Bulger case and the trauma of the visible • Criminological concordats: On the single mother and the criminal child • Fatal frames: HIV/AIDS as spectacle in criminal justice • Afterthoughts: The imagination of crime • References • Index
[from the cover] This book offers [a] reading of the 'crimino-legal complex'—criminology, criminal law, criminal justice, the media, everyday experience—in the light of cultural studies and feminist theory.

Through an exploration of the crisis engendered by the failure of the crimino-legal complex to solve the problems of crime and criminality, Alison Young exposes the cultural dimension of its institutions and practices. She analyses the far-reaching effects of the cultural value given to crime, showing it to be rooted in a powerful nexus of the body, language, the community and everyday life.

"Imagining Crime" integrates questions in criminology, criminal law and criminal justice with feminist theory, socio-legal studies and cultural studies. It is [intended] for students and scholars of criminology, socio-legal studies, criminal law and cultural studies.

Criminal Law & Criminal Adjudication

Chapters

29101. Wagenaar, Willem A. (Leiden U, Unit of Experimental & Theoretical Psychology, Leiden, Netherlands). **Autobiographical memory in court.** [In: (PA Vol 83:25361) *Remembering our past: Studies in autobiographical memory.* Rubin, David C. (Ed.). Cambridge University Press: New York, NY, 1996. viii, 448 pp. ISBN 0-521-46145-6 (hardcover).] pp. 180–196.
[from the chapter]
— the reliability of autobiographical memory has shaped all legal systems, no matter which system is ultimately adopted ◊ is the result satisfactory, in the sense that problems of reliability are sufficiently met by legal provisions ◊ [compare] the amount of precision required for legal applications to the amount of precision that is to be expected from witnesses in all sorts of situations ◊ [focus] on a single case . . . in the small village of Epe, The Netherlands [in which an adult female accused her parents and others of continual sexual abuse, illegal abortions, and murder] ◊ demonstrate in what respect the autobiographical memories of witnesses appeared to be highly inadequate for use in the criminal trial, even though, maybe, the quality of these memories was not abnormal

Mediation & Conflict Resolution

Serials

29102. Salacuse, Jeswald W. (Tufts U, Fletcher School of Law & Diplomacy, Medford, MA) **The art of advising negotiators.** *Negotiation Journal,* 1995(Oct), Vol 11(4), 391–401. —Ex-

plores the advising process as it relates to negotiators and suggests principles to guide such advising. The principles include know your client, help or at least do no harm, agree on your role, and never give a solo performance. Seven questions that should be asked to evaluate an advisor's performance are given. —*J. P. Bagato.*

Police & Legal Personnel

Serials

29103. Morris, Anne. (U California, School of Public Health, Health Policy & Administration, Berkeley, CA) **Gender and ethnic differences in social constraints among a sample of New York City police officers.** *Journal of Occupational Health Psychology,* 1996(Apr), Vol 1(2), 224–235. —Examined gender and ethnic differences in social constraints both on and off the job among 372 police officers from the New York City Housing Authority. Positive and negative social interactions with supervisors and coworkers, and perceptions of the work environment as well as support and resentment of the job from family and significant others, were included. 73% of the sample were White, 11% were Black or African American, 11% were Hispanic, and 1% were Asian American; women comprised 22% of the sample. Women and minority men reported more negative social interactions on the job, such as criticism, bias, and sexual harassment. Few differences were observed for positive social interactions on or off the job, and where differences emerged, women and minority men reported more favorable social interactions.

29104. Slama-Cazacu, Tatiana. (U Bucharest, Lab of Psycholinguistics, Romania) **The non-dialogue in political interrogations.** *International Journal of Psycholinguistics,* 1993(Jun), Vol 9(1)[25], 73–97. —Analyzes the unfolding of a dialogue between the interrogated and the interrogator before political detentions, as described in Romanian memoirs published after 1945. These demonstrate the unilateral way of communication in interrogations. Interrogations suppose an Interrogator who is all powerful, and the interrogated who is obliged to answer with no right to change the direction of this verbal act. The Interrogator aims at obtaining a presumed "confession", which is enhanced by terrifying tortures. The interrogator uses the rules of communication in his interests, in a situation that is coercive. Thus, interrogation leads to the destruction of the interrogated's personality, denial of the freedom of verbal acts, pre-collapse, and biased confessions. Such a situation ultimately results in a false act of communication and a complete deviation from the rules of a dialogue.

Police & Legal Personnel

Books

29105. Martin, Susan Ehrlich & Jurik, Nancy C. (National Insts of Health, National Inst on Alcohol Abuse & Alcoholism, Bethesda, MD). **Doing justice, doing gender: Women in law and criminal justice occupations. Women and the criminal justice system, Vol. 1.** Sage Publications, Inc: Thousand Oaks, CA, 1996. ix, 270 pp. ISBN 0-8039-5197-3 (hardcover); 0-8039-5198-1 (paperback).
TABLE OF CONTENTS (Abbreviated)
List of tables • Acknowledgments • Introduction: Changes in criminal justice organizations, occupations, and women's work • Explanations for gender inequality in the workplace • The nature of police work and women's entry into law enforcement • Women officers encountering the gendered police organization • Women entering the legal profession: Change and resistance • The organizational logic of the gendered legal world and women lawyers' responses • Women in corrections: Advancement and resistance • Gendered organizational logic and women CO response • Doing justice, doing gender, today and tommorrow: Occupations, organizations, and change • References • List of cases cited • Author index • Subject index • About the authors
[from the introduction] This book examines the organization of justice occupations along gender lines.

We examine the justice system occupations of policing, law, and corrections. We focus broadly on the field of law,

abstracted in French. While this bilingual format may be restrictive to many, this abstracting tool can help you to locate criminal justice information in other countries.

National Association of Social Workers. *Social Work Abstracts*. Washington, DC: National Association of Social Workers, 1994–.

National Association of Social Workers. *Social Work Research*. Washington, DC: National Association of Social Workers, 1993–.

CD-ROM: *Social Work Abstracts* (coverage begins with March 1991)

Social Work Abstracts and *Social Work Research* were formed from the division of *Social Work Research and Abstracts* (1977–1993), which had, in turn, continued *Abstracts for Social Workers*, 1965–1976. In addition to abstracts of journal articles and dissertations, the two referenced works offer an index to research papers. These tools offer a good deal of information directly pertaining to criminal justice issues such as family violence, fear of crime, and crime and delinquency, as well as information regarding different groups such as race, ethnic, gender, and sexual orientation.

National League of Cities. *Urban Affairs Abstracts*. Washington, DC: National League of Cities, 1971–.

Urban Affairs Abstracts covers articles from several hundred periodicals, newsletters, and journals. Each weekly issue provides a periodical guide and a table of contents, which is arranged by subject listing. Although it provides some valuable information, it is highly inaccessible. However, the annual cumulation is somewhat easier to use than the weekly issues because it includes a subject descriptor index, a periodical guide, an author index, and a geographic index.

Sage Public Administration Abstracts. Beverly Hills, CA: Sage Periodicals Press, 1974–.

This abstracting tool provides approximately 250 abstracts in each issue as well as related bibliographic citations. It is an effective tool for locating materials pertaining to administrative, social services, public service personnel, and policy-making issues.

Social Planning, Policy and Development Abstracts (SOPODA). San Diego, CA: Sociological Abstracts, 1984–.

CD-ROM: as *Sociofile*. Wellesley, MA: SilverPlatter, 1986–.

Published biannually, this abstracting tool differs from the previous one in that the focus of its abstracts tends to be practical application as opposed to theory. The format is similar with author, source, and subject indexes in each issue. The table of contents is organized by subject headings, one of which is "Crime and Public Safety." Formerly titled *Social Welfare, Social Planning/Policy and Social Development*.

Sociological Abstracts. San Diego, CA: Sociological Abstracts, 1953–.

CD-ROM: as *Sociofile*. Wellesley, MA: SilverPlatter, 1986–.

Online: OVID; DIALOG, file 37; CompuServe Knowledge Index, file SOCS1; DataStar, file SOCA; OCLC EPIC; OCLC FirstSearch Catalog.

Sociological Abstracts is organized by subject headings, which may be difficult for newcomers. However, source, author, and subject indexes are included in each issue, and the subject index is clear and easy to use. These indexes are also cumulated annually. Topics of interest to criminal justice students include drug abuse and crime. The CD-ROM version includes abstracts from *Social Planning/Policy and Development Abstracts* (cited above).

Women Studies Abstracts. New Brunswick, New Jersey: Transaction Periodicals Consortium/Rutgers University, 1972–.

Criminal justice issues pertaining to women, such as violence and crimes against women, are covered by this tool.

U.S. Department of Education. *Resources in Education*. Washington DC: U.S. Department of Education. 1975–.

CD-ROM: as part of *ERIC*.

Online: as part of ERIC; OVID; OCLC EPIC; OCLC FirstSearch Catalog; DIALOG, file 1; CompuServe Knowledge Index, file EDUC1; CARL Systems Network; DataStar.

Resources in Education is a continuation of *Research in Education*, Vol. 1–Vol. 9 (1966–1974). It offers abstracts of a broad array of literature, including periodicals, monographs, and government reports. Each issue contains an author, subject, and other indexes; semiannual indexes are also available. The Department of Education maintains a clearinghouse of information and publications in education, thus much of the literature indexed can be classified as *grey literature*. Those documents not published by the usual presses may be obtained on microfiche or ordered from ERIC (the Educational Research Information Center). This abstracting tool could be of value to criminal justice students researching topics such as drug reduction programs in schools.

PERIODICAL DIRECTORIES

Library of Congress subject headings: American periodicals—Directories; Canadian periodicals—Directories; Serial publications—Bibliography; Serial publications—Directories

Periodical directories identify and describe journals relevant to a particular field; they do not list the contents of periodical titles, but they do suggest publications that may be of interest. They are best as tools for finding out who publishes a particular journal, the current subscription price, and the address of the publisher, and where a journal is indexed. They can also lead to previously unknown publications of interest, particularly since some obscure journals are not covered in standard indexing and abstracting tools.

Directory of Electronic Journals, Newsletters and Academic Discussion Lists. 2d ed. Washington, DC: Association of Research Libraries, 1991–.

"Directory of Electronic Journals, Newsletters and Academic Discussion Lists." gopher://arl.cni.org:70/11/scomm/edir/edir95 (April 2, 1997).

> Although quite similar to *Ulrich's* (see below) in scope, this directory comprises a larger selection of newspapers and is somewhat larger overall. In addition, it lists Library of Congress classification numbers for most titles. Part 1 of this directory is an alphabetical listing of journals and newsletters; part 2 lists academic discussion list and interest groups.

Directory of Periodicals Online: Indexed, Abstracted and Full Text. Washington, DC: Federal Document Retrieval, 1985–.

> The *Directory of Periodicals Online* is particularly concerned with documenting full-text online newspapers, newsletters, and other materials in the field of law.

The Serials Directory: An International Reference Book. Birmingham, AL: EBSCO, 1986–.

> Although quite similar to *Ulrich's* in scope, *The Serials Directory* includes a larger selection of newspapers and lists Library of Congress classification numbers for most titles. Also available online and on CD-ROM.

Standard Periodical Directory. New York: Oxbridge Communications, 1964/65–.

> This directory is limited to periodicals published in the United States and Canada. Its value is in the inclusion of association publications, house organs, and more extensive coverage of newsletters. If you are searching only for North American periodicals, this is the preferred tool.

Ulrich's International Periodicals Directory. 5 vols. New York: R.R. Bowker, 1994/95–.

CD-ROM: as *Ulrich's Plus.*

Online: DIALOG.

> *Ulrich's International Periodicals Directory* is the foremost directory of serial publications. This multivolume work, published annually with quarterly updates, provides bibliographic and ordering information for more than 147,000 serials published worldwide and arranged under 967 subject headings. See exhibit 5-10 for a partial listing of periodicals classified under the topic "Criminology and Law Enforcement." Each entry gives detailed information on the publisher, address, frequency of publication, language, and price. Most entries also include the date the serial was first published, the name of the editor, former titles, circulation statistics, availability of online or mi-

croform versions, where it is indexed or abstracted, and a brief description of its scope or contents.

> Over 10,000 worldwide newspapers are included in the 1994/95 edition, and Volume 5 lists 7,000 daily and weekly U.S. newspapers. Subject-oriented newspapers are included in Volume 3, which is the "Classified List of Serials." Volume 4 contains a section on refereed serials, alphabetically listing all serials known to be refereed or peer reviewed. *Ulrich's Update* is published three times a year, and Ulrich's hotline is a toll-free number for solving serials' research problems and questions. The electronic versions offer the preferred way to search such a large directory.

ACCESS TO NEWSLETTERS

Newsletters are an important source of information for current events in criminal justice or any other discipline. They generally report results of recent studies, announce upcoming conferences, provide information on society events, and report on government activities. Although not always a citable source of information, they can be valuable for keeping you informed of developments in a discipline or literature. However, accessing newsletters is a special problem in research. Finding this type of resource is especially problematic since so few newsletters are indexed in the standard sources.

Listed below are a few sources that provide a way to identify newsletters concerning a particular topic. Newsletter directories, for example, can make finding newsletters easier. They will not list the articles published in any given newsletter, but they may lead you to newsletters in your general subject area.

Newsletters in Print. 4th ed. Detroit: Gale Research, 1988/89–.

> *Newsletters in Print* is a guide to more than 11,000 subscription, membership, and free newsletters, bulletins, digests, and updates issued in the U.S. and Canada and available in print and online. Periodicals are arranged under broad subject heading such as "Social Sciences" and "Law and the Administration of Justice." Each newsletter entry gives title, publisher name, publisher address, and telephone number. It also lists editors, a description of the periodical, the intended audience, frequency of indexing, and price.

Oxbridge Directory of Newsletters. New York: Oxbridge Communications, 1979–.

> The *Oxbridge Directory of Newsletters,* published annually, lists newsletters in subject categories, with information on address, frequency of publication, circulation, distribution, and primary readership. Relevant newsletters to criminal justice are listed under the heading "Law Enforcement and Penology."

364 289 7   US
CRIME AND JUSTICE NETWORK NEWSLETTER. 1979. q. suggested donation $5. Mennonite Central Committee, 21 S. 12th St., Box 500, Akron, PA 17501-0500. TEL 717-859-1151 FAX 717-859-2622. Ed. Howard Zehr. bk. rev. circ. 500. **Document type:** newsletter.
    Formerly: M C C Office of Criminal Network Newsletter.
    Description: Articles and resources on criminal justice, including alternatives to prison, death penalty and victim-offender reconciliation.

364   US
CRIME AND THE NATION'S HOUSEHOLDS (YEAR). (Subseries of: National Crime Victimization Survey Report) 1973. a. free. U.S. Department of Justice, Bureau of Justice Statistics, 633 Indiana Ave., N.W., 11th Fl., Washington, DC 20531. (Subscr. to: Superintendent of Documents, U.S. Government Printing Office, Box 371954, Pittsburgh, PA 15250-7954. TEL 202-783-3238. FAX 202-512-2233) stat. circ. 17,000. (also avail. in microfiche) **Document type:** government publication.

364   US   ISSN 0011-1295
KF9223.C92
CRIME CONTROL DIGEST. 1967. w. $295. Washington Crime News Services, 3918 Prosperity Ave., Ste. 318, Fairfax, VA 22031-3334. TEL 703-573-1600. Ed. Betty B. Bosarge. bk.rev.: tr.lit. (looseleaf format; also avail. in microform from UMI; reprint service avail. from UMI) **Indexed:** CJPI. **Document type:** newsletter.
    —UMI.

364   US   ISSN 0146-5759
HV7296
CRIME IN VIRGINIA.* a. Department of State Police, Uniform Crime Reporting Section, Box 27472, Richmond, VA 23261-7472. TEL 804-323-2031. (also avail. in microfiche from CIS) **Indexed:** SRI.

364   US
CRIME, LAW, AND DEVIANCE SERIES. 1979. irreg., latest 1991. price varies. Rutgers University Press, 109 Church St., New Brunswick, NJ 08901. TEL 908-932-7762. FAX 908-932-7039. (Dist. by: Rutgers University Press Distribution Center, Box 4869, Hampden Sta., Baltimore, MD 21211. TEL 410-516-6947) Ed. David Greenburg. adv.; bk.rev. **Document type:** monographic series.

364 343 360   NE   ISSN 0925-4994
HV6001   CODEN: CSCJEL
CRIME, LAW AND SOCIAL CHANGE; an international journal. (Text in English) 1977. 8/yr. fl.644($336) (effective 1994). Kluwer Academic Publishers, Postbus 17, 3300 AA Dordrecht, Netherlands. TEL 31-78-334911. FAX 31-78-334254. TELEX 29245 KAPG NL. (Dist. by: Kluwer Academic Publishers Group, P.O. Box 322, 3300 AH Dordrecht, Netherlands. TEL 31-78-524400. FAX 31-78-524474; N. America dist. addr.: Box 358, Accord Sta., Hingham, MA 02018-0358. TEL 617-871-6600. FAX 617-871-6528) Ed. Alan Block. bk.rev.; index. (also avail. in microform from UMI; reprint service avail. from SWZ) **Indexed:** A.B.C.Pol.Sci., Crim.Just.Abstr., Curr.Cont., Int.Polit.Sci.Abstr., Lang.& Lang.Behav.Abstr., Left Ind. (1982-), P.A.I.S., Sociol.Abstr., SSCI. **Document type:** academic/scholarly publication.
    —BLDSC (3487.342795); Faxon; UnCover; SWETS; UMI. **CCC.**
    Formerly: Contemporary Crises (ISSN 0378-1100); Incorporates (1986-1992): Corruption and Reform (ISSN 0169-7528)
    Refereed Serial

364.4   UK
CRIME PREVENTION NEWS. 1969. q. Home Office, 50 Queen Anne's Gate, London SW1H 9AT, England. TEL 071-273-2946. circ. 65,000. **Document type:** government publication.

364   AT   ISSN 1031-5330
CRIME PREVENTION SERIES. irreg. price varies. Australian Institute of Criminology, G.P.O. Box 2944, Canberra, A.C.T. 2601, Australia. TEL 06-274-0256. FAX 02-274-0260. (Dist. in US by: Criminal Justice Press, Box 249, Monsey, NY 10952) **Document type:** monographic series.

364   US   ISSN 1065-7029
▼CRIME PREVENTION STUDIES. 1993 s-a. $47.50 Criminal Justice Press, Box 249, Monsey, NY 10952. TEL 914-354-9139. FAX 914-362-8376. Ed. Ronald V. Clarke. **Document type:** academic/scholarly publication.
    Description: Covers international research and practice on situational crime prevention and other measures to limit opportunities for crime. Papers include preventive-oriented analyses of specific crime problems, evaluations of crime-prevention programs, and theoretical discussions of the philosophy and methods of situational crime prevention.

364   US   ISSN 0884-5107
KF9763.A15
CRIME VICTIMS DIGEST. 1983. m. $75. Washington Crime News Services. 3918 Prosperity Ave., Ste. 318, Fairfax, VA 22031-3334. TEL 703-573-1600. Ed. Susan Kernus. (looseleaf format) **Indexed:** CJPI. **Document type:** newsletter.

364   UK   ISSN 0070-1521
KD7865.A2
CRIMINAL APPEAL REPORTS. 1908. 6/yr. (in 2 vols., 3 nos./vol.). £190. Sweet & Maxwell, South Quay Plaza, 7th Fl., 183 Marsh Wall, London E14 9FT, England. TEL 071-538-8686. FAX 071-538-9508. Ed. Rebecca Hough. adv. contact: Jackie Wood. index. **Document type:** bulletin.
    ●Also available online. Vendor(s): Mead Data Central, Inc.
    —BLDSC (3487.346000).

CRIMINAL BEHAVIOUR AND MENTAL HEALTH. see *MEDICAL SCIENCES — Psychiatry And Neurology*

365   UK
CRIMINAL JUSTICE. 1970. 4 /yr. £10 membership. Howard League. 708 Holloway Rd., London N19 3NL, England. TEL 071-281-7722. Ed. Frances Crook. adv.; bk.rev.; illus. circ. 2,000. (also avail. in microform from UMI) **Indexed:** C.L.I., CJPI, Hum.Ind.
    Formerly (until 1983): Howard League for Penal Reform Newsletter.
    Description: Reports on prison facilities and administration.

345   US
KFI1762.A15I55
CRIMINAL JUSTICE (SPRINGFIELD). 1957. bi-m. $16 to members. Illinois State Bar Association, Section on Criminal Justice, Illinois Bar Center, Springfield, IL 62701. TEL 217-525-1760. FAX 217-525-0712. Ed.Bd. circ. 3,200. (looseleaf format; back issues avail.)

364 150   US   ISSN 0093-8548
HV9261   CODEN: CJBHAB
CRIMINAL JUSTICE & BEHAVIOR; an international journal. 1974. q. $47 to individuals; institutions $140 (effective 1994). (American Association of Correctional Psychologists) Sage Publications, Inc., 2455 Teller Rd., Thousand Oaks, CA 91320. TEL 805-499-0721. FAX 805-499-0871. (Subscr. to: Sage Publications, Inc., Box 5084, Thousand Oaks, CA 91359; Overseas subscr. to: Sage Publications, Ltd., 6 Bonhill St., London EC2A 4PU, England; Sage Publications India Pvt. Ltd., P.O. Box 4215, New Delhi 110 048, India) (Affiliate: American Correctional Association) Ed. David S. Glenwick. adv.; bk.rev.; index. circ. 1,600. (also avail. in microfiche from WSH; microfilm from UMI,WSH,PMC; back issues avail.; reprint service avail. from KTO,UMI) **Indexed:** Abstr.Bk.Rev.Curr.Leg.Per., ASSIA, C.I.J.E., C.L.I., CJPI, Crim.Just.Abstr., Curr.Cont., Excerp.Med., L.R.I., Leg.Cont., Mid.East: Abstr.& Ind., Mult.Ed.Abstr., P.A.I.S., PHRA, Psychol.Abstr., Psychol.R.G., Sage Fam.Stud.Abstr., Sage Urb.Stud.Abstr., Soc.Sci.Ind., Sociol.Abstr., Sp.Ed.Needs Abstr., SSCI. **Document type:** academic/scholarly publication.
    —BLDSC (3487.348000); Faxon; UnCover; SWETS; UMI. **CCC.**
    Supersedes: Correctional Psychologist (ISSN 0589-8218)
    Description: Covers criminal justice relating to mental health, personality assessment, and changes.

364   US   ISSN 0889-5724
CRIMINAL JUSTICE DIGEST. 1982 ~ $140. Washington Crime News Services. 3918 Prosperity Ave., Ste. 318, Fairfax, VA 22031-3334. TEL 703-573-1600. Ed. Betty B Bosarge. bk.rev (looseleaf format; also avail. in microfilm from WSH) **Indexed:** Abstr.Bk.Rev.Curr.Leg.Per., C.L.I., Crim.Just.Abstr., L.R.I., Leg.Per **Document type:** newsletter.
    —UMI.
    Formerly (until 1985): Criminal Justice Journal (Springfield).

CRIMINAL JUSTICE ETHICS. see *PHILOSOPHY*

364.9   US   ISSN 0194-0953
HV7921
CRIMINAL JUSTICE HISTORY; an international annual. 1980. a. $59.50. Greenwood Press. Inc. (Subsidiary of: Greenwood Publishing Group Inc.). 88 Post Rd., W., Box 5007, Westport, CT 06881-9990. TEL 203-226-3571. FAX 203-222-1502. Ed.Bd. **Indexed:** Amer.Hist.& Life, Hist.Abstr.
    —BLDSC (3487.350200); UnCover

364   US
CRIMINAL JUSTICE INFORMATION EXCHANGE DIRECTORY. 1982. a. $13. U.S. Department of Justice, National Institute of Justice. National Criminal Justice Reference Service. Box 6000, Rockville, MD 20850. TEL 800-851-3420.

CRIMINAL JUSTICE JOURNAL. see *LAW — Criminal Law*

364   US   ISSN 0045-9038
K3
CRIMINAL JUSTICE NEWSLETTER. 1970. s-m. $198. Pace Publications, 443 Park Ave. S. New York, NY 10016. TEL 212-685-5450. FAX 212-679-4701. Ed. Craig Fischer. bk.rev.; index. **Indexed:** C.L.I., CJPI, L.R.I. **Document type:** newsletter.
    Description: Systemwide perspective on the criminal justice system, covering law enforcement, courts, and corrections.

CRIMINAL LAW FORUM; an international journal. see *LAW — Criminal Law*

364   US   ISSN 0192-3323
K3
CRIMINAL LAW REVIEW. 1979. a. $85. Clark - Boardman - Callaghan Company Ltd.. 375 Hudson St., New York, NY 10014. TEL 212-929-7500; 800-221-9428. FAX 212-924-0460 Ed. James G. Carr. **Indexed:** ASSIA, Crim.Just.Abstr
    Description: Contains the most significant articles on criminal law published within the past year

364 362.7   US   ISSN 1066-2677
▼CRIMINAL MONITOR. 1992. bi-m. $12 4241 Florin Rd., Ste. 75-461, Sacramento, CA 95823. stat.; index. circ. 1,200. **Document type:** newsletter.
    Description: Parent-oriented crime prevention report.

364   US
CRIMINAL ORGANIZATIONS. 1985. q. $20 (membership). International Association of the Study of Organized Crime (IASOC), University of Illinois at Chicago, OICJ (M-C 777), 1033 W. Van Buren St., Chicago, IL 60607-2919. TEL 516-299-2594. FAX 516-299-2587. Ed. Patrick J. Ryan. bk.rev. circ. 600. (back issues avail.) **Document type:** bibliography.
    Formerly: International Association for the Study of Organized Crime. Update.
    Description: Includes articles, book reviews, news and notes, member network and summaries on organized crime issues.

362.8   US   ISSN 0095-5833
HV7245
CRIMINAL VICTIMIZATION IN THE UNITED STATES. (Subseries of: National Crime Victimization Survey Report) 1973. a. free. U.S. Department of Justice, Bureau of Justice Statistics, 633 Indiana Ave., N.W., 11th Fl., Washington, DC 20531. TEL 800-732-3277. (Subscr. to: Box 6000, Rockville, MD 20850) stat. circ. 17,000. (also avail. in microfiche; back issues avail.) **Document type:** government publication.

EXHIBIT 5-10

ACCESS TO NEWSPAPERS

Finding information published in newspapers can be an extremely important task in completing a research project. Your purpose for trying to find news stories will probably vary. You may need to track current events that impact on a research project or study already underway. You may also need to find an account of some past event in order to lend it perspective. Whatever your purpose, the media is a rich source of on-the-spot factual information. When focusing on twentieth-century events, the printed word is supplemented with graphical representations of events. Photographs, newsreels, and video recordings of events lend an added dimension to the reporting of facts that the printed word alone cannot.

As we said earlier in this chapter, print and online media, unlike other resources, are able to respond quickly to events and report facts. For research purposes, the importance of the press lies in its time-sensitivity. Newspapers are often the first place to read about a particular happening, and, in fact, often provide us with the most recent information on a topic. They are extremely valuable in keeping us up to date on happenings in our local area, as well as national and international occurrences. Furthermore, they provide a chronological record of events as they occur, and editorial comments in any given newspaper provide opinions on a wide range of issues. As such, newspapers are an important part of our historical record. Actually, newspapers are probably the most widely read form of publication that exists.

Several of the largest newspapers in the United States, such as the *New York Times,* have been indexed for a number of years. These indexes are in print, CD-ROM, and online formats and are generally available in libraries of various sizes. Smaller newspapers may also be indexed, but these indexes are not typically distributed for sale. The indexes of lesser-known newspapers may be available in local libraries or, more frequently, only at the offices of the newspaper itself. Access to information in news sources therefore tends to be inconsistent. This is especially true if you are researching news accounts of events that took place before and during the 1970s.

Newspaper Directories

Listed below are some directories of newspapers, both of contemporary and historical newspapers published in the United States and Canada. Even though these directories are not indexes per se, remember that many newspapers do produce an index for their own publication (e.g., *The New York Times* and *The Wall Street Journal*) and that for obscure newspapers, you should contact the newspaper itself to determine where or if it is indexed.

Early American Newspapers. New York: Readex, 1983–.

> *Early American Newspapers* is a microfilm collection of over 2,000 American newspapers published between the seventeenth and early nineteenth centuries. This excellent source is indexed by the *Index to Readex Microfilms Collection of Early American Newspapers* (1990), compiled by Lydia S. Kellerman and Rebecca A. Wilson.

Editor & Publisher International Year Book. New York: Editor & Publisher, 1920–.

> This annual publication provides a geographical listing of newspapers published throughout the world. For each, the circulation, political focus, and type of newspaper is given. Also available on CD-ROM.

Fulltext Sources Online: For Periodicals, Newspapers, Newsletters, Newswires, and TV- Radio Transcripts. Needham, MA: BiblioData, 1995.

> *Fulltext Sources Online,* published twice yearly in January and July, lists sources available online alphabetically by title. The most relevant subject headings are "Government/Law," "News/Current Events," and "Sociology," and it has a subject index.

Gale Directory of Publications and Broadcast Media. Detroit: Gale Research, 1880–.

> This Gale directory, published annually, provides a listing of newspapers, popular magazines, and broadcast media in the United States, Canada, and some foreign countries. Entries are listed geographically, first by state or province, then by city. Check relevant entries by referring to the subject index, which will lead you to the full entry under the correct geographical area. There is a also a master index listed by title and keyword. Entries list publisher, subscription rates, and circulation data. Previously published as the *Ayer Directory of Publications.*

Special Libraries Association. *Directory of Newspaper Libraries in the U.S. and Canada.* New York: Special Libraries Association, 1976.

> Despite its age, this resource is a valuable geographic guide to libraries—usually newspaper company libraries—that retain back issues of local newspapers. Information includes the titles of the newspapers archived, address, telephone number, the date the library was formed, library hours, resources available, services available, and how unaffiliated users may access files. See exhibit 5-11 for a sample page from this resource.

U.S. Library of Congress. *Newspapers in Microform: Foreign Countries, 1948–1983.* Washington, DC: U.S. Library of Congress, Catalog Publications Division, 1984.

Tucson Daily Citizen

```
CITIZEN (e)


4850 S. Park Ave.
(P.O. Box 26887)
Tucson, AZ  85726                    602/294-4433 ext 257


   Charlotte Nusser, Librarian
   Jeannie Jett, Asst. Librarian

Circ.:  60,320 (e)

Group:  Independent

Library founded:  1939           Staff:  9

Library hours:

   Mon.-Fri.  6:00a.m.-midnight
   Sat.       6:30a.m.-noon


Resources:

   Clippings     1 million     Periodical titles        80
   Photos & art    100,000     Pamphlet drawers          10
   Negatives        50,000     Microforms (Jackets)  10,000
   Cuts/Veloxes                Film from               1870
   Books               400
   Indexes

Special collections:


Services:

   Copy machine, reader/printer


Services available to unaffiliated users (except newsmen):


Automation:
```

DIRECTORY OF NEWSPAPER LIBRARIES IN THE U.S. AND CANADA. NEW YORK: SPECIAL LIBRARIES ASSOCIATION, 1976.

EXHIBIT 5-11

U.S. Library of Congress. *Newspapers in Microform: United States, 1948–1983.* Washington, DC: U.S. Library of Congress, Catalog Publications Division, 1984.

   Updated by annual and quarterly supplements, these are two union lists of more than 100,000 newspapers held in libraries in the United States and elsewhere according to geographic region. Annotations indicate particular library holdings.

Newspaper Indexes and Abstracts

Most printed newspaper indexes offer a brief description of article content, date published, and page and column where it can be located. Most of these indexes are classified and cross-referenced by subject, geographic, organizational, and personal name headings. Headings are arranged alphabetically with specific entries arranged chronologically. Some indexes, such as the *New York Times Index,* include more information.

However, for several reasons their use is decreasing, and CD-ROM and online versions are becoming preferred. Print versions only index a single newspaper, whereas electronic versions index more than one; printed indexes are labor intensive to update; and you must look through several bound volumes if you are researching an event in the current year (because they have not yet been indexed).

The DIALOG Online Information Retrieval Service (see chapter 3, page 77, for more information) is by far the single most inclusive and comprehensive source for newspaper index and abstract information. DIALOG also offers very powerful searching capabilities. For instance, while it offers both bibliographic and full-text formats of databases, DIALOG searching capabilities enable you to search both formats simultaneously if you so desire. It also offers manual and menu-guided searching. Because DIALOG charges by time, quicker bibliographic searches are less expensive than full-text searches.

DIALOG databases can be searched by abstract, company name, caption, descriptor, named person, product name, or title. There are approximately 30 additional specific or detailed indexes that can help narrow search parameters.

Listed below are a variety of newspaper indexes in various forms including print and electronic.

IAC National Newspaper Index [online database]. Foster City: CA Information Access Co., 1979–.

"*IAC National Newspaper Index* provides front-to-back indexing of the *Christian Science Monitor,* the *Los Angeles Times,* the *New York Times,* the *Wall Street Journal,* and the *Washington Post.*"

IAC Newsearch [online database]. Foster City, CA: Information Access Co. Current 45 days.

Online: DIALOG, file 211.

Newsearch, updated daily, indexes the most current articles and wire stories from over 1,700 newspapers, wire services, magazines, business publications, and computer and legal periodicals. The file is limited to the most current two to six weeks of indexing. At midmonth, all records added to *Newsearch* during the previous month are removed from the file and form the basis for longer term archival files such as the *National Newspaper Index* (file 111).

National Newspaper Index [online database]. Foster City, CA: Information Access, .

Online: InfoTrac.

National Newspaper Index, updated monthly on the InfoTrac online service, is a source of abstracted information for newspapers. Entries cover articles, news reports, editorials, letters to the editor, obituaries, biographies, and reviews. Although this index abstracts fewer newspapers than *Newspaper Abstracts Ondisc* (see below), its strength lies in the fact that it provides coverage of five major newspapers for an extended period of time. For research focusing on the 1970s, this would be the most appropriate reference for this medium. For research that only dates back to 1985, *Newspaper Abstracts Ondisc* is the preferred resource since it comprises more information from a greater number of sources. Newspapers covered by *National Newspaper Index* include *Christian Science Monitor,* 1970–, *Los Angeles Times,* 1982–, *New York Times,* 1970–, *Wall Street Journal,* 1970–, *Washington Post,* 1982– and items transmitted over the PR Newswire.

New York Times Index. New York: New York Times, 1851–.

The printed *New York Times Index* indexes and summarizes the contents of the *New York Times* newspaper. Also provides abstracts of the significant news, editorial matter, and special features cited.

Newspaper Abstracts [online database]. Ann Arbor, MI: UMI Co. 1984–1988.

Newspaper Abstracts comprises indexes and abstracts of materials for 1984–88 from regional, national, and international major newspapers.

Newspaper Abstracts Ondisc [CD-ROM]. Ann Arbor, MI: University Microfilms International, 1985–.

Newspaper Abstracts Ondisc is updated monthly and is searchable by subject, companies/organizations, names, authors/reviewers, sources, geographic places, products, article type, and keywords/basic index. It comprises abstracts and indexing of nine major newspapers for the following types of articles: international, national, regional, state, and local news; business, financial, and economic articles; editorials, op-ed columns, and editorial cartoons; letters to the editor from prominent people; obituaries of prominent people; reviews of books, plays, movies, restaurants, and performances; special series and supplements; and, sports as news features, profiles, or results of big events. Newspapers indexed include *New York Times,* 1985–, *Wall Street Journal,* 1985–, *Washington Post,* 1989–, *Christian Science Monitor,* 1985–, *Los Angeles Times,* 1985–, *Chicago Tribune,* 1985–, *Boston Globe,* 1985–, *Atlanta Constitution,* 1985–, *USA Today,* 1985–, and selected commentary from *Atlanta Journal,* 1889–.

The next title, *Facts on File,* is a little different from the other abstracting sources mentioned in this section. While the others summarize news events and provide references to the sources, *Facts on File* provides summaries without references to specific sources. It is frequently used as a reference source for basic information about an event rather than for thorough coverage and additional resources.

Facts on File. New York: Facts on File, 1940–.

CD-ROM: as *Facts on File News Digest CD-ROM* (coverage begins with 1980).

Online: LEXIS-NEXIS; CARL Systems Network; as *Facts on File World News Digest* (coverage begins with 1975).

> All three versions of this publication provide summaries of news events from throughout the world. Topics covered include politics, foreign affairs, government, business, the economy, arts, sports, and medicine. Its sources include U.S. and foreign newspapers and periodicals, as well as Commerce Clearing House and Congressional Quarterly publications, presidential documents, and official press releases.
>
> *Facts on File,* the printed version, is published in 52 weekly issues and four quarterly indexes. See exhibit 5-12 for a summary of "Whitewater" events for the week of July 13, 1995, from the print version. With electronic versions, searching is available by date, index topic, keyword, and with Boolean logic. The CD-ROM is updated annually and the online version, weekly.

Full-Text Newspaper Sources

"Ecola's Newsstand." http://www.ecola.com/news/press/ (April 7, 1997).

> "Ecola's Newsstand" is a World Wide Web site that provides access to hundreds of newspapers and magazines throughout the world. For U.S. newspapers, it allows you to browse state by state for newspaper sites and includes links to alternative and business news sources.

KROnDisc [CD-ROM]. Knight-Ridder Information, n.d.

> The Knight-Ridder Information company offers full-text versions of many DIALOG and DataStar newspaper databases on CD-ROM. Dates of data coverage, frequency of updates, and prices vary. All are easy to use and offer a range of search options.

NewsBank/Readex [CD-ROM]. NewsBank CD-News Company, n.d.

> This CD-ROM covers 50 individual newspapers and 3 types of regional compilations. The regional compilations are a composite of 7 full-text newspapers from a particular state or region specified by the subscriber. There is also a nationwide compilation covering the *Atlanta Journal, Atlanta Constitution, Boston Globe, Chicago Tribune, Dallas Morning News, Los Angeles Times, Washington Post,* and *Christian Science Monitor.*

Full-Text Online Services for Newspapers

Carl Systems Network. The CARL Systems Network is strictly a vender—it does not publish any databases on its own. It does provide access to the *National Newspaper Index,* and *Facts On File World News Digest.*

DataTimes Corporation. DataTimes is a comprehensive database that provides access to 120–130 full-text newspapers. You may search all of the newspapers simultaneously by author, title, subject, or keyword for free. This search will produce a list of article headlines, dates of publication, and sources. One drawback to this method is that you must select articles for viewing based upon headline alone—an abstract would be of much greater benefit. This is especially true given the number of newspapers available.

DIALOG Online Information Retrieval Service. DIALOG (Knight-Ridder) provides access to the full text of news stories, editorials, features, letters to the editor, columns and wire stories from 61 state, regional, and national newspapers. Refer to DIALOG's printed catalog (see page 77) for a complete list. Full-text searching is time consuming and thus costly. Each of the 61 newspapers identified has a corresponding file number, and DIALOG allows you to search up to 40 files simultaneously.

Dow Jones Text Library. The Dow Jones Text Library is a full-text source of national, international, and business news. Newspaper sources include *Barron's,* the *Wall Street Journal,* and *Washington Post.* Additional information is compiled from the Dow Jones News Files (selected articles from *Barron's, Wall Street Journal,* and the Dow Jones News Service ["Broadtape"]); the Business Library (complete text of 200 business periodicals and the PR Newswire and the McGraw-Hill Library (complete text of business journals published by McGraw-Hill). Coverage is from 1984 to the present, focusing primarily on the United States and Canada, as well as some international news. A command version (TEXT) as well as a menu version (TEXM) are available to facilitate searching.

NEXIS News Sources. The NEXIS library is another voluminous source of newspaper information. It contains abstracted and full-text information from over 160 newspapers, for many as far back as the mid-1980s. Searches may be conducted by specifying keyword, headline, or author. Searches may be conducted on the entire collection of newspapers simultaneously for a higher fee, or specific files may be searched individually. After identifying an article, you can

tration in the so-called Whitewater affair. [See pp. 499B1, 411D1]

Brown's attorney, Reid Weingarten, July 6 said he was pleased by the selection of Pearson, whom he called "scholarly, experienced and fair." But he reiterated his client's claim of innocence and charged that the accusations against Brown were "politically inspired." ∎

Whitewater Affair

Clinton Ally Hubbell Sentenced. U.S. District Judge George Howard Jr. in Little Rock, Ark. June 28 sentenced Webster L. Hubbell, a former high-ranking Justice Department official and long-time confidant of President Clinton's, to 21 months in prison for tax evasion and mail fraud. Hubbell in December 1994 had pleaded guilty to charges stemming from his fraudulent billing of personal expenses to his clients at Little Rock's Rose Law Firm, where he and Hillary Rodham Clinton had been senior partners. [See p. 211C1; 1994, p. 914E1]

Howard also sentenced Hubbell to three years' probation and community service upon his release from prison and ordered him to pay $135,000 in restitution to the parties he had defrauded.

Hubbell, 47, was the most prominent person thus far to be convicted as a result of the federal inquiry into the so-called Whitewater affair, the tangle of real-estate and financial dealings involving the Clintons.

Hubbell had been a top adviser to Clinton during the 1980s, when Clinton was governor of Arkansas, and he had served briefly as chief justice of the state's Supreme Court. He had gone on to hold the third-highest ranking post in the U.S. Justice Department, as associate attorney general in President Clinton's administration. Hubbell resigned that post in March 1994 amid controversy over his billing practices at the Rose firm.

At Hubbell's sentencing hearing, prosecutors and Hubbell's attorneys submitted documents showing that Hubbell had defrauded the Rose firm and about 15 clients out of a total of $482,410 between 1989 and 1992. By failing to report the embezzled money as income, Hubbell had avoided paying $143,747 in taxes, court records showed.

In an emotional statement at the hearing, Hubbell conceded that he had knowingly broken the law after becoming "overwhelmed" by personal debts. "This is not the man I want my children to love and admire," he said of himself.

Probe Cooperation Preceded Sentence— Hubbell's 21-month prison term was the minimum sentence allowed by federal guidelines. Kenneth W. Starr, the independent counsel investigating the Whitewater case, had deferred Hubbell's sentencing so that Hubbell could cooperate with his inquiry.

Sentences in plea-bargain cases commonly were reduced if the defendant provided useful information to investigators. Although Hubbell reportedly had pro-

vided Starr's team with more than 100 hours of testimony, Starr did not petition Judge Howard to reduce Hubbell's sentence. ∎

Land Venture Report Boosts Clintons. A confidential study commissioned by federal regulators had found evidence to support claims by President Clinton and First Lady Hillary Rodham Clinton that they had been only passive investors in the Whitewater Development Corp. real-estate venture, it was reported June 26. The study reportedly had found that the couple had "little direct involvement" in legally questionable transactions in the 1980s that were related to the venture. [See p. 210F2; 1994, p. 277C3]

The report had been prepared for the Resolution Trust Corp. by the Washington, D.C. law firm of Pillsbury, Madison & Sutro. The overseer of the inquiry was Jay B. Stephens, a former Republican federal prosecutor and vocal critic of President Clinton whose hiring for the study by the RTC in February 1994 had prompted objections from the White House. [See 1994, p. 228A1]

Among the primary issues being examined by investigators in the so-called Whitewater affair was the relationship between the real-estate enterprise and the now-defunct Madison Guaranty Savings & Loan thrift institution. James B. McDougal, Madison's owner, had also been the Clintons' partner in the Whitewater venture. The RTC and independent counsel Kenneth W. Starr had been seeking to determine whether McDougal or the Clintons had contributed to Madison's 1989 collapse by illegally diverting funds to the Whitewater concern.

Stephens's investigation reportedly had found that about $58,000 of the money that McDougal invested and eventually lost in the Whitewater venture could be traced to the assets of the Madison thrift. Stephens had been unable to determine whether those transfers by McDougal had been illegal. His inquiry had found no evidence that the Clintons knew about any of the Madison–Whitewater transactions.

The RTC report supported the president's assertion that he had been only tangentially involved with running the real-estate venture. The study noted that Hillary Clinton in the late 1980s had taken a more active role that included settling the enterprise's tax affairs and selling off some lands, but it did not implicate her in any financial misdealings.

The study concluded that the Clintons between 1978 and 1990 had lost about $42,000 on their Whitewater investment, slightly less than the $46,635 loss they had reported to the public in March 1994. [See 1994, p. 227C2]

The Clintons' attorney, David Kendall, June 27 said that the RTC report effectively upheld his clients' long-standing account of their Whitewater involvement. Republicans questioned how the Clintons could have been ignorant of key transactions involving what had been for them a large financial investment. ∎

Prosecution Rests in O. J. Simpson Murder Trial

Glove Fit Test Seen as Gaffe. The prosecution in the double murder trial of former football star O. J. Simpson rested its case July 6. Simpson was charged with two counts of first-degree murder stemming from the June 1994 fatal stabbings of his ex-wife, Nicole Brown Simpson, and a male friend of hers, Ronald Goldman. The prosecution's case had featured 92 days of testimony, 58 witnesses and 488 exhibits. [See below, p. 226G2]

Nicole Simpson and Goldman had been killed June 12, 1994 outside the doorway of Nicole Simpson's condominium in the wealthy Brentwood section of Los Angeles. There were no known witnesses to the murders, and police had not found a murder weapon. Both the victims were white; the suspect was black.

Since late March, the prosecution had presented voluminous genetic and physical evidence in an attempt to convince the jury of Simpson's guilt. The defense had tried to cast doubt on the evidence collected by authorities by suggesting that it had been tainted either by sloppy police work or by a conspiracy on the part of racist officers. Analysts said that the prosecution had committed its worst mistake in June when it had Simpson try on a pair of bloody gloves allegedly used by the killer. In a dramatic scene, Simpson seemed to have difficulty putting on the gloves. [See below]

The trial, which was being held in Los Angeles Superior Court, was presided over by Judge Lance Ito. Since the trial's January opening, Judge Ito had dismissed 10 jurors, leaving only two alternate panelists and raising the specter of a mistrial should the number of jurors fall below 12. [See below]

The current panel, which was sequestered, consisted of nine blacks, two whites and one Hispanic. Ten jurors were women, and two were men. The alternates were a black man and a black woman.

Judge Ito, who had been criticized for allowing the trial to drag on, in late April began issuing additional court orders designed to pick up the trial's pace and became less patient with the wrangling of the defense and prosecution.

*Evidence Disposal Suggested—*The prosecution March 29 suggested that Simpson might have dumped a duffel bag containing the murder weapon and bloody clothing in a Los Angeles International Airport trash can on the night of the murders. Simpson had flown to Chicago that evening. A search of the airport after the killing found no trace of the bag.

The limousine driver who drove O. J. Simpson to the airport testified March 28–29. The driver, Allan Park, said that he had helped Simpson load four bags into the limousine when he picked up the defendant at about 11:00 p.m. Park recalled seeing a fifth bag, a knapsack, in the driveway, although he never saw it loaded into the car. Park testified that

FACTS ON FILE. NEW YORK: FACTS ON FILE, INC., 1940-

EXHIBIT 5-12

browse it to see if it's relevant to your research. If you desire to print the full text of an article, there is a copying fee. You may browse an entire article, or you may select the NEXISQuick feature, which displays the 15 words before and after a specified keyword. Like DIALOG, you are not limited to searching all of the newspapers. You may specify which papers you would like to search, or you may use one of NEXIS's search categories which include "Major Papers," "Midwest Papers," "Northeast Papers," "Southeast Papers," or "West Papers." Four of these categories are geographically based; "Major Papers" are identified as those (approximately 40) in the top 25 in terms of dominant influence in an area and in the top 50 in terms of circulation.

Another tool that makes NEXIS very accessible to just about anyone is called NEXISExpress. In general most subscribers to NEXIS are large businesses, libraries, and schools. However, these institutions greatly restrict access due to the costs incurred. NEXISExpress is a service provided where nonsubscribers may call up, request a search, and, within 24 hours, receive the results via mail, fax, or e-mail.

OCLC. Like CARL, OCLC does not publish newspaper databases, but it does provide access to University Microform International's *Newspaper Abstracts* through the OCLC First Search Gateway Service. This database describes "significant items" in over 50 national and regional newspapers.

In terms of access to full text of newspapers, we would also like to mention some Internet service providers, such as CompuServe, America Online, Prodigy, and Orbit. America Online, Prodigy, and Orbit only provide access to information from one or two newspapers, but CompuServe, between the hours of 5 PM and 6 AM, allows access to *Knowledge Index*. *Knowledge Index* includes the *National Newspaper Index* and *Newsearch* (see page 113 above). Because *Knowledge Index* is a DIALOG publication, all the powerful DIALOG search options apply. Internet service providers are expanding their resources rapidly to keep pace with the popularity of online communication. It would be wise to consult one of them for your research.

NEWS SERVICES

News services provide 24-hour-a-day coverage of developing events. They are made up of a network of staff and freelance reporters who provide material for dissemination to subscribers. What makes news services unique is the fact that news is disseminated constantly, in contrast to standard media—newspapers, television, and radio—which provide news programs at regular intervals.

The Associated Press (AP). 50 Rockefeller Plaza, New York, NY. The Associated Press is the oldest and largest supplier of news in the United States and serves more than 15,000 newspaper and broadcast outlets in 115 countries around the world. AP works as a news cooperative and has access to news gathered by over 1,500 newspaper members and 6,000 radio or television members in the U.S. Being a cooperative means that AP not only has the news-gathering ability of its own staff but also that of its members, including ABC, NBC, CBS, CNN, 98 percent of all television stations with regular news broadcasts, and 51 percent of all radio stations. AP covers news stories of local interest, as well as national and international political, financial, and business news. Access to past stories can usually be obtained by researching an AP member publication or retrieving the information from an online service such as DIALOG or LEXIS-NEXIS. AP has recently started video coverage of some events and stories (APTV), which are for sale to broadcast media, and also maintains a radio news service for national and international news. The corporation itself does not maintain a library of past stories but many of the online services mentioned above are equipped to search for a particular piece.

CNN (Cable News Network)/Headline News. PO Box 105366, Atlanta, GA 30348, 404-827-1500. Created June 1980, cable television station CNN began with the ability to reach over 1.7 million cable viewers; currently it broadcasts to more than 63.4 million households. CNN maintains 29 news bureaus and covers stories broadcast in over 140 countries worldwide. CNN and CNNI (Cable News Network International) combined reach over 150 million households worldwide and can be viewed in over 210 countries 24 hours a day. The network was the first to provide Europe with 24-hour news coverage and provides such coverage now to Latin America, Africa, Asia, the Middle East, and the Indian subcontinent. Programming includes major news stories, special reports, business, medicine, finance, nutrition, science, sports, weather, and numerous other topics. CNN prides itself on live coverage of breaking events and national and international political events; it provides updates on many of these stories after the fact. CNN also broadcasts a radio signal of all its news programming, which is available to more than 500 radio stations nationwide. Transcripts are usually available for most programming. Contact the main or a local CNN office for details on a particular program.

C-SPAN/C-SPAN II (Cable Satellite Public Affairs Network). 400 North Capitol St., Suite 650, Washington, DC 20001, 202-737-3220. Created in 1979 by the emerging cable industry, cable television station C-SPAN seeks to provide live "gavel to gavel" coverage of the U.S. House of Representatives and, on C-SPAN II, the U.S. Senate. Events are broadcast live or on unedited tape to show the business of government in an unfiltered format. Other programming provided by C-SPAN includes viewer call-in programs featuring assorted federal policy makers or national public figures, coverage of political campaigns and rallies, coverage of federal and military court proceedings, and national and international coverage concerning public affairs. C-SPAN stresses a policy of providing 24-hour coverage of national political events without commentary, editorial influence, or bias. Its mission statement is to "provide elected and appointed officials and others who would influence public policy a direct conduit to the audience without filtering or otherwise distorting their point of view." Funding for C-SPAN is provided by fees charged to local cable station affiliates—no public funding is provided. C-SPAN offers several online services available through Internet service providers such as America Online and Prodigy.

General e-mail can be sent to viewer@c-span.org or cspanprogm@aol.com. Copies of previously run programming is available on videotape for a fee of $35 an hour through C-SPAN's Viewer Services department. C-SPAN broadcasts are also available on radio in particular areas.

Network News Services. All three popular entertainment networks in the U.S. maintain numerous affiliates and regional offices.

ABC (American Broadcasting Company). 77 W. 66th St., New York, NY 10023, 212-456-7777.

CBS (Columbia Broadcasting System). 51 W. 52nd St., New York, NY 10019, 212-975-4321.

NBC (National Broadcasting Company). 30 Rockefeller Plaza, New York, NY 10112, 212-664-4444

These news services are not providers of 24-hour coverage, and no facilities exist for perusal of previously broadcast stories through the corporation. Transcripts for particular news stories may be available through private companies that maintain contracts with the corporation. Detailed information such as

specific subject and date and time of broadcast would be needed, and the corporations themselves claim not to be equipped to assist in the researching of any information on past coverage. These companies do not appear to be a good source of information and do not maintain a library of previously aired material that would be accessible for academic use.

National Public Radio (NPR). 2025 M St., NW, Washington, DC 20036, 202-822-2000. National Public Radio is a supplier of radio programs to its more than 500 member stations nationwide. Based in Washington, DC, NPR has news bureaus in Chicago, New York, Los Angeles, London, and Moscow, and reporters in 15 other foreign locations. News coverage consists of national and international news programs provided to member stations by NPR, as well as local news programs produced by the individual stations in the different localities. A total of 35 newscasts are provided daily to member stations. Funding for NPR comes mainly from membership dues, grants, and sales of stock. Availability of transcripts to particular shows depends on ownership of production rights. Some transcripts are available and information on them can be received from the main office.

New York Times News Service. 229 W. 43rd St., New York, NY 10036. The *New York Times* is proud of its claim as the "newspaper of record" and is probably one of the most widely quoted sources of published information in existence. The *New York Times* maintains an index of its past publications, and many libraries make this index available to their patrons. The *Times* has been keeping this index since 1862 and in the 1960s acquired the Microfilming Corporation of America, which now makes the *Times* available from its first issue in 1851 to the present. The *Times* is a member of numerous wire services and maintains *stringers* throughout the world. The *Times* also provides its own stories via wire service to over 600 newspapers worldwide. It claims a readership of 7 to 8 million people, and the morning circulation alone tops over 1.2 million readers. The *Times* is probably one of the easiest research sources to access and can be found on numerous online services.

Reuters News Service. 1700 Broadway, New York, NY 10019, 212-603-3300; 1333 H Street NW, Suite 410, Washington, DC 20005, 212-898-8300. Reuters maintains a reputation as an international information source with bureaus across the globe in Europe, Asia, Africa, the Americas, and the Indian subcontinent. The company maintains over 100 bureaus worldwide and employs over 1,000 journalists and photographers to gather information. The coverage includes national, regional, and international political news, as well as specialized news services for banking and finance, shipping, petroleum products, and other business ventures. While Reuters delivers primarily coverage of events to other countries, it is currently trying to expand into local markets. Their services are now used by 32 of the top 50 daily newspapers in the U.S., and much of what is available on their wire services can be reached via online companies such as DIALOG and LEXIS-NEXIS.

United Press International (UPI). 1400 I St., NW, Suite 800, Washington, DC 20005, 202-898-8000. UPI was at the brink of bankruptcy in 1992 and, as a result, is dramatically scaled back from what it once was. It primarily maintains a wire service and radio network covering national and international news, some financial news, and Washington DC–based stories. The UPI wire service can be found on numerous online services, and its stories run in many of the most common daily newspapers.

REPRINTS OF SEMINAL ARTICLES

In addition to the ability to gain access to journal articles through the indexes and abstracting tools mentioned in this chapter, many publishers and enterprising individuals compile articles on specific topics taken from standard periodical sources and republish them in the form of a monograph. Such publications can be very useful in locating periodical articles on specialized topics, and some libraries purchase them to fill gaps in subject areas that may not be fully covered by their periodical collections.

These are the kinds of sources that you are likely to find by accident when searching your library catalog. If all the articles were taken from the same journal, you might search the title of the journal to locate the compilation. Many, however, draw their articles from a number of different journals. In that case, a subject search of the catalog is your only option.

The following two sources are significant because each reproduces noteworthy articles from major journals and reprints them as they appeared originally. The series by Dartmouth Publishing is ongoing, and you should look for forthcoming titles of interest because several more volumes are currently in progress.

The International Library of Criminology, Criminal Justice and Penology. Brookfield, VT: Dartmouth, 1994–.

> *The International Library* reprints important articles in contemporary criminology, criminal justice, and penology. Each volume is edited by an authority in the field and begins with an introductory essay on the subject. Titles in the series include *Drugs, Crime and Criminal Justice; Professional Criminals; Gender, Crime and Feminism; White-Collar Crime; Sex Crimes; Organized Crime;* and *Victimology.* This series is ongoing and should be consulted for classic essays on given topics.

McShane, Marilyn D., and Franklin P. Williams, III, eds. *Criminal Justice.* New York: Garland, 1997.

> A six-volume series includes published articles from 1991–1995 arranged according to the following topics: "Law Enforcement Operations and Management," "Drug Use and Drug Policy," "Criminological Theory," "The Philosophy and Practice of Corrections," "The American Court System," and "Victims of Crime and the Victimization Process." Articles were selected by the editors and a board of experts in each subject area and were selected for their excellence and contribution to the field.

Monkkonen, Eric H., ed. *Crime and Justice in American History: Historical Articles on the Origins and Evolution of American Criminal Justice.* 11 vols. Munich; London: K. G. Saur, 1992.

> This 11-volume series includes reprints of historical articles arranged into the following sections: "The Colonies and Early Republic"; "Courts and Criminal Procedure"; "Delinquency and Disorderly Behavior"; "The Frontier"; "Policing and Crime Control"; "Prisons and Jails"; "The South"; "Prostitution, Drugs, Gambling and Organized Crime"; "Violence and Theft"; "Reform"; and "Theory and Methods in Criminal Justice History."

Chapter 6
Statistical Sources

Statistics related to criminal justice cover a wide variety of topics beyond crime statistics alone. They may include statistics concerning health, environmental pollution, occupational safety, and population—for instance, age and geographic distribution—because certain types of crime are related to these factors.

Statistics also come in different varieties, and the utility of each depends on what you are looking for. *Compendia* of statistics are useful if you are looking for a statistic on a particular topic, such as the murder rate in Texas in 1972. However, if you are looking for statistics that provide more detailed information, such as trends in crime as related to other factors, you may wish to turn to *datasets,* sets of data that have been used by past researchers. These, however, usually require a level of skill beyond that of the lay user.

As a solution to this problem of accessibility, more and more Web sites offer formatted versions of datasets so the layperson can read them— i.e., statistics are set into columns as in compendiums of statistics. Some Web sites now allow you to download files (such as those with *.pdf* extensions) to your personal computer in formats that will print out on a laser printer looking exactly like a page from a book.

Both compendia and sources for dataset archives are included in this chapter. It should also be noted that many government sources make electronic as well as printed statistics available to the public. Many government Web sites can be found easily using a World Wide Web search engine. In addition, most of the major statistical sites mentioned in this chapter provide links to other statistical sites; therefore, once one has found one major site, it is usually easy to find others.

INDEXES TO STATISTICAL SOURCES

> Library of Congress subject headings: Statistics—Bibliography; Statistics—Indexes—Periodicals; United States—Statistics—Indexes; United States—Statistical services

Indexes to statistical sources can tell you exactly which source is most likely to contain the information you need. Therefore, you should begin your quest for statistical information with the statistical indexes listed below. Each source recommended has a standard of excellence and will serve you well. These sources not only can lead a researcher to criminal justice statistical sources, but they also can prove invaluable for locating related statistical information, e.g., employment data, economic data, and educational data. Data not specific to criminal justice can, nonetheless, enhance a report or paper with interesting and relevant data.

Balachandran, M., and S. Balachandran, eds. *State and Local Statistics Sources: A Subject Guide to Statistical Data on States, Cities, and Locales.* 2d ed. Detroit, MI: Gale Research, 1990/91–.

> Updated biennially, *State and Local Statistics* offers more than 60,000 references to statistical sources for state, county, city, and local data. Individual chapters cover each of the 50 states, as well as the District of Columbia, Guam, Puerto Rico, and the Virgin Islands. Chapters are divided into subject headings, and appendixes include (1) a listing of nonprint sources of state and local data and (2) an alphabetical, descriptive listing of all data sources used.

Index to Current Urban Documents. Westport, CT: Greenwood Press, 1972–.

> Primarily covering larger cities and counties in the U.S., *Current Urban Documents* is a tool for locating specific criminal justice statistical sources, e.g., city reports, for city and county jurisdictions. It is published quarterly, with annual and biennial cumulations. Documents noted in this source are available in Greenwood Press's *Urban Documents Microfiche Collection.*

Monthly Catalog of United States Government Publications. Washington, DC: U.S. Government Printing Office, 1895–.

> The *Monthly Catalog* is a good source for locating the numerous statistical publications of the U.S. government. Start with the subject index and check under relevant criminal justice headings, e.g., crime and criminals, criminal statistics, parole, and probation. (See page 149 for a fuller description of this source.)

Wasserman O'Brien, J., and S. Wasserman. *Statistics Sources 1995: A Subject Guide to Data on Industrial, Business, Social, Educational, Financial and Other Topics for the United States and Internationally.* Detroit: Gale Research, 1995.

> *Statistics Sources* is an excellent guide to current sources of factual, quantitative information on more than 20,000 subjects. Approximately 95,000 references from over 2,000 sources lead researchers to a variety of print, nonprint, published, unpublished, and other U.S. and international statistics.
>
> The main section consists of entries on general subjects and political entities, including states and individual countries, arranged together alphabetically. Under each of these headings, sources of statistical information are listed alphabetically by issuing organization. For political entries, two key types of references are immediately provided: the first is for the national statistical office if one exists; the second is for the country's major printed sources of statistics. Following these, references are arranged by subject, enabling the researcher to pinpoint sources by subject for each country. For example, under the entry titled "Australia" there are subsections titled "Crime and Criminal Research," each of which is followed by a list of alphabetically arranged sources.

Three sections precede the main section. A bibliography provides an annotated guide to a selected group of general statistical compendia and related works, and it includes dictionaries of terms, almanacs, census publications, periodical sources, and guides to machine-readable and online sources. Both governmental and nongovernmental sources are listed, and the availability of online database or machine-readable forms is noted.

The "Telephone Contact" section provides the names and telephone numbers of individuals and agencies within the U.S. federal government with expertise in identifying the most current statistical data. Three pages of this section are devoted to the subject of crime.

The "Federal Statistical Data Bases" section identifies the most significant U.S. government statistical files available in machine-readable form, including tape, disc, and CD-ROM. This section is arranged by subject, identifies the issuing agency, and indicates how to obtain the file. Five pages are devoted to criminal justice topics comprising approximately 200 databases.

The following three publications form a triad of indispensable aids in locating statistical information. Also available together on a single CD-ROM, each is produced by the Congressional Information Services company and is similar in arrangement to the others. Once you become familiar with one of these sources, you can use the same search strategies with the other two.

Statistical Masterfile, ASI, SRI, & IIS on CD-ROM. Bethesda, MD: Congressional Information Services, n.d.

> This is the CD-ROM version of the following three publications. If available to the user, this source provides excellent access to the three publications in a handy format.

American Statistics Index. Bethesda, MD: Congressional Information Services, 1973–.

> The *American Statistics Index,* or *ASI,* is a comprehensive monthly abstracting and indexing publication covering thousands of statistical reports and publications prepared and issued by the U.S. government. This set is issued monthly, with quarterly, annual, and five-year cumulations. Two volumes are issued each year, one *Abstracts* volume and one *Index* volume. The *Abstracts* volume, arranged by issuing agency, contains concise, descriptive abstracts of statistical sources. Since most criminal justice statistics are issued by the U.S. Department of Justice, you may turn directly to this issuing agency in the *Abstracts* volume. To discover other agencies that also issue reports of interest, use the *Index* volume, which provides excellent access by subject, name, category (e.g., sex, age, or geographic area), title, and report number. As with the other volumes in this triad, most reports referred to in this publication are also available in a companion microfiche set. Available on CD-ROM as part of *Statistical Masterfile* (see above). Also available online via DIALOG, file 102.

Index to International Statistics. Washington, DC: Congressional Information Services, 1983–.

> The *Index to International Statistics,* or *IIS,* is a comprehensive abstracting and indexing publication covering English-language statistical information published by international organizations such as the United Nations, the Organization of American States, and approximately 100 other important intergovernmental agencies. Of particular interest to the criminal justice user are the social statistics, but economic, demographic, and industrial data can be helpful as well. The *Index* volume is arranged by subject, name, geographic area, issuing agency, and category (e.g., industry). *IIS* is published monthly, with quarterly, annual, and five-year cumulations. Available on CD-ROM as part of *Statistical Masterfile* (see above).

Statistical Reference Index. Bethesda, MD: Congressional Information Services, 1980–.

> The *Statistical Reference Index,* or *SRI,* is designed to provide a reliable, centralized way to access the large body of business, financial, and social statistical data produced each year by thousands of private U.S. organizations and state government agencies. (U.S. federal organizations are covered in the *ASI* listed above.)
>
> The *SRI* surveys and reviews current statistical publications issued by major U.S. associations and institutions, business organizations, commercial publishers, independent research centers, state government agencies, and universities. It then identifies current publications containing substantial statistical material of general research value.
>
> Publications in which data appear are cataloged, and full bibliographic data and availability information are provided for each entry. Full descriptions of the contents of the publications are given, and the information is indexed by subject, category, issuing source, and title.
>
> Criteria for data selection are based on the objective of covering a wide array of data publishing organizations and subject matter. Emphasis is placed on coverage of currently published sources of statistics and on continuing time series data. Priority is also given to maintaining coverage of basic social, governmental, economic, and demographic data for each of the 50 states and the District of Columbia. Geographic coverage includes national, statewide, foreign, and local data.
>
> Use of the *SRI* is fairly simple. Consult the user guide in the forward of the *Index* volume. The guide provides a step-by-step procedure to utilize this source.
>
> The abstracts provided in *SRI* are based on examination of the entire document. They differ in the degree of detail depending on the type of publication and the kind of data being described. The objective of the abstract is to describe a source fully enough to allow the researcher to determine if the publication is likely to contain the data he or she seeks. The abstract further allows the user to determine how the contents of the publication are organized and provides bibliographic data and availability information. The *SRI* includes printed abstracts and indexes and a companion microfiche collection of source data. The *SRI* is published monthly, with annual cumulations.

Another source for this type of information is *Who Knows What: A Guide to Experts* (Washington, DC: Washington Researchers). This annual publication lists government experts by subject areas and department.

GENERAL STATISTICAL SOURCES

> Library of Congress subject headings: United States—Statistics; Local government—Statistics; Cities and towns—United States—Statistics; Statistics—Indexes—Periodicals; Reference books—Statistics—Indexes; Statistics—Tables—Indexes

County and City Extra: Annual Metro, City, and County Data Book. Lanham, MD: Bernan Press, 1992–.

> This annual publication augments the *County and City Data Book.* Data collected by government and private agencies are presented for every county, state, city, and metropolitan area in the United States. The *Extra* is also available on CD-ROM as *County and City Plus.* A companion volume is *Places, Towns, and Townships.*

County and City Compendium [CD-ROM]. Washington, DC: Slater Hall Information Products.

> A CD-ROM version of *County and City Extra,* containing additional county data. Published annually.

"New York State Division of Criminal Justice Services." http://criminaljustice.state.ny.us (April 7, 1997).

> State agencies are now providing statistical and other information on their World Wide Web sites. The Division of Criminal Justice Services of New York State offers searchable data on missing children as well as various criminal justice data at the regional and county level for New York State.

Reddy, Marlita, ed. *Statistical Abstract of the World.* Detroit, Gale Research, 1994.

> The first edition of this reference source covers a wide range of topics, including labor, employment, income, and law enforcement statistics from nearly 200 countries.

Slater, Courtenay M., and George E. Hall, eds. *Places, Towns, and Townships.* Lanham, MD: Bernan Press, 1992–.

> Using a variety of census data from 1987 and 1990, this provides statistical information for many smaller geographical areas in the United States. It consists primarily of two tables: the first for places with a population of 10,000, and the second for smaller areas with a population under 10,000. Subjects covered include population, race, age, income, poverty, education, and employment.

U.S. Bureau of the Census. *County and City Data Book.* Washington, DC: U.S. Bureau of the Census, 1947–.

> Published every five years, the *County and City Data Book* provides demographic, economic, and government data

for counties, cities, and towns of 2,500 population or greater. This source is also available via the Census Bureau's Web server (http://www.census.gov/stat_abstract/ ccdb.html [June 4, 1997]) and on CD-ROM (US.GPO).

U.S. Bureau of the Census. *Historical Statistics of the United States: Colonial Times to 1970.* 2 vols. Washington, DC: U.S. Bureau of the Census, 1975.

Historical Statistics is the major source of historical data for the United States, compiling data from annual series from colonial times to 1970. The "Crime and Corrections" subsection in the general "Social Statistics" section provides data on crime and crime rates (1967–1970), urban crime (1937–1957), homicide and suicide (1900–1970), police officers killed (1945–1970), persons arrested (1932–1970), criminal justice expenditures (1902–1970), and persons lynched (1882–1970).

U.S.Bureau of the Census. *State and Metropolitan Area Data Book.* Washington, DC: U.S. Bureau of the Census, 1979–.

Provides current and historical statistics for states and standard metropolitan areas (SMAs) on population, crime, education, employment, and housing, for instance. It is also available online through CENDATA but is published irregularly.

U.S. Bureau of the Census. *Statistical Abstract of the United States.* Washington, DC: U.S. Bureau of the Census, 1879–.

U.S. Bureau of the Census. "Statistical Abstract of the United States." http://www.census.gov:80/ stat_abstract/

Published annually since 1897, the *Statistical Abstract of the United States* is probably the most widely available and regularly used source of statistical data from U.S. government sources and includes some data collected by private organizations as well. The section entitled "Law Enforcement, Courts, and Prisons" provides specific data on crimes committed, victims of crimes, arrests, criminal violations, and the criminal justice system and general data on social, economic, and political issues. Original sources are noted for data tables, thus this source acts as an index to more comprehensive statistical sources. Also available on CD-ROM (U.S. GPO) and the World Wide Web (www.census.gov/stat_abstract [June 6, 1997]. The Web version provides only selected statistics.)

U.S. Bureau of the Census. *USA Counties.* [CD-ROM]. Washington, DC: U.S. Bureau of the Census, Data User Services Division, 1994.

USA Counties gives demographic, economic, and governmental data for 1969–1990. This latest edition includes some 2,080 items.

A growing number of statistical sources can also be found on the Internet. One of the values of the World Wide Web in particular is that some Web sites offer links to other sites with relevant information for the convenience of their users. It is a good idea to find and create bookmarks for sites that provide this kind of service. An example of such a site is that of the School of Criminal Justice at the University at Albany.

"School of Criminal Justice at the University at Albany."

http://www.albany.edu/scj/links.html#stats (April 11, 1997)

Below is a sample listing of the statistical links this site provides.

Bureau of Justice Statistics
CERN/ANU—Demography and Population Studies
Danish Data Archives (DDA)
Council of European Social Science Data Archives
GESIS Social Science Research Gopher
Home Office—Research and Statistics
National Archive of Criminal Justice Data
National Criminal Justice Reference Service
Norwegian Social Science Data Services (NSD)
Sourcebook of Criminal Justice Statistics
SSD's Home Page
Statistical Resources on the Web
Statistics Canada
University of Alberta, Data Library
The World Wide Web Virtual Library: Research Resources
The World Wide Web Virtual Library: Statistics

STATISTICAL SOURCES ON CRIME

Library of Congress subject headings: Corrections—United States—Statistics; Crime and criminals—United States—Statistics; Criminal statistics—United States—Periodicals; Criminal justice, administration of—United States—Statistics; Law enforcement—United States; Victims of crimes—United States—Periodicals; Subject heading—Statistics

Generally, the first place you look for criminal justice statistics is the FBI's *Uniform Crime Reports for the United States* (see entry below under U.S. Federal Bureau of Investigation), the most-often-used source for crime statistics. Although most other criminal justice statistics are published by the agencies of the U.S. Department of Justice (see description on page 143), the authors also provide fine sources below that present different perspectives, compilations of crime statistics, or foci on a particular issue. The publications noted in this section focus on nationwide statistics; most appear annually, and a few are of special interest. Remember that certain reports may be more difficult to locate but should not be overlooked because of the specialized information they contain.

Dobrin, Adam, Brian Wiersema, Colin Loftin, and David McDowall, eds. *Statistical Handbook on Violence in America.* Phoenix, AZ: Oryx Press, 1996.

> This statistical sourcebook provides information on violence in the U.S., using data from both published and unpublished sources. Chapter titles are "Fatal Violence in America," "Other Interpersonal Violence in America," "Groups and Situations," "Impact of Violence," and "Opinions about Violence."

Gall, Timothy L., Daniel M. Lucas, Peter C. Kratcoski, and Lucille Dunn Kratcoski, eds. *Statistics on Crime & Punishment.* Detroit: Gale, 1996.

> This includes a "selection of statistical charts, graphs and tables about crime and punishment from a variety of published sources with explanatory comments." Entries are arranged under two broad subject headings—crime and punishment—and numerous subheadings. For each entry, there is a suitable chart, graph, or table, followed by comments from the editors, the source for the statistics, and a contact agency for future information. A brief glossary and geographical/subject index are included.

Garoogian, Rhoda, and Andrew Garoogian, eds. *Crime in America's Top-Rated Cities: A Statistical Profile.* Boca Raton, FL: Universal Reference Publications, 1995/1996.

> The first edition of this companion volume to *America's Top-Rated Cities* focuses on the 75 American cities that are rated as the best places for business and living. It includes 20 years of statistics in all major crime categories, as well as statistics on illegal drugs, correctional facilities, inmates and HIV/AIDS, the death penalty, and gun laws. Easy-to-read tables compare numbers of crime and crime rates for the metropolitan area and suburbs.

Hollinger, Richard C. *National Retail Security Survey.* Gainesville, FL: Security Research Project, Department of Sociology, University of Florida, 1990–.

> This annual series focuses on retail loss-prevention and security activities. Its purpose is to determine the level of inventory shrinkage experienced by the retailing community—excluding restaurants, bars, vehicle dealers, auto service stations, and direct catalog sales. Numerous charts and graphs make this a highly usable data source.

Insurance Theft Report. Washington, DC: Highway Loss Data Institute, 1986–.

> Insurance companies supply the Highway Loss Data Institute with the information used to publish this series of reports on passenger vehicle thefts, which began publication in 1986. Information includes overall theft losses by vehicle type and body style, vehicles with the best and worst theft losses, theft losses by calendar period, insurance losses and theft coverage for yearly models, and overall theft losses for recent years.

O'Leary Morgan, Kathleen, Scott Morgan, and Neal Quitno, eds. *City Crime Rankings: Crime in Metropolitan America.* Lawrence, KS: Morgan Quitno, 1995–.

> Using statistics derived from *Crime in the United States*, *City Crime Rankings* presents key crime data as of 1993 for 274 U.S. metropolitan areas and the 100 largest cities in an easy-to-use format. This reference tool is organized into three sections: part 1 reports crime statistics for metropolitan areas, part 2 reports crime statistics and police data for the 100 target U.S. cities, and part 3 consists of appendixes that provide population tables for cities and metro areas as well as cross-reference tools that describe which cities and counties make up specific metropolitan areas.

O'Leary Morgan, Kathleen, Scott Morgan, and Neal Quitno. *Crime State Rankings: Crime in the 50 United States.* Lawrence, KS: Morgan Quitno, 1994–.

> *Crime State Rankings* "reports state crime information and rankings on juvenile and adult arrests, corrections, law enforcement personnel and expenditures, offenses, crime clearances, courts, and drug and alcohol prevention and treatment programs." The 1996 edition contains 502 tables presented in two ways: alphabetically and rank order, from highest to lowest. Includes a subject index.

U.S. Arson Trends and Patterns. Quincy, MA: National Fire Protection Association, 1986–.

> *U.S. Arson Trends and Patterns* presents annual data on incendiary and suspicious fires for a given year. Sections include information on structure fires, vehicle fires, outdoor fires, arson and suspected arson structure fires by community size, criminal justice aspects of arson (clearances and arrests, convictions, sentences, and motives of offenders), arson and suspected arson by property type and area of origin, arson as a weapon of gangs and drug rings, and myths of arson.

U.S. Federal Bureau of Investigation. *Uniform Crime Reports for the United States: Crime in the United States.* Washington, DC: U.S. Federal Bureau of Investigation, 1930–.

U.S. Federal Bureau of Investigation. **"Uniform Crime Reports for the United States: Crime in the United States."** http://www.fbi.gov/publish.htm (April 7, 1997).

> The FBI's *Uniform Crime Reports* (*UCR*), updated annually with a mid-year update, is based solely on crimes reported to the police. *UCR* reports "index crimes" in part 1 (also called "part 1 offenses" by the publication), which is subdivided into two categories: violent personal crimes (murder, rape, robbery, and aggravated assaults) and prop-

erty crimes (burglary, larceny, motor vehicle theft, and arson). Information regarding these crimes is given for the United States as a whole; geographic divisions; states; metropolitan statistical areas (MSAs); cities, towns, and counties; and college and university campuses.

In addition to reported crime data, *UCR* also furnishes data on all arrests, except for traffic violations, by age, sex, and race of arrestee according to crime category. Useful tables include city arrest trends, suburban county arrests, arrests by state, and police disposition of juvenile offenders taken into custody. Another section gives valuable statistics on numbers of law enforcement employees, including sworn personnel, civilian employees, and law enforcement officers killed and assaulted.

UCR has recently undergone a number of significant changes; for instance, a number of "index offenses" have been redefined as "incident driven." Such offenses are now reported by the National Incident-Based Reporting System (NIBRS), which is designed to "collect data on each single incident and arrest within 22 crime categories." This redefinition was adopted to provide greater detail in reporting. *UCR* is also now available on the World Wide Web as listed above.

As stated earlier, many of the statistical sources in criminal justice are produced by the U.S. Bureau of Justice Statistics (BJS), which is a bureau of the U.S. Department of Justice. While most of these reports are issued annually with the same title each year, BJS also publishes series which address specific issues, present shortened versions of fuller annual reports, or summarize research reports funded by the federal government. Some of these series are titled *Bureau of Justice Statistics Bulletin, Research in Action, Juvenile Justice Bulletin, OJJDP Update on Programs, Drugs and Crime Data—Factsheets, Bureau of Justice Statistics Special Reports, Program Focus Reports,* and *Crime Data Briefs.* Many of these statistical publications can be accessed via the Web site: http://www.ojp.usdoj.gov:/bjs/).

In addition, the U.S. Bureau of Justice Statistics uses the National Crime Victimization Survey (NCVS), begun in 1972, to complement the FBI's annual *Uniform Crime Reports.* The NCVS was designed to present a detailed picture of crime in the U.S. from the victim's perspective. Each year approximately 50,000 households with more than 100,000 individuals age 12 or older are surveyed regarding their recent experiences as victims of crime. The major difference between the NCVS and *UCR* is that the National Crime Victimization Survey includes unreported as well as reported crime. Specifically, it measures crime rates for selected personal crimes which involve direct contact between the victim and offender (e.g., rape, robbery, assault, and larceny) and

selected household crimes (e.g., burglary, larceny, and motor vehicle theft). The NCVS does not measure the following crimes: murder, kidnapping, commercial burglary and robbery, public drunkenness, drug abuse, prostitution, illegal gambling, con games, buying of stolen property, embezzlement, and blackmail.

As with *UCR*, there have been some major design changes in the NCVS. A new questionnaire has been developed to help respondents more accurately recall and report incidents. In addition, information on domestic violence and sexual crimes is now included. Publications from the Bureau of Justice Statistics that use data from the NCVS indicate such in the annotation text.

U.S. Bureau of Justice Statistics. *Compendium of Federal Justice Statistics.* Washington, DC: U.S. Department of Justice, Bureau of Justice Statistics, 1989–.

> Beginning with statistics from 1984, this annual report describes all phases of U.S. federal criminal processing during years covered. Data appear both in narrative-form tables on the prosecution, conviction, and incarceration of offenders. Data are obtained from operational agencies and are linked together on the basis of name, birth data, identifying numbers, and other personal identifiers.

U.S. Bureau of Justice Statistics. *Crime and the Nation's Households.* Washington, DC: U.S. Department of Justice, Bureau of Justice Statistics, 1975–.

> *Crime and the Nation's Households* reports annually on the households-touched-by-crime data derived from NCVS statistics. It offers information on households victimized by crime, including race and ethnicity of household, family income, household size, and place and region of residence. (Earlier editions in this series were entitled *Households Touched by Crime.*)

U.S. Bureau of Justice Statistics. *Criminal Victimization in the United States.* Washington, DC: U.S. Department of Justice, Bureau of Justice Statistics, 1974–.

U.S. Bureau of Justice Statistics. *Criminal Victimization in the United States: Trends.* Washington, DC: U.S. Department of Justice, Bureau of Justice Statistics, 1980–.

> These two sources comprise an annual report and a summary report based upon the annual, both in the NCVS series.

U.S. Bureau of Justice Statistics. *Highlights from 20 Years of Surveying Crime Victims: The National Crime Victimization Survey, 1973–92.* U.S. Department of Justice, Bureau of Justice Statistics, 1993.

Highlights, another summary report in the NCVS series, is a compendium of 20 years of victimization statistics.

U.S. Bureau of Justice Statistics. *Justice Expenditure and Employment.* Washington, DC: U.S. Department of Justice, Bureau of Justice Statistics, 1973–.

> *Justice Expenditure and Employment* presents detailed statistics on public expenditure and employment related to civil and criminal justice activity in the United States, including police protection, judicial activities, legal services and prosecution, public defense, corrections, and other costs. This publication first appears in a short version as part of the *Bureau of Justice Statistics Bulletin* series; the more detailed edition follows. Unfortunately, full report is generally several years behind; for instance, as of 1996, only a short version exists for 1992. The latest full edition is for 1988. (Previous title for this series was *Trends in Expenditure and Employment Data for the Criminal Justice System.*)

U.S. Bureau of Justice Statistics. *Report to the Nation on Crime and Justice.* 2d ed. Washington, DC: U.S. Department of Justice, Bureau of Justice Statistics, 1988.

> The second edition of *Report to the Nation* includes data from the NCVS, *Uniform Crime Reports,* the Bureau of the Census, the National Institute of Justice, the Office of Juvenile Justice and Delinquency Prevention, and other research and reference sources. Because it analyzes these and other data sources, this report serves the general public as well as criminal justice practitioners, researchers, and educators. Easy-to-read charts and graphs and a good subject index make this an effective reference aid.

U.S. Bureau of Justice Statistics. *Sourcebook of Criminal Justice Statistics.* Washington, DC: U.S. Bureau of Justice Statistics, 1973–.

U.S. Bureau of Justice Statistics. **"Sourcebook of Criminal Justice Statistics."** http://www.albany.edu/sourcebook/ (April 7, 1997).

> The *Sourcebook* is an invaluable source for criminal justice research; the field is fortunate to have such a resource. It is a collection of U.S. crime and criminal justice data published by hundreds of public and private agencies, academic institutions, public opinion polling firms, and other groups. Information is compiled from a variety of sources and is intended to be accessible to a wide audience. All data presented are nationwide in scope and where possible, displayed by region, state, and city, which is valuable for local decision making and comparative analyses. Criteria for data inclusion are soundness of methodology with respect to sampling procedures, data collection methods, estimation procedures, and reliability of information.
>
> The sourcebook is organized into six sections: "Characteristics of the Criminal Justice System," "Public Attitudes toward Crime and Criminal Justice Topics," "Nature and Distribution of Known Offenses," "Characteristics and Distribution of Persons Arrested," "Judicial Processing of Defendants," and "Persons under Correctional Supervision." Each of the sections opens with an overview of its contents. Tables and figures indicate source publications, and annotations include complete bibliographic information, frequency of publication, dates of tabular information, summary contents of publication, and a list of tables and figures selected for inclusion. Addresses of publishers follow annotations. Appendixes are included to add clarity or more information for more complex data presentation.
>
> The sourcebook attempts to provide the most recent data available and, when possible, compares them with earlier data to show trends. However, the publisher acknowledges that many reports are based on data published elsewhere and are, therefore, already several years old. The sourcebook is by nature somewhat out of date. To find out if more recent statistics exist for a given topic, ask your librarian whether a more current edition of the source of the data exists. A more recent edition should present you with more recent data. The only thing lacking from this source is a more substantial index.

U.S. Bureau of Justice Statistics. *State Justice Sourcebook of Statistics and Research.* Washington, DC: U.S. Department of Justice, Bureau of Justice Statistics, 1992.

> The *State Justice Sourcebook* is a useful reference on state jurisdictions and was designed to meet the needs of criminal justice practitioners, policy makers, and researchers at the federal, state, and local levels. The volume is divided into three sections. The first presents a profile of the criminal justice system of each state, beginning with an overview of the state system and continuing with information on law enforcement, prosecution and defense, victims' rights and assistance, adjudication, corrections, and statutory provisions. The second section recounts the mission and goal of each state's statistical analysis center. The third section is a directory of criminal justice issues and research in each state. An appendix provides the names and address of the directors and research contacts for each center.

U.S. Federal Bureau of Investigation. *Hate Crime Statistics.* Washington, DC: U.S. Federal Bureau of Investigation, 1990–.

> With the passage of the 1990 Hate Crime Statistics Act, states began reporting crimes motivated by hate and bias to the FBI for inclusion in this separate annual report. A preliminary release generally precedes a full version in this series. Hate crime statistics are now included in the *Uniform Crime Reports.*

STATISTICAL SOURCES ON CAPITAL PUNISHMENT

NAACP Legal Defense and Education Fund. *Death Row, U.S.A.* New York: NAACP Legal Defense and Education Fund, 1973–.

This quarterly publication gives a listing of the total number of known death row inmates; dispositions since January 1, 1973; jurisdictions with capital punishment statutes; jurisdictions without capital punishment statutes; capital cases before the U.S. Supreme Court; the total number of executions since 1976, including name of defendant, date of execution, state where executed, and race and gender of victim; and an execution breakdown by state.

National Criminal Justice Information and Statistics Service. *Capital Punishment.* Washington, DC: National Criminal Justice Information and Statistics Service, 1974–.

Streib, Victor L. *Capital Punishment of Female Offenders: Present Female Death Row Inmates and Death Sentences and Executions of Female Offenders.* Ada, OH: Ohio Northern University, Claude W. Pettit College of Law, 1988–.

The *Capital Punishment of Female Offenders* series documents more than 20 years of death penalty sentencing of female offenders under current U.S. death penalty statutes. Tables report death sentences imposed upon female offenders, 1973 to date; characteristics of offenders and victims in female death penalty cases; female death sentences imposed, by year, offender's name, race and state; and case summaries for current female death row inmates.

Streib, Victor L. *The Juvenile Death Penalty Today: Present Death Row Inmates under Juvenile Death Sentences and Death Sentences and Executions for Juvenile Crime.* Ada, OH: Ohio Northern University, Claude W. Pettit College of Law, 1986–.

This report, published irregularly, documents juvenile death sentencing under current U.S. death penalty statutes, reporting the number of juveniles executed since January 1, 1973, to the present; the legal context of juvenile death penalty statutes; states with minimum death penalty statutes; death sentences imposed for crimes committed as juveniles; and a state-by-state breakdown of juvenile death sentences. *The Juvenile Death Penalty Today* presents a very detailed picture of this unique population.

U.S. Bureau of Justice Statistics. *Capital Punishment.* Washington, DC: U.S. Department of Justice, Bureau of Justice Statistics, 1981–.

U.S. Bureau of Justice Statistics. *Correctional Populations in the United States.* Washington, DC: U.S. Department of Justice, Bureau of Justice Statistics, 1985–.

The *Capital Punishment* series began with statistics for 1971/1972 published by the National Criminal Justice Information and Statistics Service. It continues today in two forms, both published by the Bureau of Justice Statistics. One is an abbreviated version issued annually in the "Bulletin Series"; the other is the complete version but has a different title, *Correctional Populations in the United States.* The annual bulletin edition is generally more up to date.

STATISTICAL SOURCES ON CORRECTIONS

American Correctional Association. *Juvenile and Adult Correctional Departments, Institutions, Agencies, and Paroling Authorities, United States and Canada.* Lanham, MD: American Correctional Association, 1979–.

Although this annual source is primarily regarded as a directory for correctional agencies (in all 50 states, the District of Columbia, the Federal Bureau of Prisons, U.S. territories, military correctional facilities, Canada, New York City, Cook County [Chicago], and Philadelphia), it also includes summary statistics on personnel, fiscal expenditures, correctional populations, and capacity of institutions, as well as descriptive information on the various agencies and institutions. This title continues publication of the *Directory of Juvenile and Adult Correctional Departments, Institutions, Agencies, and Paroling Authorities.*

American Correctional Association. *National Jail and Adult Detention Directory.* Lanham, MD: American Correctional Association, 1979–.

Although primarily a directory, this source also provides meaningful information on correctional salaries, fiscal expenditures, physical plant characteristics, security staff, and the average daily population for jails and adult detention facilities. The most current edition is dated 1996–1998.

American Correctional Association. *Probation and Parole Directory.* Lanham, MD: American Correctional Association, 1981–.

The most current edition (1995–1997) of this directory includes information on probation and parole commissions, boards, and local offices plus state, district, and satellite offices. Entries are arranged by state, and after a brief narrative on parole and probation structures, state agencies are listed, followed by an alphabetical listing of all other providers. A typical entry includes the following information: address, programs and services, fiscal information, beginning salary ranges, personnel, and client caseload.

American Correctional Association. *Vital Statistics in Corrections.* Lanham, MD: American Correctional Association, 1979–.

This report is based on a salary survey of corrections professionals. Although its primary focus is on salary and personnel issues in both adult and juvenile facilities, it also includes information on correctional expenditures, correctional facilities, and correctional populations in both state and federal systems.

Cahalan, Margaret Werner. *Historical Corrections Statistics in the United States, 1850–1984.* Washington, DC: U.S. Department of Justice, Bureau of Justice Statistics, 1986.

Historical Corrections Statistics presents summary tables and commentary for published national government reports on corrections statistics for the U.S. from 1850 to 1984.

Center for Studies in Criminology and Law. *Private Adult Correctional Facility Census.* Gainesville, FL: Center for Studies in Criminology and Law, University of Florida, 1989–.

> The annually published *Private Census* presents data on privately managed correctional institutions in the United States, Australia, and the United Kingdom, such as the number of facilities, ownership of facilities, population, and security level.

Corrections Compendium. Lincoln, NE: CONTACT. 1976–.

> Each issue of this monthly periodical contains a survey of interest to corrections professionals. Recent surveys cover prison violence and escapes, inmate population projections, and prison construction.

Criminal Justice Institute. *Corrections Yearbook.* South Salem, NY: Criminal Justice Institute, 1981–.

> The *Corrections Yearbook* offers a concise picture of correctional data based on information collected by the Criminal Justice Institute. Detailed data on correctional populations, expenditures, and personnel, for example, are presented in summary form. Later editions of this compendium are issued is four separate pocket-sized volumes: *Probation and Parole, Jail Systems, Adult Corrections,* and *Juvenile Corrections.*

Langan, Patrick A., ed. *Race of Prisoners Admitted to State and Federal Institutions, 1926–1986,* Washington, DC: U.S. Department of Justice, Bureau of Justice Statistics, 1991.

> *Race of Prisoners* provides documentation on the racial composition of U.S. prisoners from 1926—the year the federal government began keeping detailed annual records on prison admissions—to 1986.

Langan, Patrick A., et al, eds. *Historical Statistics on Prisoners in State and Federal Institutions, Yearend 1925–86.* Washington, DC: U.S. Department of Justice, Bureau of Justice Statistics, 1988.

> This report brings together year-end prison population counts from annual published reports for 1925 through 1986. It shows the prison population of each state, the District of Columbia, and the federal government on December 31 for each year covered.

U.S. Bureau of the Census. *Prisoners in State and Federal Prisons and Reformatories 1926–.* Washington, DC: U.S. Bureau of the Census, 1929–1949.

> Based on voluntary reporting, this series provided data on inmates in state and federal correctional institutions, including the geographical distribution of prisoners and demographic characteristics of inmates. The series was discontinued in 1949 but was continued by a number of publications with similar titles, such as *Prisoners in State and Federal Institutions for Adult Felons, Prisoners in State and Federal Institutions, Correctional Populations in the United States,* and various bulletins issued by the Bureau of Justice Statistics.

U.S. Bureau of Justice Statistics. *Census of Local Jails.* Washington, DC: U.S. Department of Justice, Bureau of Justice Statistics, 1970–.

> The *Census of Local Jails* was first published in 1970, then in 1978, 1982, and 1983, and is currently updated every five years. The latest edition in the series, *Census of Local Jails: 1988,* consists of five volumes: a summary volume and four separate volumes, one for each geographical region in the United States (*Volume 2: The Northeast, Volume 3: The Midwest, Volume 4: The South,* and *Volume 5: The West*). Census information is given on jail detention authority; capacity; court orders; facility age and use of space; medical accommodations; facility programs, inmate sex, race, and conviction status; staff sex, race, and occupation; and expenditures. This census is also reported in annual bulletins issued by the Bureau of Justice Statistics.

U.S. Bureau of Justice Statistics. *Correctional Populations in the United States.* Washington, DC: U.S. Department of Justice, Bureau of Justice Statistics, 1985–.

> This annual source combines four previously separate publications that presented data on U.S. correctional populations: *Prisoners in State and Federal Institutions, Capital Punishment, Characteristics of Persons Entering Parole,* and *Parole in the United States.* It provides statistical information on persons under the supervision of various components of the correctional system: probation, parole, jail, prison, and capital punishment. Although some of these statistics are still issued in brief reports from the Bureau of Justice Statistics, this report emphasizes connections between these segments of the corrections system and is a handy one-volume compilation.

U.S. Bureau of Justice Statistics. *HIV in Prisons, 1994.* Washington, DC: U.S. Department of Justice, Bureau of Justice Statistics, 1996.

> A number of publications have been issued in this annual series addressing the issue of HIV and AIDS in the correctional population. This publication is represented in most library catalogs as a monograph whose titles vary slightly from year to year.

U.S. Bureau of Justice Statistics. *Jail Inmates.* Washington, DC: U.S. Department of Justice, Bureau of Justice Statistics, 1982–.

> Issued as part of the *Bureau of Justice Statistics Bulletin* series, *Jail Inmates* provides estimates of the nation's jail inmate population for the year of publication. This series is issued in the years between the nationwide jail census.

U.S. Bureau of Justice Statistics. *Probation and Parole.* Washington, DC: U.S. Department of Justice, Bureau of Justice Statistics, 1981–.

The National Probation and Parole Reporting program collects annual data on state and federal probation and parolee populations. The *Probation and Parole* series contained data from this program including numbers and characteristics of persons under supervision, admissions and release by method of entry and discharge, demographic information, time served, and conviction offenses. This same information is now released as part of the Bureau of Justice Statistics *Bulletin* series and as part of the larger report entitled *Correctional Populations in the United States* (above).

U.S. Bureau of Justice Statistics. *State and Federal Prisoners, 1925–85.* Washington, DC: U.S. Department of Justice, Bureau of Justice Statistics, 1986.

This brief report presents 60 years of data on prison populations from the statistical series *Prisoners in State and Federal Institutions.* Along with these data, a discussion of trends and the development and expansion of the series is presented.

U.S. Department of Justice. *National Corrections Reporting Program.* Washington, DC: U.S. Department of Justice, 1985–.

This annual publication details the characteristics of individuals admitted to and released from U.S. prison and parole systems. Data are gathered from participating states, the District of Columbia, and the Federal Bureau of Prisons. Data are gathered from official statistics and the University of Michigan's National Archive of Criminal Justice Data. Numerous tables provide details for state and federal prisons regarding sex, race, ethnicity, and education of persons leaving or entering prison or parole; conviction offense; sentence length; admission type; time served; and prison and parole release method. Year-to-year comparisons are provided.

U.S. Federal Bureau of Prisons. *Facilities, Federal Bureau of Prisons.* Washington, DC: U.S. Federal Bureau of Prisons, 1974–.

Facilities is primarily an annual directory of correctional institutions operated by the Federal Bureau of Prisons, but the profiles given for each facility are beneficial to the criminal justice researcher.

U.S. Federal Bureau of Prisons. *Statistical Report.* Washington, DC: U.S. Federal Bureau of Prisons. 1930/31–.

The annual *Statistical Report* presents Federal Bureau of Prisons employment data and data on prisoners under its jurisdiction. Prisoner data are given for age, race, ethnicity, sex, offense, sentence length, and security level. Title varies.

U.S. Federal Bureau of Prisons. *State of the Bureau.* Washington, DC: U.S. Federal Bureau of Prisons, 1988–.

State of the Bureau reviews the activities of the Federal Bureau of Prisons and provides a list of institutions. Helpful information on the characteristics of the federal inmate population, prison capacity of individual institutions, cost of imprisonment, time served, and personnel characteristics is offered.

U.S. Office of Justice Programs. *Census of State and Federal Correctional Facilities.* Washington, DC: U.S. Office of Justice Programs, 1984–.

The latest edition (1990) of this quinquennially published series reports on the third national census of state correctional facilities conducted in 1979. It records information on the men and women in custody in 1,287 state and federal correctional facilities on June 29, 1990, including information on the institutions, inmates, programs, staff, and expenditures for each facility.

STATISTICAL SOURCES ON JUVENILE JUSTICE

American Correctional Association. *National Juvenile Detention Directory.* Lanham, MD: American Correctional Association, 1992–.

Although this is primarily a directory of administrators of juvenile detention facilities in the United States and their addresses, it also contains facts about juvenile facilities, listed by state, offenders' average length of stay, average per capita costs, and various breakdowns of the juvenile inmate population.

Krisberg, Barry, Robert DeComo, and Norma C. Herrara. *National Justice Custody Trends, 1978–1989.* San Francisco, CA: National Council on Crime and Delinquency, 1992.

National Justice Custody Trends provides data on juvenile offenders in public and private correctional facilities from 1978 to 1989, such as the number of admissions and admission rates, number in custody, reason for custody, characteristics of private and public juvenile facilities, actual and inflation-controlled expenditures by total and per facility type, average length of stay, average daily population, and one-day rates and counts.

Snyder, Howard N., and Melissa Sickmund. *Juvenile Offenders and Victims: A Focus on Violence.* Washington, DC: U.S. Office of Juvenile Justice and Delinquency Prevention, 1995.

Using nontechnical writing and easy-to-understand graphics and tables, this report addresses the following issues: juvenile population characteristics, juvenile victims, juvenile offenders, juvenile justice system structure and process, law enforcement and juvenile crime, juvenile courts and juvenile crime, and juveniles in correctional facilities. While the data are gathered from other published sources, its easy-to-use format makes this report significant. Includes annual updates.

Snyder, Howard N., and Melissa Sickmund. *Juvenile Offenders and Victims: A National Report.* Washington, DC: U.S. Office of Juvenile Justice and Delinquency Prevention, 1995.

Modeled after the Bureau of Justice Statistics's *Report to the Nation on Crime and Justice, Juvenile Offenders and Victims* presents a picture of the juvenile justice system in a clear, nontechnical style. Numerous tables and graphs summarize information on juvenile crime, juvenile victimization, and the juvenile justice system. A subject index is included.

Stekette, Martha Wade, Deborah Alice Willis, and Ira M. Schwartz. *Juvenile Justice Trends, 1977–1987.* Ann Arbor, MI: University of Michigan School of Social Work, 1990.

Juvenile Justice Trends is a study of trends in juvenile justice in the U.S. between 1977 and 1987, analyzing data from government statistics such as the Juvenile Detention and Correctional Facility censuses, the 1987 Survey of Youths in Custody, and the 1978 and 1983 National Jail censuses, and selected editions of *Uniform Crime Reports.*

U.S. Bureau of Justice Statistics. *Children in Custody.* Washington, DC: U.S. Department of Justice, Bureau of Justice Statistics, 1974–.

This publication presents a broad overview of trends and statistical data on children in public and private juvenile facilities for the years stated in the title. From 1945 to 1967 the U.S. Children's Bureau was responsible for compiling and publishing statistics on children in reception or diagnostic centers; training schools; and ranches, forestry camps, or farms. Beginning in 1971, this series was replaced by various publications in the *Children in Custody* series.

U.S. Office of Juvenile Justice and Delinquency Prevention. *Arrests of Youth.* Washington, DC: U.S. Office of Juvenile Justice and Delinquency Prevention, 1992.

Prepared by the U.S. Office of Juvenile Justice and Delinquency Prevention (formerly the National Center for Juvenile Justice), *Arrests of Youth* analyzes data on arrests and long-term arrest trends of individuals under age 18, as reported in *Crime in the United States* and a companion document, *Age-Specific Arrest Rates and Race-Specific Arrest Rates for Selected Offenses.*

U.S. Office of Juvenile Justice and Delinquency Prevention. *Juvenile Court Statistics.* Washington, DC: U.S. Office of Juvenile Justice and Delinquency Prevention, 1929–.

This series, first published by the U.S. Department of Labor in 1929, described cases handled in 1927 by 42 courts. The series has undergone many changes during the years, but now contains detailed, case-level descriptions of delinquency and status-offense cases handled by U.S. courts with juvenile jurisdiction. It reports offenses involved, sources of referral, detention practices, and dispositions ordered. A database and analysis package of this publication is available as *Easy Access to Juvenile Court Statistics 1989–1993* from the National Center for Juvenile Justice, which is the agency responsible for the compilation of these data.

U.S. Office of Juvenile Justice and Delinquency Prevention. *Juveniles Taken into Custody.* Washington, DC: U.S. Office of Juvenile Justice and Delinquency Prevention,1989–.

Although *Children in Custody (CIC)* data have been collected and published at various intervals since 1945 and the titles in this series have changed over the years, the recent publication in the series is titled *Juveniles Taken into Custody.* This current publication provides data on juveniles taken into custody and describes custody trends for recent years. In addition to the number and characteristics of juveniles taken into custody, this work furnishes rates at which juveniles are taken into custody, the number of juveniles who have died in custody, and the circumstances of their deaths. Analysis is presented separately for delinquent offenders, status offenders, and juvenile nonoffenders, and the data are disaggregated by specific types of facilities and selected characteristics.

STATISTICAL SOURCES ON LAW ENFORCEMENT

Although the focus of this section is federally funded reports and series, remember that a number of state and local policing authorities issue their own annual reports. Two sources, listed first in this section, can help you identify such reports.

Index to Current Urban Documents. Westport, CT: Greenwood, 1972–.

An excellent source for accessing the reports of state and local authorities, this publication is arranged by place and then by issuing agency. The Urban Documents Microfiche Collection, 1973–, reproduces the documents indexed by this set.

International City Management Association. *The Municipal Yearbook.* Washington, DC: International City Management Association, 1991/92–.

Another source for statistics on police department and personnel is *The Municipal Yearbook.* This source can be found in most library collections.

U.S. Bureau of Justice Statistics. *Law Enforcement Management and Administrative Statistics: Data for Individual State and Local Agencies with 100 or More Officers.* Washington, DC: U.S. Bureau of Justice Statistics, 1992–.

The U.S. Bureau of Justice Statistics began the *Law Enforcement Management and Administrative Statistics (LEMAS)* program in 1987 with a survey of the nation's state and local law enforcement agencies. The latest volume provides data on 661 state and local law enforcement agencies employing 100 or more officers. Data are presented on personnel, expenditures, pay, operations, equipment, computer and information systems, and policies and programs. Agencies are listed alphabetically by state and county. For each county, the county police and sheriffs' departments are listed first, followed by the municipal police and special police agencies operating within the county. This is a significant source for law enforcement data.

U.S. Bureau of Justice Statistics. *Sheriffs' Departments*. Washington, DC: U.S. Bureau of Justice Statistics, 1990–.

> Yet another product of the *LEMAS* program (see above), *Sheriffs' Departments* presents summary data on sheriffs' departments such as expenditures, personnel, educational requirements, salaries, authorized use of semiautomatic sidearms, and requirements to wear protective body armor.

U.S. Bureau of Justice Statistics. *State and Local Police Departments*. Washington, DC: U.S. Bureau of Justice Statistics, 1990–.

> Another publication of the *LEMAS* program (see above), *State and Local Police Departments* summarizes responses from local and state police departments, providing information such as operating expenditures, personnel, salaries, education requirements, use of semiautomatic sidearms, and requirements to wear protective body armor.

U.S. Federal Bureau of Investigation. *Killed in the Line of Duty: A Study of Selected Felonious Killings of Law Enforcement Officers*. Washington, DC: U.S. Federal Bureau of Investigation, Uniform Crime Reports, 1992.

> This study examines the offenders, victims, and events leading to the deaths of 54 law enforcement officers over a three-year period.

U.S. Federal Bureau of Investigation. *Law Enforcement Officers Killed and Assaulted*. Washington, DC: U.S. Federal Bureau of Investigation, 1982–.

> The annual *Officers Killed and Assaulted* notes the number of law enforcement officers, including federal officers, killed or assaulted during a given year, reporting, for example, weapon type, time of incident, and circumstances surrounding the incident.

STATISTICAL SOURCES ON COURTS

Most states issue annual reports for their particular jurisdiction, but reports for federal courts as well as compilations of state court statistics are issued by the U.S. Administrative Office of the United States Courts, the U.S. Bureau of Justice Statistics, and the National Center for State Courts. Resources from these organizations are listed below.

The following two publications are the work of the Court Statistics Project of the National Center for State Courts. This project is funded by the State Justice Institute and the U.S. Bureau of Justice Statistics;

its purpose is "to translate diverse state court caseload statistics into a common framework in order to identify and analyze national trends in court activities."

National Center for State Courts. *Examining the Work of State Courts: A National Perspective from the Court Statistics Project*. Williamsburg, VA: National Center for State Courts, 1995–.

> *Examining the Work of State Courts* is an annual nontechnical report from the Court Statistics Project designed to present a simple picture of the work of the nation's state courts. Information for this report is derived from data reported in a companion volume, *State Court Caseload Statistics* (below). Of particular interest are the sections on juvenile caseloads in state trial courts, criminal caseloads in state trial courts, and felony caseloads in state trial courts.

National Center for State Courts. *State Court Caseload Statistics*. Williamsburg, VA: National Center for State Courts, 1993–.

> This national caseload database is derived from published and unpublished sources submitted by state court administrators and appellate court clerks. The following are furnished by this noteworthy annual report: an examination of state trial court caseloads for the current year; a description of the volume and trends in state appellate court caseloads; a detailed listing of caseload statistics for appellate and trial courts, including trends in the volume of case filings and dispositions, trends in the volume of case filings and dispositions, and trends in felony case filings; a one-page chart describing the overall structure of each state court system; and a list of state court practices that may affect the comparability of caseload information reported by the courts. This resource continues the *State Court Caseload Statistics Annual Report*, which was published from 1975 to 1992.

U.S. Administrative Office of the United States Courts. *Annual Report of the Director*. Washington, DC: U.S. Administrative Office of the United States Courts, 1940–.

> This annual report is divided into three sections: the current year proceedings of the Judicial Conference of the United States, a narrative section on the activities of the Administrative Office of the United States Courts, and a section on the judicial business of the U.S. courts. This third section is the most significant because it contains data on civil and criminal cases filed, terminated, and pending. Helpful tables furnish information on disposition of criminal cases, the length of civil and criminal trials, the number of prisoner petitions, and juror utilization.

U.S. Administrative Office of the United States Courts. *Federal Court Management Statistics*. Washington, DC: U.S. Administrative Office of the United States Courts, 1983–.

> *Management Statistics* presents workload and performance statistics for both civil and criminal cases for the U.S. courts of appeals and U.S. district courts.

U.S. Administrative Office of the United States Courts. *Federal Judicial Workload Statistics.* Washington, DC: U.S. Administrative Office of the United States Courts, 1989–.

> This resource, published annually, reports workload statistics for the U.S. courts of appeals and U.S. district courts for a 12-month period for civil cases, criminal cases, persons on probation, and bankruptcy code petitions and cases. For criminal cases, data include number of cases commenced and terminated by major offense.

U.S. Administrative Office of the United States Courts. *Federal Offenders in the United States District Courts, 1963–.* Washington, DC: U.S. Administrative Office of the United States Courts, 1962/63–.

> *Federal Offenders,* published annually, gives the disposition of defendants in criminal cases for the current 12-month period. Part 1 is a narrative with graphs or tables of case filings, defendant proceedings, and dispositions. Additional sections provide tables and graphs on various topics of interest, as well as historical data on sentencing and disposition for selected offenses.

U.S. Administrative Office of the United States Courts. *Grand and Petit Juror Services in United States District Courts.* Washington, DC: U.S. Administrative Office of the United States Courts, 1982–.

> Following a narrative section and summary tables on grand and petit juror services, this resource provides the following information on grand and petit juror services: estimates of expenditures for juror services, individual profiles of relevant juror statistics for each district, and a summary of historical data on factors influencing a district's statistics. (Previous title was *Juror Utilization in the United States District Courts,* published between 1974 and 1981.)

U.S. Administrative Office of the United States Courts. *United States District Court Sentences Imposed Chart.* Washington, DC: Administrative Office of the United States Courts, 1976/77–.

> This annually published report presents a compilation of sentences imposed in the U.S. district courts for the current year.

The U.S. Bureau of Justice Statistics (BJS), housed in the Department of Justice, is the primary source for federal criminal justice statistics. In order to provide policy makers with critical data, BJS collects, analyzes, and publishes information on crime, criminal offenders, and victims of crime at all levels of government. Some of the data reported by the bureau are collected by the U.S. Bureau of the Census, but statistics collected by Department of Justice programs and the Bureau of Justice Statistics provide crime data in addition to basic census data. The BJS Clearinghouse is the source for information and publications on crime and justice statistics published through the department.

Bureau of Justice Statistics Clearinghouse
633 Indiana Avenue N.W.
Washington, DC 20531
Toll-free: 800-732-3277

World Wide Web: http://www.ojp.usdoj.gov/bjs/
> CD-ROM available for a nominal fee (not a full-text publication—contains ASCII files that require the use of specific statistical software packages).

U.S. Bureau of Justice Statistics. *Federal Criminal Case Processing.* Washington, DC: U.S. Department of Justice, Bureau of Justice Statistics, 1989–.

> Covers details about the prosecution, adjudication, and sentencing of federal criminal cases. Numerous tables provide information on suspects prosecuted, defendants, offenders convicted, and prisoners released from federal prison. The first report in this series covered 1980–88; subsequent annual reports update this information.

U.S. Bureau of Justice Statistics. *Federal Drug Case Processing, 1982–1991.* Washington, DC: U.S. Department of Justice, Bureau of Justice Statistics, 1994.

> *Federal Drug Case Processing* reports on federal drug case processing in the U.S. federal criminal justice system. Data describe initial prosecution decisions, referrals to magistrates, court dispositions, sentencing outcomes, lengths of incarceration, sentences imposed, and length of time served in prisons. Tables present the number of defendants and the percentages of subjects, defendants, or offenders at each stage of processing.

Two important Bureau of Justice Statistics programs that collect and publish data about the nation's court system are the *National Judicial Reporting Program* and the *State Court Processing Statistics Program* (formerly known as the *National Pretrial Reporting Program*). The Bureau of Justice Statistics initiated the *National Judicial Reporting Program* (NPRP) in 1988. This program conducts a survey of state courts in a nationwide sample concerning the criminal history, pretrial processing, adjudication, and sentencing of felony defendants. Surveys are conducted every two years following the first, which was in 1986. The most current survey, conducted in 1992, was based on a sample of 300 counties selected as representative of the nation. The State Court Processing Statistics Program collects data on the criminal justice processing of persons charged with felonies in 40 jurisdictions, which are representative of the 75 largest counties in the nation. It tracks felony defendants from charging by prosecutors to case dispositions or for a maximum of 12 months. Data obtained include demographic characteristics, arrest offense, criminal justice status at the time of arrest, prior arrests and convictions, bail and pretrial release, court appearance record, rearrests while on pretrial release, type and outcome of adjudication, disposition of case, and type and length of sentence.

Executive Office for United States Attorneys. *Statistical Report.* Washington, DC: Executive Office for United States Attorneys, 1979– .

> This annual report summarizes the civil and criminal caseloads of the U.S. attorney's offices. Section 2, the most beneficial, presents data on criminal cases opened, filed, pending, disposed of, and appealed.

U.S. Bureau of Justice Statistics. *Felony Defendants in Large Urban Counties* Washington, DC: U.S. Department of Justice, Bureau of Justice Statistics, 1990–.

> *Felony Defendants* describes the demographic characteristics, criminal history, pretrial release information, and sentencing for felony offenders in the 75 most populous counties in the U.S.

U.S. Bureau of Justice Statistics. *Felony Sentences in State Courts.* Washington, DC: U.S. Department of Justice, Bureau of Justice Statistics, 1989–.

> *Felony Sentences* presents data on felony sentences imposed by state courts for the current year and makes comparisons using 1986 data to present data. Data include number of felony convictions, types of sentences imposed, sentence length and time served, demographic characteristics of persons convicted, methods of felony convictions, number of days between arrest and sentencing, and information on specific penalties such as restitution and treatment.

U.S. Bureau of Justice Statistics. *Felony Sentences in the United States.* Washington, DC: U.S. Department of Justice, Bureau of Justice Statistics, 1989–.

> Issued as part of the *Bureau of Justice Statistics Bulletin* series, *Felony Sentences* compares sentencing statistics in state and federal courts, including the number of convictions for drug offenses, type of sentence, sentence length, and estimated time to be served.

U.S. Bureau of Justice Statistics. *National Judicial Reporting Program.* Washington, DC: U.S. Department of Justice, Bureau of Justice Statistics, 1988–.

> This biennial publication describes the number and characteristics of felons convicted in state courts across the nation and in the largest counties. Each of four sections addresses a different aspect of felony convictions in state courts. The first section covers felony sentences in state courts, including the number of felony offenders in state courts and the sentences they received; the second section gives a profile of felons convicted in state courts, includ-

ing the sex, race, age, and other characteristics of convicted felons; the third section reports on felons sentenced to probation in state courts, focusing on the most frequent type of sentence and probation; and the fourth section covers felony case processing in state courts, describing the number of felons convicted by trial and by guilty plea in state courts, comparing sentences in cases convicted by these different methods, and presenting the average time required to process felony cases. *The National Judicial Reporting Program* is the basis for three reports on felony sentencing in state courts cited above.

U.S. Bureau of Justice Statistics. *Pretrial Release of Federal Felony Defendants.* Washington, DC: U.S. Department of Justice, Bureau of Justice Statistics, 1994.

> *Pretrial Release of Federal Felony Defendants,* one in the National Pretrial Reporting Program (NPRP) series, provides pretrial release data on felony defendants in a representative number of counties in the U.S. It presents number of felony defendants released before case disposition, financial and nonfinancial release, type of offense, bail amounts, number of prior convictions, number of rearrests prior to case disposition, time from pretrial release to rearrest, time from arrest to adjudication, adjudication outcome, and sentencing outcome.

U.S. Bureau of Justice Statistics. *Pretrial Release of Felony Defendants.* Washington, DC: U.S. Department of Justice, Bureau of Justice Statistics, 1991–.

> Another product of the NPRP, *Pretrial Release of Felony Defendants* provides information on criminal history, pretrial processing, pretrial misconduct, adjudication, and sentencing of felony defendants.

U.S. Bureau of Justice Statistics. *Profile of Felons Convicted in State Courts.* Washington, DC: U.S. Department of Justice, Bureau of Justice Statistics, 1990.

> Produced as part of the National Judicial Reporting Program, *Profile of Felons Convicted* provides a profile of felons convicted in state courts. Data are gathered for a nationally representative sample comprising 100 counties in 37 states located in all regions of the country.

U.S. Bureau of Justice Statistics. *Prosecution of Felony Arrests.* Washington, DC: U.S. Department of Justice, Bureau of Justice Statistics, 1983–.

> Beginning with statistics for 1977, this annual series describes the prosecution of adult felony arrests in urban prosecutors' offices for a given year, providing statistics on what happens to criminal cases between arrest and incarceration and explaining the role of the prosecutor in the felony disposition process. (Previous title was *A Cross-City Comparison of Felony Case Processing*, edited by Kathleen Brosi, 1979.)

U.S. Bureau of Justice Statistics. *State Court Organization.* Washington, DC: U.S. Department of Justice, Bureau of Justice Statistics, 1980–.

> *State Court Organization,* published periodically, describes how state courts in the U.S. operate and provides some corresponding information about the federal courts. Tables and charts are presented in eight topical areas: "Courts and Judges"; "Judicial Selections and Services"; "Governance, Funding, and Administration of Judicial Branches"; "Jurisdiction, Staffing, and Procedures of the Appellate Courts"; "Trial Court Administration and Procedures"; "Juries"; "Sentencing Contexts"; and "Court Structures."

STATISTICAL SOURCES ON DRUGS

The U.S. Office of National Drug Control Policy has established the Drugs and Crime Clearinghouse, which is an excellent source for data about illegal drugs. The clearinghouse disseminates the federal publications listed below relating to drugs and crime, produces national directories of state and local drug-related agencies, and maintains a reading room, where you can peruse numerous documents on drugs and crime, and a bibliographic database, containing statistical and research reports, books, and journal articles on drugs and crime.

Drugs and Crime Clearinghouse

U.S. Office of National Drug Control Policy

P.O. Box 6000

Rockville, MD 20849-6000

Toll-free: 800-666-3332

> World Wide Web: http://www.whitehouse.gov/WH/ EOP/ondcp/html/ondcp.html

Johnston, Lloyd D., Patrick M. O'Malley, and Jerald G. Bachmahn. *National Survey Results on Drug Use from the Monitoring the Future Study, 1975–1995.* Washington, DC: U.S. National Institute on Drug Abuse, 1996.

> This publication reports survey results from questions about drug use and related attitudes of high school students, college students, and young adults in the U.S.

National Narcotics Intelligence Consumers Committee. *The NNICC Report: The Supply of Illicit Drugs to the United States.* Washington, DC: National Narcotics Intelligence Consumers Committee, 1978–.

> Prepared by the National Narcotics Intelligence Consumers Committee (NNICC), this annual publication assesses the current situation of worldwide illicit drugs. Sections of the report examine issues such as laundering of drug money and availability, use, and trafficking of cocaine, opiates, cannabis, and other dangerous drugs in the United

States and internationally. Numerous graphs and maps make this report easy to use.

U.S. Bureau of International Narcotics Matters. *International Narcotics Control Strategy Report.* Washington, DC: U.S. Department of State, Bureau of International Narcotics Matters, 1984–.

> *International Narcotics Control,* published annually with a midyear update, presents country profiles concerning the national narcotics situation. Each profile contains a summary, status of country, country action against drugs for the current year, agreements and treaties, demand reduction programs, and U.S. policy initiatives and programs. Tables on seizures, arrests, and users conclude the country profile.

U.S. Bureau of Justice Statistics. "Drugs and Crime Facts." Washington, DC: U.S. Department of Justice, Bureau of Justice Statistics, 1987–.

> This booklet summarizes drug-related crime issues discussed in the various reports issued by the Bureau of Justice Statistics. It includes information on drug use by offenders at the time of offense, drug-related crime, drug law enforcement, drug offenders in correctional populations, recidivism of drug law violators, drugs and youth, and other drug data.

U.S. Bureau of Justice Statistics. *Drugs, Crime, and the Justice System: A National Report.* Washington, DC: U.S. Department of Justice, Bureau of Justice Statistics, 1992.

> Presented in a nontechnical format, *Drugs, Crime, and the Justice System* provides a comprehensive, statistical description of drugs, crime, and drug-control efforts. Topics include the drug-crime connection; the extent of illegal drug use; the business of illegal drug cultivation, manufacture, and merchandising; the history of domestic drug-control efforts; and a description of the justice system's response to illegal drugs. Data were obtained from federal agency reports, state governments, and private sources.

U.S. Department of Health and Human Services. *National Household Survey on Drug Abuse.* Rockville, MD: U.S. Department of Health and Human Services, 1985–.

> The annual *National Household Survey* reports on drug use by U.S. households for populations age 12 and older, including statistics on those who have never used drugs, the number of drug users for the past year, and those who have used drugs during the last month. Data are presented according to age groupings: youths (12 to 17 years old), young adults (18 to 25), middle adults (26 to 34), and older adults (35 and older). This survey consists of separate sections titled "Main Findings," "Highlights," and "Population Estimates." The "Main Findings" report contains the most detailed information, while the "Highlights" report uses graphs to summarize the main findings of the full survey. The "Population Estimates" report contains information on the number and percentage of drug users by

age, sex, race, and geographic area for all drugs and each drug type.

U.S. Drug Enforcement Administration. *Worldwide Cocaine Situation Report.* Washington, DC: U.S. Drug Enforcement Administration, 1990–.

This annual publication reports on cocaine trafficking in both the United States and foreign countries. Although most of the work is in narrative form, it does provide a glimpse into the world of cocaine trafficking.

U.S. National Institute of Justice. *Drug Use Forecasting.* Washington, DC: U.S. National Institute of Justice, 1987–.

To present a picture on drug use by persons arrested, *Drug Use Forecasting* presents data collected quarterly and annually on adult male and female arrestees as well as juvenile male arrestees and detainees from selected sites. A brief summary of all the data and summaries of essential data from each of the *Drug Use Forecasting* sites are presented with graphs and charts.

U.S. National Institute of Justice. *Searching for Answers: Annual Report on Drugs and Crime.* Washington, DC: U.S. National Institute of Justice, 1989–.

With the passage of the Anti-Drug Abuse Act of 1988, the National Institute of Justice was required to report on the effectiveness of federally funded drug-enforcement efforts. The resulting report, *Searching for Answers,* is presented in narrative form.

U.S. Office of National Drug Control Policy. *Pulse Check: National Trends in Drug Abuse.* Washington, DC: U.S. Office of National Drug Control Policy, 1994–.

Pulse Check is designed to give a quick glimpse of overall drug use in the United States. Based on quarterly conversations with police, ethnographers, epidemiologists, and drug treatment providers, this work provides a brief picture of trends in drug use for heroin, cocaine, marijuana, and emerging drugs.

In addition to the reports listed here, a number of reports on the drug situation in various countries are issued by the U.S. Department of State. The best way to locate these reports is through indexes to government reports such as the ones listed in chapter 7. Remember also that various articles, books, and agency reports contain information on drug issues. These materials can be found by using the various indexing and abstracting tools relevant to criminal justice such as the ones listed in chapter 5.

STATISTICAL SOURCES ON TERRORISM

U.S. Bureau of Alcohol, Tobacco and Firearms. *Explosives Incidents Report.* Washington, DC: U.S. Bureau of Alcohol, Tobacco and Firearms, 1976–.

The annual *Explosives Incidents Report* covers explosives incidents reported to or investigated by the Bureau of Alcohol, Tobacco, and Firearms. (Previous title was *Explosives Incidents.*)

U.S. Department of State. *Patterns of Global Terrorism.* Washington, DC: U.S. Department of State, 1976–.

Patterns of Global Terrorism provides a once-a-year, narrative review of international terrorist acts organized by country, region, and pattern. Appendixes include a chronology of significant terrorist incidents, background information on major groups discussed in the report, a statistical review in chart form, and a map of terrorist incidents for the year.

U.S. Federal Bureau of Investigation. *Bomb Summary.* Washington, DC: U.S. Federal Bureau of Investigation, 1973–.

This annual publication gives a summary and analyses of incidents involving explosive and incendiary devices reported to the Federal Bureau of Investigation for the current year. It includes statistics on hoax devices, recoveries of explosives, and accidental explosions.

U.S. Federal Bureau of Investigation. *Terrorism in the United States.* Washington, DC: U.S. Federal Bureau of Investigation, Counterterrorism Section, Criminal Investigative Division, 1981–.

This annual publication reports on the number and types of terrorist events in the United States. A narrative format gives the user a summary of the year's incidents, suspected incidents, and preventions.

STATISTICAL SOURCES ON WHITE-COLLAR CRIME

Recent attention paid by criminologists to *white-collar crime* and crimes of environmental pollution require the criminal justice researcher to focus on data produced by agencies ordinarily not thought of as concerned with criminal justice, such as the Department of Labor's Occupational Safety and Health Administration (OSHA) and the Environmental Protection Agency (EPA). Substantial amounts of data concerning criminal violations of health and safety regulations can be obtained from these and other agencies listed below.

Department of Labor Occupational Safety and Health Administration (OSHA). OSHA works in partnership with state governments, more than 100 million working men and women, and their 6.5 million employers to save lives, prevent injuries, and protect the health of America's workers. To use its limited resources effectively, OSHA seeks to stimulate management commitment and employee participation in comprehensive workplace safety and health programs. You can obtain a complete listing of OSHA materials as well as single free copies of the publications listed below from the U.S. Government Printing Office or from OSHA Publications. OSHA standards, interpretations, directives, interactive expert compliance assistance, and additional information are now also available on CD-ROM and the World Wide Web.

OSHA Publications
P.O. Box 37535
Washington, DC 20013-7535
World Wide Web: http://www.osha.gov/ and http:// www.osha-slc.gov/
Government Printing Office
Telephone: 202-219-4667

Environmental Protection Agency (EPA). The main Web site, or home page, for the EPA is probably enough for the beginning researcher; however, a special page for researchers and scientists is also full of valuable information and links to other sites related to white-collar crime, environmental crime, or crimes against the environment. Below is a partial listing of topics, displayed in full on the research page, for which information is available from the EPA.

- Catalog of Hazardous and Solid Waste Publications, 9th Edition
- Data Systems and Software
- Doing Business with EPA: Contracts and RFPs
- Environment—Pollution Prevention Initiative
- Environmental Monitoring and Assessment Program (EMAP)
- Environmental Test Methods and Guidelines
- EPA Office of Air Quality Planning and Standards (OAQPS)
- Government Information Locator Service (GILS)
- Grants and Fellowship Information
- Library Resources
- National Center for Environmental Publications and Information (NCEPI)
- National Center for Environmental Research and Quality Assurance

- National Environmental Supercomputing Center (NESC)
- Offices, Regions, and Laboratories
- Office of Research and Development
- Office of Research and Development (ORD) Publications
- Office of Science and Technology (Office of Water)
- Publications Catalog
- Research Programs
- Regulatory Information
- Science Advisory Board
- Solvents and Petroleum Studies
- Technical Documents
- Technology Transfer Network (TTN) Technical Information Areas
- World Wide Web (home page): http://www.epa.gov
- World Wide Web (research page): http:// www.epa.gov/epahome/research.htm

Centers for Disease Control (CDC). Extensive data are collected by the CDC, some of which are related to criminal justice, in particular, the data collected on violence and causes of death. Such data can be accessed via the CDC World Wide Web site listed below. From this home page you can select the link Data and Statistics, then the link titled CDC WONDER, or you can go directly to the CDC WONDER page as indicated below. CDC WONDER provides a single point of access to a variety of CDC reports, guidelines, and even numeric public health data, and it has a search and query function for CDC databases—both numeric datasets (e.g., U.S. mortality, natality, AIDS, STDs, cancer) and certain text-based databases (e.g., MMWR). The CDC Web site offers information on related Internet resources as well as links to health-related Web resources. Sorted by protocol, you will find a list of FTP, Gopher, HTTP, Mailto, and Telnet sites and services. Below is a sample of the topics and information available.

- Birth Defects Surveillance
- CDC and Agency for Toxic Substances and Diseases Registry (ATSDR) Electronic Information Resources for Health Officers
- Data from Death Investigations
- Hazardous Substance Release/Health Effects Database (HAZDAT)
- HIV/AIDS

- Information and Surveillance Systems
- Laboratory Standardization, Quality Assurance, and Quality Control programs
- Laboratory Studies and Programs
- National Center for Health Statistics
- Sexually Transmitted Diseases
- Surveillance Report
- The Year 2000 Issue—Implications for Public Health
- World Wide Web (home page): http://www.cdc.gov/cdc.html
- World Wide Web (CDC WONDER): http://wonder.cdc.gov/

National Center for Health Statistics (NCHS).
World Wide Web: http://www.cdc.gov/nchswww/nchshome.htm

OPINION POLLS AND SURVEYS

Library of Congress subject headings: Public opinion polls—Bibliography; Public opinion polls—Periodicals; Public opinion—United States—Bibliography; Public opinion—United States—Indexes—Periodicals; Social surveys—Bibliography; Social Surveys—United States—Bibliography

The issue of crime is of major concern to the American public, and this fact has not escaped the pollsters. Articles concerning public attitudes toward a wide range of criminal issues appear regularly in various news sources. For locating these articles, one should use the indexes listed here. It should also be noted that some organizations specialize in conducting opinion polls, i.e., Louis Harris Associates, Gallup, and Roper. The following sources will give the user access to public opinion on a variety of criminal justice issues.

American Public Opinion Index. Boston: Opinion Research Service, 1981–. Annual.

Currently indexes more than 250 sources of polling information. This source "lists questions asked in periodic and special surveys and opinion polls administered nationwide, statewide and locally." Relevant entries are under broad subject categories, i.e., crime, death penalty, prisons, and violence. Each entry gives you the question asked, the date the poll was taken, and the poll in which the question was asked. Responses to the questions cited can be found in a companion microfiche set, *American Public Opinion Data.*

Cantril, Hadley. *Public Opinion, 1935–1946.* Princeton, NJ: Princeton University Press, 1951.

An index to over 12,000 polls from 23 organizations in 16 countries for the time period given, this source's entries include a summary of the results and indicates the source for the entry.

Gallup, George Horace. *The Gallup Poll: Public Opinion, 1935–1971.* New York: Random House, 1971. 3 vols.

Gives findings of the Gallup Polls conducted from 1935–1971. Updated by a supplement covering 1972–1977 (Wilmington, DE: Scholarly Resources, 1978), by annual publications, and the *Gallup Poll Monthly.*

The Gallup Poll: Public Opinion. Wilmington, DE: Scholarly Resources, 1978–. Annual.

This annual continues the cumulative indexes cited above. It reports the annual public opinion polls conducted by Gallup. Most useful will be those questions dealing with social issues. Start with the detailed subject index.

The Gallup Poll Monthly. Princeton, NJ: The Gallup Poll, 1989–.

A monthly publication that includes short survey articles on current topics. Recent articles include: "Wrapping Up the O. J. Simpson Case" (Nov. 1995); "Majority Advocate Death Penalty for Teenage Killers" (Sept. 1994); and "Black Americans See Little Justice for Themselves" (March 1995).

General Social Surveys, 1972–. Storrs, CT: The Roper Center for Public Opinion Research, University of Connecticut, 1973–. Annual.

This is actually a data file of all General Social Surveys administered from 1972 to the present in machine-readable form. The survey questions include several on criminal justice issues, including capital punishment, crime, guns, and law enforcement.

The Harris Poll. Los Angeles: Creators Syndicate, Inc. 1988–.

This consists of weekly news releases of public opinion research on various current issues.

Index to International Public Opinion. Westport, CT: Greenwood Press, 1978/79–. Annual.

The latest volume of this index includes data from opinion surveys covering 98 countries and geographical areas. Some 166 research firms contributed data to this most recent volume, making this a very useful resource.

This is an example of what exists on the international level. Look for other indexes that provide international coverage, such as the Gallup international public opinion polls on France and Great Britain.

In addition to the regularly published public opinion sources, several agencies and states now routinely publish monographs that address criminal justice issues. Some examples include *A Survey of Experiences, Perceptions, and Apprehensions About Guns Among Young People in America,* by LH Research,

Inc. (Cambridge, MA: School of Public Health, Harvard University, 1993); *Punishing Criminals: Pennsylvanians Consider the Options* (New York: Public Agenda Foundation, 1993); and *Americans View Crime and Justice: A National Public Opinion Survey,* edited by Timothy J. Flanagan and Dennis R. Longmire (Thousand Oaks, CA: Sage, 1996). Also, articles concerning public opinion on a wide range of criminal justice issues appear in the various criminal justice journals. To locate these surveys and articles, consult one of the abstracts and indexes sources described in chapter 4.

DATASET ARCHIVES

Inter-university Consortium for Political and Social Research. The Inter-university Consortium for Political and Social Research (ICPSR), located within the Institute for Social Research at the University of Michigan, Ann Arbor, Michigan, is a membership-based, not-for-profit organization serving member colleges and universities in the United States and abroad. The ICPSR provides access to the world's largest archive of computerized social science data, training facilities for the study of quantitative social analysis techniques, and resources for social scientists using advanced computer technologies. The archive comprises an enormous collection of datasets that have been carefully evaluated and *cleaned.* The ICPSR Web site allows the user to search by type of dataset, project title, principle investigator, and other key terms.

The National Archive of Criminal Justice Data (NACJD) was established in 1978 under the auspices of the ICPSR and the Bureau of Justice Statistics (BJS). Its central mission is to facilitate and encourage research in the field of criminal justice through the preservation and sharing of data resources and the provision of specialized training in quantitative analysis of crime and justice data. The NACJD currently contains over 500 data collections relating to criminal justice, and the NACJD Web site provides browsing and downloading access to most of this data and documentation. Current NACJD sponsors include BJS, the National Institute of Justice, and the Office of Juvenile Justice and Delinquency Prevention. To order data or to obtain a list of datasets available as part of this archive, contact the ICPSR or the NACJD via mail, telephone, or directly through their respective Web addresses.

National Archive of Criminal Justice Data
Inter-university Consortium for Political and Social Research
Institute of Social Research
University of Michigan
P.O. Box 1248
Ann Arbor, MI 48106-1248
Telephone: 800-999-0960
ICPSR World Wide Web: http://www.icpsr.umich.edu
NACJD World Wide Web: http://www.icpsr.umich.edu/nacjd

Chapter 7

Government Agencies as Generators of Criminal Justice Information

Federal and State Legislatures
- Legislative Histories
- Tracking Federal Bills
- State Legislative Histories
- Tracking State Bills

The Police Agencies
- Federal Law Enforcement

The Prosecution System
- Federal Prosecution
- State Prosecution
- Local Prosecution

The Courts
- Federal Courts
- State Courts

The Corrections System
- Security Rankings

Government Documents or "Grey Literature"
- Federal Government Documents
- Guides to Federal Government Documents
- State and Local Government Documents

The documents produced by state and federal agencies are sometimes referred to as *grey literature* or *fugitive literature* because a large proportion is unpublished and often the only way to obtain them is through the agencies themselves. The *United States Government Manual* (see page 31) is a primary source for finding agencies likely to be in possession of information you need for your research. Athough government documents are not as readily identifiable or available as commercial publications, the amount of *bibliographic control* exercised over them is increasing. Although you may have to go to greater lengths to find the documents you need, they can be obtained.

This chapter begins with a general overview of the structure of the criminal justice system in the United States, providing you with a basic map of where to go in the system for information. While specific bibliographic sources are also given, the authors' emphasis here is less on the titles of sources than on the processes and terminology involved in finding them. Be aware that this chapter covers the realm of government information sources with very broad strokes. If you are interested in exhausting this area of research, we recommend reading some of the standard works listed here. We also recommend that you refer to the most helpful resources for finding information generated by government agencies—knowledgeable government documents reference librarians and archivists. Take the time and the effort to develop a healthy respect for these information professionals.

The American criminal justice system is composed of numerous federal, state, county, city, and local agencies that, in total, generate a tremendous volume of information that may be quite useful to the criminal justice researcher.

The basic components of the American criminal justice system are the police, prosecution, courts, and corrections. The legislature represents a backdrop to this system by setting the boundaries for the scope and effect of the various components.

138

FEDERAL AND STATE LEGISLATURES

The role of legislatures is to make law, to define the conduct that is prohibited by law, and to determine the penalties for violation of law. In addition, legislatures can modify or repeal laws should those laws prove to be unclear or vague in their application. Along with the power to create laws, legislatures are given the authority to define procedural aspects of law, such as rules for arrest, search, posting bail, and trial proceedings. Finally, legislatures are responsible for allocating resources required to carry out its laws. In a federal system like that of the the United States, both the federal and state legislatures have these powers at their respective levels.

In addition to the sources listed in this chapter, the sources for finding information about legislatures are covered in several parts of the work. Directory and biographical information on representatives to Congress and the state legislatures is covered in chapter 2. News sources that may include information about the activities of the legislatures are included in chapter 5, and sources where one will find the text of laws passed by the federal and state legislatures are listed in chapter 8.

Also keep in mind that the U.S. House of Representatives and the Senate both maintain Web sites at "http://www.house.gov/" and "http://www.senate.gov/" respectively. Both sites are a resource for information on the Congress and information on the legislative process. State legislatures also maintain Web sites, and in many instances, provide background information on the legislative process.

Legislative Histories

The day-to-day record of of legislatures is often an important element in understanding laws and, more to the point, what was intended in the passage of those laws. The United States is peculiar in its use of *legislative intent* in judging how laws should be applied. Judges in the federal and state courts will often try to determine the legislature's intent in framing a law in order to properly adjudicate a case that falls under it.

To determine legislative intent, researchers compile *legislative histories*. A legislative history culls together documents that were produced as part of the legislative process. Because this process differs from jurisdiction to jurisdiction, the documents that are printed pursuant to and in recording the passage of legislation, vary. But typical documents that one might attempt to find include transcripts of hearings before legislative committees and subcommittees, reports or studies commissioned by committees, studies referred to by the legislature as part of the legislative process, transcripts of debate on the floor of the legislature, and various versions of bills as they passed through the process.

The compilation of legislative histories of bills before the U.S. Congress has become simplified by the availability of several sources. The following sources are easiest to find and provide the most complete information.

Congressional Information Service. Washington, DC: Congressional Information Service, 1970–.

> The *Congressional Information Service* (*CIS*) indexes all the publications issued by the Congress, including prints, documents, hearings, reports and laws passed. *CIS* is a useful resource for compiling legislative histories, not only of laws that have passed, but also of those that did not, *CIS* is divided into two annual volumes—"Index" and "Abstracts"—which, in turn, are gathered into 5-year cumulations. The indexes can help you identify the documents by subject as well as by bill number, public law number, and other points of access. "Legislative History" volumes have been compiled in recent years. These volumes gather CIS citations to documents related to all legislation passed or proposed.
>
> Each index volume entry provides an abstract number, which begins with an "S" for the Senate or an "H" for the House. See exhibit 7-1 and the entry "Alien Criminals Deportation Procedures, revision, H523-5" (under the subject heading "Crime and Criminals") for an example of this coding scheme. Each abstracts volume provides a brief summary of the documents as well as some useful bibliographic information and the item's Superintendent of Documents (SuDoc) number. Exhibit 7-2 shows the entry from the index volume as it appears in the abstract volume, which you were referred to by the H523-5 identification number.
>
> *CIS* provides a related service that reproduces the documents on microfiche. Libraries can subscribe to the index/abstract volumes separately from the microfiche version. When the fiche service is available, the researcher can obtain the full text of the item by using the item number located in the index and the abstract volumes. (In our example, H523-5.) If the document service is not available in the library, the SuDoc number from the abstract can be used to find materials in most Government Documents Depository Libraries. In exhibit 7-2, the SuDoc number is preceeded by a degree sign (°) and reads "Y1-1/8:104- 22/CORR."

Congressional Record. Washington, DC: Government Printing Office, 1873–.

> First published during the 43rd Congress, the *Congressional Record* provides a transcript of the debate before the respective houses of Congress. It is divided into two

Corporate credit unions financial condition, investment practices, and regulation, H241–37

Financial condition of credit union industry and deposit insurance fund, H241–12

Financial instns and Fed deposit insurance funds financial condition and regulation issues, S241–35.1

Natl Credit Union Admin Central Liquidity Facility programs, FY95 approp, S181–1.3

Natl Credit Union Admin Central Liquidity Facility programs, FY96 approp, H181–28.3, S181–44.7

Regulation revisions, S243–2

Creed, Gordon

Land conveyance in Hopewell Township, Pa, to nonprofit economic dev corp, H641–30.1

Cregan, Teena

USPS retired workers temporary reemployment in rural areas, pension reduction exemption estab, H621–10.4

Crestar Bank

Credit availability to minority small businesses, data collection and disclosure requirements, H241–36.2

Crews, Clyde W., Jr.

DOE power mktg admins privatization issues, H651–30.2

Crime and criminals

Alien criminals deportation procedures, revision, H523–5

Alien criminals deportation process review, H521–76

Alien criminals, problems and Fed identification and deportation efforts, rpt, S403–7

Assault weapons control measures estab, H521–55

Budget proposal, FY96, H180–7

Children and youth response to surveys or questionnaires, parent consent requirements estab, H403–6

"Coming Anarchy: How Scarcity, Crime, Overpopulation, Tribalism, and Disease Are Rapidly Destroying the Social Fabric of Our Planet", H521–11.3

Corp for Natl and Community Service crime prevention activities, project list and rpt, S181–8.4

Crime against small businesses and workplace violence, H721–36

"Crime and Management: An Interview with New York City Police Commissioner Lee P. Brown", S521–5

Criminal history records interstate database ops review, S401–56

Criminal history records unauthorized use or disclosure, H521–5

Criminal justice laws and programs, revision and expansion, H523–4

Criminal justice laws, technical amendments, H523–39

"Drug Abuse Control Policy From a Crime-Control Perspective", H401–39.2

Drug abuse trends, prevention methods, and law enforcement efforts, H401–39.3

Drug control strategy effectiveness, assessment rpt, S522–1

Gambling economic and social impacts and regulatory issues, Fed study commission estab, H523–42

Immigration laws enforcement improvement measures, Pres message, H520–6

Immigration policies impact on State and local govts, review, H401–50

Internet computer network access to pornographic materials, child protection issues, H701–52.2

Justice Dept and Judicial br programs, FY96 approp, H181–72

Law enforcement assistance to State and local govts, block grants estab, H523–7

Pipeline safety programs, extension and revision, H273–10, H753–2

"Prevention of Relapse in Sex Offenders" regarding pedophilia, H181–76.14

Public housing crime prevention measures, expansion, H241–6, H241–16

Public housing crime problems and reduction measures in Chicago, review, H241–25

Safe and Drug-Free Schools and Communities Act, text, H322–6

Small businesses in Buffalo, NY, crime impact, H521–41

Treas Dept Financial Crimes Enforcement Network programs, FY95 approp, S181–7.6

Treas Dept Financial Crimes Enforcement Network programs, FY96 approp, H181–62.12

Vietnam veterans psychiatric disorders and incarceration, possible relationship, H761–4.2

see also Air piracy
see also Arson
see also Black market
see also Child abuse
see also Compensation of crime victims
see also Corruption and bribery
see also Counterfeiting
see also Crime insurance
see also Crimes against humanity
see also Criminal procedure
see also Drunk driving
see also Extradition
see also Federal aid to law enforcement
see also Forgery
see also Fraud
see also Gambling
see also Homicide
see also Hostages
see also International crime
see also Juvenile delinquency
see also Kidnapping
see also Law enforcement
see also Money laundering
see also Narcotics and drug traffic
see also Obscenity and pornography
see also Organized crime
see also Prostitution
see also Rape
see also Rehabilitation of criminals
see also Robbery and theft
see also Sentences, criminal procedure
see also Smuggling
see also Suicide
see also Tax fraud and evasion
see also Terrorism
see also War crimes
see also White collar crime

Crime Control Act

Youth-related provisions, text, H322–4

Crime insurance

Property reinsurance program for minority and low-income neighborhoods, estab, H241–29.1

EXHIBIT 7-1

H523-5	**CRIMINAL ALIEN DEPORTATION IMPROVEMENTS ACT OF 1995.**

Feb. 6, 1995.   104-1.
30 p. Corrected print.
H Doc Rm   CIS/MF/3
•Item 1008-C; 1008-D.
H. Rpt. 104-22.
*Y1.1/8:104-22/CORR.
MC 95-17001.

Recommends passage, with an amendment in the nature of a substitute, of H.R. 668, the Criminal Alien Deportation Act of 1995, to amend the Immigration and Nationality Act, the Violent Crime Control and Law Enforcement Act of 1994, and the Immigration and Nationality Technical Corrections Act of 1994 to revise procedures for expediting the deportation of criminal aliens.

   Also designates various immigration-related offenses as predicate crimes under the Racketeer Influenced and Corrupt Organizations Act.

   Includes additional views (p. 29-30).

   H.R. 668 is related to H.R. 3.

CONGRESSIONAL INFORMATION SERVICE ABSTRACT.
WASHINGTON, DC: CONGRESSIONAL INFORMATION
SERVICE, 1970-

EXHIBIT 7-2

parts—"House" and "Senate." An index provides subject access to debate, but citations to debate are also provided by *U.S. Code, Congressional and Administrative News* (the "Legislative History" section) as well as other sources. A frequent source of frustration for researchers is that the page numbers in the daily edition are different from those found in the bound edition. Thus, if you have a citation to the daily edition and the library retains a backfile of the bound edition, a new subject search will be in order. This problem occurs only when your search involves historical research. Be aware that the text one finds in the *Congressional Record* does not always reflect exactly what the legislator said. Senators and Members of the House may add or revise comments to the *Record*.

In the case of major legislation, legislative histories are frequently compiled by private publishers and are available in libraries. Compiled legislative histories typically reproduce all the documents related to a law or act, although some provide only a bibliography of the related documents. Several sources can be used to identify compiled legislative histories, including your library catalog and online services such as RLIN and OCLC. Bibliographies of compiled legislative histories—such as the following—are also useful:

Johnson, Nancy P. *Sources of Compiled Legislative Histories: A Bibliography of Government Documents, Periodical Articles, and Books, 1st Congress–94th Congress.* Littleton, CO: Published for the American Association of Law Libraries by F. B. Rothman Co., 1979–.

   This bibliography is published in loose-leaf format and is supplemented after each session of Congress. It is in tabular

form and indicates if the compiled legislative history includes the actual documents or just citations to the documents.

Reams, Bernard D. *Federal Legislative Histories: An Annotated Bibliography and Index to Officially Published Sources.* Westport, CT: Greenwood Press, 1994.

   This annotated bibliography describes approximately 255 legislative histories compiled from the 37th Congress, 1862, through the 101st Congress, second session, 1990. Five indexes provide access by author of the document, popular name of the public law, Congressional session law numbers before 1901, public law numbers after 1900, and bill number. Abstracts of the legislative histories include a wealth of information for those trying to identify the documents themselves, including SuDoc number, CIS number (see *Congressional Information Service*, 1970– above), and other identifying information.

United States Code, Congressional and Administrative News (USCCAN). St. Paul, MN: West Publishing 1952–.

   First published to cover the 82nd Congress, second session, *USCCAN* is published for each session of the Congress and may be used to find the text of *laws that have passed.* It is also valuable because it provides extracts of documents that comprise the legislative histories of the acts of Congress during that session. Some information that is not reproduced in *USCCAN*, such as debate, is referenced at the beginning of the legislative history. Generally, the extracted sections of reports and prints are those that the publisher believes best illustrate Congress's intent in passing the law.

Online systems, such as LEXIS and WESTLAW, also provide documents one can use to determine legislative intent. They also provide bill tracking services.

Tracking Federal Bills

The sources listed above are useful when attempting to compile a legislative history, either of an act that has passed the legislature or one that has died in either house. On occasion, however, you may need to trace a piece of legislation that is currently before Congress. The resources listed below can be used to find the current status of a bill.

Commerce Clearing House. *Congressional Index.* Chicago, IL: Commerce Clearing House, 1937/38–

   The *Congressional Index*, first published after the 75th Congress, is a loose-leaf service that tracks federal bills through the entire legislative process. It is updated weekly and provides tracking in two volumes—one for the Senate and one for the House of Representatives. Entries for each bill include a title, a brief description of the bill, and its current stage in the legislative process.

Many online services publish or provide access to databases that report on the status of bills. As mentioned earlier, LEXIS-NEXIS and WESTLAW offer such databases. A few others are cited below. (For a comprehensive listing of online legislative services, refer to the *Gale Directory of Databases*, page 76.)

LEGI-SLATE. Washington, DC: Legi-Slate, Inc.
> Online service provides a synopsis of every bill and resolution, committee and subcommittee actions, house and senate floor actions and votes.

The World Wide Web is a growing source of information on bills and legislative action. Without a doubt the best compendium site for locating information on legislation is the Library of Congress site.

U.S. Library of Congress. **"Thomas, Legislative Information on the Internet."** http://thomas.loc.gov (May 5, 1997).

State Legislative Histories

Legislative histories of acts passed by state legislatures are another matter. As mentioned earlier, the state legislative process varies from jurisdiction to jurisdiction. Therefore, the documentary evidence of legislative activities varies too. If you are attempting to compile a legislative history for an act of a state legislature, you would do well to contact the state library, state law library, state legislative reference library, and/or archives department. The *American Library Directory* (see chapter 2, pages 28–29) can be used to identify the proper state agency.

Another helpful source for compiling state legislative histories are state legal research guides. These are most often written by individuals who are very knowledgeable about legal research within specific states. Given the importance of legislative intent in all jurisdictions, these works usually have a chapter covering the mechanics of doing a legislative history as well as information about where one can obtain the documents.

Infosource. *The Legal Researcher's Desk Reference.* Teaneck, NJ: Infosources, 1990–.
> The annual *Legal Researcher's Desk Reference* includes a bibliography of state legal research guides and manuals, as well as other useful information, such as a listing of state libraries and archives departments.

The World Wide Web also provides information about legislative action within states. A number of sites provide links to all 50 states, and most states are beginning to provide legislative information on their own sites. Two of the many sites that have gathered together links to state government are as follows:

Lex Mundi. "Hieros Gamos." http://www.hg.org/ usstates-govt.html (May 6, 1997).

"State and Local Government on the Net." http:// www.piperinfo.com/state/states.html (May 28, 1997).

Tracking State Bills

In regards to tracking state bills, most states also provide a digest with information about bills before their state legislature. Many states also make the online bill-tracking services that are used by the legislature available to the public. Commercial databases that provide the same function are also available. The following list represents a fraction of those that are available. Some of these provide bill tracking and legislative history for selected states, or only one.

WESTLAW database. *LEGIS-ALL*. St. Paul, MN: West Publishing Co.

You may also want to try some Web sites as a source of legislative information.

Hoebeke, Anna M. **"Current Legislation."** http:// www.law.sc.edu/st_cur.htm (May 6, 1997).
> An exemplary local page compiled by Anna M. Hoebeke, this page contains links to as many state legislative sites as are available.

THE POLICE AGENCIES

In general, the roles of law enforcement authorities (police, etc.) are to enforce the laws of their jurisdiction, to protect the citizenry from the threat of crime, and to investigate and apprehend suspects of crime and deliver those suspects to court. However, because the police department often represents the only 24-hour-a-day social service agency in many localities, the great majority of police services often fall outside the realm of law enforcement, e.g., in health assistance, traffic control, and crowd control. There are thousands of policing agencies at the federal, state, and local levels in the United States. In addition, there are several thousand private security and other policing agencies.

Federal Law Enforcement

At the federal level, several government departments and agencies perform law enforcement duties. These organizations include the Department of Justice, Treasury Department, and Central Intelligence Agency.

Department of Justice

The Department of Justice (DOJ) represents the official policing arm of the federal government. It is headed by an attorney general, who is appointed by the president with the approval of the Senate. The attorney general is assisted by the deputy general and several assistant attorneys general who head different sections or bureaus of the Department of Justice.

The department is composed of several law enforcement organizations that investigate violations of federal law. Among these organizations are the Federal Bureau of Investigation (FBI), the Drug Enforcement Administration (DEA), the Immigration and Naturalization Service (INS), and the United States Marshals Service (USMS).

Federal Bureau of Investigation (FBI). The FBI was created and funded by the Department of Justice Act of 1908 and was originally known as the Bureau of Investigation. In March 1935, the name was changed to the Federal Bureau of Investigation. The FBI is responsible for investigating violations of federal criminal law. Its primary objective is to reduce criminal activity through investigation; cooperation with other federal, state, and local investigative agencies in cases of mutual interest; and research offered by its laboratory and training facilities. Further, because of its greater jurisdictional scope, the FBI assists local police authorities with the tracking of fleeing suspects, missing persons, and accident victims.

The Drug Enforcement Administration (DEA). The DEA, formerly the Bureau of Narcotics, was established in 1930 under the umbrella of the Treasury Department. In 1968, the Bureau of Narcotics was transferred to the Department of Justice and was renamed the Bureau of Narcotics and Dangerous Drugs. In 1973, the current name, Drug Enforcement Agency, was coined. The DEA shares jurisdiction with the FBI. Major responsibilities of the DEA are the full investigation and prosecution of drug law violations; the development of overall federal drug law-enforcement strategies; cooperation with foreign, state, and local agencies on joint drug-enforcement strategies; and the regulation of the legal manufacture of drugs and other controlled substances. DEA agents are authorized to carry weapons, make arrests, and seize property in connection with federal drug law violations.

Immigration and Naturalization Service (INS). The Immigration and Naturalization Service was created in 1940 as a division of the Department of Justice. Under the McCarren-Walter Act of 1952, the INS was charged with three goals: the reunification of families, the immigration of persons with necessary labor skills, and the protection of the domestic labor force. Perhaps the most visible component of the INS is the Border Patrol, originally created to patrol the borders between the United States and Canada and Mexico. Its main function now is to stop the illegal entry of aliens. INS agents have the authority to carry weapons, to arrest, and to search and seize evidence in violation of federal border and immigration law.

The United States Marshals Service (USMS). The United States Marshals Service was established under the Judiciary Act of 1789. In 1974, the Marshals Service became a bureau of the Department of Justice with one U.S. marshal designated as chief administrative officer for each of the 94 judicial districts in the country. These U.S. marshals are assisted by the chief deputy marshal and deputy marshals. The primary responsibility of the Marshals Service is to serve federal judges by issuing summons and warrants for arrest, by handling international extradition, by providing detention of suspects, and by offering protection to witnesses of crime (as per the Witness Protection Program introduced in 1984).

The National Institute of Justice is the research arm of the Department of Justice. One of its most useful publications is the database compiled by the National Criminal Justice Reference Service described in chapter 5. Another source that will provide information about current research activities of the DOJ is *Criminal Justice Research: Biennial Report of the National Institute of Justice* (National Institute of Justice, 1979–). This publication is useful in identifying the research efforts of the institute.

Treasury Department

Several law enforcement agencies are encompassed by the Treasury Department, such as the Bureau of Alcohol, Tobacco and Firearms(ATF); Customs Service; International Revenue Service (IRS); and United States Secret Service.

The Bureau of Alcohol, Tobacco and Firearms (ATF). The Bureau of Alcohol, Tobacco and Firearms was created in 1972 by order of the Treasury Department. Under this order, the ATF was given authority to enforce Treasury laws regulating the manufacture, sale, and distribution of alcohol, tobacco, firearms, and explosives, including the issuance of licenses for firearms dealers, importers, and exporters. In 1976, the ATF was given the additional power to enforce violations of federal wagering and gambling laws.

Customs Service. The first Customs Service was created in 1789 under the Traffic Act, which authorized the collection of duties on goods and merchandise. Under Article 19 of the *U.S. Code*, the Customs Service is authorized to conduct searches and inspections on all ships, aircraft, and vehicles entering United States' territory. The Customs Service has the power to arrest and seize evidence in violation of federal law.

Internal Revenue Service (IRS). The Internal Revenue Service, created in 1862, is the largest department of the Treasury. Its main role is to monitor and collect federal income taxes from individuals and businesses, including filing, examining, and auditing tax returns. The IRS also has a Criminal Investigation Division (CID), which investigates violations of federal tax law.

United States Secret Service. The United States Secret Service originated in 1865 as the Secret Service Division. In 1908, this agency was placed under the Justice Department, and in 1965 it was moved to the Treasury Department. Since 1901, the Service was given the task of protecting the president, the vice president, and former presidents and their families. In addition, the Secret Service is responsible for investigating crimes of counterfeiting, credit card fraud, and computer-related crimes. The Secret Service also has a uniformed division which provides protection to the White House, Treasury Building, Offices of the President, and Missions of Foreign Governments.

Central Intelligence Agency (CIA)

The National Security Act of 1947 established the National Security Council. The goal of this act was to provide a program for future security of the United States. Soon after, the Central Intelligence Agency was created by the CIA Act of 1949. Since its inception, the CIA has earned notoriety for its sophisticated covert operations. The functions of the CIA include the collection, production, and dissemination of foreign intelligence and counter-intelligence and the collection and dissemination of information on drug trafficking and terrorism.

Other federal policing agencies include the Organized Crime and Racketeering Section (OCR), the Postal Inspection Service, and the U.S. Coast Guard.

State, County, and City Level Law Enforcement

Law enforcement efforts at the state level vary greatly from state to state. However, all states, with the exception of Hawaii, have a state police organization. They are charged with enforcing the laws of the state and with assisting in highway and traffic patrols. In addition to these more common law-enforcement tasks, many state police organizations assist with the collection of state taxes and revenues. Further, some states have investigative organs analogous to the FBI. At the county and municipal level, there are various policing agencies whose scope is normally focused on law enforcement within its borders.

All of these agencies keep records and are often required to report information such as statistics to local, state, and federal agencies. Sources such as *Crime in America*, commonly known as *Uniform Crime Reports*, publish this kind of information. (See pages 123–24.) Likewise, law enforcement agencies keep internal records that may be available for research. The terminology applied to these documents varies from state to state, but some common terms are *uniform crime reports*, *annual reports*, and *statistical reports*.

THE PROSECUTION SYSTEM

The basic functions of the prosecution are threefold: (1) to make a decision whether to bring criminal charges against an accused suspect; (2) to present the accusation in the proper form and place it before the appropriate judicial body; and (3) to produce evidence before the court in an attempt to establish the guilt of the accused. The American prosecution system is divided into federal, state, and local levels.

There are several phases in a typical prosecution. The duties of a prosecutor, regardless of their level, are the following:

1. To decide whether to charge the accused upon receipt of an arrest report.

2. To determine the offense with which the suspect will be charged.

3. To coordinate the investigation of the case, which includes gathering evidence and interviewing witnesses.

4. To present the facts to the grand jury for its determination of prosecutorial viability.

5. To make recommendations as to whether the defendant should be released on bail.

6. To make recommendations to the court for the possibility of a pretrial diversion (i.e., treatment program).

7. To attempt to settle the case through negotiations with the defense lawyer (i.e., "plea bargaining").

8. To prepare the case for trial and to participate, if necessary, in the selection of the jury.

9. To make recommendations about the sentencing.

Federal Prosecution

The United States federal government has a prosecution system that is entirely separate and distinct from that of the 50 states. This federal system is divided into 94 districts throughout the country, each coordinated by a United States attorney who manages the daily work of the office. These officials are appointed by the president for a period of four years on the advice and consent of the Senate. The primary purpose of the U.S. attorney is to represent the federal government in the prosecution of persons charged with federal law violations within the district. The U.S. attorney must hold a law degree and is aided by other lawyers called assistant U.S. attorneys.

Although the U.S. attorney offices tend to function fairly independently, they are part of the federal Department of Justice, which is headed by the attorney general, a member of the presidential Cabinet. The Department of Justice is very complex, composed of various bureaus and divisions such as the Federal Bureau of Investigation, Anti Trust Division, and Criminal Division. Each division is headed by an assistant attorney general, who is charged with setting general policies and managing the routine tasks of the divisions.

Because the U.S. attorneys represent the government in trials against those accused of crimes, much of the output of these offices are in the form of briefs, at least at the appellate level. We discuss how to obtain briefs in the section dealing with the courts.

The attorney general, however, publishes many documents that will be of use to the researcher including the *Annual Report of the Attorney General* and *Opinions of the Attorney General of the United States*. These publications have a long history and are very useful in historical research, but there have been a number of title changes over the years. You may need to ask for the assistance of a librarian.

State Prosecution

Each of the 50 states in the United States has an attorney general, a state-level counterpart to the United States attorney general. The state attorneys general are the chief legal officers of the states. Their role is to supervise the prosecution of all violations of their state's penal code. Occasionally, these state attorneys general also make major rulings on criminal procedure. While the federal attorneys general may be appointed by the president, the state attorneys general may be publicly elected.

State attorneys general, like the attorney general of the United States, also file annual reports and write opinions on legal matters. These annual reports are sometimes printed with those of other agency heads.

Local Prosecution

The local prosecutor, also known by different names such as the district attorney (DA), state's attorney, county prosecutor, commonwealth lawyer, circuit attorney, and solicitor, is at the core of the American prosecution system, handling most criminal cases that arise under state law. (Some district attorneys' offices have special units to deal with particular crimes.) As a rule, the Office of the Local Prosecutor is reasonably autonomous and is not administratively subordinate to any other office. The offices are truly political in that these local level prosecutors, or DAs, are frequently elected officials servings terms of two to four years in salaried posts. Because of their high visibility and political sensitivity, these offices often attract young lawyers with political aspirations.

In most urban areas, elected district attorneys have little to do with the day-to-day prosecution of cases, as most of the functions are carried out by assistant district attorneys (ADAs).

THE COURTS

As a federal system, the United States has a dual system of courts, with a common hierarchy at both state and federal levels. While the federal judiciary enforces federal laws, each state judiciary enforces its laws often with an eye to abiding by the legal minimum established at the federal level. State courts vary considerably in regard to policies, size, and constitutional or statutory scope. Yet, despite these differences, there are some basic similarities in structure and in authority to resolve disputes.

Federal Courts

The Judiciary Act of 1789 created a three-tiered system of federal courts: the Supreme Court, circuit courts of appeal, and district courts. The highest court was named the Supreme Court, originally consisting of a chief justice and five associate justices. (There are now eight associate justices.) The second level, the circuit courts, consisted of two justices from the Supreme Court and one district judge. Federal district courts, each presided over by a district judge, represented the third level. As the *court of final record*, the Supreme Court had the power to interpret federal law and to balance the interests between the states. The circuit courts were appellate in nature and reviewed the decisions of the federal district courts.

The Supreme Court. The Supreme Court is the *court of first instance* in all controversies that arise between states and in proceedings against ambassadors and public ministers of foreign lands. However, the primary function of the Supreme Court is appellate in nature, with most of its time devoted to reviewing the decisions of lower federal courts and state supreme courts. Subject to the approval of the Senate, justices of the Supreme Court are appointed for a term of life by the president. Because of the duration of the term and the power vested in the Supreme Court, these appointments often reflect the political interests of the appointing president and the ideology of the party to which he or she belongs. At present, there is one chief justice and eight associate justices of the Supreme Court.

The Courts of Appeal. Before the Judiciary Act of 1789, the only federal courts in the United States were circuit courts, each presided over by three judges known as "circuit riders." Over the years, various reforms occurred in the structure and administration of the circuit court system. The current scheme was created by the Judiciary Act of 1891. As of 1989, there are 13 judicial circuit courts with a total of 168 circuit judges. Each judge is appointed by the president, with the advice of the Senate, for a term of life.

The courts of appeals have appellate jurisdiction over all federal district courts in a geographically defined circuit. Panels of these judges convene at regular intervals to hear appeals from federal district courts.

Federal District Courts. The jurisdiction of the federal district court system is considerable. Since all violations of federal criminal and civil law are tried in these courts, they are the major trial courts of the United States. Federal district court judges are also appointed by the president for a term of life. Some of the jurisdictional parameters and duties of the federal district courts are to hear civil cases where the dispute exceeds $10,000; to try cases regarding citizenship; to hear cases in relation to bankruptcy, copyright, patent rights, and unfair commercial competitions; to hear cases of revenue, tax, and customs disputes; and to hear cases regarding civil and human rights violations.

The federal court system is the source of a large amount of information on the disposition of criminal cases. The record of a case itself can be an important part of your research. Records and briefs are often available for appeals cases in law libraries, including cases before the U.S. Supreme Court and for the courts of appeals. The record of a case includes arguments put forward by the counsel on both sides, motions and pleadings, and frequently submitted documentary and photographic evidence. The originals of these documents are kept in the court clerk's office at the courthouse where the trial took place. In addition to the cases found in the traditional sources (discussed in chapter 8), federal court decisions and court records are also available online through various court record systems such as PACER, which we cite in chapter 2.

State Courts

The structures of the courts of individual states are diverse and complicated, so it is difficult to generalize. However, there are certain basic components common to each system. The highest court in each state is normally called the "supreme court." Variations include the "Supreme Judicial Court" (Massachusetts), the "Court of Appeals" (New York), and the "Supreme Court of Appeals" (West Virginia). In over two-thirds of the states, intermediate appellate courts sit below the supreme court. These courts hear appeals directly from trial courts. Under the intermediate appellate court are trial courts of various nomenclature: superior courts or circuit courts or courts of common pleas, or simply lower courts. There are also several courts with limited or special jurisdiction, such as probate courts, municipal courts, and domestic relations courts. At the lowest level are courts presided over by justices of the peace and police magistrate courts, both with limited jurisdiction in civil and criminal matters. Again, this description of the structure of state courts is very general. Many states differ in their court organization, with variations in jurisdiction, nature of processing cases, and nomenclature.

As with the record of cases before the federal courts, the records and briefs of cases before state appellate courts are often available in law libraries. These local law libraries may be funded by bar associations or the state. Records take many forms, either bound or microform, and contain the same kinds of information and documents as federal records and briefs. Like federal cases, transcripts of the cases are also available at local courthouses.

THE CORRECTIONS SYSTEM

As with the other components of the criminal justice system, there are two separate correctional systems in the United States: the Federal Bureau of Prisons and the various state-level systems. In general, the dominant form of punishment in the U.S. involves incarceration in a prison or jail. Prisons are designed to hold felons, those individuals convicted of offenses carrying sentences of one year or more. Jails are institutions designed to hold persons awaiting trial and those charged with offenses carrying sentences of less that one year (misdemeanors).

Prisons are normally self-contained structures occupying large areas, with security as a main component of their design (e.g., high walls, electric fences, and guard towers). Prisons are normally maintained by federal and state taxes and are operated by civil employees and administrators.

Jails are normally city or county operated and often fall under the administration of the local law enforcement agencies.

In addition to incarceration in prisons and jails, a number of states employ a broad spectrum of alternative methods of punishment and social control, ranging from capital punishment to probation and parole supervision to electronic monitoring and home incarceration to mandated drug and alcohol counseling to community service to victim-offender mediation and to restrictive court orders.

State and federal prisons and corrections departments keep statistics and written reports on a large number of topics, including recidivism rates, parole, staff, and inmates. Directories of information about prison authorities are covered in chapters 2 and 6.

Security Rankings

Prisons are ranked according to the degree and intensity of their level of custody, from minimum security to medium security to maximum security. For example, the Federal Bureau of Prisons uses a scale ranging from one to six to describe the level of security of its prisons, with Level One representing an honor farm, or minimum-security camp facility, and Level Six representing a maximum-security penitentiary with severely restricted movement and interaction among inmates. Prisoners are assigned to prisons depending on their past behavior, the nature of their offenses, and a prediction of their in-prison behavior.

Some characteristics of maximum-security prisons include the following: inmates can be kept in administrative or punitive isolation if necessary; inmates are extensively monitored by the correctional staff; inmate movement is severely restricted; and inmate privileges are greatly curtailed. Nearly 40 percent of all prisons in the U.S. are considered maximum facilities. Inmates are often idle (i.e., simply "doing time").

Medium-security prisons sometimes offer dormitory-like accommodations. The inmates have greater freedom of movement and may engage in rehabilitative and educational programs.

Minimum-security prisons are designed for prisoners who are nonviolent or are not likely to pose a threat to other inmates. Normally, inmates live in more "normal" housing arrangements and privileges and opportunities are common.

Refer to the American Correctional Association's *Directory of Juvenile and Adult Correctional Departments, Institutions, Agencies and Paroling Authorities United States and Canada* for security ranking information. The directory is cited fully in chapter 6.

GOVERNMENT DOCUMENTS, OR "GREY LITERATURE"

Government documents are the primary source of information about the work product of the agencies discussed above. Such information can be found in the text of laws, agency reports, legal briefs, statistical reports, resolutions, discussion drafts, written policies and procedures, court decisions, policy recommendations, memoranda, white papers (even green papers), and a number of other documents that contain written transcripts of administrative activities. Government publications may be issued by all levels of governments: international, federal, intergovernmental, state, and local.

Quite often, these kinds of publications can be very elusive and difficult to find. They fall into a body of publications known as *grey literature*, or, perhaps more appropriately for criminal justice, *fugitive literature*. These terms are generally applied to those kinds of publications that, because they are not published nor distributed by the *normal* means, are difficult to identify and locate. This problem is changing as most libraries and documentation centers have cataloged their collections on online union catalogs such as OCLC, RLIN, and WLN. There is now enough bibliographic control of these materials that their identification is rather easy.

Despite these improvements in bibliographic control and access, a very large proportion of government agency information is unpublished, and the only source of this information is the agencies themselves. The *United States Government Manual*, mentioned below, is a primary source for finding which agencies are likely to be in possession of information that you need for your research. In most instances, an agency of the government will provide access to information that you need, but this has not always been the case.

During the 1960s, the Congress passed the Freedom of Information Act (FOIA). The act's intention was to secure citizens' rights to have access to government information against arbitrary government secrecy. Under the act, unclassified government documents must be provided to citizens who request them. The agencies that refuse access must offer some sort of proof as to why they cannot provide that document. Each agency has published the procedures by which a citizen may proceed with a request for information under the FOIA in the *Federal Register*. States have also passed freedom of information acts that guarantee the same rights of access to state agency information.

In the next few pages, the authors attempt to give you a grounding in government publications. Remember, however, that as with legal research, a thorough understanding is better gained from the major works and guides on the subject, which are listed later in this chapter.

Federal Government Documents

In chapter 5 of this work, we covered two criminal justice sources that are useful in identifying and locating federal and state agency publications: the *National Criminal Justice Reference Service* and *Criminal Justice Abstracts*. NCJRS is particularly valuable because it not only indexes these documents, but, through its *Documents Collection*, provides microform copies

to subscribing libraries. The NCJRS World Wide Web site, also mentioned in chapter 4, provides access to the full text of more than 400 documents that are the result of federal criminal justice agency activities. These files can be downloaded and printed at your convenience.

Guides to Federal Government Documents.

> Library of Congress subject headings: Government publications—United States; Government publications— United States—Handbooks, manuals, etc.; Government publications—United States—Bibliography; Government information— United States—Computer network resources

The works listed below are guides to finding federal government documents.

Herman, Edward. *Locating United States Government Information: A Guide to Sources.* Buffalo, NY: W.S. Hein, 1983.

Maxwell, Bruce. *Washington Online: How to Access the Federal Government on the Internet, 1995.* Washington, DC: Congressional Quarterly, 1995.

Morehead, Joe, and Mary Fetzer. *Introduction to United States Government Information Sources.* 4th ed. Englewood, CO: Libraries Unlimited, 1992.

Robinson, Judith Schiek. *Tapping the Government Grapevine: The User-Friendly Guide to U.S. Government Information Sources.* 3d ed. Phoenix, AZ: Oryx Press, 1998.

Sears, Jean L., and Marilyn K. Moody. *Using Government Information Sources: Print and Electronic.* 2d ed. Phoenix, AZ: Oryx Press, 1994.

The Federal Government Depository System

The federal government is a prolific publisher of information. It issues everything from a three-fold pamphlet by the Department of Agriculture on growing tomatoes to official sources of the Constitution of the United States. All of these publications are, as you might expect, produced at public expense. Government documents are available for purchase, but they are also made available to the public through the Federal Depository Library System. The depository system is a web of libraries in the U.S. which receive, retain, and provide access to publications of the federal government. As part of their agreement to be depository libraries, these institutions must process and make their document collections available to the general public. Thus, a depository library may prohibit the general public from using its other resources, but it cannot bar the public access to documents that it receives as a depository library.

Depository libraries are of two types: regional and selective. Regional depositories collect all publications that are made generally available, and they retain them in the archival sense. Selective depositories have the option of choosing certain kinds of publications, which they process and keep indefinitely, but for no less than five years. Depositories may be public, special, or academic libraries. All American Bar Association-accredited law school libraries are part of the depository system. The *American Library Directory* and many other sources provide information about depository libraries, including whether they are selective or regional and the length of time the library has been a depository.

Depository libraries most often provide access to government documents through the library's catalog. Many libraries also classify these documents using whatever classification scheme is in use. Many others, however, arrange government documents on the shelf by a special classification scheme developed by the Government Printing Office (GPO) called the Superintendent of Documents Classification Scheme (SuDoc, for short). Government documents libraries using the SuDoc classification keep their documents in a separate collection. When you visit a depository library, ask a reference librarian about how to access government documents.

Unfortunately, not all depository libraries provide access to their documents collections through the catalog. When this is the case, you will have to refer to the *Monthly Catalog of United States Government Publications*.

Monthly Catalog of United States Government Publications. Washington, DC: U.S. Government Printing Office, 1895–.

CD-ROM: Cumulative coverage usually begins with July 1976.

Online: DIALOG, file 66; OCLC EPIC file 10; OCLC FirstSearch Catalog file GPO; CARL Systems Network, Government Publications. (Online coverage also begins in 1976.)

The *Monthly Catalog*, as the name implies, is a catalog of publications issued by the Government Printing Office. In its current form, it provides card catalog-like entries for published documents. (See exhibit 7-3.) Entries provide the name of the author, title of the publication, and date of publication, as well as the SuDoc number. The

catalog is arranged by agency, and each entry has an id number, for example, 95-4931. The author, subject, and title indexes provide access through these entry numbers. The December issue of each year provides a cumulative index to publications described in the preceding 12 monthly issues. The *Monthly Catalog* has gone through several changes of format, and so the researcher should approach it somewhat cautiously, especially when doing historical research. Before 1951, the title of the *Monthly Catalog* was *United States Government Publications Monthly Catalog*.

Two other sources currently identify government publications.

American Statistics Index. Washington, DC: Congressional Information Service. 1973–.

The *American Statistics Index* includes all federal publications that contain primary data of research value or secondary data collected on a special subject, special study, or analysis. The format is the same as that of the *Congressional Information Service (CIS)* described earlier. Each annual is divided into two volumes: "Index" and "Abstracts." Monthly supplements provide access to current publications. The "Index" volume provides subject access to documents, and the "Abstracts" volume includes full descriptions of the content and format (such as electronic) of each publication.

Index to U.S. Government Periodicals. Chicago, IL: Infordata International, 1970–1987.

Indexed more than 150 U.S.-Government-published periodicals. Subject and author indexing provided for some titles that were not distributed to depository libraries.

In addition to these sources, *Public Affairs Information Service*, *National Criminal Justice Reference Service*, and *Criminal Justice Abstracts* can help identify government publications. These indexes are described in chapter 5. There is also a number of guides and bibliographies which one may use to identify government publications pertinent to your research. We discuss a few of these sources below.

State and Local Government Documents

Publication by state agencies is rarely a regularized activity. As many, if not more, state publications come off photocopiers as commercial duty presses. They tend, therefore, to be considered as "not for general distribution."

There are two problems associated with working with state agency publications: first, identifying that they exist, and second, once you have identified one, finding a copy. The reason for this situation is due, in large part, to the fact that they are not widely distributed. Some states do not even require their agencies to

95-4928

J 28.24:D 84/12

Wellisch, Jean.

Drug-abusing women offenders : results of a national survey / by Jean Wellisch, Ph.D., Michael L. Prendergast, Ph.D., and M. Douglas Anglin, Ph.D. — [Washington, D.C.] : U.S. Dept. of Justice, Office of Justice Programs, National Institute of Justice, [1994]

19 p. ; 28 cm. — (Research in brief) Caption title. Shipping list no.: 94-0351-P. "October 1994." Includes bibliographical references (p. 18-19). ●Item 0718-A-03 S/N NCJ 149261 @ NIJ

1. Female offenders — Drug use — United States — Statistics. 2. Female offenders — Rehabilitation — United States — Statistics. 3. Drug abuse surveys — United States. I. Prendergast, Michael L., 1946- II. Anglin, M. Douglas. III. National Institute of Justice (U.S.) IV. Title. V. Title: Drug abusing women offenders. VI. Series. OCLC 31428550

95-4929

J 28.24/3:C 15

Cronin, Roberta C.

Boot camps for adult and juvenile offenders : overview and update / Roberta C. Cronin ; with the assistance of Mei Han. — Washington, D.C. : U.S. Dept. of Justice, Office of Justice Programs, National Institute of Justice, [1994]

ii, 67, 6 p. ; 28 cm. — (Research report) "A final summary report presented to the National Institute of Justice." "Supported under award number 92-DD-CX-K043, award to the American Institutes for Research"—T.p. verso. Shipping list no.: 94-0338-P. "October 1994." Includes bibliographical references (p. 63-67). ●Item 0718-A-3 S/N NCJ 149175 @ NIJ

1. Shock incarceration — United States. 2. Alternatives to imprisonment — United States. 3. Criminals — Rehabilitation — United States. 4. Juvenile delinquents — Rehabilitation — United States. I. Han, Mei. II. National Institute of Justice (U.S.) III. American Institutes for Research. IV. Title. V. Series: Research report (National Institute of Justice (U.S.)) OCLC 31404442

95-4930

J 28.31/2:994

National Criminal Justice Reference Service document data base [computer file] / U.S. Department of Justice, National Institute of Justice. Rockville, Md. : NCJRS, NCJRS, Box 6000, Rockville, MD 20850

computer laser optical disks ; 4 3/4 in.

Semiannual Other title: NCJRS document data base System requirements: IBM PC or compatible; 512K; DOS 3.0 or later; MS-DOS CD-ROM extensions (version 2.0 or later); CD-ROM drive and hard disk. Disk characteristics: CD-ROM. Written in ISO 9660 format. Shipping list no.: 94-0042-E. June 1994. Description based on: June 1994; title from title screen. ●Item 0718-D-01

1. Criminal justice, Administration of — United States — Bibliography — Databases — Periodicals. 2. Criminals — United States — Bibliography — Databases — Periodicals. I. National Criminal Justice Reference Service (U.S.) II. National Institute of Justice (U.S.) sn-94028493 OCLC 31458893

JUSTICE STATISTICS BUREAU
Justice Dept.
Washington, DC 20531

95-4931

J 29.2:D 84/2/994

State drug resources, ... national directory / U.S. Department of Justice, Office of Justice Programs, Bureau of Justice Statistics. Washington, D.C. : The Bureau ; Rockville, MD : Drugs & Crime Data Center & Clearinghouse [distributor], Drugs & Crime Data Center & Clearinghouse, 1600 Research Blvd., Rockville, MD 20850

v. ; 28 cm.

Biennial

Began with Mar. 1990. Shipping list no.: 94-0345-P. 1994. Description based on: 1992. ●Item 0717-R-01 S/N NCJ-147709 @ BJS

1. Narcotics, Control of — United States — States — Directories. 2. Drug abuse — United States — States — Prevention — Directories. 3. Drug abuse — Treatment — United States — States — Directories. I. United States. Bureau of Justice Statistics. II. Drugs & Crime Data Center & Clearinghouse (U.S.) HV5825.S66 92-660680 362.29/18/02573 /20 OCLC 22250455

95-4932

J 29.2:IN 3/6

Profile of inmates in the United States and in England and Wales, 1991 / James P. Lynch ... [et al.]. — Washington, D.C. : U.S. Department of Justice, Office of Justice Programs, Bureau of Justice Statistics, [1994]

iii, 23 p. : ill. ; 28 cm. "An international comparision of persons held in prisons and jails: offenses; sentences; sex, race, and age; prior sentences; family characteristics; employment and educational status"—Cover. Shipping list no.: 94-0353-P. "October 1994." Includes bibliographical references (p. 22-23). ●Item 0717-R-01 S/N NCJ-145863 @ BJS

1. Criminal statistics — United States. 2. Criminal statistics — Wales. 3. Prisoners — United States — Statistics. 4. Prisoners — Wales — Statistics. 5. Prisoners — England — Statistics. I. Lynch, James P. (James Patrick), 1949- II. United States. Bureau of Justice Statistics. HV7245.L853 1994 OCLC 31428344

95-4933

J 29.11/13:992

National corrections reporting program / U.S. Department of Justice, Office of Justice Programs, Bureau of Justice Statistics. Washington, D.C. : The Bureau, 1990- Justice Statistics Clearinghouse/NCJRS, U.S. Dept. of Justice, Box 6000, Rockville, MD 20850

v. ; 28 cm.

Annual

1985- Shipping list no.: 94-0357-P. 1992. ●Item 0968-H-12 S/N NCJ-145862 @ BJS

1. Corrections — United States — Statistics — Periodicals. I. United States. Bureau of Justice Statistics. HV8482.A34 91-641541 365/.6/0973021 /20 OCLC 23007469

95-4934

J 29.14/2:993-94

United States. Bureau of Justice Statistics.

Bureau of Justice Statistics publications catalog / U.S. Department of Justice, Office of Justice Programs, Bureau of Justice Statistics. Washington, D.C. : The Bureau, 1994- Bureau of Justice Statistics Clearinghouse, P.O. Box 179, Annapolis Junction, MD 20701-0179

v. ; 28 cm.

Annual

deposit a copy of their publications in a central archive, such as the state library or archives department. For this reason, state publications tend not to appear in many library catalogs. This situation is changing as states have begun to recognize the importance of their publications and as agencies such as state libraries are beginning to catalog state publications.

State Depository Library Systems and State Libraries

Like the federal government, many states also have a depository system. These systems are often not as well supported or organized as the federal depository system, but they nonetheless fulfill a need to access state publications. In states where agencies are required to place a copy with a state library or archive, your chances of finding a document are improved, especially if these institutions catalog all their documents. When libraries catalog state documents, these cataloging records sometimes appear on online union catalogs such as OCLC and RLIN. Sometimes, however, a state depository maintains its state publications separately from the rest of its collection and does not catalog these materials. Others maintain proprietary checklists which may be available only at that library. In most instances, however, these checklists are distributed to libraries around the state, making identification easier.

State libraries in the twentieth century have become centers for the maintenance of state records and accumulation of state publications. Archives departments collect and preserve records of state government activities, usually in the form of originals or copies of memoranda and internal publications or documents. These documents are rarely distributed, but they might be accessible nonetheless. Access to government archives is greatly enhanced by the archivists who work for these departments. Many archives departments keep checklists or catalogs of the materials in their control. Some of these documents are not individually cataloged but rather are described as "collections" of documents regarding a particular topic, or they might be documents of a particular type such as transcripts of hearings before legislative committees.

Most states now have promulgated written record retention guidelines. In some instances, these guidelines have the force of law (i.e., they may be written into the state's code of laws or regulations). When a state has records retention guidelines, these guidelines may also apply to local government entities as well.

The best bet for finding state publications is to contact the state library or archives and ask about the availability of catalogs and checklists as well as where to find the documents themselves. Making personal contact and maintaining a good working relationship with a knowledgeable documents librarian are also important.

Bibliographic Sources for State Documents

Criminal Justice Issues in the States. Washington, DC: Justice Research and Statistics Association, 1984–.

"The directory compiles efforts by the State Statistical Analysis Centers. It describes programs at the state level, research in progress, and publications produced in each year. It indicates, by jurisdiction, many of the justice-related issues and problems examined throughout the country. It also summarizes substantive and methodological research undertaken by the Statistical Analysis Centers in response to issues and problems."

The directory has several valuable features including a tabular summary of the issues for which State Statistical Analysis Centers produced data or conducted research during the calendar year. The body of the directory is a state-by-state listing of criminal justice agency activities and research. An index provides subject access on 39 broad subject headings. There is a listing of SAC publications by state, with the date of the most recent issue, and a directory of Statistical Analysis Centers. (See exhibit 7-4 for a sample page.) (Formerly titled: *Directory of Criminal Justice Issues in the States.*)

Index to Current Urban Documents. Westport, CT: Greenwood Press, 1972–.

This index includes citations of local government publications only. State documents that deal specifically with a city or county and federal congressional documents that deal with governance of Washington, DC, might be included. It has two indexes: a geographic index arranged alphabetically by city or region and a subject index. An accompanying document delivery service provides microfiche copies of the documents indexed.

Monthly Checklist of State Publications. Washington, DC: Library of Congress, U.S. Government Printing Office, 1910–1994.

The *Monthly Checklist* was the "national bibliography of U.S. state publications." Although it ceased publication in 1994, it continues to be of value, especially for the historical researcher. It lists state publications that were received by the Library of Congress from 1910 to 1994. Each monthly issue includes entries for monographic publications of the states. The June and December issues include entries for state-published periodicals. Publications of associations of state officials and regional organizations appear at the end of the listings for monographs. It ceased publication in 1994, because approximately 75 percent of

NEBRASKA

AFIS Research Committee

A cooperative effort of the Sheriffs' Association, Police Officers' Association, Omaha Police Department, Lincoln Police Department, Nebraska State Patrol, Police Chiefs Association, and the Crime Commission pursued a statewide, multiagency Automated Fingerprint Information System (AFIS) for several years. The Research Committee disseminated information and sought funding which was obtained in 1994. The SAC was involved also in the RFP assessment, benchmarking, and procurement and currently is on the AFIS Policy Review Board.

Data
Sources: AFIS, Police Departments, Sheriffs' Departments

Date of
Completion: Continuing Activity

Contact: Michael Overton
(402) 471-2194

Criminal Justice Data Information Clearinghouse

Through a cooperative agreement with BJS, the SAC maintains a clearinghouse that serves as a central repository of information resources and as an interface with Federal statistical resources.

Data
Sources: Courts, Corrections Departments, Jail Information Systems, Juvenile Information System, Police Departments, Probation/Parole, Survey, UCR

Date of
Completion: Continuing Activity

Contact: Michael Overton
(402) 471-2194

Criminal Justice Directory

The SAC *Directory* lists all criminal justice-related State and local agencies, and is organized in the following categories: Courts/Adjudication Process, Corrections, Victim/Witness, Domestic Violence, Education, and Law Enforcement. Contact persons are identified for each agency.

Data
Sources: Courts, Corrections Departments, Jail Information Systems, Police Departments, Probation/Parole, Prosecutors, Sheriffs' Departments

Date of
Completion: Continuing Activity

Contact: Michael Overton
(402) 471-2194

Criminal Justice Film Library

The Criminal Justice Film Library houses approximately 800 16-mm films and videocassettes covering 62 subject areas, and several slide/tape presentations. Criminal justice agencies are eligible to borrow films for up to seven days for a $3 fee; other agencies and individuals are charged $15 per film per showing day.

Date of
Completion: Continuing Activity

Contact: Darlene Snitly
(402) 471-2194

Criminal Justice Information Systems (CJIS) Advisory Committee

The CJIS Advisory Committee was formed by the Crime Commission to facilitate the coordination and improvement of data systems throughout State and local agencies. The Committee is involved in the NCHIP activities and a data architecture study.

Date of
Completion: Continuing Activity

Contact: Michael Overton
(402) 471-2194

Drug Program Evaluation

This is an ongoing activity to focus on projects funded through the Crime Control Act as well as general components related to the State's drug strategy.

Data
Sources: Police Departments, Prosecutors, Survey

Date of
Completion: Continuing Activity

Contact: Michael Overton
(402) 471-2194

Jail Admission and Release System (JARS)

The JARS system provides an ongoing database of statistical information on the typology and flow of inmates through local criminal detention facilities. The system enhances sound recordkeeping practices by local officials.

Data
Sources: Jail Information Systems

Date of
Completion: Continuing Activity

Contact: Michael Overton
(402) 471-2194

Juvenile Court Reporting Program (JCR)

The JCR program provides data collected during the calendar year on young people who were processed by courts with jurisdiction over juveniles, including 90 county courts and the three separate juvenile courts of Douglas, Lancaster, and Sarpy Counties. The forms sent in by the courts are based on a juvenile's disposition date. Statistics include referral and disposition information.

Data
Sources: Courts, Juvenile Information System

Date of
Completion: Continuing Activity

Contact: Michael Overton
(402) 471-2194

Uniform Crime Statistics Reporting/Nebraska Incident Based Reporting System

Training is provided to law enforcement agencies in Uniform Crime Reporting (UCR) classification, program methods, and procedures; the processing of UCR data; and the preparation of monthly, quarterly, and yearly UCR reports.

Data
Sources: Police Departments, Sheriffs' Departments, UCR

Date of
Completion: Continuing Activity

Contact: Marilyn Keelan
(402) 471-2194

NEW HAMPSHIRE

Comprehensive Crime Control Act of 1984 and Anti-Drug Abuse Acts of 1986 and 1988

The New Hampshire SAC has been assisting the Office of the Attorney General in implementing the Comprehensive Crime Control Act of 1984 and the Anti-Drug Abuse Acts of 1986 and 1988. The Governor designated the Office of the Attorney General as the responsible agency for administering these programs. Federal funds from BJA and the Office of Victims of Crime are made available to selected subgrantees whose activities have the greatest impact in crime-prone areas of New Hampshire.

Data
Sources: Courts, Corrections Departments, Police Departments, Probation/Parole, Prosecutors, Sheriffs' Departments, Survey, School Systems, Treatment Centers

Date of
Completion: Continuing Activity

Contact: Mark Thompson
(603) 271-3658

DWI Plea Bargaining

DWI plea bargaining cases reported to the Office of the Attorney General are analyzed according to specific areas of concern, such as witness problems and Blood Alcohol Collection suppressions. This report is tabulated on a monthly basis and published annually.

Data
Sources: Police Departments, Prosecutors

Date of
Completion: Continuing Activity

CRIMINAL JUSTICE ISSUES IN THE STATES. WASHINGTON, DC: JUSTICE RESEARCH AND STATISTICS ASSOCIATION, 1984–.

EXHIBIT 7-4

all state publications appeared in OCLC and RLIN online union catalogs before they appeared in the *Checklist.*

Municipal Government Reference Sources: Publications and Collections. New York: Bowker, 1978.

This guide book concentrates on large urban areas. Arrangement is by state, subdivided by municipality. It attempts to identify municipal reference sources and includes published local newspaper indexes, databases available to the public, and descriptions of collections of municipal documents whenever possible. *Municipal Government Reference Sources* is useful for tracking down collections of local government publications as well as the titles of major publications and series.

State Government Research Checklist. Lexington, KY: Council of State Governments, 1979–.

State Government Research Checklist is an excellent source for locating current information on criminal justice research being carried on by the states. This bimonthly periodical identifies documents that originate from the legislative, judicial, and executive branches of state government, but many also come from national nonprofit organizations as well. Document citations are arranged by subject, and each one includes author, title, place, publisher, date of publication, and paging for the items included.

State Reference Publications. Topeka, KS: Government Research Service, 1991–.

This annual is a "bibliographic guide to state bluebooks, legislative manuals, and other general reference sources." Most of the titles in this bibliography represent generally published and distributed reference sources. They are, therefore, the kinds of items that are generally available in academic, public, and special libraries within the states covered.

Other publications that are useful for locating state publications follow.

Checklist of State Publications. Englewood, CO: Information Handling Service, 1977.

Dow, S.L. *State Document Checklists: A Historical Bibliography.* Buffalo, NY: William S. Hein & Co., 1990.

Lane, M. *State Publications and Depository Libraries: A Reference Handbook.* Westport, CT: Greenwood Press, 1981.

Parish, D.W. *State Government Reference Publications: An Annotated Bibliography.* 2d ed. Littleton, CO: Libraries Unlimited, 1981.

Guides to State Government Documents.

Library of Congress subject headings: State government publications—United States—Bibliography; State government publications—*Geog.*—Bibliography; *Geog.*—Government publications—Bibliography;

The Librarian's Guide to Public Records. Tempe, AZ: BRB Publications, 1996.

This very useful guide belongs in the library of anyone who does primary source research in state records. It is divided into four sections. Section 1 is a "Comprehensive Review" of public records and accessing them. It discusses issues of privacy and how to search records, even how to use a vendor to perform records searches. Section 2 is a state-by-state, county-by-county directory of addresses and phone numbers of the agencies where local public records of different sorts may be located. Section 3 deals with state records, and section 4 with federal court records.

Occasional Papers Series; Chicago, IL: American Association of Law Libraries, No. 3.

The American Association of Law Libraries publishes this series of state document bibliographies as part of its *Occasional Papers Series.* Many of the bibliographies are in revised editions, and one has been prepared for each state. These bibliographies carry their own unique titles and were formerly entered under the series title *Annual State Documents Bibliography.*

The Sourcebook of State Public Records: The Definitive Guide to Searching for Public Record Information at the State Level. Tempe, AZ: BRB Publications, 1994.

Resources for Individual States' Documents

For the individual states, the following resources are helpful in identifying documents:

Alabama

Checklist of Alabama State Publications. Montgomery, AL: Department of Archives and History, 1973–.

Alaska

Some Books about Alaska Received in . . . . Juneau, AK: Department of Education. Division of State Libraries and Museums, 1963–.

State and Local Publications Received. Juneau, AK: Division of State Libraries and Museums. Documents Section.

Alaska State and Local Publications. Juneau, AK: Division of State Libraries, 1985–.

Arizona

Checklist of Publications of the State of Arizona. Phoenix, AZ: Department of Library, Archives and Public Records. 1986–.

Arkansas

Arkansas Documents. Little Rock, AR: State Library. Documents Services, 1981–.

Checklist of Arkansas State Publications Received by the University of Arkansas Library. Fayetteville, AR: University of Arkansas, 1943–.

California

California State Publications. Sacramento, CA: California State Library. 1947–.

Colorado

Accessions Checklist: Colorado State Publications. Denver, CO: Colorado State Publications Depository and Distribution Center, 1989–.

Checklist of Colorado State Publications Available in Microfiche. Denver, CO: Colorado State Publications Depository and Distribution Center, 1986–.

Colorado Checklist. Denver, CO: Division of State Archives and Public Records, 1971–.

Connecticut

Checklist of Publications of Connecticut State Agencies. Hartford, CT: Connecticut State Library, 1984.

Delaware

Delaware Documentation. Dover, DE: Bureau of Archives and Records Management, 1974–.

District of Columbia

Checklist of District of Columbia Titles. Washington, DC: Martin Luther King Library.

Florida

Florida Public Documents. Tallahassee, FL: Florida State Library, 1968–.

Hawai'i

Hawai'i Documents. Honolulu, HI: Hawai'i State Library, 1967–.

Idaho

Monthly Checklist of Idaho Government Publications. Boise, ID: Idaho State Library, 1994–.

Illinois

Illinois Documents List. Springfield, IL: Illinois State Library, Documents Branch, 1971–.

Publications of the State of Illinois. Springfield, IL: Illinois State Library, Documents Section, 1961–.

Indiana

Checklist of Indiana State Documents. Indianapolis, IN: Indiana State Library, 1974–.

Iowa

Iowa Documents Index. Des Moines, IA: State Library of Iowa, 1979–.

Kansas

State Documents of Kansas Catalog. Topeka, KS: Kansas State Library, 1977–.

Kentucky

Kentucky Checklist of State Publications. Frankfort, KY: Public Records Division, 1990–.

Lousiana

Public Documents Issued in Accordance with R.S. 25:123. Baton Rouge, LA: Louisiana State Library.

Public Documents of Louisiana. Baton Rouge, LA: Louisiana State Library, 1951–.

State of Louisiana Official Publications. Baton Rouge, LA: Louisiana State Library, 1935–.

Maine

Government Publications Checklist. Augusta, ME: Maine State Library, 1979–.

Index to Maine State Documents. Augusta, ME: Maine State Library, 1985–.

Maryland

The Crab. Baltimore, MD: Maryland Library Association, 1971–.

Maryland Documents. Baltimore, MD: General Assembly, State Department of Legislative Reference, Library and Information Services Divisions, 1977–.

Maryland State Publications: Documents Received by the State Publications Depository and Distribution Program. Baltimore, MD: State Publications Depository and Distribution Program, 1983–.

Massachusetts

Massachusetts State Publications Checklist. Boston, MA: State Library of Massachusetts, 1989–.

Michigan

Michigan Documents. Lansing, MI: State Library Services, 1978–.

Minnesota

Miscellaneous Checklist. St. Paul, MN: Minnesota State Law Library, 1973–.

Mississippi

Mississippi State Government Publications. Jackson, MS: Mississippi State Library Commission, 1975.

Missouri

Cumulative Index to Missouri Government Publications. Jefferson City, MO: Missouri State Library, Documents Division, 1979–.

Missouri State Government Publications. Jefferson City, MO: Missouri State Library, 1972–.

Montana

List of State Publications Received by Montana State Library. Helena, MT: Montana State Library, 1988.

Nebraska

Nebraska State Publications Checklist. Lincoln, NE: Nebraska Publications Clearinghouse, 1973–.

Nevada

Nevada Official Publications List. Carson City, NV: Nevada State Library and Archives, 1988–.

New Hampshire

Checklist of New Hampshire State Departments' Publications. Concord, NH: New Hampshire State Library, 1944–.

New Jersey

Checklist of Official New Jersey Publications. Trenton, NJ: New Jersey State Library, 1965–.

New Jersey Bibliography. Trenton, NJ: New Jersey State Library, 1981–.

Selected New Jersey Documents. Trenton, NJ: New Jersey State Library, 1981–.

New Mexico

Annual List of State Publications Sent to New Mexico State Depository Libraries. Santa Fe, NM: New Mexico State Library, 1986–.

Publications Filed with the State Records Center . . . . Santa Fe, NM: State Rules and Publications Division, 1979–.

New York

A Checklist of Official Publications of the State of New York. Albany, NY: New York State Library, 1947–.

Dictionary Catalog of Official Publications of the State of New York. Albany, NY: New York State Library, 1973–.

North Carolina

Checklist of Official North Carolina State Publications. Raleigh, NC: Division of the State Library, 1980–.

North Dakota

Publications of North Dakota State Departments Monthly Checklist. Bismarck, ND: North Dakota State Library, 1978–.

Publications of the State of North Dakota Received by the State Library . . . . Bismarck, ND: North Dakota State Library, 1965–.

Publications of the State of North Dakota Received by the State Library Microfilmed and Indexed. Bismarck, ND: North Dakota, State Library Commission, 1978–.

Ohio

Ohio Documents, A List of Publications of State Departments. Columbus, OH: Ohio State Library, 1971.

Oklahoma

Oklahoma Government Publications. Oklahoma City, OK: Oklahoma Publications Clearinghouse, 1981–.

Oklahoma Government Publications, Subject Index. Oklahoma City, OK: Oklahoma Publications Clearinghouse, 1984–.

Oregon

Oregon State Library Catalog: ORDOCS Checklist. Salem, OR: Oregon State Library, 1979–.

Pennsylvania

Checklist of Official Pennsylvania Publications. Harrisburg, PA: State Library of Pennsylvania, 1963–.

State Publications Directory. Harrisburg, PA: Pennsylvania, Department of General Services, 1987–.

Rhode Island

Checklist of Rhode Island State Documents. Providence, RI: Rhode Island State Library, 1983–.

South Carolina

Checklist of South Carolina State Publications. Columbia, SC: South Carolina State Library, 1950–1988.

South Dakota

South Dakota State Government Publications Checklist. Pierre, SD: South Dakota State Library, 1975.

Tennessee

A List of Tennessee State Publications. Nashville, TN: Tennessee State Library and Archives, 1954–.

Texas

New Publications of Texas State Agencies Available for Check-out in the Library. Austin, TX: Texas Legislative Reference Library, 1972–.

Texas State Publications. Austin, TX: Texas State Publications Clearinghouse, 1993–.

Texas State Publications Periodicals Supplement. Austin, TX: Texas State Publications Clearinghouse, 1988–.

Utah

Utah under Cover, Checklist of Utah State Agency Publications. Salt Lake City, UT: Utah State Library, 1984–.

Vermont

Checklist of Available Vermont State Publications. Montpelier, VT: Department of Libraries, 1970–.

Virginia

Quarterly Check-list of Virginia State Publications Received by the Virginia State Library. Richmond, VA: Virginia State Library and Archives, 1978–.

Virginia State Documents. Richmond, VA: Virginia State Library and Archives, 1991–.

Washington

Washington State Publications, Monthly Checklist. Olympia, WA: Washington State Library, 1978–.

West Virginia

West Virginia Publications Checklist. Charleston, WV: Archives and History Library, 1979–.

Wisconsin

Wisconsin Public Documents. Madison, WI: State Historical Society of Wisconsin, 1964–.

Wyoming

Outrider. Cheyenne, WY: Wyoming State Library, 1968–.

REFERENCES

Adler, Freda, Gerhard O.W. Mueller, and William S. Laufer (1994). *Criminal Justice.* New York: McGraw-Hill, Inc.

Anderson, Patrick R., and Donald J. Newman. *Introduction to Criminal Justice.* New York: McGraw-Hill, Inc., 1994.

Blumberg, Abraham S.. *Criminal Justice: Issues and Ironies.* New York: New View Points, 1979.

Edwards, John L.J. *The Attorney General, Politics, and the Public Interest.* London: Sweet & Maxwell, 1984.

Karlen, Dalmar. *Anglo-American Criminal Justice.* Oxford: Oxford University Press, 1967.

Glick, Henry R. *Courts, Politics, and Justice.* New York: McGraw-Hill, Inc., 1993.

Levine, James P., Michael C. Musheno, and Denis J. Palumbo. *Criminal Justice in America: Law in Action.* New York: John Wiley & Sons, 1986.

Chapter 8
Legal Research

Nothing challenges the researcher as much as the complexities of the law and legal research. It is complex because of the refined and sometimes confounding vocabulary of the law, issues of jurisdiction over criminal matters, the variety of sources for the law, the dynamic nature of the law, and the variety of resources in which the law is published.

The authors' purpose in this chapter is not to give the reader a thorough knowledge of legal research. You can better achieve such knowledge by using one of the classics on the subject (listed directly below in this subsection) or any one of the dozens of fine manuals and abridgments. We do, however, hope to give the occasional legal researcher a grounding in the resources that explain and analyze the law; that is, secondary sources, or books about the law. These sources are the same as those used by expert legal researchers when they begin a research project. These sources, in addition to explaining the law, refer to primary sources such as cases, statutes (or codes), and regulations. We also identify the most commonly used primary sources in the latter part of this chapter. Equipped with both types of resources, you should be able to access and analyze the documents in which the law is recorded.

The following sources are considered classic works on legal research.

Cohen, Morris L., Robert C. Berring, and Kent C. Olson. *How to Find the Law.* 9th ed. St. Paul, MN: West Publishing, 1989.

Jacobstein, J. Myron, Roy M. Mersky, and Donald J. Dunn. *Fundamentals of Legal Research.* 6th ed. Westbury, NY: Foundation Press, 1994.

Price, Miles O., Harry Bitner, and Shirley Raissi Bysiewicz. *Effective Legal Research.* 4th ed., Boston: Little, Brown, 1979.

THE CONTEXT OF LEGAL RESEARCH

Before beginning legal research, a summary view of the context within which legal research is conducted is valuable. This background is important because you will be better prepared to filter the information that results from your research.

Jurisdiction

Criminal law in the United States is the purview of all levels of government—local, state, and federal. Within the legal realm, each one places sanctions upon criminal activity and adjudicates cases that result from the apprehension of those suspected to be involved in crimes. One of the first requirements to doing legal research, then, is to determine which law governs in each situation: federal, state, or local. Issues of legal jurisdiction can be extremely complex, but the resources we cover in this chapter should make them reasonably clear.

Legal Authority

In chapter 2, the authors made a distinction between *cognitive* and *performative authority* (see pages 8–9). A recognition of the difference between the two is important. But in the practice of legal research, the concept of authority is somewhat more refined.

The definition of cognitive authority in the law is the same as elsewhere. It is bestowed upon individuals and institutions by their peers because of *what they know, their understanding of a subject,* or *what their experiences have been.* This type of authority is more likely to be questioned and tested. Failure to yield to cognitive authority does not result in a legal sanction. In this discussion of legal research, the authors have included "secondary sources": those which analyze or comment on the law and those which make statements *about* the law. These secondary sources are not the sources of the law itself but are simply explanations of the law. Cognitive authority in the law is always referred to as "persuasive authority" (read "cognitive persuasive authority"). It has the power to persuade, but only at the discretion of those who have performative authority to decide what the law really is (for example, judges); depending on the circmcumstances, it may be ". . . no authority at all"[1].

Performative authority grows out of the legal status of an individual or institution to determine what the law is or to make the law. Congress and representatives to Congress, as well as courts and judges, administrative agencies, and officials, have performative authority. The individual members of institutions have performative authority when acting in their official capacity. Thus a judge or a court has the authority to decide the outcome of a dispute. Failure to obey performative authority usually evokes some kind of legal sanction. The sources in which the pronouncements of performative authorities are published are referred to as "primary sources." They contain the text of the law. These include sources such as court reports, statutes, regulations, and decisions of administrative agencies. While secondary sources are only persuasive, the primary sources can be persuasive or "mandatory."

In the courtroom, the term *performative authority* is rarely, if ever, used. The focus revolves around what is "persuasive" and what is "mandatory." *Mandatory authority* is the law or authority which *must* be deferred to. The concept of mandatory, or binding, authority is limited by two factors: the jurisdiction (subject or geographic) in which the law is applied, and the relative stature of the document, or governmental institution, within the *hierarchy of legal authority* that made the rule. Very briefly stated, a rule of law must be followed within the bounds of its geographic jurisdiction (for example, within a state) on all matters to which it was intended to apply, and it must be upheld by all documents or governmental institutions that are subordinate to that which created it. Thus, the Alaska District Court, the lowest Alaska court, must defer to legal pronouncements of the Alaska Superior Court, which in turn must abide by those of the Alaska Court of Appeals, which must defer to the decisions of the Alaska Supreme Court, which must defer to legislation properly enacted by the Alaska General Assembly, which must be consistent with principles established by the Constitution of Alaska.

The decisions of the Alaska Supreme Court are binding, or mandatory, upon the decisions of all the courts below it in the hierarchy of Alaska courts. But, what about the authority of a lower-court decision on the Alaska Supreme Court?

A second source of *persuasive authority* exists which is critical to an informed reading of the law and your ability to evaluate it. While the Alaska Court of Appeals is bound by the decisions of the Alaska Supreme Court, the Alaska Supreme Court is not bound by those of the Alaska Court of Appeals. The former is free to overturn the decisions of the latter. Thus, when used as precedent to argue a case before the Supreme Court of Alaska, decisions and interpretations of Alaska law made by the Court of Appeals are not mandatory. They may, however, be persuasive. Likewise, law established outside of Alaska is not mandatory on Alaska courts (assuming it is not a

---

[1] Late Hon. Sidney Wernick, Justice of the Maine Supreme Judicial Court.

federal matter) because it is not Alaska law. Thus, Illinois state law, for example, is not mandatory. It may be raised in the Alaska Supreme Court, but it too is only persuasive. In the absence of a law to address a particular situation, persuasive authority, either from other geographic jurisdictions or from lower levels in the hierarchy of legal authority, may provide an example of how others have settled similar disputes or how they have interpreted or applied a similar law. Therefore, for purposes of this book, the authors coin the phrase "exemplary persuasive authority."

Sources of the Law

In addition to considering issues of jurisdiction and legal authority, the legal researcher must distinguish between different types of law. Law in the United States emerges from three sources: constitutions, legislation, and common law. These sources are introduced below but are given a more in-depth treatment on pages 175–81 of this chapter. Primary sources of each of these three sources of the law are given in that section.

Constitution. A constitution is the fundamental legal document of a jurisdiction. It may be referred to by various names, including *charter* and *fundamental law*. It establishes the structure of government and how legislative law will be made and, traditionally, places limits on governmental activity vis-a-vis those who fall within the boundaries of its jurisdiction. It is a statement of general principles of law.

Legislation. Legislation, or *positive law,* is the product of legislative bodies. Depending on the jurisdiction, that legislative body could be Congress, state legislatures, county legislatures, city councils, or other bodies charged with the responsibility of making rules. The authority of the positive law enacted by a legislative body extends only to the boundaries of its geographical jurisdiction. Thus, state laws are valid only within state lines. Legislative bodies frequently delegate the authority to make law to administrative agencies, then referred to as "regulations." This authority is usually limited to specific subject matters, such as the environment or taxes. Although they are not the product of legislative bodies, regulations nonetheless have the authority of law.

Common law. The United States and each of the states within it are referred to as *common law jurisdictions. Common law* is that body of rules that is typically, but erroneously, referred to as "judge-made law." The concept of common law has its roots in the *customary law* that was used to resolve disputes in the British Isles before the reign of William the Conqueror. Common law was the law "discovered" by William's judges to be governing Anglo-Saxon social relationships. Common law, then, is more accurately described as "judge-discovered law." Common law operates on the principle of *stare decisis*, or the idea that the rules used to settle one dispute should also be used to settle all subsequent disputes growing out of similar fact situations. Thus, it is imperative that the decisions of the courts be reported.

The courts provide an adjudicative function. They apply the law (legislated and common) to specific fact situations, render judgments, and sometimes write opinions. The rulings of judges in criminal cases, as well as cases involving criminal procedure and statutory and constitutional interpretation, comprise a large proportion of what we know as *criminal law*.

Publishing, Updating, and Citing the Law

Acts of legislatures and pronouncements of the courts are published in chronological order. This is partly because these law-making bodies act through time, but it is also because the public must know what the law is—in a timely manner—if it is going to be held accountable to it. The actions of the courts and legislatures also change existing law. Therefore, it is critical that the public be notified when the law has changed and that there be a means of keeping current with those changes.

The history of the Anglo-American legal system is such that a clear and uniform system of citation is required for the law to be efficiently located and applied. The rules of legal citation are extremely well developed, and, to the initiated, they clearly indicate the jurisdiction that promulgated the law or decision, the source of the law, the legal authority of the source, and when the law was made. In other words, legal citation addresses all of the contextual issues discussed above.

Although a complete examination of legal citation method is well beyond the scope of the current work, the authors do briefly describe how to read a legal citation and provide sources for further research later in this chapter. One of the principles of legal citation is brevity. Therefore, citations to legal materials are replete with abbreviations, and to identify a source being cited, you may have to refer to a list of abbreviations. Two sources mentioned later in this chapter, *Black's Law Dictionary* and *Corpus Juris Secundum*, include lists of common legal abbreviations. An exhaustive list of abbreviations for law books can be found in the source listed below. Companion volumes to this work include legal abbreviations reversed and instructions on citing specific sources.

Prince, Mary Miles. *Bieber's Dictionary of Legal Abbreviations: Reference Guide for Attorneys, Legal Secretaries and Law Students.* 4th ed. Buffalo, NY: William S. Hein & Co., 1993.

Resources for Finding the Law

Mere publication might have been sufficient notice of law at one time in human history. However, society, and with it the law, has become incredibly complex. The amount of legal information has grown to such a degree that it is no longer possible for anyone to know all the law, nor is it possible for anyone to find the law by simply leafing through the primary sources—there is just too much of it. Because of the amount of legal publication and the fact that publication is in chronological order, there is a need for subject access to the acts of legislatures, the regulations of administrative agencies, and the decisions of the courts.

The need for subject access to the law has led to the development of indexing and citation tools and the subject arrangement of primary sources, for example: (1) *digests* (see page 181), which are subject indexes to court decisions, or common law; (2) *codes* (see pages 176–77), which are the full text of legislation currently in force arranged by subject; (3) indexes for accessing codes and secondary sources, such as encyclopedias, law review articles, and treatises (see pages 162–75); and (4) *citators* (see pages 178–81) for finding how the courts and legislatures have treated the law subsequent to its promulgation.

BEGINNING A RESEARCH PROJECT

Like most disciplines, including criminal justice, the law has its own vocabulary. It is, however, considerably more refined than others, and it has a much longer history. It includes Latin terms as well as some English ones that may seem foreign. But one's ability to navigate through the law, just like one's ability to negotiate a foreign language, is a matter of building a vocabulary. That usually involves starting with general and familiar concepts, then building on them.

For the novice or occasional legal researcher, the course of doing legal research should be viewed as a learning experience. Just as in learning anything else, you might wish to begin with the aid of a dictionary and read encyclopedic works on the subject of your research. These kinds of sources frequently cite other related works that you might want to read as well. Each one is a step in building knowledge in a subject. After additional reading and vocabulary development, your subject and its vocabulary, become more and more familiar.

Law Dictionaries

A law dictionary is an important element of legal research, not only to the novice but also to the expert. The reason for this reliance on legal dictionaries is that the legal definition of a term is often very specific; it may vary from jurisdiction to jurisdiction and from common parlance. Legal definitions of words have their roots in either positive law or common law, wherever the definition of a term or phrase was required to settle a legal dispute. Listed below are some legal dictionaries beneficial to your research.

Ballentine, James Arthur. *Ballentine's Law Dictionary: With Pronunciations.* 3rd ed. Rochester, NY: Lawyers Cooperative Publishing Co., 1969.

Ballentine's Law Dictionary is also a valuable resource for the definition of legal terms and phrases. It may be, however, a better resource for the criminal justice student or professional who only does occasional legal research. Although *Ballentine's* cites the cases or codes that provide the definition of a word, it also makes frequent references to *American Jurisprudence* (see page 63), *American Law Reports* (see page 166), and other secondary sources. See exhibit 8-1 for the definition of *criminal assault* (with a reference to *American Jurisprudence*) and, at the end of the second paragraph, citations to a Maine case and to an annotation in *American Law Reports*. These citations give the researcher a valuable point of reference for further study of a term or concept. It also includes a list of abbreviations to American and British legal resources.

Black, Henry Campbell. *Black's Law Dictionary: Definitions of the Terms and Phrases of American and English Jurisprudence, Ancient and Modern.* 6th ed. St. Paul, MN: West Publishing, 1990.

Black's is probably the most widely used law dictionary. It includes the legal definitions of terms and phrases as found in case law and other sources such as the *Model Penal Code.* Most definitions include citations to the case or code upon which it is based. Through the publication of new editions, it attempts to keep up with changes in legal concepts and doctrines. *Black's* also includes a list of commonly used abbreviations to law sources. (See exhibit 8-2 for a sample entry.)

Words and Phrases. (Permanent Ed., 1658 to date. St. Paul, MN: West Publishing, 1940–.

Words and Phrases, the consummate legal dictionary, comprises "[a]ll judicial constructions and definitions of words

crime of moral turpitude. See moral turpitude.

crime of omission. An offense in the form of failure to perform a required act, rather than the doing of a prohibited act. 21 Am J2d Crim L § 6.

crime of reputation. A crime predicated by statute on reputation, such as the offense of keeping, frequenting, or being an inmate of premises reputedly used for designated unlawful purposes. 21 Am J2d Crim L § 5.

crime of status. A crime, such as vagrancy, living in adultery, or living in fornication, predicated on a status, condition, or mode of life. 21 Am J2d Crim L § 5.

criminal (krim'i-nal). Adjective: Relating to or having the character of crime. People v Bradley, 60 Ill 390, 402. Noun: A person who has committed a crime, especially, if he is a recidivist or the crime is a serious or violent one. In the eyes of the law, a person is a criminal who has been adjudged guilty of a crime, and he continues to be a criminal so long as the judgment remains in force. Re Molineux, 177 NY 395, 69 NE 727.

criminal act. Any act which is punishable as a crime.

criminal action. An action by the sovereign, that is the state or the United States, or instituted on behalf of the sovereign, against one charged with the commission of a criminal act, for the enforcement of the penalty or punishment prescribed by law. 1 Am J2d Actions § 43.

criminal anarchy. The doctrine that organized government should be overthrown by force, violence, assassination of the executive head, or of other executives of the government, or by any unlawful means. 47 Am J1st Sedit etc. § 3.

criminal appeals. Appeals from judgments in criminal cases. 4 Am J2d A & E § 159.

criminal assault. An assault for which the assailant may be criminally prosecuted. 6 Am J2d Asslt & B § 8.
  A statute which provides that whoever unlawfully attempts to strike, hit, touch, or do any violence to another, however small, in a wanton, wilful, angry, or insulting manner, having an intention and existing ability to do some violence to such person, is guilty of an assault, and that if such attempt is carried into effect, he is guilty of assault and battery, and upon conviction shall be subject to a penalty within maximum limits, and when the offense is of a high and aggravated nature, shall be subject to a greater penalty, is merely declaratory of the common law. Rell v State, 136 Me 322, 9 A2d 129, 125 ALR 602.

criminal attempt. See attempt.

criminal bail. Bail given in a criminal case. See bail.

criminal business. For the purposes of a venue statute, the term "criminal business" means the criminal matters occupying the attention and labor of men engaged in legal affairs, coming into being or notice in any county. Sherman v Droubay, 27 Utah 47, 74 P 348.

criminal capacity. The capacity to commit a crime, that is, legal mental capacity, whereunder responsibility for the commission of an act prohibited by law and susceptibility to punishment provided by law attaches to the wrongdoer. 21 Am J2d Crim L § 26. Substantial capacity either to appreciate the criminality of one's act and to conform to the re-

BALLENTINE, JAMES ARTHUR. *BALLENTINE'S LAW DICTIONARY: WITH PRONUNCIATIONS.* 3D ED. ROCHESTER, NY: LAWYERS COOPERATIVE PUBLISHING CO., 1969.

EXHIBIT 8-1

tional Government League, 1 Wash.2d 635, 96 P.2d 588, 591, 125 A.L.R. 1100. The word is defined as of the nature of or involving a crime; more generally, of the nature of a grave offense; wicked. Van Riper v. Constitutional Government League, 1 Wash.2d 635, 96 P.2d 588, 591, 125 A.L.R. 1100.

Criminal abortion

See Abortion.

Criminal act

A term which is equivalent to crime; or is sometimes used with a slight softening or glossing of the meaning, or as importing a possible question of the legal guilt of the deed. The intentional violation of statute designed to protect human life is criminal act. State v. Agnew, 202 N.C. 755, 164 S.E. 578, 579.

Criminal action

The proceeding by which a party charged with a public offense is accused and brought to trial and punishment is known as a "criminal action." Pen.Code Cal. § 683. A criminal action is (1) an action prosecuted by the state as a party, against a person charged with a public offense, for the punishment thereof; (2) an action prosecuted by the state, at the instance of an individual, to prevent an apprehended crime, against his person or property. Code N.C. 1883, § 129, C.S. § 395.

Criminal assault and battery

An accused may be guilty of a "criminal assault and battery" if he intentionally does an act which by reason of its wanton and grossly negligent character exposes another to personal injury and in fact causes injury. State v. Linville, 150 Kan. 617, 95 P.2d 332, 334.

Criminal case

An action, suit, or cause instituted to punish an infraction of the criminal laws. State v. Smalls, 11 S.C. 279; People v. Iron Co., 201 Ill. 236, 66 N.E. 349; Wilburn v. State, 140 Ga. 138, 78 S.E. 819, 820; Hankamer v. Templin, 143 Tex. 572, 187 S.W.2d 549, 550. The phrase has various meanings according to context and purpose of constitutional provision or statute. Ex parte Tahbel, 46 Cal. App. 755, 189 P. 804, 806; Childs v. City of Birmingham, 19 Ala.App. 71, 94 So. 790; Barnett v. Atlanta, 109 Ga. 166, 34 S.E. 322.

Criminal charge

An accusation of crime, formulated in a written complaint, information, or indictment, and taking shape in a prosecution. U. S. v. Patterson, 150 U.S. 65, 14 S.Ct. 20, 37 L.Ed. 999; Eason v. State, 11 Ark. 482; People v. Ross, 235 Mich. 433, 209 N.W. 663, 666.

Criminal contempt proceeding

"Criminal contempt proceedings" are brought to preserve the power and vindicate the dignity and integrity of the court and to punish for disobedience of its orders. O'Malley v. United States, C.C.A.Mo., 128 F.2d 676, 683.

BLACK, HENRY CAMPBELL. *BLACK'S LAW DICTIONARY: DEFINITIONS OF THE TERMS AND PHRASES OF AMERICAN AND ENGLISH JURISPRUDENCE, ANCIENT AND MODERN.* 6TH ED. ST. PAUL, MN: WEST PUBLISHING CO., 1990.

EXHIBIT 8-2

and phrases by the State and Federal courts from the earliest times, alphabetically arranged and indexed." It includes over 40 volumes of legally defined words and phrases, and each definition includes a citation to its source. It is kept up to date with pocket supplements. Because it collects definitions from all jurisdictions, *Words and Phrases* is extremely useful in determining how different jurisdictions have defined a word. It is also helpful when trying to find a case in which the definition of a word is an important element.

Unfortunately, *Words and Phrases* itself cannot always be found in local law libraries. However, most state digests include a volume or part of a volume labeled "Words and Phrases," which is generally an index to the legal definitions of words and phrases as used within that state.

Legal Encyclopedias

If you don't know anything about a subject and need to learn some basic information, you would undoubtedly go to an encyclopedia. If you wanted to learn something about law, you might refer to the *Encyclopedia Americana* or the *Encyclopedia Britannica*, where you would find information about the history of law and perhaps some basic principles. When engaging in legal research, however, you need more thorough explanations than these sources can provide. For a more complete, but still encyclopedic, treatment of a legal subject, turn to one of several legal encyclopedias listed below.

Legal encyclopedias can help define the scope of a legal problem. They are an excellent source of background information, a good introduction to a topic, and can help to place a subject in context. They are secondary sources that filter information found in primary sources and make simple statements about what the law is. Thus, they provide you with a basic vocabulary in your topic. However, the importance of beginning your legal research in an encyclopedia extends beyond obtaining a good grounding in concepts and vocabulary. Within the text of encyclopedias, you will find numerous footnotes to primary sources of the law. These sources are the legal authority upon which the encyclopedia authors relied to make their statements. In many instances, you should follow up your research by reading the cases and other sources cited there. Thus, beginning with encyclopedias is also an excellent way to identify the most important primary sources in your research. Keep in mind, however, that encyclopedias are not legal authority unto themselves; they simply restate laws and the pronouncements of the courts.

American Jurisprudence. 2d ed. Rochester, NY: Lawyers Cooperative Publishing Co., 1962–.

Abbreviated and cited as *Am.Jur.2d.*, *American Jurisprudence* is easier for the layperson to read than the other standard legal encyclopedia. *American Jurisprudence* provides a statement of the law in more than 430 topics. Each topic opens with a general and a detailed outline and includes a thorough scope note with cross-references to other topics. These outlines can aide in a quick survey of how subtopics relate to each other within a topic. See exhibit 8-3 for an example. *American Jurisprudence* also has a subject index, as well as statutes, rules, and regulations indexes and tables, which provide a way to determine how specific statutes, rules, and regulations fit within the scheme of the law. They are also a useful way to find a treatment and examination of documents within the context of your subject. *American Jurisprudence* is kept up to date with annual pocket supplements.

The editorial policy of the Lawyers Cooperative Publishing Company is to cite only to the most authoritative sources of the law. Thus, *American Jurisprudence* focuses more on the statement of the law than on citing authorities. By the same token, if you prefer to let the publisher make judgment calls as to the best documents, then *American Jurisprudence* is also a good source. You can be assured that the cases cited in the text are illustrative.

American Jurisprudence is also useful as a stepping stone to more information than just primary sources. The publisher makes copious references to other publications such as *American Law Reports* (see page 166) and law review articles, which provide you with even more analysis of your subject. *American Jurisprudence* is often referenced by other Lawyers Cooperative publications such as the *United States Code Service* and *Ballentine's Law Dictionary*.

Corpus Juris Secundum. St. Paul, MN: West Publishing Co., 1936–.

Abbreviated and cited as *C.J.S.*, *Corpus Juris Secundum* (*CJS*) is subtitled "A Complete Restatement of the Entire American Law as Developed by All Reported Cases," a fact that West Publishing's editors currently concede is impossible given the output of the courts. Just the same, *CJS* is an extremely well footnoted source. For that reason, it is a good way to find the law on a given subject. *CJS* categorizes the law of the United States in 400 broad topics. Each topic opens with a general and detailed outline. *CJS* has a multivolume subject index but does not include a table of statutes cited. It is also referenced in primary sources such as the *United States Code Annotated.* (See page 176.) Citations to *CJS* can also be found in many state codes as well as in West Publishing's system of digests. (See page 181.) It comprises over 150 volumes and is kept up to date with cumulative annual pocket parts.

Another feature of *CJS,* which makes it a valuable starting point for legal research, is its frequent use of West Publishing's topic and key numbering system, which we describe briefly below. See exhibit 8-4 for a sample page from *CJS*. Note the number of footnotes and case references; also note that following section 2, you will find a "Research Note" and "Library Reference." The library reference to Arrest, Key Numbers 1 and 58, are West's Digests' topic and key numbers under which you locate more cases on the subject within West's Digests.

Guide to American Law: Everyone's Legal Encyclopedia. St. Paul, MN: West Publishing, 1983–.

The *Guide to American Law* is a layperson's encyclopedia. Although it cites primary sources of the law and provides good background information, its coverage of legal topics is very general and does not approach the kind of

coverage provided by *American Jurisprudence* and *CJS* described above.

State Encyclopedias

In addition to the encyclopedias mentioned above, which are national in scope, there are a number of encyclopedias that cover the laws of individual states. These encyclopedias are found under a variety of names including "Jurisprudence," for example, *New York Jurisprudence* and *South Carolina Jurisprudence*; "Index," for example, *Strong's North Carolina Index*; or "Encyclopedia," for example, *Encyclopedia of Georgia Law*. As you might expect, these titles are a rich source of information and citations to the law of

---

5 Am Jur 2d   ARREST

Outline

   I. INTRODUCTION [§§ 1–7]

  II. IN CRIMINAL CASES [§§ 8–72]
     A. IN GENERAL [§§ 8, 9]
     B. WITH WARRANT [§§ 10–36]
     C. WITHOUT WARRANT [§§ 37–72]

 III. IN CIVIL CASES [§§ 73–91]
     A. IN GENERAL [§§ 73–75]
     B. PARTICULAR ACTIONS [§§ 76–84]
     C. PROCEDURE [§§ 85–91]

 IV. MANNER OF, AND PROCEDURE IN, MAKING ARRESTS [§§ 92-127]
     A. IN GENERAL [§§ 92–104]
     B. FORCE AND RESISTANCE [§§ 105–116]
     C. ENTERING PRIVATE PROPERTY TO MAKE ARREST [§§ 117–127]

  V. PRIVILEGE OR EXEMPTION FROM ARREST [§§ 128–143]
     A. IN GENERAL [§§ 128–131]
     B. PERSONS ENGAGED IN OFFICIAL BUSINESS OR ATTENDING OFFICIAL PROCEEDINGS [§§ 132–141]
     C. PROCEDURE [§§ 142, 143]

 VI. LIABILITIES CONNECTED WITH ARREST [§§ 144–149]

VII. EFFECT OF ILLEGALITY OF ARREST [§§ 150, 151]

I. INTRODUCTION

§ 1. Generally
§ 2. Definition; what constitutes arrest
§ 3. —Objective test
§ 4. —Physical force or submission required
§ 5. —Investigative stop distinguished
§ 6. Constitutional law aspects
§ 7. —Seizures not amounting to arrest

II.   IN CRIMINAL CASES

A. IN GENERAL

AMERICAN JURISPRUDENCE, 2D ED. ROCHESTER, NY: LAWYERS COOPERATIVE PUBLISHING CO., 1962 (OUTLINE OF ARREST, 5 AM JUR 2D PP. 659 AND 660)

EXHIBIT 8-3

---

§ 8.   Generally
§ 9.   Requirement of probable cause

B. With Warrant

1. In General

§ 10.   Nature of warrant
§ 11.   Warrant requirement; generally
§ 12.   Validity of warrant; effect of errors or invalidity
§ 13.   Effect of prior vacation or satisfaction of warrant
§ 14.   Use of search warrant as warrant of arrest

2. Issuance of Warrant

§ 15.   Who may issue warrant
§ 16.   Showing of probable cause
§ 17.   —Required showing where defendant has been indicted
§ 18.   Oath or affirmation
§ 19.   —Who may take oath or affidavit
§ 20.   —Requisites and sufficiency of affidavit or complaint
§ 21.   —Information and belief
§ 22.   Discretion of court
§ 23.   Duty to issue; mandamus to compel issuance
§ 24.   —Standing of private citizen to seek mandamus

3. Elements of Warrant

§ 25.   Generally
§ 26.   Facts establishing jurisdiction
§ 27.   Description of offense
§ 28.   Designation of person to be arrested

4. Execution and Return of Warrant

§ 29.   Execution of warrant; generally
§ 30.   Who may execute warrant
§ 31.   Service upon defendant
§ 32.   Return of warrant
§ 33.   Effect of failure to make proper return

5. Territorial Extent of Power to Arrest with Warrant

§ 34.   Generally
§ 35.   Execution of warrant in county other than that in which issued
§ 36.   Execution of warrant in state other than that in which issued

C. Without Warrant

1. In General

§ 37.   Generally
§ 38.   Statutory provisions

660

AMERICAN JURISPRUDENCE, 2D ED. ROCHESTER, NY: LAWYERS COOPERATIVE PUBLISHING CO., 1962 (OUTLINE OF ARREST, 5 AM JUR 2D PP. 659 AND 660)

EXHIBIT 8-3 (continued)

---

their respective jurisdictions. If there is an encyclopedia covering your jurisdiction, it would be worth your while to investigate it.

Subject Specific Encyclopedias

General encyclopedias, such as the *Britannica*, cover the entire topic of the law in several hundred pages, and criminal law in just a few. *CJS* (cited above) covers all of criminal law, including criminal proce-dure, in five volumes. LaFave and Israel's *Criminal Procedure* (see page 175), an encyclopedia of another sort, covers the subject of criminal procedure alone in three volumes. As the breadth of coverage of an encyclopedia narrows, its treatment of a subject deepens. Listed below is a selection of encyclopedic works which treat their subjects with greater depth than the general legal encyclopedias discussed above.

6A C. J. S.

ARREST §§ 1-2

I. INTRODUCTION

§ 1. Scope of Title

This title includes the treatment of the law concerning the taking and keeping of persons in legal custody to answer civil demands or criminal charges or to prevent the commission of a crime, the nature and scope of the remedy, privilege from arrest, grounds of arrest and jurisdiction over and proceedings to obtain arrest. Also discussed herein is the issuance, requisites and validity of writs, warrants, orders of arrest, etc., in civil actions and the amendment thereof; authority to arrest, making arrests and service of writs, warrants etc.; quashing, vacating, or setting aside process or orders for arrest, and other relief against arrest. Liabilities on, and enforcement of, securities to procure arrest and the liabilities of persons other than officers in wrongfully procuring or making arrests are also considered.

Subjects which are covered in other titles and not treated in this title include admission to, and rights and liabilities of, bail,[1] arrest as a means of commencing civil actions,[2] constitutional prohibitions of imprisonment for debt,[3] writs of habeas corpus and ne exeat,[4] liabilities for illegal arrest,[5] and motions in arrest of judgment.[6]

Also treated elsewhere are offenses committed in making or resisting arrest or delivering prisoners from custody,[7] and officers' duties and liabilities in regard to arrests, care and custody of prisoners, escapes, etc.;[8] liability of particu-lar classes of persons to arrest,[9] review of decisions in civil actions relating to arrest,[10] arrest of vessels,[11] and warrants for arrest in criminal prosecutions.[12]

§ 2. Definitions and Nature in General

An arrest is the taking, seizing, or detaining the person of another either by touching, or by any act which indicates an intention to take him into custody and subject the person arrested to the actual control and will of the person making the arrest.

Research Note

Nature and purpose of arrest on criminal charges and in civil actions are discussed respectively infra §§ 4, 73. What constitutes an arrest is considered infra §§ 43, 44, and investigatory detention, infra § 38.

Library References

Arrest ☞1, 58.

An arrest is the taking, seizing, or detaining the person of another either by touching, or by any act which indicates an intention to take him into custody and subject the person arrested to the actual control and will of the person making the arrest,[13] or any deprivation of the liberty of one person by another or any detention of him, for however short a time, without his consent, and against his will, whether it was by actual violence, threats, or otherwise.[14] The word "arrest" is derived from the French "arreter," meaning to stop or stay, and signifies a restraint of the person.[15] The terms "arrest" and "apprehension" have been by some courts used interchangeably as meaning the same thing when employed

---

1. See C.J.S. Bail.

2. See C.J.S. Process.

3. See C.J.S. Constitutional Law.

4. See C.J.S. titles Habeas Corpus and Ne Exeat.

5. See C.J.S. False Imprisonment.

6. See C.J.S. titles Criminal Law and Judgment.

7. See C.J.S. titles Assault and Battery, Escape, Homicide, Obstructing Justice, and Rescue.

8. See C.J.S. titles Clerks of Courts, Sheriffs and Constables, and Prisons.

9. See C.J.S. Infants and other specific titles.

10. See C.J.S. Appeal and Error.

11. See C.J.S. Admiralty.

12. See C.J.S. Criminal Law.

13. Mont.—State v. District Court of Eighth Judicial Dist. in and for Cascade County, 225 P. 1000, 1001, 70 Mont. 378.

Tenn.—Corpus Juris Secundum cited in West v. State, 425 S.W.2d 602, 221 Tenn. 178—Corpus Juris Secundum cited in Robertson v. State, 198 S.W.2d 633, 636, 184 Tenn. 277.

14. Ky.—Pratt v. Gross, 92 S.W.2d 788, 263 Ky. 521—Great Atlantic & Pacific Tea Co. v. Billups, 69 S.W.2d 5, 253 Ky. 126.

Similar definitions
(1) An arrest is a restriction of the right of locomotion or a restraint of the person.

D.C.—Price v. U. S., Mun.App., 119 A.2d 718.

(2) Term "arrest" may be applied to any case where a person is taken in custody or restrained of his full liberty, or where detention of a person in custody is continued for even a short period of time.

D.C.—U. S. v. Willis, D.C., 248 F.Supp. 265—U. S. v. Scott, D.C., 149 F.Supp. 837.

(3) Restraint, however slight, on another's liberty to come and go, constitutes arrest.

D.C.—Turney v. Rhodes, 155 S.E. 112, 42 Ga.App. 104.

N.Y.—People v. Esposito, 194 N.Y.S. 326, 118 Misc. 867.

15. Ill.—People v. Mirbelle, 276 Ill.App. 533.

Ohio.—Alter v. Paul, 135 N.E.2d 73, 101 Ohio App. 139.

5 C.J. p 385 note 2 [b].

Corpus Juris Secundum. St. Paul, MN: West Publishing Co., 1936-

FIGURE 8-4

Encyclopedia of the American Constitution. New York: Macmillan, 1986.

> This source seeks to "bridge the disciplines of history, law, and political science. . . . The subjects fall into five general categories: doctrinal concepts of constitutional law (about 55 percent of the total words); people (about 15 percent); judicial decisions, mostly of the Supreme Court of the United States (about 15 percent); public acts, such as statutes, treaties, and executive orders (about 5 percent); and historical periods (about 10 percent)."

Encyclopedia of the American Judicial System: Studies of the Principal Institutions and Processes of Law. New York: Scribner's, 1987.

> The topics covered by this encyclopedia constitute a broad range of legal and procedural issues. Although not considered authoritative in the legal sense of the word, this work provides an excellent historical and general treatment of many topics of concern to the criminal justice researcher. Each article is signed by the author.

The above works include the word *encyclopedia* in their titles. They are, therefore, easily identified as such. A number of other works provide an encyclopedic treatment of their subjects as well. Examples of such works are listed below.

LaFave, Wayne R., and Jerold Israel. *Criminal Procedure.* St. Paul, MN: West Publishing, 1984–.

LaFave, Wayne R. *Search and Seizure: A Treatise on the Fourth Amendment.* 3d ed. St. Paul, MN: West Publishing, 1996–.

Annotated Law Reporters

The words *annotation* and *annotated* have several meanings in legal research. (The authors define *annotated code* on page 176.). In this section the authors use *annotation* to mean an article or essay on some point of the law. Annotations of this sort usually take a relatively narrow subject and give it an in-depth, almost encyclopedic treatment. Such annotations consider all sides of a topic and all jurisdictions that might address the issue, and they give references to primary and secondary sources. They also point to, or raise, all issues related to the topic. For this reason, they are a fruitful source of context and analysis.

The only annotated law reporters for recent law in the United States are *American Law Reports; ALR Federal;* and *United States Supreme Court Reports, Lawyers Edition,* all listed below. Because these titles are so valuable to those who only occasionally use legal resources, we will describe them thoroughly.

American Law Reports. Rochester, NY: Lawyers Cooperative Publishing Co.

1st Series, Vol. 1–175 (1919–1948).

2d Series, Vol. 1–100 (1948–1965).

3d Series, Vol. 1–100 (1965–1980).

4th Series, Vol. 1–90 (1980–1991).

5th Series, Vol. 1– (1992–).

ALR Federal. Vol. 1-(1969–).

> Abbreviated and cited as *ALR, ALR 2d, ALR 3d, ALR 4th, ALR 5th,* and *ALR Fed.,* respectively, the above sources contain annotations as well as the full text of cases that Lawyers Cooperative Publishing has identified as addressing legal issues not yet resolved or representing a new direction in the law. *ALR* is supplemented with pocket parts at the end of each volume wherein the editors refer to new sections added to annotations, references to new cases, *ALR* annotations, and other sources of related information. Until 1969, subjects that fell under federal and state jurisdiction were treated in *ALR,* but in that year, federal issues were addressed exclusively by cases and annotations published in *ALR Federal.*
>
> In all of these series, Lawyers Cooperative Publishing preserves its editorial policy for *American Jurisprudence,* citing only "the most authoritative sources of the law." The cases published in the *ALR* volumes are the starting points for annotations, which provide comprehensive analyses of relatively narrow topics and use leading cases from as many jurisdictions as possible. In most instances, therefore, researchers who are restricted by jurisdiction can find some local case law treating their subjects.
>
> *ALR* annotations, like encyclopedia articles, provide references to primary sources of the law that address the issues. They are, therefore, complete with footnotes and citations to cases and collateral authorities. Several features of *ALR* annotations are especially helpful in completing research. Each annotation opens with the title and name of the responsible editor. The by-line is followed by an outline to the topic. (See exhibit 8-5. Notice the way the subject is analyzed and all possible sides of the topic are considered.) The outline is followed by various indexes to the annotation. The subject index provides subject access within the topic. (See exhibit 8-6.) Indexes and outlines are of different length, depending on the complexity of the law that addresses the topic and the length of the annotation itself. These two features provide subject access to the contents of the annotation.
>
> Exhibit 8-7 shows the "Table of Jurisdictions Represented," which can be used by those interested in determining how individual jurisdictions have treated a subject. Note that those interested in knowing how Pennsylvania has treated some portion of a subject will find Pennsylvania cases cited in §§4[a] and 9[b]. Notice in exhibit 8-8 that §1[b] cites *ALR* annotations that treat "Related Matters." These cross-references can be used to broaden or narrow the focus of your research. Finally, look at the text and footnotes of exhibit 8-9, where you will find references to cases, law review articles, *American Jurispru-*

dence, and other sections of the annotation in the footnotes and text. *In-text* references to cases and other sources of analysis and the law can also be found throughout.

You can find an *ALR* annotation several ways. First, other Lawyers Cooperative publications, such as *American Jurisprudence* (see page 162) and the *United States Code Service* (see page 176), indicate if an *ALR* annotation treats a related subject. Second, *ALR* has a subject index (supplemented with a pocket part), which provides access to annotations in *ALR 2d* through *ALR 5th, ALR Fed.*, and those appearing in *United States Supreme Court Reports, Lawyers Edition* (see below). (Most of the annotations found in *ALR* [first series] have now been superseded by the subsequent series, thus indexing for the first is not critical. The issue of superseded annotations is addressed below.) *ALR* annotations can also be located through references in other *ALR* annotations.

Access to *ALR* annotations is also provided by a series of tables found in the last of the index volumes. If you are researching a section of the *United States Code, Code of Federal Regulations, Federal Court Rules, State Laws, Uniform Laws, Model Acts,* or *Restatement of the Law*, these tables provide references to annotations which treat them. See exhibit 8-10 for a sample page noting the references to annotations dealing with the *California Penal Code*.

As mentioned above, *ALR* annotations are sometimes superseded. This is a direct result of changes in the law made by legislatures and courts; annotations are subsequently rewritten. In most instances, *ALR's* pocket supplements indicate when an annotation has been superseded and refer to the article that superseded it. In many cases, however, the novice legal researcher has already spent valuable time reading old law before referring to the supplement. The final volume of the "ALR Index" provides an "Annotation History" table. Before reading an annotation—unless it is very recent—refer to this table and determine if the annotation you are about to read has been superseded. This table is also supplemented in the pocket parts.

United States Supreme Court Reports, Lawyers Edition. Rochester, NY: Lawyers Cooperative.
1st Series, Vol. 1–Vol. 100 (1926–1956).
2d Series, Vol. 1– (1956–).

Abbreviated and cited as *L.Ed.* and *L.Ed.2d., Lawyers Edition* reports the full text of all the cases of the Supreme Court but also provides annotations where the Court's decisions are considered especially important. Access to annotations in *L.Ed.* is provided as to *ALR*. Like *ALR*, annotations are supplemented in pocket parts at the back of each volume. (See page 178 for further information about *L.Ed.* as mentioned in a discussion about decisions of the United States Supreme Court.)

Legal Periodicals

Legal periodical articles are another excellent source of analysis of the law. Several kinds of publications fall under the broad rubric of *legal periodical*, including law reviews, subject-oriented law reviews, bar journals, and legal newspapers. Law reviews, published by law schools, tend to be scholarly in both choice of subjects and treatment of those subjects. Most deal with theoretical issues and often take a narrow area of the law and give it in-depth treatment. They are especially useful when researching a "cutting-edge" legal topic. Law review articles are copiously footnoted with citations to primary and secondary sources. They are also generally more analytical and critical in their approach to topics. They are, therefore, an excellent resource. Annual surveys of the law and special subject-oriented issues are a feature of some law school reviews. The first issue of each volume of the *South Carolina Law Review*, for example, is titled "Annual Survey of South Carolina Law." Here you might find an article dealing with important developments in South Carolina criminal law or procedure.

Annual surveys are extremely helpful to criminal justice research. The following source provides a bibliography of annual surveys of the law.

Annuals and Surveys Appearing in Legal Periodicals: An Annotated Listing. Littleton, CO: F. B. Rothman, 1987–.

This publication is issued in loose-leaf format and compiles citations to surveys of the law of all 50 states, the federal courts, and subjects such as criminal law and criminal procedure.

Subject-oriented periodicals, such as the *Criminal Law Bulletin*, limit their subject coverage, although articles vary in their focus on that topic. These reviews are traditionally published by private publishers but are being produced more and more by law schools as well. You can rely on these kinds of publications to cite relevant law.

Bar journals are practice oriented and are usually published by bar associations. Although they tend to deal with matters of interest to the legal practitioner, they can be a good source of information for criminal justice research—especially when dealing with practical issues such as the defense function.

Articles from legal newspapers are frequently picked up by indexing services. Although many of the articles might sound on point, you should be aware that legal newspapers do just that—publish the news.

ANNOTATION

PEACE OFFICER'S CIVIL LIABILITY FOR DEATH OR PERSONAL INJURIES CAUSED BY INTENTIONAL FORCE IN ARRESTING MISDEMEANANT

by

James O. Pearson, Jr., J.D.

I. PRELIMINARY MATTERS

§ 1. Introduction:
  [a] Scope
  [b] Related matters
§ 2. Summary and comment:
  [a] Generally
  [b] Practice pointers

TOTAL CLIENT-SERVICE LIBRARY® REFERENCES

5 Am Jur 2d, Arrest §§ 80, 112, 114; 6 Am Jur 2d, Assault and Battery § 148; 15 Am Jur 2d, Civil Rights § 269

2 Am Jur Pl & Pr Forms (Rev ed), Assault and Battery, Forms 101–103, 283–285; 22 Am Jur Pl & Pr Forms (Rev ed), Sheriffs, Police and Constables, Forms 131–134

2 Am Jur Proof of Facts 81, Assault and Battery; 9 Am Jur Proof of Facts 2d 363, Police Officer's Use of Excessive Force in Making Arrest

15 Am Jur Trials 556, Police Misconduct Litigation—Plaintiff's Remedies

42 USCS § 1983

US L Ed Digest, Arrest § 1; Civil Rights §§ 4.5, 12.5; Sheriffs and Constables §§ 1, 4

ALR Digests, Arrest §§ 6, 11; Civil Rights § 1.3; Police § 7; Sheriff § 7

L Ed Index to Annos, Arrest; Assault and Battery; Civil Rights; Police

ALR Quick Index, Arrest; Assault and Battery; Discrimination; Misdemeanors; Police

Federal Quick Index, Arrest; Assault and Battery; Civil Rights; Misdemeanor; Police

---

Consult POCKET PART in this volume for later cases

AMERICAN LAW REPORTS. ROCHESTER, NY: LAWYERS COOPERATIVE PUBLISHING CO.

EXHIBIT 8-5

83 ALR3d   ARREST OF MISDEMEANANT—INTENTIONAL FORCE
83 ALR3d 238

INDEX

FIGURE 8-5 (continued)

ARREST OF MISDEMEANANT—INTENTIONAL FORCE   83 ALR3d
83 ALR3d 238

EXHIBIT 8-6

TABLE OF JURISDICTIONS REPRESENTED
Consult POCKET PART in this volume for later cases

US: §§ 2[a], 3, 4[a, b], 6[a], 7[c], 9[a, b], 13, 14[b]
Ala: §§ 2[b], 3, 4[a, b], 7[b]
Ark: §§ 2[b], 4[b], 9[b], 12[b], 14[b]
Cal: §§ 5, 7[c], 13, 14[a]
Colo: § 12[b]
Conn: § 9[a]
Fla: § 2[b]
Ga: §§ 2[a], 3, 4[b], 6[a]
Iowa: §§ 2[b], 3, 4[a, b]
Ky: §§ 2[a, b], 3, 4[a, b], 6[a], 7[a], 9[c]
La: §§ 2[b], 8[a, b], 9[a, b], 11[a]
Mass: § 12[c]
Mich: § 9[a]
Miss: §§ 2[a], 3, 4[a, b], 7[c], 8[a], 13
Mo: §§ 2[b], 9[a, b], 13
Neb: §§ 2[b], 9[a]

NJ: §§ 2[a, b], 3, 4[b], 6[a]
NM: §§ 3, 4[b], 6[a]
NY: § 14[b]
NC: §§ 2[a], 3, 6[b]
ND: §§ 2[b], 3, 4[a], 12[a]
Ohio: §§ 2[a], 4[a], 9[c]
Okla: § 4[b]
Or: § 14[b]
Pa: §§ 4[a], 9[b]
RI: §§ 9[b], 14[a]
Tenn: §§ 2[a, b], 3, 4[b], 6[a], 9[a]
Tex: § 14[b]
Utah: §§ 3, 6[a], 10[b]
Wash: § 3
W Va: §§ 2[a], 9[c], 11[b]
Wis: §§ 2[b], 8[a], 10[a]

I. Preliminary matters

§ 1. Introduction

[a] Scope

1. The annotation entitled "Degree of force that may be employed in arresting one charged with a misdemeanor" at 3 ALR 1170, supplemented at 42 ALR 1200, need no longer be consulted for cases within the scope of the present annotation.

2. Included are federal civil rights actions under 42 USC § 1983 in which the claim of a deprivation of constitutional rights was based on death or personal injuries suffered by the suspect, if such cases are otherwise within the scope of the present annotation. See generally the annotation entitled "Police action in connection with arrest as violation of Civil

This annotation[1] collects and analyzes the cases in which a civil[2] action was initiated against a peace officer[3] to recover damages for death or per-

Rights Act, 42 USC § 1983," at 1 ALR Fed 519.

3. The term "peace officer" includes all public law-enforcement officers, such as sheriffs, deputy sheriffs, marshalls, policemen, and constables.

The present annotation is concerned only with the liability of a peace officer, not with the liability either of his employer or of the surety on his official bond. These subjects are covered in the annotation entitled "Municipal liability for personal injuries resulting from police officer's use of excessive force in performance of duty," at 88 ALR2d 1330, and in 70 Am Jur 2d, Sheriffs, Police, and Constables §§ 141, 143–145, respectively.

EXHIBIT 8-7

§ 1[a]   ARREST OF MISDEMEANANT—INTENTIONAL FORCE   83 ALR3d
83 ALR3d 238

sonal injuries caused by the officer's use of intentional[4] force in arresting or attempting to arrest[5] a person suspected of having committed a misdemeanor.[6]

Since relevant statutory provisions are treated herein only insofar as they are discussed in the reported cases, the reader is advised to consult the most current statutes of the jurisdiction in which he is interested.

[b] Related matters

Modern status: Right of peace officer to use deadly force in attempting to arrest fleeing felon. 83 ALR3d 174.

Right to resist excessive force used in accomplishing lawful arrest. 77 ALR3d 281.

Liability of municipal corporation for shooting of bystander by law enforcement officer attempting to enforce law. 76 ALR3d 1176.

Modern status of rules as to right to forcefully resist illegal arrest. 44 ALR3d 1078.

What constitutes obstructing or resisting an officer, in the absence of actual force. 44 ALR3d 1018.

Municipal liability for personal injuries resulting from police officer's use of excessive force in performance of duty. 88 ALR2d 1330.

Truant or attendance officer's liability for assault and battery or false imprisonment. 62 ALR2d 1328.

Personal liability of policeman, sheriff, or other peace officer, or bond, for negligently causing personal injury or death. 60 ALR2d 873.

Civil liability, under federal civil rights statute (42 USC § 1983) of state officers who coerce or attempt to coerce confessions or pleas of guilty. 55 ALR2d 512.

Civil liability of sheriff or other officer charged with keeping jail or prison for death or injury of prisoner. 14 ALR2d 353.

Degree of force that may be employed in arresting one charged with a misdemeanor. 42 ALR 1200, supplementing 3 ALR 1170.

---

4. The term "intentional" includes all touchings of the suspect which the officer deliberately caused, as well as those acts which were so reckless and certain to involve a touching of the suspect that the court has treated them as constituting an intentional tort. It is not necessary that the officer have intended to cause the death or personal injuries suffered by the suspect. For discussion of an officer's liability for negligently causing personal injury or death, see the annotation entitled "Personal liability of policeman, sheriff, or other peace officer, or bond, for negligently causing personal injury or death," at 60 ALR2d 873.

5. The present annotation is concerned with an officer's civil liability for the use of intentional force in arresting a misdemeanant only where the attempted arrest is lawful. Furthermore, rules governing a peace officer's use of force in situations not directly relating to arrests, such as force applied to extract a confession or

force exerted against prisoners generally, are beyond the scope of this annotation. See the annotations entitled "Civil liability, under federal civil rights statute (42 USC § 1983) of state officers who coerce or attempt to coerce confessions or pleas of guilty," at 55 ALR2d 512, and "Civil liability of sheriff or other officer charged with keeping jail or prison for death or injury of prisoner," at 14 ALR2d 353, respectively.

6. In cases of which the court has not specified whether the offense in question was a misdemeanor or felony, minor offenses, such as breach of the peace and traffic violations, which are normally classified as misdemeanors, have been treated as constituting misdemeanors for purpose of inclusion within the present annotation, while such offenses as murder, treason, robbery, and larceny, which are normally classified as felonies, have likewise been treated as felonies herein.

242

EXHIBIT 8-8

Police action in connection with arrest as violation of Civil Rights Act, 42 USC § 1983. 1 ALR Fed 519

◆

Moreland, The Use of Force in Effecting or Resisting Arrest. 33 Neb L Rev 408 (1954).

◆

C. Torcia, Wharton's Criminal Procedure (12th ed, 1974), §§ 80, 81.

§ 2. Summary and comment

[a] Generally

The basic rule governing the conduct of a peace officer in making an arrest is that he may use whatever force is necessary to effect the arrest, but he may not use excessive force.[7] This rule is, of course, generally applicable to arrests involving misdemeanants. However, despite the broad implications of such rule, it has been universally held that a peace officer may not use deadly force against a fleeing misdemeanant even though such force is necessary to prevent the suspect's escape.[8] The justification most often given for this restriction on the force available to an arresting officer is that, as a matter of social policy, allowing persons committing minor crimes to escape is preferable to taking or endangering their lives.[9] In addition, some courts have emphasized the high probability that escaping misdemeanants will be recaptured at a later time.[10]

Even when a misdemeanant is resisting arrest, rather than fleeing, not all courts have carried to its logical conclusion the general rule allowing an officer to use whatever force is necessary to effect an arrest. For example, with respect to the use of deadly force against a resisting misdemeanant, numerous courts, applying traditional principles of self-defense, have permitted the use of such force only when the officer was in danger of losing his life or suffering great bodily harm.[11] In so holding, these courts have not focused on whether the use of deadly force was necessary to effect the resisting misdemeanant's arrest, but instead have examined the reasonableness of the officer's belief that deadly force was required to save his own life.[12]

Other courts, apparently in the minority,[13] have not limited the use of deadly force against a resisting misdemeanant to situations involving self-

---

7. See 5 Am Jur 2d, Arrest § 80.

8. § 3, infra.

9. See, for example, Palmer v Hall (1974, DC Ga) 380 F Supp 120, affd in part and revd in part on other grounds (CA5 Ga) 517 F2d 705, reh den (CA5 Ga) 521 F2d 815 (applying Georgia law).

10. See, for example, Sossamon v Cruse (1903) 133 NC 470, 45 SE 757 (ovrld on other grounds State v Mobley, 240 NC 476, 83 SE2d 100).

11. § 4[b], infra.

12. See, for example, Holland v Martin (1952) 214 Miss 10, 58 So 2d 62.
It has been suggested that this rule is logical for the reason that if an officer is not justified in taking the life of a fleeing misdemeanant, then he should likewise not be permitted to take the life of a resisting misdemeanant unless his own life is in danger. See the note, The Application of Deadly Force to Effectuate an Arrest, in 5 Washburn L J 262 (1967).

13. See the notes, The Civil Liability of Peace Officers for Wounding or Killing, in 28 U Cin L Rev 488 (1959), and The Application of Deadly Force to Effectuate an Arrest, in 5 Washburn L J 262 (1967), wherein both commentators stated the basic rule to be that an arresting officer may only kill a resisting misdemeanant in self-defense.

243

EXHIBIT 8-9

TABLES

Title and section	Vol. and page	Title and section	Vol. and page
CALIFORNIA—Cont'd		**CALIFORNIA—Cont'd**	
Civ Proc Code—Cont'd		**Ins. Code—Cont'd**	
1190.0	4 ALR5th 772 § 43	790.03(h)	6 ALR5th 297 § 40[b], 41[b], 43, 49[b]
1190.0(h)	4 ALR5th 772 § 12[b], 73[a]	790.03(h)(1)	6 ALR5th 297 § 40[a]
1190.1	4 ALR5th 772 § 12[a], 32, 36, 37[b], 39, 45[b], 46, 51, 53[a], 75, 77[b], 79[b]	790.03(h)(2)	6 ALR5th 297 § 43
		790.03(h)(3)	6 ALR5th 297 § 12, 34[a], 43
1190.1(h)	4 ALR5th 772 § 4[e], 32, 34, 36, 38, 51, 53[a], 59[b], 73[b], 76, 109	790.03(h)(5)	6 ALR5th 297 § 4[b], 7[b], 18[b], 37, 41[a], 43, 45[a]
1190.1(h) (1963)	4 ALR5th 772 § 81[a]	790.03(h)(13)	6 ALR5th 297 § 41[a], 43
1191.1	4 ALR5th 772 § 75	1063 et seq	6 ALR5th 297 § 26
1192.1	4 ALR5th 772 § 75, 78, 101, 106	1063.2	6 ALR5th 297 § 12, 50
1193	4 ALR5th 772 § 63[a]	1063.12(a)	6 ALR5th 297 § 50
1194	4 ALR5th 772 § 74, 77[a], 77[b]	1158.2 [11580.2]	3 ALR5th 746 § 5, 10[a]
1195	4 ALR5th 772 § 74, 77[b]	11580.2	2 ALR5th 922 § 3; 3 ALR5th 746 § 5, 6
1197	4 ALR5th 772 § 74, 77[b]	11580.2, subdivision (g)	3 ALR5th 746 § 12[a]
1197.1	4 ALR5th 772 § 36, 43, 46, 53[a], 75	**Lab Code**	
1197.1(a)	4 ALR5th 772 § 4[e], 12[b], 34	1720-1775	5 ALR5th 470 § 6[b]
1308	3 ALR5th 590 § 7[a]	1726	7 ALR5th 444 § 3
1312	3 ALR5th 590 § 7[a]	1727	7 ALR5th 444 § 3
1330	3 ALR5th 590 § 7[a]	1770 et seq	7 ALR5th 400 § 9[a]
1333	3 ALR5th 590 § 7[a]	1775	7 ALR5th 444 § 3
1710.15	8 ALR5th 653 § 9[a]	3202	4 ALR5th 585 § 3, 16[a]
3264	4 ALR5th 772 § 32	3351	8 ALR5th 798 § 3[a]
Fin Code		3357	8 ALR5th 798 § 3[a]
7152	4 ALR5th 772 § 76	3600	4 ALR5th 443 § 5[a], 6[b], 10[a]
7153	4 ALR5th 772 § 76	3601	4 ALR5th 443 § 5[a], 6[b]
7154	4 ALR5th 772 § 76	3602	6 ALR5th 297 § 43
7156	4 ALR5th 772 § 76	**Penal Code**	
Gov Code		7(4)(2)	6 ALR5th 733 § 12[a]
3205	107 ALR Fed 21 § 57[a]	220	8 ALR5th 254 § 7[b]
14376	4 ALR5th 772 § 59[a]	243(e)(5)	5 ALR5th 243 § 19
14402	4 ALR5th 772 § 59[a]	288	8 ALR5th 254 § 10[b], 15
65302 subd (c)	1 ALR5th 662 § 11[a]	288a	1 ALR5th 776 § 11; 8 ALR5th 254 § 7[b], 10[b]
65583	1 ALR5th 662 § 11[a]	288a(b)(2)	8 ALR5th 254 § 10[b]
65587	1 ALR5th 662 § 11[a]	422.6(b)	8 ALR5th 254 § 13[b]
65700 subd (a)	1 ALR5th 662 § 11[a]	594	8 ALR5th 254 § 13[b]
Health & Safety Code		597	6 ALR5th 733 § 11[b], 16[b]
11003	4 ALR5th 1 § 18, 28[a]	597(a)	6 ALR5th 733 § 3, 12[a], 29[a]
11003.1	4 ALR5th 1 § 18, 28[a]	597(b)	6 ALR5th 733 § 11[a], 16[b]
11350	4 ALR5th 1 § 33[a]	597b	6 ALR5th 733 § 6, 26[a]
11377	4 ALR5th 1 § 37	597f	6 ALR5th 733 § 11[b], 16[a], 18[a]
11500	4 ALR5th 1 § 17[d], 33[a], 34[c], 36	647(c)	7 ALR5th 455 § 3[a, b], 4, 6[b]
11530	4 ALR5th 1 § 17[a], 18, 21[b], 22[b], 26, 28[a], 29	653M(a)	8 ALR5th 254 § 13[b]
11910	4 ALR5th 1 § 18, 30, 31, 37	654	4 ALR5th 273 § 23
26250	2 ALR5th 189 § 6[a]	667	7 ALR5th 263 § 7[d]
28689	2 ALR5th 966 § 4[a], 5	667 subd (a)	7 ALR5th 263 § 3[a], 4[a], 5[a, b], 7[d]
Ins. Code		667.5 subd (b)	7 ALR5th 263 § 7[d]
533	8 ALR5th 254 § 10[a, b], 14, 15		
790-790.10	6 ALR5th 297 § 4[b], 7[b]		

AMERICAN LAW REPORTS. ROCHESTER, NY: LAWYERS COOPERATIVE PUBLISHING CO.

EXHIBIT 8-10

little of the information found there is substantive. But as we said in our discussion of periodicals in chapter 5, these kinds of publications have a legitimate place. If the topic of your research is current or if you are looking for alternative coverage of some event, they will be beneficial. To find articles from legal periodicals, use one of the indexes covered in chapter 5. You will also find frequent references to legal periodical articles in *ALR* annotations, annotated codes, and other sources of the law.

Legal Treatises

The sources examined thus far represent an increasingly detailed level of analysis of the law. Legal treatises and comprehensive books about legal topics are the final type of secondary source to address in this progression. Here, too, the uniqueness of legal vocabulary—even in the way it identifies books—reveals itself. Books on legal topics are generally called "treatises." In fact, all published materials about the law with an identifiable author could be called a treatise. *Hornbooks*, however, are a distinct type of legal treatise; generally they are one-volume works written by prominent legal scholars that treat relatively broad topic areas. These works are often referred to as a source of "black letter law," or a simple statement of generally accepted principles of law based on leading cases and statutory authorities. As with encyclopedias and annotations, hornbooks are a source of analysis and citations to primary sources. What is particularly important about them is that they bear the name of a prominent legal scholar, which may give them greater weight than an encyclopedic work.

A few important hornbooks in criminal law are listed below.

LaFave, Wayne R., and Austin W. Scott, Jr. *Criminal Law.* 2d ed. St. Paul, MN: West Publishing, 1986.

LaFave, Wayne R., and Jerold H. Israel. *Criminal Procedure.* 2d ed. St. Paul, MN: West Publishing, 1992–.

Whitebread, Charles H., and Christopher Slobogin. *Criminal Procedure: An Analysis of Cases and Concepts.* 3d ed. Westbury, NY: Foundation Press, 1993.

Beyond the realm of hornbooks are several worthy multivolume treatises on criminal law, some of which we cited in our treatment of encyclopedias. All offer the same expert analysis of the law and, of course, copious footnotes to primary sources.

PRIMARY SOURCES OF THE LAW

Up to this point, the authors have covered some of the most valuable publications for analyses of the law and citations to primary source documents. These materials are best used in instances when you need an explanation of the law in order to understand it. In some kinds of writing, such sources could be used as quotable sources; however, in scholarly research, as in the practice of law, considerable judgement must be used in a decision to cite them. When they are cited, these secondary sources constitute only persuasive authority, not mandatory authority. Those that are cited are usually the more scholarly types such as law review articles and important treatises. In this case, references are made because the author is of sufficient stature and his or her interpretation should be respected.

In essence, however, legal research is a search for primary sources of the law—constitutions, legislation, and common law—which can be found in a number of different publications. Some of these are published by government agencies and are considered *official* publications. Commercial publishers are also involved in the publication of primary legal resources. Generally, these privately published resources are considered *unofficial,* but some governments may authorize private companies to print the official version of their laws.

For academic research purposes, the difference between official and unofficial publications can generally be ignored. In fact, for criminal justice research, the use of privately published legal resources is recommended because private publishers enhance research in the law with devices such as indexing aids, historical notes, and references to related cases, statutes, and law review articles.

Listed below you will find primary sources of the law organized into the three types outlined above.

Constitutions

The text of the Constitution of the United States can be accessed through a variety of ways—everything from encyclopedias and almanacs to the calendar hanging in your kitchen. The most authoritative publication of any government's constitution is always the official one published by that government. This official version can be relied upon as evidence of law as long as your copy is the current version and is up to date with the latest amendments.

The official version of the U.S. Constitution is as follows:

The Constitution of the United States of America. Washington, DC: U.S. Government Printing Office, 1987.

The Constitution of the United States can also be located in *United States Code Annotated* and *United States Code Service* (both discussed later on this page) and at various Web sites, such as the two listed below.

"Cornell University, Legal Information Institute." http://www.law.cornell.edu/constitution/constitution.overview.html (April 21, 1997).

"Emory Law School." http://www.law.emory.edu/FEDERAL/usconst.html (April 21, 1997).

Authoritative versions of state constitutions are often published with the states' respective codes. Many other state publications, such as *registers* and *legislative manuals*, also contain copies of their respective state's constitution.

Legislation

Legislation falls into two categories: *session laws* and *codes*. Session laws are those laws or acts passed by individual sessions of a legislative body usually numbered and printed in chronological order as they are passed. For example, Public Law 91-452 is the 452d law passed by the 91st U.S. Congress and signed by the president. Different jurisdictions number their session laws in different ways and refer to their laws with different terminology. Although *session law* is a good generic term when referring to resources such as these, be aware that other terms are used as well, including *statutes, statutes at large, acts, public acts, laws,* and *public laws*.

Code is a generic term that applies to the subject arrangement of all the laws currently in force within a jurisdiction. Codes are important resources for two reasons: First, as we said above, session laws are arranged in chronological order, thus accessing them by subject can be a daunting task. To find a federal law by subject, you would have to look through the index of every volume of the *Statutes at Large*. Because codes organize the law by subject, all criminal law may be located in one place rather than spread throughout all the volumes of published session laws. Second, finding the law is complicated by the fact that legislatures amend and repeal laws that they have already passed in earlier sessions. Thus, the current version of the Organized Crime Control Act might be very different today from the law as it was originally passed. To determine what the law says currently using session law sources, you would have to find each amendment, then piece the language of the law together from the original and all changes. Codes, on the other hand, incorporate all amendments into a single form. Like session laws, codes are referred to by a number of terms that vary from jurisdiction to jurisdiction: *statutes, revised statutes, general statutes, general laws, code, compiled laws,* or *consolidated laws*.

Annotated codes are especially helpful in legal research. As mentioned earlier in this chapter, the word *annotation* is used in various ways in legal research; when used in the context of a code, it usually means that the code includes aids that can assist in further research. Annotated versions of the U.S. and state codes can include library references, cross references to other code sections, history notes on how the law has changed through various amendments, references to texts and law review articles that might give a description or analysis, and references to cases that have either interpreted the code section or dealt with the same subject.

Federal Code

There are three versions of the *U.S. Code*, one official and two unofficial. They all use the same numbering system to identify code sections.

The United States Code. Washington, DC: U.S. Government Printing Office, 1940–.
> Abbreviated and cited *USC*, this is the official version of the *U.S. Code*. Although official, it is not the most effective way to access the law. The schedule for recompilation lags too far behind the passage of laws; therefore, research for current law has to be carefully updated.

United States Code Annotated. St. Paul, MN: West Publishing, 1927–.
> Abbreviated and cited *USCA*, this is a privately published annotated version of the *U.S. Code*. It is kept up to date with annual and quarterly supplementation. Although not official, most researchers consider it to be an authoritative source of the law. References to cases that interpret code sections are extensive. You can rely on finding a large number of references to sources such as *Corpus Juris Secundum*.

United States Code Service. Rochester, NY: Lawyers Cooperative, 1972–.

Abbreviated and cited *USCS*, this is an annotated, privately published version of the *U.S. Code*. It is kept up to date with quarterly and annual supplements and a session law service for new legislation. References to sources such as *American Law Reports* (see page 166) and *American Jurisprudence* (see page 162) are copious; case notes are used more conservatively. Lawyers Cooperative Publishing makes an effort to refer users to what it considers only the most important cases.

The U.S. Code is also available on the World Wide Web.

"Cornell University, Legal Information Institute." http://www.law.cornell.edu/uscode (April 21, 1997).

U.S. House of Representatives, Internet Law Library. **"U.S. Code."** http://law.house.gov/usc.html (April 21, 1997).

Delegated legislation, or regulations, promulgated by agencies of the federal government are first published in chronological order in the *Federal Register,* then are codified in the *Code of Federal Regulations*.

State Codes

Like the federal government, each of the states has codes. These codes are published in a variety of formats; some states have official and unofficial codes, most are annotated to one degree or another, and cite cases interpreting state code sections. All state codes are kept up to date with supplementation. State codes are accessible through their indexes as well as references from various sources such as *ALR* (*American Law Report*) annotations.

In the study of criminal justice, a frequent topic of legal research involves the comparison of related state laws. Under normal circumstances, you would have to work through the indexes of all 50 state codes, but in many instances, sources such as the following provide citations to the laws of all jurisdictions by subject. Thus, if you need to compare criminal statutes of limitation for the states, you might turn to one of the resources listed below.

Comparative Statutory Sources: U.S., Canadian, Multinational. 3d ed. Buffalo, NY: William S. Hein & Co., 1987.
> This guide attempts to provide an index to comparative national provisions of statutes on specific subjects. It limits itself to sources that are updated frequently, such as periodicals and loose-leaf services. Therefore, although the current edition was published in 1987, the sources cited are likely to be current.

National Survey of State Laws. 2d ed. Detroit, MI: Gale Research, 1997.

The *National Survey of State Laws* provides citations to state laws on given topics, as well as simple analyses of the law in a convenient tabular format. Under the topic heading "Criminal Statutes of Limitation," for example, the table refers to the code section, the length of time for statutes of limitation for felonies and misdemeanors, and a description of acts that toll the statute. Under "Illegal Drugs: Marijuana," the table cites the appropriate section of the code and definitions of *possession, sale,* and *trafficking.*

Subject Compilations of State Laws. Westport, CT: Greenwood Press (and various other publishers), 1960–.
> This publication is a bibliography of books, articles, and federal and state publications that contain compilations of state laws on approximately 200 subjects. Subjects include crime control, crime victims, criminal commitment, criminal conversation, criminal law, criminal procedure, and police.

Uniform and Model State Laws

In chapter 2 the authors mentioned the National Conference of Commissioners on Uniform State Laws (see page 38), which is composed of individuals in the legal profession appointed by the states' governors. Their mission is to promote uniformity among state laws on subjects where uniformity is deemed desirable and practicable; thus, the terms *uniform* and *model* are used. These individuals are responsible for drafting the *Model Penal Code,* the *Uniform Controlled Substances Act,* and the *Criminal Extradition Act*, to name a few. State legislatures, in turn, are left to adopt these acts at their own discretion via the usual legislative processes. These uniform or model laws— as drafted by the conference—can be found in the following publication:

Uniform Laws Annotated. Master ed. St. Paul, MN: West Publishing, 1967–.
> This 13-volume set contains the full text of uniform laws and includes tables describing how each has been adopted by the states, comments as to how the states have made variations on the laws, and descriptions of how the laws have been treated in the courts, law review articles, and other secondary sources.

Uniform laws go through an extended deliberative process before being offered to the states for promulgation. As part of this process the National Conference of Commissioners offers various drafts for comment. These drafts can be found in law libraries or at the following World Wide Web site:

National Conference of Commissioners on Uniform State Laws. **"Drafts of Uniform and Model State Acts."** http://www.law.upenn.edu/library/ulc/ulc.htm (April 21, 1997).

In some instances, states adopt a uniform act but make changes to suit their individual needs. Model or uniform laws that have been adopted by a state, whether changed or not, are published in that state's code (see page 177 for states' codes).

Common Law

The courts are called upon to adjudicate conflicts by applying the law. Part of judges' responsibility is to settle conflicts that grow out of human relationships such as contracts. As it relates to criminal justice, their work is focused on the application and interpretation of law and procedure in the investigation, arrest, trial, and final determination of criminal cases. As such, judges may have to interpret legislative law and constitutional limits thereupon.

The decisions of courts are published in *reporters*. The opinions of the highest courts of each jurisdiction, and sometimes the lower courts, can be found in official and unofficial versions of these reporters. As mentioned above, common law operates on the principle of *stare decisis*, the idea that the legal rules used to settle one dispute should be used to settle all subsequent similar disputes. Thus, it is imperative that decisions and opinions of the courts be reported.

Federal Reporters

Opinions of the U.S. Supreme Court are published officially in *United States Reports* and unofficially in *U.S. Supreme Court Reports, Lawyers' Edition* and the *Supreme Court Reporter* (see below for both). These reporters publish the full text of all opinions rendered by the Court.

Supreme Court Reporter. St. Paul, MN: West Publishing, 1882–.

Abbreviated and cited *S.Ct.,* this is an unofficial reporter of Supreme Court opinions. Unlike the others, however, it is not retrospective and begins its coverage of the Court's decisions with the October term of 1882. Each opinion includes headnotes composed by West's staff, which summarize the important law and issues dealt with by the case. *Supreme Court Reporter* includes the use of West's key numbering system (see page 162–63) for the classification of case law by subject.

United States Reports: Cases Adjudged in the Supreme Court. Washington, DC: Government Printing Office, 1754–.

Abbreviated and cited *U.S.,* this official reporter of U.S. Supreme Court opinions dates back to the first opinion rendered by the Court and includes cases from Pennsylvania before the Revolution. Cases are accompanied by a *syllabus* written by the official reporter of decisions, which provides a good summary of the facts, issues, and law used

to resolve the dispute before the Court. Unfortunately, like many official publications, the reporting of opinions in this source may lag as long as three years.

United States Supreme Court Reports, Lawyers Edition. Rochester, NY: Lawyers Cooperative.
1st Series, Vol. 1–Vol. 100 (1926–1956).
2nd Series, Vol. 1– (1956–).

Abbreviated and cited *L.Ed.* and *L.Ed.2d,* this unofficial reporter of Supreme Court decisions is popularly referred to as *Lawyers Edition.* Although it began publication in 1926, *Lawyers Edition* is completely retrospective in its coverage of Supreme Court opinions. Editorial features that enhance the use of this reporter include *headnotes,* or more detailed summaries of the important issues and legal rules used to decide the case; summaries of the briefs and arguments of counsel in cases; and *annotations.*

U.S. Supreme Court opinions are available at the following World Wide Web sites:
"Cornell University, Legal Information Institute." http://www.law.cornell.edu/supct/supct.table.html (April 21, 1997) (Cases from 1990 to date).
"Findlaw." http://www.findlaw.com/casecode/ supreme.html (April 21, 1997) (Cases from 1937 to date).

Here is a sample U.S. Supreme Court case citation:

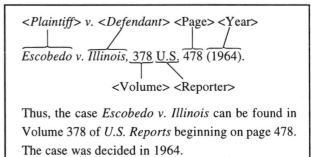

Thus, the case *Escobedo v. Illinois* can be found in Volume 378 of *U.S. Reports* beginning on page 478. The case was decided in 1964.

Opinions of the federal courts of appeals and district courts are published officially and unofficially as well. Unlike the reporters of Supreme Court decisions, reporters of the lower federal courts do not publish all the opinions available.

Federal Reporter. St. Paul, MN: West Publishing.
1st Series, Vol. 1–Vol. 300 (1880–1924)
2nd Series, Vol. 1–Vol. 999 (1924–1993)
3d Series, Vol. 1– (1993–).

Abbreviated and cited *F., F.2d, F.3d,* this reporter began its coverage of the intermediate appellate courts in 1880. It currently reports the decisions of the U.S. Court of Appeals as well as those of various other courts of limited subject matter jurisdiction. From 1880 to 1932, it included opinions of the federal district courts and other courts of first instance as well. It also uses West Publishing's key numbering system.

The following is a sample citation from a U.S. Court of Appeals case:

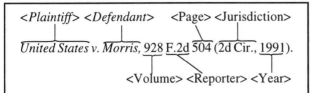

The decision in the case *U.S. v. Morris* is reported in Volume 928 of the *Federal Reporter,* 2d series, beginning on page 504. It was heard in the Second Circuit of the U.S. Court of Appeals and decided in 1991.

Recent decisions of the U.S. Court of Appeals are also available on various Web sites. The easiest way to access these cases is through one of many compendium sites at law schools, such as the one below:

The University of South Carolina Law Center. **"Federal Reference Desk."** http://www.law.sc.edu/refdesk1.htm (April 21, 1997).

With the expansion of the Web, the decisions of many courts are available online. The following site provides a search engine for accessing the decisions of the U.S. Court of Appeals. As with all developing World Wide Web resources, the user should pay close attention to the time period covered.

Law Journal Extra. **"Search the Federal Courts."** http://search.ljx.com/ (April 21, 1997).

District court cases can be found in the following source:

Federal Supplement. St. Paul, MN: West Publishing, 1932–.
> Abbreviated and cited *F. Supp.* or *F.S.*, the *Federal Supplement* began coverage of federal district opinions in 1932. It also makes use of the key numbering system (see page 162–63).

A sample Federal Supplement citation follows:

State Reporters

The opinions of state courts can be found in official publications dating back to the beginning of the courts. State opinions can currently be found in both official and unofficial form. Almost all opinions of the highest state courts are published; opinions of the intermediate appellate courts and trial level courts are selectively published.

West Publishing is the largest publisher of opinions of the courts of all jurisdictions in the United States. As part of its National Reporter System, it publishes unofficial reports of decisions for all the state courts, as well as the federal courts. It also acts as the official reporter for some states. Those portions of the National Reporter System that report state decisions are sometimes referred to as "regional reporters." Because the coverage of the regional reporters is not completely retrospective, the historical researcher must refer to official reporters for the years before approximately 1880. These regional reporters, which also use West's key numbering system, are listed below.

Atlantic Reporter. St. Paul, MN: West Publishing.
1st Series, Vol. 1–Vol. 200 (1885–1938).
2d Series, Vol. 1– (1938–).
> Abbreviated and cited *A.* and *A.2d*, this reporter covers all decisions of the courts of last resort and selected opinions of intermediate appellate courts, beginning in 1885, from the states of Connecticut, Delaware, Maine, Maryland, New Hampshire, New Jersey, Pennsylvania, Rhode Island, and Vermont.

California Reporter. St. Paul, MN: West Publishing.
1st Series, Vol. 1–Vol. 286 (1960–1992).
2d Series, Vol. 1– (1992–).
> Abbreviated and cited *Cal.Rptr* and *Cal.Rptr 2d,* this reporter covers all decisions of the California Supreme Court and decisions approved for publication from the lower appellate courts. Until 1960, decisions of all of these courts were published in the *Pacific Reporter* (see below). Since 1960, only decisions of the California Supreme Court are also published in the *Pacific Reporter.*

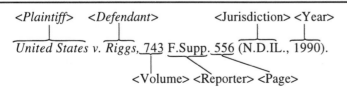

The decision in the case *U.S. v. Riggs* can be found in Volume 743 of the *Federal Supplement*, beginning on page 556. It was decided by the U.S. District Court for the Northern District of Illinois in 1990.

New York Supplement. St. Paul, MN: West Publishing.

1st Series, Vol. 1–Vol. 300 (1888–1938).

2d Series, Vol. 1– (1938–).

Abbreviated and cited *N.Y.S.* and *N.Y.S.2d,* this reporter covers all decisions of the court of last resort and intermediate appellate courts of the state of New York. The *North Eastern Reporter* (see below), by comparison, reports only the decisions of the New York Court of Appeals, New York's highest court.

North Eastern Reporter. St. Paul, MN: West Publishing.

1st Series, Vol. 1–Vol. 200 (1885–1936).

2d Series, Vol. 1– (1936–).

Abbreviated and cited *N.E.* and *N.E.2d,* this reporter covers all decisions of the courts of last resort and selected opinions of intermediate appellate courts, beginning in 1885, from the states of Illinois, Indiana, Massachusetts, New York, and Ohio. See also *New York Supplement* above.

North Western Reporter. St. Paul, MN: West Publishing.

1st Series, Vol. 1–Vol. 300 (1879–1942).

2d Series, Vol. 1, (1942–).

Abbreviated and cited *N.W.* and *N.W.2d,* this reporter covers all decisions of the courts of last resort and selected opinions of intermediate appellate courts, beginning in 1879, from the states of Iowa, Michigan, Minnesota, Nebraska, North Dakota, South Dakota, and Wisconsin. It also reports cases from the Dakota Territory.

Pacific Reporter. St. Paul, MN: West Publishing.

1st Series, Vol. 1–Vol. 300 (1883–1931).

2d Series, Vol. 1– (1931–).

Abbreviated and cited *P.* and *P.2d,* this reporter covers all decisions of the courts of last resort and selected opinions

of intermediate appellate courts, beginning in 1883, from the states of Arizona, California, Colorado, Idaho, Kansas, Montana, Nevada, New Mexico, Oklahoma, Oregon, Utah, Washington, and Wyoming. See also *California Reporter* above.

South Eastern Reporter. St. Paul, MN: West Publishing.

1st Series, Vol. 1–Vol. 200 (1887–1939).

2d Series, Vol. 1– (1939–).

Abbreviated and cited *S.E.* and *S.E.2d,* this reporter covers all decisions of the courts of last resort and selected opinions of intermediate appellate courts, beginning in 1885, from the states of Georgia, North Carolina, South Carolina, Virginia, and West Virginia.

South Western Reporter. St. Paul, MN: West Publishing.

1st Series, Vol. 1–Vol. 300 (1886–1928).

2d Series, Vol. 1– (1928–).

Abbreviated and cited *S.W.* and *S.W.2d,* this reporter covers all decisions of the courts of last resort and selected opinions of intermediate appellate courts, beginning in 1885, from the states of Arkansas, Kentucky, Missouri, Tennessee, and Texas.

Southern Reporter. St. Paul, MN: West Publishing.

1st Series, Vol. 1–Vol. 200 (1887–1941).

2d Series, Vol. 1– (1941–).

Abbreviated and cited *So.* and *So.2d,* this reporter covers all decisions of the courts of last resort and selected opinions of intermediate appellate courts, beginning in 1885, from the states of Alabama, Florida, Louisiana, and Mississippi.

A sample citation that one might find for a state case follows. Note that two sources are identified, one official, the other unofficial.

```
<Plantiff>  <Defendant>                <Year>

State v. Escobedo, 28 Ill.2d 41, 190 N.E.2d 825 (1963).

           <Official Citation> <Parallel Citation>
```

This citation refers to *Escobedo v. Illinois* when it was still in the state courts. It later became a familiar federal case, and the citation to the decision of the federal courts refers to the reporters of federal cases. Most state decisions have an official citation and a parallel citation; that is, the same opinion is published in official and unofficial sources. Thus, *Escobedo* can be found in Volume 28 of *Illinois Reports*, 2d series, beginning on page 41. It can also be found in Volume 190 of *North Eastern Reporter*, 2d series, beginning on page 825.

The opinions of the federal and state courts are also offered through LEXIS-NEXIS and WESTLAW database services. (See page 77.) As mentioned, searches for databases can be performed using keywords or citations. The WESTLAW service also permits use of West Publishing's key numbering system. Coverage, however, is not as retrospective as with the printed reporters.

Court cases from states are also beginning to be published on Web sites. Refer to various sites that have gathered links to state court opinions, including the University of South Carolina Web site at http://www.law.sc.ed.

DIGESTS

Digests are indexes to common law as transcribed in court cases, and their use is a complicated venture. Instead of attempting to explain how to use them in detail or listing references, the authors will give some background and a brief description of a few of their features.

As stated, digests are indexes to common law or case law. The dominant digests used for finding the case law of the United States are those published by West Publishing. West's digests classify the law according to the publisher's topic and key numbering system, and citations to cases are accompanied by a brief description of the law that the case presents.

There are several kinds of digests in use. State digests provide access to cases from the state courts as well as federal cases that arose in the state. The five federal digests cover different time periods and provide access to all cases adjudicated by the federal courts. Regional digests classify state court cases published in the regional reporters. Finally the *American Digest* and its constituent parts—*Century Digest, Decennial Digests,* and *General Digest*—provide access to all state and federal cases.

Always use the digest that provides the quickest access; that is, if you know the case is from a state court, go to that state's digest. If that state digest is not available, go to the regional digest including that state. If the regional digest is not available, use the *American Digest.* If you are looking for a federal case and you know in which state it originated, try that state's digest first. If it is not available or if you don't know the state of origin, use the federal digest for the

time period during which the decision was published. If it is not available, use the *American Digest.* There are also two digests of U.S. Supreme Court decisions, one published by West, the other by Lawyers Cooperative Publishing. If you know your case is a Supreme Court case, you will find it fastest by using the case tables from one of these two digests.

Features of digests that you will find useful are a "Table of Cases," a "Defendant-Plaintiff Table of Cases," and "Words and Phrases" volumes. Quite frequently you only have the names of the two parties involved in a case—the plaintiff and the defendant. When this occurs, you can use the "Table of Cases" or the "Defendant-Plaintiff Table of Cases" for the appropriate digest to look up the names of the parties. There you will find the complete citation to the case. "Words and Phrases" volumes of West digests, as for dictionaries, contain definitions, or citations to cases which define legal terms and phrases. The *American Digest* is the only one of the West digests that does not include a "Words and Phrases" volume. For a comprehensive coverage of all judicially defined words and phrases in all American courts, refer to the title "Words and Phrases" described above.

All digests are supplemented in some way. The updates of state, regional, and federal digests are found in pocket parts, which are, in turn, supplemented with quarterly or biennial pamphlets. The *American Digest* is supplemented with the *General Digest.*

THE DYNAMIC NATURE OF THE LAW

The law is constantly changing. Laws are always being enacted or rewritten; courts are always deciding new cases or revisiting old ones. This constant change presents the legal researcher with a special problem—keeping his or her legal research up to date.

Shepardizing

Shepardizing is a process that every researcher concerned about the current authority of a case or statute should learn. For case law, Shepards citators provide a complete listing of all cases that have cited a case in question. It provides an analysis of how the citing cases treated it and access to *ALR (American Law Reports)* annotations and selected law review articles that have cited them. Most important, where Shepards analyzes the treatment of a case, it indicates if a case has been reversed or if the principle of law used to guide the decision of the court has been overruled. For legislation, Shepards citators provide a listing of statutes or code sections, again accompanied by subsequent cases citing the original. It also lists all session laws that have amended or repealed a code section.

Supplementation of Law Books

Making certain that your legal research is current, especially for primary source material, is critical. Law book publishers keep up with the ever-changing law through various updating tools. The authors cannot stress enough the importance of seeking out supplements of various forms when doing legal research. A few of the kinds of supplementation you will find that accompany law books are outlined below.

Many official codes are kept up to date with the publication of revised volumes. Because revisions tend to be published long after first editions, you might have to use session law services to access current code.

Annotated and privately published codes are most frequently updated through supplements referred to as *pocket parts* or *pocket supplements*. These supplements are slipped into a pocket in the back cover of each bound volume to keep the information therein current. Pocket parts may be further supplemented by quarterly or biennial pamphlets.

Cumulative supplements, bound volumes that stand next to texts on the same shelf, is another way of updating the law. This kind of supplementation is usually used with secondary sources.

Loose-leaf publication is another way to keep legal information—both primary and secondary source materials—up to date. Revised pages are simply removed and replacements inserted. Some loose-leaf publications also take advantage of cumulative supplements, which are filed in the front or back of ring or post binders.

Finally, advance sheets are used most frequently to keep case reporters up to date. They are pamphlet-size publications that report only a few cases. After a sufficient number of advance sheets have been issued, the publisher prints a bound volume covering those same cases. The advance sheets can then be discarded.

Chapter 9

International Criminal Justice Information

So far, the current work has focused primarily on criminal justice information sources in the United States. However, you should be aware that there is a great deal of information produced outside those borders. This chapter is intended as a means of guiding you through this complicated international arena.

DIRECTORIES AND GUIDES TO INTERNATIONAL CRIMINAL JUSTICE INFORMATION

One of the great challenges of finding information produced outside the United States is simply locating the relevant agencies and documents. Directories and guides to organizations and publications, such as those listed below, can be valuable in this search.

Encyclopedia of Associations: International Organizations. Detroit, MI: Gale Research, 1989–. Also a CD-ROM version which includes this volume and other volumes in the encyclopedia series. Additional information available electronically at http://www.gale.com/gale.html/

> Gale's *International Organizations* covers more than 15,000 multinational and national membership organizations including U.S.-based organizations with binational or multinational membership. Entries provide the names of directors, executive officers, and other personal contacts; telephone, fax, telex, electronic mail, and bulletin board numbers and addresses; the group's history, governance, staff, membership, budget, and affiliations; the goals and activities of the international organization, including research, awards, certification, education, promotion, lobbying, and other important activities; and publication and convention information. Entries are arranged in 15 general subject chapters allowing users to browse. A free supplement keeps the user up to date between issues. Three indexes—geographic, executive, and keyword—help speed research.

Hajnal, Peter I., comp. *Directory of United Nations Documentary and Archival Sources.* New York: Academic Council of the United Nations System; Kraus International Publications, 1991.

Prepared in cooperation with the United Nations Dag Hammarskjold Library, this directory includes annotations and an introduction by the compiler. "The purpose of this *Directory* is to assist teaching, research, and documentation and library work in the field of international relations as well as in a wide variety of subject fields in the purview of the United Nations system of organization. The *Directory* provides to concerned individuals and organizations an annotated guide to major documentary and archival sources of those organizations. In addition to material originating from organizations of the UN system itself, the *Directory* includes entries for items of reference or informational value published commercially, academically or by governments" (preface, v).

Hajnal, Peter I., ed. *Guide to United Nations Organization, Documentation and Publishing*. Dobbs Ferry, NY: Oceana Publications, 1978.

"The twofold purpose of this *Guide* is to aid researchers, students, librarians and others whose work involves an awareness of United Nations activities and the use of United Nations publications and related secondary material; and to whet the appetite of those who are not familiar with the multifarious activities of the world organization" (introduction, xxvii).

Hajnal, Peter I., ed. *International Information: Documents, Publications, and Information Systems of International Governmental Organizations*. Englewood, CO: Libraries Unlimited, 1988.

"The purpose of the book is to aid researchers, librarians, documentalists, information professionals, and other readers to understand, select, organize, and use efficiently a most important resource: the publications, documents and computerized information systems of international governmental organizations" (preface, xxiii).

Union of International Associations. *Yearbook of International Organizations*. 33d ed. München; New Providence; London; Paris: K. G. Saur Verlag, 1996/97.

Also CD-ROM version.

Additional information available electronically at http://www.uia.org/

Since 1910, the *Yearbook of International Organizations* has provided the most extensive coverage of nonprofit international governmental and nongovernmental organizations. The *Yearbook* provides information on over 30,000 international organizations in 300 countries and territories. It includes all types of organizations, from formal structures to informal networks and from professional bodies to recreational clubs. It does not include for-profit enterprises. Its four volumes are *Organization Descriptions and Cross-References* (Volume 1), *International Organization Participation* (Country Directory of Membership) (Volume 2), *Global Action Networks* [Subject Guide and Index] (Volume 3), and new for the 1996/97 edition, *International Organizations Bibliography and Resources* (Volume 4).

United Nations Interregional Crime and Justice Institute. *A World Directory of Criminological Institutes*. 6th ed. Rome: United Nations Interregional Crime and Justice Institute, 1995.

One of the great challenges of finding information produced outside the United States is simply locating the relevant agencies. This directory lists more than 470 institutes representing some 70 countries. Entries were prepared on the basis of responses to a questionnaire distributed to approximately 1,000 institutes and other bodies worldwide, including a number of agencies in developing countries that are not criminological institutes per se but may, nonetheless, be worthwhile resources for the researcher.

THE UNITED NATIONS

The United Nations was founded in 1945 as a mechanism for reducing the likelihood of the recurrence of the atrocities of the Second World War. Essentially, the four objectives of the United Nations are to keep peace throughout the world; develop friendly relations among nations; work together to solve economic, social, cultural, and humanitarian problems; and be the focal point for helping nations achieve these goals. It is the only organization in the world with an entirely international mandate.

Below you will find a list of U.N. offices and agencies, including contact information. As evidenced by the information given below, the United Nations and various interregional and regional organizations have recently been making information and documents available electronically via the World Wide Web.

United Nations Headquarters
1 United Nations Plaza
New York, NY 10017
USA
Telephone: 212-963-1234
World Wide Web main site: http://www.un.org/
Locator for United Nations organizations: http://www.unsystem.org/index.html

Of particular note are the Statistics Division, which maintains a large collection of demographic, economic, and development data at the global level, and the Office for Legal Affairs, Treaties Section, which maintains an extensive compilation of multilateral treaties that have been deposited with the Secretary-General of the U.N.

Although it is possible to connect to every online United Nations information source around the world through either one of the Web sites listed, for the researcher unfamiliar with the United Nations and its many agencies, the main site is a better starting point. For those who know the location of the agency from which they wish to retrieve information, the other major offices of the United Nations (Vienna and Geneva) maintain independent Web sites (see below). Each contains information related to its local constituent agencies as well as links to the other United Nations offices. Therefore, it is possible to access any site via any of the other sites.

United Nations Office at Geneva (UNOG)

Palais de Nations
1211, Geneva 10
Switzerland
Telephone: 41-22-917-1907 or 41-22-917-1234
World Wide Web: http://www.unog.ch/

Of particular note are the Centre for Human Rights and the Centre for Disarmament, and the Institute for Disarmament Research.

United Nations Office at Vienna (UNOV)

Vienna International Centre
P.O. Box 500
Vienna 1400
Austria
Telephone: 43-1-21345-94
World Wide Web main site: http://www.un.or.at/

"United Nations International Drug Control Programme." http://undcp.or.at/index.html

"United Nations Crime and Justice Information Network." http://www.ifs.univie.ac.at/~uncjin/uncjin.html

The United Nations Office at Vienna is host to the United Nations International Drug Control Programme (UNDCP) and the United Nations Crime Prevention and Criminal Justice Division. The Division maintains the United Nations Crime and Justice Information Network (UNCJIN); its main Web site includes links to UN sites, as well as other agencies in the Vienna International Centre. The UNDCP produces information on demand reduction, supply reduction, research, treaty implementation, and legal affairs.

The UNCJIN site, maintained by the Crime Prevention and Criminal Justice Division in Vienna, provides access to other U.N. sources such as the United Nations Development Programme (UNDP), the United Nations International Drug Control Programme (UNDCP), the United Nations Research Institute on Social Development (UNRISD), and the World Health Organization (WHO), as well as to other non-U.N. sources. UNCJIN also maintains an electronic discussion list (UNCJIN-L) for several hundred criminal justice practitioners, researchers, and officials. The goal of the UNCJIN is to establish a worldwide network to enhance dissemination and the exchange of information concerning criminal justice and crime prevention issues. It was established in 1989 on a limited budget in an attempt to implement United Nations Resolution 1986/11: "To establish, in cooperation with the United Nations Institutes and other entities concerned, a global crime prevention and criminal justice information network . . . including a mechanism for the centralization of inputs from nongovernmental organizations and scientific institutions" (para. 5(a), U.N. Economic and Social Council).

Documents available through the UNCJIN Web site include:
- United Nations Standards and Norms
- United Nations Charter
- Standard Minimum Rules for the Treatment of Prisoners
- Declaration Against Torture and Other Cruel, Inhumane, or Degrading Treatment or Punishment
- Safeguards Guaranteeing Protection of the Rights of Those Facing the Death Penalty
- Resolution on Measures against International Terrorism

Proceedings from Conference and Meetings
- Eighth UN Congress on the Prevention of Crime and the Treatment of Offenders
- Ninth UN Congress on the Prevention of Crime and the Treatment of Offenders
- Fourth UN World Conference on Women, Beijing, China
- UN International Conference on Population and Development (ICPD), Cairo, Egypt
- World Summit for Social Development, Copenhagen, Denmark
- Fifth Session of the Commission on Crime Prevention and Criminal Justice, Vienna, Austria, with reports in English, French, and Spanish

Newsletters and Journals
- Trends: UNCJIN Crime and Justice Letter
- International Review of Criminal Policy
- United Nations Crime Prevention and Criminal Justice Newsletter

Statistical Information
- World crime surveys covering 1970–1990
- Criminal justice country profiles

Treaties and Constitutions
- Database on Bilateral Agreements on Extradition, Judicial/Legal Assistance, Control of Narcotic Drugs, and Prisoner Transfer by Country
- Various National Constitutions

United Nations Educational, Scientific, and Cultural Organization, or UNESCO

7, place de Fontenoy
75352 Paris 07 SP
France
Telephone: 33-1-45-68-10-00
Fax: 33-1-45-67-16-90
World Wide Web: http://www.unesco.org

The main objective of UNESCO is to contribute to peace and security in the world by promoting collaboration among nations through education, science, culture, and communication in order to further universal respect for justice, the rule of law, human rights, and the fundamental freedoms of the peoples of the world—without distinction of race, sex, language, or religion.

United Nations Crime Prevention and Criminal Justice Programme Network

Since its inception, the United Nations has become a large, multilevel bureaucracy with many offices, sections, and units involved in a wide range of activities from farming and irrigation systems development to peace-keeping operations. In addition, the United Nations is very much involved with the issue of crime prevention and criminal justice.

The Economic and Social Council (ECOSOC) was established by the U.N. Charter as the principal organ to coordinate the economic and social work of the U.N. and its specialized agencies and institutes. Its most relevant subsidiary body for the purpose of research in criminal justice is the Commission on Crime Prevention and Criminal Justice. Membership in this Commission consists of 40 member states elected by the ECOSOC on the basis of equitable geographic distribution. The Commission responds and makes recommendations to ECOSOC, which, in turn, reports to the U.N. General Assembly, whose law defines the activities of the various bodies of the United Nations.

The primary group of agencies that assist the Commission is the United Nations Crime Prevention and Criminal Justice Programme Network. The Crime Prevention and Criminal Justice Division (hereafter referred to as the Division) acts as the chief coordinating entity of a larger programme composed of various regional and interregional affiliated institutes. At present, regional institutes affiliated with the United Nations serve Asia and the Pacific region, Latin America, Europe, and Africa, and an interregional institute is located in Rome. There are also U.N.-associated institutes serving the Arab states, North America, and the South Pacific.

Below you will find a list of the agencies of the U.N. Crime Programme. Because the amount of material produced by these agencies is truly voluminous and no directory or index already exists, the authors have compiled—in appendix B—a complete bibliography of all resolutions, reports, documents, and publications of the United Nations Crime Prevention and Criminal Justice Programme network.

African Institute for the Prevention of Crime and the Treatment of Offenders (UNAFRI)

P.O. Box 10590

Kampala
Uganda
Telephone: 25641-285-236 or 25641-221-119 or 25641-222-623
Fax: 25641-222-628 or c/o UNDP 25641-244-801
E-mail: unafri@mukla.gn.apc.org
Established: 1989, Kampala, Uganda

Arab Security Studies and Training Centre (ASSTC)

c/o UNDP Field Office
P.O. Box 558
King Faysal Street (Olaya Street)
Riyadh 11421
Saudi Arabia
Telephone: 9661-491-2032
Fax: 9661-246-4713

A collaborative agreement was signed between the Crime Prevention and Criminal Justice Division (then Branch) and the Arab Security Studies and Training Centre (ASSTC) in 1986. The ASSTC also has inter-governmental organization status (ECOSOC decision 1989/165).

Asia and Far East Institute for the Prevention of Crime and the Treatment of Offenders (UNAFEI)

1-26 Harumicho
Fuchu, Tokyo 183
Japan
Telephone: 81-423-337021
Fax: 81-423-68-8500
E-mail: LDJ00272@niftyserve.or.jp
Established: 1961, Fuchu, Tokyo, Japan

Australian Institute of Criminology (AIC)

GPO Box 2944
Canberra ACT 2603
Australia
Telephone: 616-260-9200
Fax: 616-260-9201
E-mail: front.desk@aic.gov.au
World Wide Web: http://www.aic.gov.au

The Australian Institute of Criminology (AIC) at Canberra, Australia. Memorandum of Understanding signed by the Director of AIC, the Chairman of the Board of Management of the AIC, and the Director-General of United Nations Office at Vienna on July 7, 1988.

Centro Nazionale di Prevenzione e Difesa Sociale (International Scientific and Professional Advisory Council)

Palazzo communale delle scienze sociali
Piazza Castello 3
I-20l2l Milano
Italy

Telephone: ++39-402-8646-0714

Fax: ++39-402-2686-4427

E-mail: Cnpds.Ispac@agora.stm.it

> Memorandum of Understanding signed between the Secretary-General of the Centro and the Under Secretary General of the United Nations Office at Vienna, on 20 December 1990.

Helsinki Institute for Crime Prevention and Control (HEUNI)

P.O. Box 161

Kasarmikatu 46-48, 5th floor

FIN-00131 Helsinki

Finland

Telephone: 3580-1825-7881

Fax: 3580-1825-7890

E-mail: heuni@joutsen.pp.fi

Established: 1981, Helsinki, Finland

Institute of Human Rights and Humanitarian Law

University of Lund

Sankt Annegatan 4

S-223 50 Lund

Sweden

Telephone: ++4646-222-7000 (exchange); 4646-222-4310 (secretariat)

Fax: ++4646-222-4445

> Memorandum of Understanding signed by the Director of the RW Institute and the Director-General of the United Nations Office at Vienna on April 28, 1994.

International Centre for Criminal Law Reform and Criminal Justice Policy

1822 East Mall

Vancouver, British Colombia

Canada VT IZI

Telephone: 604-822 -9323 or 604-822-9875

Fax: 604-822-9317

E-mail: prefont@law.ubc.ca

> The initial Memorandum of Understanding signed by the Ambassador of Canada to the United Nations in Vienna and the Under-Secretary General of the United Nations Office at Vienna on July 11, 1991. A second Memorandum of Understanding signed between the Ambassador of Canada to the United Nations in Vienna and the Chief, Crime Prevention and Criminal Justice Branch, United Nations Office at Vienna, on July 6, 1995.

International Centre for the Prevention of Crime

507, Place d'Armes, Bureau 2100

Montreal, Quebec

Canada H2Y 2W8

Telephone: 514-288-6731

Fax: 514-288-8763

E-mail: cipc@web.apc.org

No written agreement as yet.

International Institute of Higher Studies in Criminal Sciences

Via S. Agati

12-96100 Siracusa

Italy

Telephone: ++39-931-365-11

Fax: ++39-931-442-605

> Memorandum of Understanding signed by the President of the Institute and the Director-General of the United Nations Office at Vienna on July 20, 1992.

Latin American Institute for the Prevention of Crime and the Treatment of Offenders (ILANUD)

10071-1000 San José

Costa Rica

Telephone: 506-233-7471

Fax: 506-233-7175

E-mail: ilanudcd@sol.racsa.co.cr

Established: 1975, San José, Costa Rica

National Institute of Justice (NIJ)

Office of Justice Programmes

United States Department of Justice

633 Indiana Avenue, NW

Washington, DC 20531

USA

Telephone: 202-307-2942

Fax: 202-307-6394 or 202-307-2942

E-mail: hillsman@OJP.USDOJ.GOV

> Memorandum of Understanding signed by the Director of NIJ and the Director-General of the United Nations Office at Vienna on April 24, 1995.

United Nations Interregional Crime and Justice Research Institute (UNICRI)

Via Giulia 52

00186 Rome

Italy

Telephone: 396-6877437

Fax: 396-6892638

E-mail: UNICRI.ORG@AGORA.STM.IT

E-mail: UNICRI@delphi.com

Established: 1968, Rome, Italy

REGIONAL AND INTERREGIONAL ORGANIZATIONS

In addition to the United Nations, there are a number of other organizations working to coordinate the activities of governments regionally and interregionally. Below you will find a list of the dominant agencies.

Council of Europe
67075 Strasbourg Cedex
France
Telephone: 33-88-412000
Fax: 33-88-41-27-93
World Wide Web: http://stars.coe.fr/

Founded May 5, 1949, the Council of Europe identifies new trends in society and new challenges to be addressed through concerted action at the European level. Its activities have led to the *European Convention on Human Rights*, the *Social Charter*, the *Water Charter*, the *European Cultural Convention*, and conventions on the conservation of wildlife and natural habitats, transfrontier cooperation, the suppression of terrorism, and the prevention of torture, as well as many other international legal instruments which serve as a reference for democratic governments.

Of particular interest for the study of criminal justice is the *Penological Bulletin* (formerly *Prison Information Bulletin*, annual, 1983–), which regularly includes statistics on the prison population of the member states and the criminological research series of the European Committee on Crime Problems.

The committees of the Council of Europe include the Political Affairs Committee; Committee on Economic Affairs and Development; Social, Health, and Family Affairs Committee; Committee on Legal Affairs and Human Rights; Committee on Culture and Education; Committee on Science and Technology; Committee on the Environment, Regional Planning, and Local Authorities; Committee on Migration, Refugees, and Demography; Committee on Rules of Procedure; Committee on Agriculture and Rural Development; Committee on Relations with European Non-Member Countries; Committee on Parliamentary and Public Relations; and Committee on the Budget and the Intergovernmental Work Programme.

Alliance for Non-Governmental Organizations on Crime Prevention and Criminal Justice
PO Box 81826
Lincoln, Nebraska 68501-1826
USA
Telephone: 402-464-0602
Fax: 402-464-5931

The Alliance for Non-Governmental Organizations (NGOs) on Crime Prevention and Criminal Justice, formed in 1972, is a coalition of international NGOs with *consultative* status with the United Nations Economic and Social Council. The goals of the Alliance are to plan international policy in crime prevention and criminal justice by providing a line of communication between the United Nations Secretariat and the international NGO community; to offer assistance to the U.N. in identifying issues and making recommendations for action; and to

strengthen the Alliance through the exchange of information and cooperation.

European Commission
Rue de la Loi 200
1049 Brussels
Belgium
Telephone: 32-2-299-11-11
Fax: 32-2-295-11-38
World Wide Web: http://www.echo.lu/

Established August 25, 1951, the European Commission functions as a policy-making body for European Community actions. It acts as a mediator between governments, steering its proposals through the Council of Europe, and as a monitor, bringing as the last resort governments or firms before the European Court of Justice for breaches of European Community law.

European Union
Contact through the European Commission
World Wide Web: http://www.cec.lu

The European Union (EU) was established on November 1, 1993, on entry into force of the Treaty of European Union (Maastricht Treaty, 1992). The goals of the European Union are the promotion of economic and social progress, the assertion of its identity in the international scene, and the protection and promotion of the interests of the member states and their citizens through the introduction of EU citizenship.

International Criminal Police Organization
50, Quai Achille LIGNON
BP-6041
69006 Lyon
France
Telephone: 33-72-44-70-00
Fax: 33-72-44-71-63

The International Criminal Police Organization (INTERPOL) aims to ensure and promote the widest possible mutual assistance between all criminal police authorities within the limits of the laws existing in different countries and in the spirit of the Universal Declaration of Human Rights. INTERPOL maintains information on offenders, drug seizures, counterfeit currency, and stolen property, for example. Publications include *International Criminal Police Review* (six times annually); *INTERPOL Information Bulletin*; *Counterfeits and Forgerie*; *International Crime Statistics* (annual); and various other reports.

North Atlantic Treaty Organization
Office of Information and Press
1110 Brussels
Belgium
Telephone: 32-2-728-4111 or 32-2-728-4599
Fax : 32-2-728-5057 or 32-2-728-5229
Gopher: //nato.int/

Established on the basis of the North Atlantic Treaty, signed April 4, 1949, the Atlantic Alliance is a defensive political and military alliance of independent countries in accordance with the terms of the United Nations Charter. The North Atlantic Treaty Organization (NATO) is the organization that allows the goals of the Alliance to be implemented. Publications include the *NATO Review* (periodical) and various nonperiodic publications describing Alliance programs and policies.

The NATO Integrated Data Service (NIDS) is a public information dissemination and retrieval project, the goals of which are to (1) make NATO-produced information available electronically through listservers and menu-driven navigation tools such as gopher (2) establish a global electronic contacts network of governmental agencies and other nongovernmental organizations, media, and individuals; and (3) search and retrieve electronic data relevant to NATO headquarters.

Organization for Economic Cooperation and Development

2, rue Andre-Pascal
75775 Paris CEDEX 16
France
Telephone: 33-1-45-24-82-00
Fax: 33-1-45-24-85-00
World Wide Web: http://www.oecd.org/

Established September 30, 1961, the Organization for Economic Cooperation and Development (OECD) promotes policies designed to achieve the highest sustainable economic growth and employment, as well as a rising standard of living for member countries, with a view to establishing sound and harmonious fiscal development.

INTERNATIONAL HUMAN RIGHTS

The amount of material produced in the field of human rights is truly massive. Below you will find a selective list of human rights resources related to criminal justice, electronic information sources on human rights, and human rights organizations.

Bouloukos, Adam C., and Dennis C. Benamati. *Selected Online Human Rights Information Sources.* Ottawa, Canada: Human Rights Internet, 1995.

This publication offers information on discussion lists, databases, and commercial networks. In addition, the publication offers some basic skills training for the electronic information novice.

"DIANA Human Rights Electronic Text Project" http://www.law.uc.edu/Diana/ (August 4, 1997).

DIANA is a collection of human rights bibliographies and documents originating from the U.N. and various regional human rights organizations. The database can be searched by keyword, or titles may be browsed.

Harvard Law School. *Guide to Human Rights Research.* Cambridge, MA: Harvard Law School, 1994.

This is a comprehensive guide to all manner of research in the field of human rights, from the work of intergovernmental agencies to non-governmental agencies, research institutions, and online sources.

Lawson, Edward. *Encyclopedia of Human Rights.* Washington: Taylor and Francis, 1991.

Written in response to the 1988 United Nations World Public Information Campaign for Human Rights, this extensive, single volume brings together the numerous standard-setting and monitoring activities of many organizations, including the United Nations, various intergovernmental bodies, and other independent organizations.

United Nations. *Manual on Human Rights Reporting,* E.91.XIV.1.

This manual has its origins in a series of five regional training courses on human rights reporting held for government officials responsible for the preparation and drafting of reports as required under international human rights treaties. The manual was designed to provide an element of continuity among governmental departments responsible for human rights monitoring and reporting.

United Nations. *United Nations Action in the Field of Human Rights,* 1980. E.88.XIV.2.

Drafted on the 40th anniversary of the Universal Declaration of Human Rights, this text offers a detailed summary of developments relating to human rights within the United Nations system. Topics include specialized agencies, international instruments, self-determination, elimination of racism, advancement of women, economic rights, and political rights.

"United Nations Centre for Human Rights." http://www.unog.ch/ (August 18, 1997). www.unhchr.ch/HTML/hchr.htm

(See organization listing on the next page.)

United Nations. Department of Public Information. *The United Nations and Human Rights, 1945–1995,* 1995.

This book represents a comprehensive account of United Nations activities in fact-finding, monitoring, advising, and providing a forum for appeal in the field of human rights. Included are a chronology of major events, a list of reproduced documents, and texts of documents, as well as a subject index to the documents.

United Nations Educational, Scientific and Cultural Organization. *Access to Human Rights Documentation: Documentation, Databases and Bibliographies on Human Rights.* Paris: United Nations Educational, Scientific and Cultural Organization, Division of Human Rights and Peace, 1991.

This work was drafted to facilitate the work of institutions or individuals carrying out research in human rights.

HUMAN RIGHTS ORGANIZATIONS

There are several agencies worldwide that work exclusively in the field of human rights. Because they devote all their energy to this issue, they are often a strong starting point for your research activities.

Amnesty International

1 Easton Street
London WC1X8DJ
United Kingdom
Telephone: 44-1-833-1771
Fax: 44-1-833-5100

Amnesty International (AI) is a human rights movement as well as an organization. AI works toward the release of all prisoners of conscience; urges immediate and fair trials of political prisoners; seeks to end torture, executions, and other inhuman forms of cruel or degrading treatment or punishment; and seeks to end extrajudicial executions and disappearances. AI publishes the annual *Amnesty International Report*; the monthly *Amnesty International Newsletter* (in Arabic, English, French, and Spanish); and various books, leaflets, reports, and documents on human rights issues.

Council of Europe: Human Rights Information Centre

6075 Strasbourg Cedex
France
Fax: 33-88-41-27-93
World Wide Web: http://stars.coe.fr/ (August 4, 1997)

The European Convention on Human Rights (ECHR), drawn up by the Council of Europe in 1950, is a human rights protection instrument at the international level. The Council of Europe Parliamentary Assembly, which brought the Convention into being, made the reform of the control machinery one of its priority tasks, and its efforts have resulted in an additional protocol to the ECHR (Protocol No. 11), which replaces the present structures (European Commission and Court of Human Rights) with a single, permanently sitting court. Protocol No. 11 was opened for signature on May 11, 1994 in Strasbourg and will enter into force once ratified by all the states parties to the ECHR. The Human Rights Information Centre provides material on these developments as well as on other activities of the Council of Europe in this field.

Human Rights Information and Documentation System

Secretariat
2 Rue Jean-Jaquet
1201 Geneva
Switzerland
Telephone: 41-22-741-1767
Fax: 41-22-741-1768

The Human Rights Information and Documentation System (HURIDOCS) is an international network established as a decentralized clearinghouse for human rights information. HURIDOCS's main activities are to hold workshops and training courses on human rights information handling and to develop compatible tools for recording and exchanging information.

Human Rights Internet

8 York Street Suite 202
Ottawa, Ontario K1N 5S6
Canada
Telephone: 1-613-789-7407
Fax: 1-613-789-7414
World Wide Web: http://www.hri.ca/

Human Rights Internet (HRI) is a documentation center and international non-governmental organization, which promotes and seeks to stimulate human rights education, research, and the building of international solidarity. HRI maintains several databases on human rights funding sources, bibliographic abstracts, human rights awards, and the rights of the child.

Human Rights Watch

435 Fifth Avenue
New York, NY 10017-6104
USA
Telephone: 1-212-972-8400
Fax: 1-212-972-0905

Human Rights Watch conducts regular, systematic investigations of human rights abuses in over 70 countries around the world. In addition to producing the annual report *Human Rights Watch Global Report*, Human Rights Watch publishes several topic- and country-specific reports, for example, *Human Rights Watch Global Report on Prisons, The Expulsion of the Bulgarian Turks,* and *Land Mines in Angola.*

International Institute for Human Rights Policy Studies

Lancaster House
33 Islington High Street
London N1 9LH
United Kingdom
Telephone: 44-171-278-3230
Fax: 44-171-278-4334

Established in June 1996, this new organization intends to conceptualize and develop a common agenda for the international human rights community, to provide a forum to stimulate discourse and cooperation on human rights, and to serve as a resource for governments and agencies working in the field.

United Nations Centre for Human Rights

United Nations Office at Geneva

Palais de Nations

1211, Geneva 10

Switzerland

Telephone: 41-22-917-1907 or 41-22-917-1234

World Wide Web: http://www.unhchr.ch/HTML/ hchr.htm

As the primary United Nations agency entrusted with promoting and coordinating the global application of human rights in all arenas, the United Nations Centre for Human Rights produces numerous documents and maintains a World Wide Web database facility on the topic.

INTERNATIONAL STATISTICS

A significant portion of research in criminal justice makes use of statistical information as addressed in chapter 6. International criminal justice information is no different. Thus, the authors have provided a list of various primary and secondary sources of international crime and criminal justice statistics, including several potentially useful noncrime sources. Data have been drawn from most or all United Nations member states unless otherwise noted (i.e., "72 countries"). Sales publication or document reference numbers are provided when available. For annual publications, reference information refers to the current edition.

Index to International Statistics, 1995. Bethesda, MD: Congressional Information Service, 1996.

Comprehensive International Statistical Sources

Department for Economic and Social Information and Policy Analysis and United Nations Centre for Human Settlements. *Compendium of Human Settlement Statistics,* 1995. E.95.XVII. I 1.

Topics include urban population estimates; rates of reported criminal offenses against life, limb, or property; and percentages of sentenced perpetrators of criminal offenses by type of offense. First published in 1974 as the *Compendium of Housing Statistics.*

United Nations. *Crime Trends and Criminal Justice Operations at the Regional and Interregional Levels: Results of the Third United Nations Survey of Crime Trends, Operations of Criminal Justice Systems and Crime Prevention Strategies,* 1993. E.941V.2.

Covers 78 countries or areas from 1980 to 1986.

United Nations. *Trends in Crime and Criminal Justice, 1970–85, in the Context of Socioeconomic Change: Results of the Second United Nations Survey of Crime Trends, Operations of Criminal Justice Systems and Crime Prevention Strategies,* 1992. E.92.IV.3.

Covers 80 countries or areas from 1970 to 1985.

United Nations. Economic and Social Council. *Statistical Report on the State of Crime, 1937–46,* 1950. E/CN.5/204.

This *Statistical Report* illustrates the data collection efforts of the nascent United Nations in the field of criminal justice. Topics include international comparisons in the field of criminal statistics, indices of offenses, and implications. Covers 37 countries.

United Nations General Assembly. *Crime Prevention and Control—Report of the Secretary General,* 1977. A/32/199.

This report is the root of what is now the *U.N. Survey of Crime Trends.* Covers 64 countries from 1970 to 1975.

United Nations. Secretariat. Seventh United Nations Congress on the Prevention of Crime and the Treatment of Offenders. *New Dimensions of Criminality and Crime Prevention in the Context of Development: Challenges for the Future,* 1985. A/ CONF.121/18.

This is the preliminary result of the *Second U.N. Survey on Crime Trends, Operations of Criminal Justice Systems and Crime Prevention Strategies.* Covers 65 countries from 1975 to 1980.

United Nations. Secretariat. Eighth United Nations Congress on the Prevention of Crime and the Treatment of Offenders. *Crime Prevention and Criminal Justice in the Context of Development—Realities and Perspectives of International Co-operation,* 1990. A/CONF. 144/6.

This is a preliminary analysis of data from the *Second and Third U.N. Surveys of Crime Trends, Operations of Criminal Justice Systems, and Crime Prevention Strategies.* Covers 78 countries from 1975 to 1986. (Titles vary.)

United Nations. Secretariat. Ninth United Nations Congress on the Prevention of Crime and the Treatment of Offenders. *Interim Report by the Secretariat: Results of the Fourth United Nations Survey of Crime Trends and Operations of Criminal Justice Systems,* 1994. A/CONF. 169/15.

This interim report on the *Fourth U.N. Survey of Crime Trends, Operations of Criminal Justice Systems,* all these titles vary frequently and offers a preliminary review of the changes in patterns and dynamics of crime, including violent and property crime. Covers 100 countries or areas from 1986 to 1990.

United Nations. Secretariat. Ninth United Nations Congress on the Prevention of Crime and the Treatment of Offenders. *Interim Report by the Secretariat—Results of the Supplement to the*

Fourth United Nations Survey of Crime Trends and Operations of Criminal Justice Systems, on Transnational Crime, 1995.A/CONF. 169/15/ Add. 1.

> This supplement to the interim report of the same name explores the extent and impact of transnational crime. Covers 50 countries from 1988 to 1990.

United Nations. United Nations Office at Vienna, Crime Prevention and Criminal Justice Division, and United Nations, Statistics Division. *United Nations Survey of Crime Trends and Operations of Criminal Justice Systems,* 1986–.

> This survey, conducted by the Crime Prevention and Criminal Justice Division of the United Nations Office at Vienna, presents international comparative statistics for participating countries. The current (fourth) edition covers 1970–1990. Three previous surveys cover 1970–1975, 1970–1985, and 1980–1986. The fifth survey is currently underway.

Data from the surveys are available from the Chief, Crime Prevention and Criminal Justice Division, United Nations Office at Vienna, P.O. Box 500, A-1400 Vienna, AUSTRIA; Fax: 43(l) 232156 or 43(l) 21345 5898; email: <evetere@unov.un.or.at>. Please indicate which survey is required. The data from each edition of the survey are also available in various electronic formats, such as ASCII, SPSS/PC+, and Lotus 1-2-3. These survey data can also be obtained electronically through the United Nations Crime and Justice Information Network (UNCJIN) at its World Wide Web site listed earlier in this chapter.

In addition to these global reports, regional reports, such as the three listed below, have also been produced using data from the *U.N. Survey of Crime Trends, Operations of Criminal Justice Systems, and Crime Prevention Strategies.*

African Institute for the Prevention of Crime and the Treatment of Offenders. *Report on African Data of the Fourth United Nations Survey of Crime Trends and Operations of Criminal Justice Systems, 1986–1990,* n.d.

Pease, Ken, and Kristiina Hukkila, eds. Helsinki Institute for Crime Prevention and Control. *Criminal Justice Systems in Europe and North America,* 1990. HEUNI Publication Series, No. 17.

United Nations Asia and Far East Institute and Australian Institute of Criminology. *Crime and Justice in Asia and the Pacific: A Report on the Third United Nations Survey of Crime Trends, Operations of Criminal Justice Systems and Crime Prevention Strategies, 1980–86,* 1990.

Example of Statistics Available for Individual Countries

When a student or researcher thinks of writing about crime in another country, it is invariable that one looks for statistics to give a picture of the crime situation for that country. The most frequently used sources in the compilation of international crime statistics come from INTERPOL.

However, there are many other useful sources. Books, as well as journal articles, frequently include statistics on the problem being addressed. Individual countries keep their own statistics, and while many libraries may not keep these in their collection, they are available. With the advent of the Internet and the World Wide Web, many countries maintain Web sites, and more are sure to do so in the coming years. To illustrate the range of publications that are available from other countries, let us use the example of Japan. Listed here are some regularly issued publications for that country. Each of these is published in English.

Asia Crime Report No. 1. Tokyo, Japan: Ministry of Justice, Research and Training Institute (with the United Nations Asia and Far East Institute for the Prevention of Crime and the Treatment of Offender and the Asia Crime Prevention Foundation), 1993.

> *Asia Crime Report* analyzes and arranges data from the published crime and corrections statistics of Hong Kong, India, Indonesia, Japan, Republic of Korea, Malaysia, Republic of the Philippines, Sri Lanka, and Thailand.

Bulletin of the Criminological Research Department. Tokyo, Japan: Ministry of Justice, Research and Training Institute. Annual.

> This bulletin describes the research activities of the Institute.

Community-Based Treatment of Offenders in Japan. Tokyo, Japan: Ministry of Justice Rehabilitation. (Issued irregularly. Latest edition is 1995.)

> *Community-Based Treatment* focuses on probation and parole in Japan.

Correctional Institutions in Japan. Tokyo, Japan: Ministry of Justice, Correction Bureau. (Issued irregularly. Latest issue is 1995.)

> *Correctional Institutions in Japan* describes correctional administration in Japan. Section topics are correctional administration, penal institutions, juvenile training schools, juvenile classification homes, and the Women's Guidance Home.

Summary of the White Paper on Crime. Tokyo, Japan: Ministry of Justice, Research and Training Institute, 1960–. Annual.

Summarizes crime trends and criminal justice system activities related to the treatment of offenders in Japan. In addition, each annual report focuses on a special topic. For 1996 the topic was "the heinous crimes of homicide and robbery, in response to the people's growing fear of being victimized by these grave offences."

White Paper on Police (excerpt). Tokyo, Japan: Police Association. Annual.

> This publication is intended to keep the Japanese public informed on the current state of police activities.

Or you can reach the Home Page of the Japan Criminal Policy Society on the Internet. The address is http://www.tokyoweb.or.jp/JCPS/index-e.htm.

This will give the reader some idea of what is available from other countries. Of course, one will not always find an English summary, but with the help of translators, a friend who reads the language, or a good foreign language dictionary, the reader will usually be able to decipher some of the information if the only available source is in a foreign language.

International Statistical Reports by Subject

Noncrime Statistics

The United Nations publishes various statistical resources on topics not related to crime, including social, demographic, industrial, construction, national-accounts, and energy data. Other specialized agencies also provide statistical sources, for example, ILO's *Yearbook of Labour Statistics*, the International Monetary Fund's *Balance of Payments Yearbook*, UNESCO's *Statistical Yearbook*, and the World Health Organization's *World Health Statistics Annual*. For more information on U.N. and intergovernmental organizations documentation, see Hajnal, 1978, 1988, and 1991, page 183–84.

United Nations. Department for Economic and Social Information and Policy Analysis. *World Economic and Social Survey: Current Trends and Policies in the World Economy,* 1948–. [last two digits of year]. II.C.1.

> The *World Economic and Social Survey* includes topics such as the state of the world economy, current developments and policies, international resource transfers and financial development, energy, employment, and population dynamics. Published annually since 1948.

United Nations Development Programme (UNDP). *Human Development Report.* New York: Oxford University Press, 1990–.

The *Human Development Report* contains national-level information on life spans, fertility, life expectancy, work load, disease ratios, commercial energy production, and raw materials, for example. It attempts to address the level of equality of opportunity between people and among nations. Data from the *United Nations Survey of Crime Trends and Operations of Criminal Justice Systems* are published annually since 1990.

United Nations. Statistics Division. *Demographic Yearbook,* 1996. ST/ESA/STAT/SER.R/-.

> The *Demographic Yearbook* is a collection of demographic statistics from several hundred geographical entities around the world. Tables provide population, mortality, natality, nuptuality, divorce, and migration statistics. Published annually since 1948.

United Nations. Statistics Division. *Statistical Yearbook,* 1948–. ST/ESA/STAT/SER.S/-.

United Nations. Statistics Division. *Monthly Bulletin of Statistics,* 1947–. ST/STAT/SER.Q/-.

> The *Statistical Yearbook* is a summary of country statistics on population, manpower, agriculture, finance, industry, manufacturing, energy, and trade, for example. Data are presented in a series of tables grouped into chapters by subject. The sources of data (national statistical offices and intergovernmental bodies) are cited and tables are accompanied by copious notes, glossaries, and explanatory remarks. Published annually since 1948. The *Monthly Bulletin of Statistics* keeps the *Statistical Yearbook* up to date.

Capital Punishment

Data on the use of capital punishment have been compiled in quinquennial reports, beginning with the period 1969–1973. Topics include enforcement of the death penalty, ratification of international instruments, and implementation and dissemination of safeguards guaranteeing protection of the rights of those facing the death penalty.

United Nations. Economic and Social Council. *Report of the Secretary General on Capital Punishment,* 1975. E/5616.

> Covers 49 countries from 1969 to 1973.

United Nations. Economic and Social Council. *Report of the Secretary General on Capital Punishment,* 1980. E/1980/9.

> Covers 62 countries from 1974 to 1978.

United Nations. Economic and Social Council. *Report of the Secretary General on Capital Punishment,* 1985. E/1985/43.

> Covers 47 countries from 1979 to 1983.

United Nations. Economic and Social Council. *Report of the Secretary General on Capital Punishment,* 1990. E/1990/38/Rev.1.

Covers 55 countries from 1984 to 1988.

United Nations. Economic and Social Council. *Report of the Secretary General on Capital Punishment and Implementation of the Safeguards Guaranteeing the Protection of the Rights of Those Facing the Death Penalty,* 1996. E/CN. 15/1996/19.

Covers 69 countries from 1989 to 1993.

Criminal Justice Expenditures

United Nations. *National Accounts Statistics: Main Aggregates and Detailed Tables, 1989–,* 1992 or 1994. ST/ESA/STAT/SER.X/2 1. or 1982– E.95.XVII.4.

Illicit Narcotics

United Nations International Drug Control Programme (UNDCP). Commission on Narcotic Drugs. *Annual Reports Questionnaire for the Commission on Narcotic Drugs,* Parts 1-3.

The *Annual Reports Questionnaire* comprises three parts: part 1, "Legislative and Administrative Measures and Socioeconomic Action," part 2, "Drug Abuse," and part 3, "Illicit Traffic and Supply."

United Nations International Drug Control Programme (UNDCP). Commission on Narcotic Drugs. *Illicit Traffic and Supply, Including Reports from Subsidiary Bodies: Statistics on Illicit Trafficking in and Supply of Narcotic Drugs and Psychotropic Substances in 1994,* 1996. E/CN.7/1996/CRP.6.

Illicit Traffic and Supply is the comprehensive report compiled from questionnaire data that is presented annually to the Commission on Narcotic Drugs.

United Nations Social Defence Research Institute. *Drugs and Punishment: An Up-to-Date Interregional Survey on Drug-Related Offenses,* 1988. No. 30.

This is a survey of penal regulations for drug-related offenses, including topics such as models of penal measures related to drug abuse, analyses of national legal systems, trends in sentencing practice, and recidivism with recommendations for action. Covers 31 countries from 1980 1984.

Regional Reports

Council of Europe. *European Sourcebook of Crime and Criminal Justice Statistics, Draft Model.* Paper prepared for the European Committee on Crime Problems, 44th Plenary Session (29 May–2 June, 1995). Strasbourg, France: Council of Europe, 1995.

The *European Sourcebook* was prepared by a group of specialists on trends in crime and criminal justice statistics. Topics include police statistics, prosecution and court statistics, correctional statistics, and historical trends in reported crime for the member states of the Council of Europe.

United Nations Asia and Far East Institute for the Prevention of Crime and the Treatment of Offenders. *Criminal Justice Profiles of Asia: Investigation, Prosecution, and Trial,* 1995.

This work comprises profiles of 12 countries, including information on agencies, processes, and functions of the criminal justice systems of each.

Treatment of Prisoners

Data on the treatment of prisoners have been compiled in quinquennial reports based on survey responses received from countries on the use and application of "Standard Minimum Rules for the Treatment of Prisoners." Topics include results of the survey, the role of non-governmental organizations, and technical assistance. The reports noted below provide information on general trends with regard to the treatment of prisoners, including overviews of general principles of imprisonment and prison services in United Nations member states.

United Nations. Economic and Social Council. *Report of the Secretary General on Use and Application of the Standard Minimum Rules for the Treatment of Prisoners,* 1996. E/CN. 15/1996/ 16/Add. 1.

Covers 72 countries for the year 1993.

United Nations. Fourth United Nations Congress on the Prevention of Crime and the Treatment of Offenders. *Working Paper Prepared by the Secretariat on the Standard Minimum Rules for the Treatment of Prisoners in the Light of Recent Developments in the Correctional Field,* 1970. A/CONF.43/3.

Covers 44 countries.

United Nations. Fifth United Nations Congress on the Prevention of Crime and the Treatment of Offenders. *Working Paper Prepared by the Secretariat on the Treatment of Offenders, in Custody or in the Community, with Special Reference to the Standard Minimum Rules for the Treatment of Prisoners Adopted by the United Nations,* 1975. A/ CONF.56/6.

Covers 62 countries from 1970 to 1974.

United Nations. Sixth United Nations Congress on the Prevention of Crime and the Treatment of Offenders. *Working Paper Prepared by the Secretariat on the Implementation of the United Nations Standard Minimum Rules for the Treatment of Prisoners,* 1980. A/CONF.87/1 I and Add. 1.

Covers 37 countries from 1975 to 1979.

United Nations. Seventh United Nations Congress on the Prevention of Crime and the Treatment of Offenders. *Report of the Secretary General on Implementation of the United Nations Standard Minimum Rules for the Treatment of Prisoners,* 1985. A. CONF. 121/15 and Add. 1.

Covers 62 countries from 1980 to 1984.

United Nations. Eighth United Nations Congress on the Prevention of Crime and the Treatment of Offenders. *Report of the Secretary General on Implementation of the United Nations Standard Minimum Rules for the Treatment of Prisoners,* 1990. A/CONF. 144/1 1.

Covers 49 countries from 1985 to 1989.

Victims of Crime

The International Crime (Victim) Survey (IC[V]S) is coordinated by the United Nations Interregional Crime and Justice Research Institute (UNICRI) and the Ministry of Justice of the Netherlands. The IC(V)S provides information on theft from cars, theft of cars, vandalism to cars, household burglaries, sexual incidents, assaults, and robbery, for example. The publications listed below present data gathered by this survey.

del Frate, Anna Alvazzi, and Angela Patrignani, eds. UNICRI. *Women's Victimisation in Developing Countries.* Rome: United Nations Publication, 1995.

del Frate, Anna Alvazzi, and Ugljesa Zvekic, eds. UNICRI. *Criminal Victimisation in the Developing World.* Rome: United Nations Publications, 1995.

del Frate, Anna Alvazzi, Ugljesa Zvekic, and Jan J. M. van Dijk, eds. UNICRI. *Understanding Crime: Experiences of Crime and Crime Control.* Rome: United Nations Publications, 1993.

van Dijk, Jan J. M., Pat Mayhem, and Martin Callas. *Experiences of Crime across the World—Key Findings from the 1989 International Crime Survey.* Deventer, Netherlands: Kluwer Law and Taxation Publishers, 1990.

OTHER VALUABLE INTERNATIONAL RESOURCES

While international organizations such as Interpol, the Council of Europe, and the United Nations are excellent sources for international statistics and information concerning criminal justice, the researcher will find other valuable resources in many of the sources discussed earlier in this book. Let us take particular note of some of the more useful ones.

Indexes and Abstracts

Consult chapter 5 for a description of relevant indexes and abstracting services in the social sciences, criminal justice, and law. When using print, CD-ROM, or online versions of any of these tools, include a geographical descriptor and you will locate numerous articles, books, and monographs covering the international literature. If you are checking print sources, such as *Criminal Justice Abstracts* or *Criminology, Penology, and Police Science Abstracts,* the printed index for each of these abstracting services uses geographical locations as major headings in their subject index. Of course, it will be a lot easier and prove more fruitful if you combine a geographical location with other descriptors in a CD-ROM or online version of a given index.

Almanacs, Encyclopedias, and Handbooks

General encyclopedias (see chapter 3), such as *Encyclopedia Britannia* and *Encyclopedia Americana,* provide excellent background material on various countries of the world. This information can be useful to your project, as it will supply population, demographic, economic, and various other components of the larger picture of a given country. Another excellent source for a brief account of this type of information is the *World Almanac and Book of Facts* (New York: World-Telegram, 1868–).

But there are some specific criminal justice encyclopedias and handbooks that are particularly relevant. These are noted in chapter 3, but here is a listing of some of titles that have an "international" focus.

Andrade, John. *World Police & Paramilitary Forces.* New York: Stockton Press, 1985 (p. 18).

Becker, Harold K., and Donna Lee Becker. *Handbook of the World's Police.* Metuchen, NJ: Scarecrow, 1986.

Davis, Nanette J. *Prostitution: An International Handbook on Trends, Problems, and Policies.* Westport, CT: Greenwood Press, 1993.

Ingleton, Roy D. *Police of the World.* New York: Scribner's, 1979.

Johnson, Elmer H., ed. *International Handbook of Contemporary Developments in Criminology.* Westport, CT: Greenwood Press, 1983.

Kurian, George T. *World Encyclopedia of Police Forces and Penal Systems.* New York: Facts on File, 1989.

MacDonald, Scott B., and Bruce Zagaris, eds. *International Handbook on Drug Control.* Westport, CT: Greenwood Press, 1992.

Shoemaker, Donald J., ed. *International Handbook on Juvenile Justice.* Westport, CT: Greenwood Press, 1996.

For many years the Library of Congress has published a series of country profiles under the name of *Area Handbooks.* This series is now entitled *Country Study Series* and can be found in most large library collections. Although these present an overview of the country as a whole, most volumes in the series contain a section devoted to criminal justice. This series can be found on the Internet on the Library of Congress Web site at http://lcweb.2.loc.gov/frd/cs/schome.html.

In addition, be sure to check the following Web sites: *UNCJIN-Countries of the World* http://www.ifs.univie.ac.at/~uncjin/country.html and the *World Factbook of Criminal Justice Systems* maintained by the U.S. Bureau of Justice Statistics (http://www.ojp.usdoj.gov/bjs/abstract/wfcj.htm). Each of these sites provides extensive information on the criminal justice systems in a number of countries.

Textbooks

With the increased interest in international crime, colleges and universities have added courses in comparative and international criminal justice. To serve this interest, several textbooks have begun to appear in this area. Using one of these is often a good way to see how a country profile is presented and to gain an overview of a given system. Here is an annotated listing of the textbooks that are currently in use.

Cole, George F., Stanislaw J. Frankowski, and Marc G. Gertz, eds. *Major Criminal Justice Systems: A Comparative Survey.* 2d ed. Newbury Park, CA: Sage, 1987.

Each chapter in this introductory textbook is written by a distinguished scholar who describes the administration of the penal justice in his or her native land. The book discusses common law systems, civil law systems, and social law systems. Countries included are the United States, England, and Nigeria (common law systems); the Federal Republic of Germany, Sweden, and Japan (civil law systems); and the Union of Soviet Socialist Republics and Poland (socialist law systems).

Ebbe, Obi N. Ignatius, ed. *Comparative and International Criminal Justice Systems: Policing, Judiciary and Corrections.* Boston, MA: Butterworth-Heinemann, 1996.

This reader contains articles introducing national criminal systems in comparative perspective. It includes articles on the following topics: a summary of the U.S. system; a discussion of nondiscriminatory policy and practice in British and American policing; a description of the treatment of offenders in Denmark and Brazil; the development of penal policy in the former British West Africa; a description of the criminal justice system of Sierra Leone; an overview of the Chinese criminal justice system; an overview of the court system in the People's Republic of China; a review of the police system in the People's Republic of China; and an overview of Japan's prison industries.

Fairchild, Erika. *Comparative Criminal Justice Systems.* Belmont, CA: Wadsworth, 1993.

This textbook uses a model country approach under the following chapter headings: "Criminal Justice Processes"; "Police and Community"; "Constitutional Review"; "Criminal Procedure"; "Legal Actors"; "Courts and Trials"; "After Conviction: The Sentencing Process"; "After Conviction: The Problem of Prison"; "Abortion Law"; "Terrorism"; and "Organized Crime and Drugs." Included as "model countries" are England, France, Germany, the former Soviet Union, Japan, and Saudi Arabia.

Fields, Charles B., and Richter H. Moore, Jr. *Comparative Criminal Justice: Traditional and Nontraditional Systems of Law and Control.* Prospect Heights, IL: Waveland, 1996.

This reader comprises 33 papers addressing the following: comparative crime and criminality; policing, law enforcement, and social control; formal and informal judicial systems; corrections and punishment; and juvenile justice systems. Appendices reprint seven international criminal justice treaties and conventions.

Reichel, Philip L. *Comparative Criminal Justice Systems: A Topical Approach.* Englewood Cliffs, NJ: Prentice-Hall, 1994.

Comparative Criminal Justice Systems focuses on the diversity of legal systems around the world, including Europe, Asia, North and South America, Latin America, Australia, and the Pacific Islands. Topics cover crime as a world problem, traditional material on American criminal law, contemporary legal traditions and relevant substantive and procedural criminal law, policing, the judiciary, corrections, juvenile justice, and the Japanese criminal justice system.

Terrill, Richard J. *World Criminal Justice Systems: A Survey.* 3d ed. Cincinnati, OH: Anderson, 1997.

World Criminal Justice Systems introduces the reader to the criminal justice systems of England, France, Sweden, Japan, and the Soviet Union. For each country, there is a discussion of the government, the police, the judiciary, the law, corrections, and juvenile justice.

Bibliographies

A few noteworthy bibliographies on international criminal justice have been published. These are included in chapter 4. Note especially the works by Piers Beirne and Joan Hill (page 84); the bibliography on criminal justice in Israel compiled by Robert R. Friedmann (page 86); the bibliography on Canadian criminal justice by Russell C. Smandych, Catherine J. Matthews, and Sandra J. Cox; and the *International Bibliography on Alternatives to Imprisonment* (page 89).

Books and Monographs

Numerous books and monographs cover various aspects of criminal justice for any given country. These can best be located using the card catalogs or indexing and abstracting services whose coverage includes book and monograph titles. Those listed here were chosen as representative of the types of materials that one can hope to find. They were chosen for their currentness and breadth of scope (each covers at least one aspect of the criminal justice system for several countries).

Das, Dilip K., ed. *Police Practices: An International Review.* Metuchen, NJ: Scarecrow Press, 1994.

Police Practices presents a comparative study of the police in Australia, Finland, India, Japan, and New Zealand. The various contributors each analyze the police as a product of their particular country's culture.

Fogel, David. *Policing in Central and Eastern Europe.* Helsinki, Finland: European Institute for Crime Prevention and Control, 1994.

Policing in Central and Eastern Europe describes policing trends for the following six nations of Eastern Europe: Czechoslovakia, Poland, Russia, Bulgaria, Hungary, and Albania.

Galway, Burt, and Joe Hudson, eds. *Restorative Justice: International Perspectives.* Monsey, NY: Criminal Justice Press; Amsterdam, Netherlands; Kugler, 1996.

Restorative Justice presents 30 papers on the theory, research, and practice of restorative justice in Australia, Canada, Germany, Japan, New Zealand, the United Kingdom, and the United States.

Graham, John, and Trevor Bennett. *Crime Prevention Strategies in Europe and North America.* 2d ed. Helsinki, Finland: European Institute for Crime Prevention and Control, 1995.

Crime Prevention Strategies presents a survey of crime-prevention measures adopted in the countries of Europe and North America. Three main categories of crime prevention are identified—criminality prevention, situational crime prevention, and community crime prevention.

Hami, Koichi, Renaud Ville, Robert Harris, Mike Hough, and Ugljesa Zvekic, eds. *Probation Around the World: A Comparative Study.* London; New York: Routledge, 1995.

Probation Around the World is a study of probation in 10 countries: Australia, Canada, Hungary, Israel, Japan, Papua New Guinea, the Philippines, Sweden, England and Wales, and Scotland.

Part I provides an overview of the origins, history, and development of probation. Part II presents material from the comparative case studies, most of it based on national reports prepared by experts in each country.

Heiland, Hans Gunther, Louise I. Shelley, and Katoh Hisao, eds. *Crime and Control in Comparative Perspectives.* Berlin; New York: Walter de Gruyter, 1992.

An anthology examines long-term trends in crime and its control in developed and developing nations. Countries covered include the Nordic countries, West Germany, Japan, the U.S., Venezuela, Caribbean nations, Nigeria, India, East Germany, Hungary, and China.

Junger-Tas, Josine. *Alternatives to Prison Sentences: Experiences and Developments.* Amsterdam, Netherlands: Kugler, 1994.

Alternatives to Prison Sentences reviews alternatives to prison for 12 Western countries: Australia, Austria, Canada, England, France, Finland, Germany, New Zealand, Norway, Scotland, Sweden, and the United States. Included in the review are mediation projects, restitution and compensation, day fines, community service, attendance and day centers, electronic monitoring, intensive supervision programs, and boot camps.

Junger-Tas, Josine, Gert-Jan Terlouw, and Malcolm W. Klein, eds. *Delinquent Behavior Among Young People in the Western World: First Results of the International Self-report Delinquency Study.* Amsterdam, Netherlands: Kugler, 1994.

Delinquent Behavior presents the first results of a self-reported study on crime and delinquency in 13 Western countries. Chapters cover self-reported delinquency in Helsinki, Finland; England and Wales; Belfast, Northern Ireland; the Netherlands; Liege, Belgium; Mannheim, Germany; Switzerland; Portugal; Spain; three Italian cities; Athens, Greece; a midwestern American city; Germany; and New Zealand.

Kangaspunta, Kristiina, ed. *Crime and Criminal Justice in Europe and North America 1986–1990.* Helsinki, Finland: European Institute for Crime Prevention and Control, 1995.

An international expert working group analyzes results of the *Fourth United Nations Survey of Crime Trends and Operations of Criminal Justice Systems* (1986–1990). Data were obtained from national responses received from countries in Europe, North America, and the former Soviet Union.

Kangaspunta, Kristiina, ed. *Profiles of Criminal Justice Systems in Europe and North America.* Helsinki, Finland: European Institute for Crime Prevention and Control, 1995.

Brief descriptions of European and North American criminal justice systems are based on data from national responses to the *Fourth United Nations Survey of Crime Trends and Operations of Criminal Justice Systems.* Profiles include information on structure and history of the criminal justice system; system operations and sentencing; statistics; sanctions; personnel and resources; selected issues; and further suggested reading.

Countries profiled are Albania, Australia, Belgium, Bulgaria, Canada, Croatia, Cyprus, Czech Republic, Denmark, England and Wales, Finland, France, Germany, Greece, Hungary, Iceland, Ireland, Israel, Italy, Luxembourg, Malta, Netherlands, Northern Ireland, Norway, Poland, Portugal, Romania, Scotland, Slovakia, Slovenia, Spain, Sweden, and the former states of the Soviet Union.

The European Institute for Crime Prevention and Control has also produced a number of small monographs, each of which offers a brief profile of a particular country. To date, the following countries have been profiled: Albania (1992); Bulgaria (1996); Canada (1996); Finland (1997); Ireland (1995); and Sweden (1995).

Mauer, Marc. *American Behind Bars: The International Use of Incarceration, 1992–1993.* Washington, DC: The Sentencing Project, 1994.

A review compares international rates of incarceration with those of the U.S. This report is updated frequently and is very useful for placing the rate of incarceration in the U.S with those of other countries.

van Zyl Smit, Dirk, and Frieder Dunkel, eds. *Imprisonment Today and Tomorrow: International Perspectives on Prisoners' Rights and Prison Conditions.* Deventer, Netherlands; Boston: Kluwer, 1991.

Imprisonment Today and Tomorrow presents the proceedings from an international seminar on problems of imprisonment held at Buchbach, Germany, in 1989.

National case studies use empirical data on the uses of incarceration to address broad questions of penal policy. The following countries are included: Austria, Belgium, Czechoslovakia, Denmark, the United Kingdom, West Germany, France, East Germany, Hong Kong, Hungary, Italy, Japan, Holland, China, Poland, South Africa, Spain, Sweden, Switzerland, U.S.S.R., and the United States.

Walmsley, Roy. *Prison Systems in Central and Eastern Europe: Progress, Problems and the International Standards.* Helsinki, Finland: European Institute for Crime Prevention and Control, 1996.

Following site visits made to Hungary, Poland, the Czech Republic, Bulgaria, Russia, Romania, and Moldova in 1994, this study examines prison systems in Central and Eastern Europe. In particular, it assesses the progress made toward compliance with the international standards on managing prisons and treatment of prisoners.

Periodicals

Articles in periodicals can be an invaluable resource for the study of international criminal justice. Several periodicals focus on a particular country or region (i.e., *British Journal of Criminology, The Australian and New Zealand Journal of Criminology,* the *Canadian Journal of Criminology,* and the *Caribbean Journal of Criminology and Social Psychology*), but several journals are designed specifically to cover the global or international scene. The ones listed here were chosen as representative of this type and are intended to alert readers to the range of periodicals that will serve their international needs.

Crime & Justice International: Worldwide News and Trends. Chicago: Office of International Criminal Justice (OICJ), 1985–.

Crime & Justice International "provides a comparative systems approach to familiarize readers with events of the world." This is more like a newsletter, but generally contains short articles of interest. This title continues *CJ Internationals,* and incorporates *CJ The Americas and CJ Europe.* Also check the OICJ Web site at http://www.acsp.edu/index.htm which includes updated information on articles of interest.

Global Journal on Crime and Criminal Law. Boxtel, Netherlands: TFLR-Institute, 1993–.

International Criminal Justice Review. Athens, GA: College of Public and Urban Affairs, Georgia State University, Vol. 1, 1991–.

International Criminal Police Review. Paris: International Criminal Police Organization, No. 1, 1946–.

International Journal of Comparative and Applied Criminal Justice. Wichita, KS: Wichita State University, Department of Administration of Justice, Vol. 1, 1977–.

International Journal of Offender Therapy and Comparative Criminology. New York: Guilford, Vol. 1, 1957–.

International Review of Criminal Policy. New York: United Nations Publications, Vol. 1, 1952–.

International Review of Victimology. Oxon, UK: A B Academic Publishers, Vol. 1, 1990–.

This is not to say that relevant articles will not be found in other periodicals. Indeed, the vigilant researcher will find many articles in other journal titles. Be sure to use whatever indexing and abstracting tools are available. When researching other countries, be sure to check international indexing sources, such as *International Political Science Abstracts* (see page 106), the *Index to Foreign Legal Periodicals* (page 97), and *PAIS International* (page 98) in addition to the more specific criminal justice tools.

Appendix: World Wide Web Sites Related to Criminal Justice

COMPILED BY JACK REED OF THE STATE UNIVERSITY OF NEW YORK AT ALBANY

The following is a collection of Web sites—U.S. federal, foreign, and international—related to criminal justice issues. The list is arranged into the following broad subjects:

- Abnormal Behavior
- Agencies Providing Criminal Justice Information and Data
- Crime Prevention and Victims Organizations
- Criminal Justice and the Media
- Criminal Justice Education
- Criminal Justice Images and Illustrations
- Criminal Violence
- Death Penalty
- Drugs and Alcohol
- Electronic Journals
- Federal Criminal Justice Agencies
- Forensics
- Guides to Criminal Justice on the Internet
- Human Rights
- International and Foreign Criminal Justice Resources
- Juvenile Delinquency
- The Law
- Militias, Cults, Bombers, Arsonists, and Federal Responses
- Obscenity, Censorship, and the Communications Decency Act
- Organized Crime
- Police Agencies and Resources
- Prisons
- Property, White-Collar, and Computer Crimes
- Prostitution, Pornography, and Satanic Crime
- Unsolved Crimes and Fugitives

ABNORMAL BEHAVIOR

Animals Crimes Resource. http://www.teleport.com/ ~acr/

Parascope News. http://www.parascope.com/ index.htm

Psychopathology. http://www.wwnorton.com/ norton/struc/chap_18/chap_18.html

Stupid Criminals. http://www.freenet.msp.mn.us/ people/norstrem/stupid.htm

Treatment for Psychopathology. http:// www.wwnorton.com/norton/struc/chap_19/ chap_19.html

AGENCIES PROVIDING CRIMINAL JUSTICE INFORMATION AND DATA

The Arkansas Crime Information Center. http:// www.acic.org/

Bureau of Justice Statistics. http:// www.ojp.usdoj.gov/bjs/

CERN/ANU - Demography and Population Studies. http://coombs.anu.edu.au/ResFacilities/ DemographyPage.html

Council of European Social Science Data Archives. http://www.uib.no/nsd/diverse/utenland.htm

Crime Statistics Page. http://www.crime.org/

Danish Data Archives (DDA). http://gate1.dda.dk/ dda.html

GESIS Social Science Research Gopher. gopher:// unix.bonn.iz-soz.de/11/en-iz-gopher/en-institute/ en-iz

The Illinois Criminal Justice Information Authority. http://www.icjia.org/

The Minnesota Planning Commission Criminal Justice Center. http://www.mnplan.state.mn.us/cj/index.html

National Archive of Criminal Justice Data. http://www.icpsr.umich.edu/NACJD/home.html

National Consortium for Justice Information and Statistics. http://www.search.org/

National Criminal Justice Association. http://sso.org/ncja/ncja.htm

National Criminal Justice Reference Service. http://www.ncjrs.org

New York State Division of Criminal Justice Services. http://criminaljustice.state.ny.us/

Norwegian Social Science Data Services (NSD). http://www.uib.no/nsd/nsd-eng.html

Questioned Document Examination Page (Handwriting Analysis). http://www.webmasters-net.com/qde/

The Rand Corporation. http://www.rand.org/

The Seattle Crime Report. http://www.accessone.com:80/~kwirth/

The Shadowsoft Criminal Justice Data. http://www.shadowsoft.com/criminal/index.html

Sourcebook of Criminal Justice. http://www.albany.edu/sourcebook/

SSD:s HomePage. http://www.ssd.gu.se/enghome.html

SSRN Abstract Database. http://www.SSRN.com/

The State Statistical Analysis Center. http://www.ch.search.org/

Statistical Resources on the Web. http://www.lib.umich.edu/libhome/Documents.center/stats.html

Statistics Canada. http://www.statcan.ca/start.html

TEXAS Department of Criminal Justice. http://corrections.tjn.com/tdcj.htm

University of Alberta, Data Library. http://datalib.library.ualberta.ca/

Vera Institute of Justice. http://broadway.vera.org/

The World-Wide Web Virtual Library: Research Resources. http://www.pitt.edu/~ian/ianres.html

The World-Wide Web Virtual Library: Statistics. http://www.stat.ufl.edu/vlib/statistics.html

Crime, Deterrence, and Right-to-Carry Concealed Handguns. http://law.lib.uchicago.edu/faculty/lott/guncont.html

CURE: Citizens United for Rehabilitation of Errants. http://www.wp.com/CURE/

Drug Law Reform. http://www.norml.org/~norml/

Drunk Driving Defense Website. http://law.net/sponsors/taylor/

False Rape, Abuse and Molest Reports. http://www.vix.com:80/pub/men/falsereport/index.html

Firearms and Liberty. http://www.shadeslanding.com/firearms/firearms.html

Forfeiture Endangers Americans Rights. http://www.fear.org/

Forfeiture. http://www.calyx.net/~fear/

Freedom of Information Center. http://www.missouri.edu/~foiwww/

Government Access Sales. http://www.financenet.gov/

JOSHUA: The Florida Court System. http://justice.courts.state.fl.us/

Jury Nullification. http://www.primenet.com/~slack/fija/fija.html

The Jury System. http://www.calyx.net/~fija/

Legal Justice Reform Network. http://www.usa.net/uclr/

Mental Health Net. http://www.cmhc.com/mhn.htm

National Center for State Courts. http://www.ncsc.dni.us/

New York State Defenders Association. http://www.nysda.org/

Not One More! Gun violence information. http://norden1.com/~jfrisk/index.html

NRA: The National Rifle Association. http://www.nra.org/

Society Against Guns in Europe. http://www.sage.org.uk/

Supreme Court of Florida. http://justice.courts.state.fl.us/courts/supct/

US Evidence Law. http://www.law.cornell.edu/topics/evidence.html

Washinton State Courts. http://www.wa.gov/courts/

Wiretap. http://cpsr.org/dox/wiretap.html

CIVIL LIBERTIES, DUE PROCESS, AND THE COURTS

ACLU. http://www.aclu.org/

Activist Groups. http://www.calyx.net/activist.html

The ARC's Access to Justice Project: The Mentally Retarded and the CJ System. http://www.metronet.com/~thearc/ada/crim.html

Court of Last Resort. http://www.sandbox.net/court/pub-doc/home.html

COMMUNITY CORRECTIONS

Correctional Management, Inc: Community Corrections Site. http://www.c-m-i.com/

Iowa Association for Dispute Resolution. http://homebuilder.com:81/iadr/

Multnomah County Department of Community Corrections - Portland, Oregon. http://www.multnomah.lib.or.us/div/correct.html

National Center on Institutions and Alternatives. http://www.igc.apc.org/ncia/

Parole Boards. http://www.nvc.org/cdir/parolbrd.htm

Restorative Justice. http://www.fresno.edu/pacs/restj1.html

Sacramento County Probation Department. http://www.calweb.com/~sacprob/sacprob.html

Secure and Community Corrections. http://orion.alaska.edu/~afdsw/prison.html

Sex Offender Supervision. http://www.teleport.com/~mleonard/index.html

Texas Probation Association. http://cust.iamerica.net/cscdadm/

Victim Offender Mediation Association. http://www.igc.org/voma/

VORP. http://www.mbnet.mb.ca/mcc/programs/crime/vorp.html

CRIME PREVENTION AND VICTIMS' ORGANIZATIONS

Abused Children's Rights. http://pw1.netcom.com/~moto2/youths.html

Access to Justice, Final Report. http://ltc.law.warwick.ac.uk/woolf/

Assault Prevention Information Network. http://galaxy.einet.net/galaxy/Community/Safety/Assault-Prevention/apin/APINintro.html

The Atlas Group: They Expose Sex Offenders in the Community. http://www.winternet.com/~prevent/

BC Institute on Family Violence Start Page. http://www.eye.net/Netizen/Progressive/bcifv

CAVEAT - Canadian victims' rights page. http://www.caveat.org/

Child Abuse Yellow Pages. http://idealist.com/cayp/

Child CyberSEARCH. http://www.childcybersearch.org/

Child Quest International. http://www.kids.org/

Citizen's Against Violent crime. http://www.webserve.com/iandi/org/cave/welcome.html

Citizens for Law & Order. http://www.deltanet.com/users/ghc/

Crime In America Network. http://www.usa.net/uclr/news/

Crime Net. http://www.fga.com:80/crimenet/

Crime Prevention (NCJRS). http://www.ncjrs.org/cphome.htm

Crime Prevention Unit. http://www.geocities.com/CapitolHill/1591/

Crime Prevention. http://www.bconnex.net/~cspcc/crime_prevention/home.html

Crime Prevention. http://www.crime-prevention.org.uk/

Crime Victims Compensation Program, NC Victim and Justice Services Division. http://vger.gcc.dcc.state.nc.us/home/vjs/cvcp0.htm

CrimeStoppers Sites. http://www.deepcove.com/crime_stoppers/cs-sites.html

CrimeWise. http://www.protect-mgmt.com/expert/crimewise/

Criminal Justice Reform in California. http://www.sonnet.com/CriminalJusticeReform/

David Baldwin's Trauma Info Pages. http://gladstone.uoregon.edu/~dvb/trauma.htm

Dignity Of Victims Everywhere. http://www.eskimo.com/~yaquii/

Don't tell your Mummy. http://www.ion.com.au/yoni/donttell.html

Global Missing Children's Directory. http://www.gmcd.org/

Homeless-Missing Persons Project. http://www.apam.com/inca/hmpp/

Indiana Sex Offender Registry. http://www.state.in.us/cji/index.html

International Child Molester Database. http://www.greatworld.com/public/query.htm

Iowa Organization for Victim Assistance. http://www.netins.net/showcase/i_weaver/iova.htm

Justice for All: Good List of Victim-Related Links. http://www.hotsites.net/fightback/jfa/

KEYEYE: Teaches Children How to Avoid Abduction. http://www.keyeye.com/

The Klaas Foundation for Children. http://www.klaaskids.inter.net/

Legal Justice Reform Network. http://www.usa.net/uclr/

McGruff & Scuff and the CRIME DOGS. http://www.mathetics.com/cpi/crimedog.html

Men Against Domestic Violence. http://www.silcom.com/%7Epaladin/madv/

Minnesota Higher Education Center Against Violence & Abuse. http://www.umn.edu/mincava/

Mothers Against Drunk Drivers. http://www.madd.org/

National Center for Missing & Exploited Children. http://www.missingkids.org/

National Committee to Prevent Child Abuse. http://www.childabuse.org/

National Crime Victims' Research and Treatment Center. http://www.musc.edu/cvc/

National Organization for Victim Assistance. http://www.access.digex.net/~nova/

National Victim Center. http://www.nvc.org/

The Nation's Missing Children Organization. http://www.cris.com/~altoren/

Neighbourhood Watch. http://ourworld.compuserve.com/homepages/nwatch/

New York Missing and Exploited Children Clearinghouse. http://criminaljustice.state.ny.us/missing/

Nonviolence Resources. http://www.igc.apc.org/nonviolence/

Office for Victims of Crime. http://www.ncjrs.org/ovchome.htm

Official Polly Klaas Foundation Web Site. http://www.pollyklaas.org/

Parents of Murdered Children. http://www.metroguide.com/pomc/

Pavnet - Partnership Against Violence Network. http://www.pavnet.org/

Publicizing Child Molester's Prison Release. http://www.ca-probate.com/molestpr.htm

Rate Your Risk of Being a Crime Victim. http://www.Nashville.Net/~police/risk/

Representing Victims of Crime: A Perspective on the Disaster of American Public Policy and Proposals for Change. http://tsw.ingress.com/tsw/talf/txt/crime.html

SAFE-T-Child Online: Protecting Your Child from Abduction and Seduction. http://yellodino.safe-t-child.com/

Sexual Assault Information Page. http://www.cs.utk.edu/~bartley/saInfoPage.html

Surviving the Workplace Jungle. http://vvv.com/m2/swj/

Survivors of Stalking. http://www.gate.net/~soshelp/

Take Back New York. http://www.users.interport.net/~wave3/tbny.html

Texas Crime Victims' Compensation Page. http://www.oag.state.tx.us/WEBSITE/CRIMINAL/cvc_prog.htm

Unofficial Wisconsin Victims' Rights Page. http://ourworld.compuserve.com/homepages/derene/

Victim Compensation and Victim Assistance: From The U.S. Code. http://www.law.cornell.edu/uscode/42/ch112.html#s10603a

Victims (NCJRS). http://www.ncjrs.org/victhome.htm

Victims' Assistance Foundation. http://www.rtt.ab.ca/rtt/personal/vaf1.htm

CRIMINAL JUSTICE AND THE MEDIA

America's Most Wanted. http://www.foxnetwork.com/amwindx.htm

Caz's Home Page: O J Simpson Page. http://www.dnai.com:80/~caz/

CNN's O J Simpson Site. http://cnn.com/US/OJ/index.html

Cops: The Fox Documentray Series. http://www.foxnetwork.com/copsindx.htm

Court TV. http://www.courttv.com/

The Crime Writer. http://www.crl.com/~mikekell/crimewriter.html

The Crimewriting Network. http://hollywoodshopping.com/Crime/letter.html

Cyberjury: America Judges OJ. http://www.micron.net/~lit/

Drugs in the Media. http://www.he.net/~storm/drugs/media.html

Free Speech Newspaper, Inc. http://www.freespeechnews.com/callme/

Media in Cyberspace. http://www.mediasource.com/study/

Media Terrorism: Focuses on Japan. http://www.race.u-tokyo.ac.jp/~mrosin/tero/index.html

The Media vs. the Mafia. http://www.nando.net/prof/freedom/1994/reports/mafia.html

The Menendez Brothers' Case. http://www.yahoo.com/Government/Law/Legal_Research/Cases/Menendez_Brothers_Case/

National Television Violence Study. http://www.igc.apc.org/mediascope/ntvs.html#5

NetCourt: Transcripts from High Profile Media Trials. http://www.vnet.net/netcourt/

Newsweek Media Research Index. http://www.vmr.com/research/index.html

O J Central: TIME Magazine's O J Simpson Files. http://pathfinder.com/pathfinder/features/oj/central1.html

O J Simpson Discussion Center. http://www.sure.net/~wedeking/

Reportage. http://acij.uts.edu.au/reportageindex.html

Simpson Court Transcripts. http://www.islandnet.com/~walraven/simpson.html

The Simpson Deposition. http://www.latimes.com/SIMPSON/

The Simpson Matter. http://www.bdsnet.com/~mevans/oj.htm

Spike Webb Net Detective. http://www.spikewebb.com

Susan Smith Case and Trial Stories. http://www.teleplex.net/SHJ/smith/ninedays/ninedays.html

True Crime and Crime Fiction. http://www.earthlink.net/~ehumes/

TV News Archive. gopher://tvnews.vanderbilt.edu/

Unsolved Mysteries. http://www.unsolved.com/

Victims and the Media. http://www.journalism.msu.edu/ccas/journalism/vicmed/victim.html

CRIMINAL JUSTICE EDUCATION

American Society of Criminology. http://sun.soci.niu.edu/~asc/. http://www.bsos.umd.edu:80/asc/address

California Lutheran University's Sociology and Criminal Justice Department. http://robles.callutheran.edu/scj/scj.html

California State U. at Stanislaus Criminal Justice. http://cjwww.csustan.edu/cj/cjhome.html

CARL on the Web. http://www.carl.org/

CARL Telnet Session. telnet://database.carl.org/

Center for Law Enforcement Ethics. http://web2.airmail.net/slf/clee.htm

Cybercrime - Jones Multimedia Encyclopedia Update. http://www.digitalcentury.com/encyclo/update/crime.html

Fayetteville State University Criminal Justice. http://www.uncfsu.edu/col/arts/sbs/crj/index.htm

Florida State University School of Criminology and Criminal Justice. http://mailer.fsu.edu/~crimdo/index.html

Institute of Criminology University of Cambridge (England). http://www.law.cam.ac.uk/crim/iochpg.htm

Jacksonville State University (AL) Criminal Justice Department. http://jsucc.jsu.edu/depart/criminal/criminal_justice.html

Job Openings in Criminal Justice Education. http://chronicle.merit.edu/.ads/.ads-by-group/.faculty/.sscience/.crj/.links.html

John Jay College of Criminal Justice. http://www.jjay.cuny.edu/

Justice Center, University of Alaska Anchorage. http://orion.alaska.edu/just/1justice.html

Justice Research Association. http://ourworld.compuserve.com/homepages/Justice_Research

Justice Resource Center, University of Alaska, Fairbanks. http://Justice.uafss.alaska.edu/

Law Enforcement Links. http://www.execulink.com/~lbwilson/lel/

Law School Admission Council. http://www.lsac.org/

Library of Congress. http://lcweb.loc.gov/homepage/lchp.html

Maryland Criminology Department. http://www.bsos.umd.edu/ccjs/cjus.html

Metropolitan State College of Denver Department Of Criminal Justice. http://www.mscd.edu/~cjc/

New Jersey Association of Criminal Justice Educators. http://WWW.covesoft.com/fire/cje.html

New York Public Library Home Page. http://www.nypl.org/

New York State Library Home Page. http://unix2.nysed.gov/library/

Northeastern College of Criminal Justice. http://www.northeastern.edu/admissions/viewbook/cj.html

OCLC Access Selection. http://www.oclc.org/

Peterson's Education Center. http://www.petersons.com/

Saint Mary's College of Minnesota Criminal Justice Department. http://www.smumn.edu/smc/dept/cj/vetter.html

The School of Justice Administration at Griffith University. http://www.gu.edu.au/gwis/hum/justice/hum_ja_home.html

Simon Fraser University, Criminology. http://www.sfu.ca/criminology/

Southwestern Law Enforcement Institute. http://web2.airmail.net/slf/slei.htm

Southwestern Legal Foundation. http://web2.airmail.net/slf/

Statistics Internet Links. http://www.cas.usf.edu/~alka/usffeb.html

Uncover WebSearch. http://www.carl.org/uncover/

University at Albany School of Criminal Justice. http://www.scj.albany.edu:90/

University of Alabama Criminal Justice Department. http://ua1vm.ua.edu:80/~bamacj/

University of South Florida Department of Criminology. http://www.cas.usf.edu/criminology/index.html

University of Toronto Centre for Criminology Library. http://library.utoronto.ca/www/libraries_crim/crimhome.htm

The Virtual Library. http://www.albany.edu/libcomp/virtual_library/virtual.html

Wadsworth Publishing Criminal Justice List. http://www.thomson.com:9966/rcenters/cj/cj.html

Washington State Institute for Community Oriented Policing. http://www.idi.wsu.edu/wsicop/

WWW Libraries v3.0. http://www.albany.net/~ms0669/cra/libs/libs.html

Yahoo - Criminal Justice Institutes. http://www.yahoo.com/Social_Science/Sociology/Criminal_Justice/Institutes/

CRIMINAL JUSTICE IMAGES AND ILLUSTRATIONS

Art Crimes. http://www.gatech.edu:/desoto/graf/Index.Art_Crimes.html

Criminal Justice Videos. http://www.filmakers.com/
    CRIME/CRIME.html
Digital Jungle Graffiti. http://www.inta.net/~dkew/
    graf.html
Graffiti In Pleasant Hill. http://www.ccnet.com/
    ~dougs/pgraf.html
Legal Clip Art. http://legal-pad.com/legalimages/
    legalart.html
National Graffiti Information Network. http://
    infowest.com/NGIN/
National Press Photographers Association. http://
    sunsite.unc.edu/nppa/index.html

CRIMINAL VIOLENCE

Anatomy of a Murder Home Page http://
    tqd.advanced.org/2760/homep.htm
Armed Robbery. http://www.ior.com/~jdmoore/
Casebook: Jack the Ripper. http://www.ftech.net/
    ~doom/casebook.html
Cease Fire: Gun Violence. http://norden1.com/
    ~jfrisk/index.html
Criminal and Psychological Profiling By Dr. Joseph
    Davis. http://somt.nu.edu/~jdavis/profile.html
Date Rape. http://www.cs.utk.edu/~bartley/acquaint/
    acquaintRape.html
Domestic Violence Index. http://www.s-t.com/
    projects/DomVio/domviohome.HTML
Dunblane Scotland Massacre. http://www.catalyst-
    highlands.co.uk/flash.htm
Husband Battering. http://www.vix.com/pub/men/
    battery/battery.html
Internet Crime Archives: Serial Killers & More.
    http://www.mayhem.net/Crime/archives.html
John F. Kennedy Assassination Archives. http://
    www.nara.gov/nara/jfk/jfk.html
Men and Domestic Violence Index. http://
    www.vix.com/pub/men/domestic-index.html
Serial Killers and Forensic Psychology. http://
    cedar.evansville.edu/~pl5/
Serial Killers v. Mass Murderers. http://
    ucsub.colorado.edu/~mcelroy/serial.html
Sexual Assault Information Page. http://
    www.cs.utk.edu/~bartley/saInfoPage.html
Zodiac Killer Research. http://bayarea.net/~restech/
    zodix.htm

DEATH PENALTY

Abolish Capital Punishment Now. http://
    www.hooked.net/users/plehner/dp/
ABOLITION NOW!!!. http://www.abolition-
    now.com/index.html

Abolitionists vs. Retentionists. http://
    www.miamicity.com/miami/literadeath.html
Amnesty International Statistics on Peak Usage of
    Death Penalty. http://www.derechos.org/amnesty/
    dp/ExecPeakUSA.html
Amnesty International. http://www.organic.com/
    Non.profits/Amnesty/
Angel on Death Row: Sister Helen Prejean. http://
    www2.pbs.org/wgbh/pages/frontline/angel/
Court TV Library: Death Penalty. http://
    www.courttv.com/library/capital/hbo.html
Dead Man Talkin'. http://monkey.hooked.net/m/hut/
    deadman/deadman.html
The Death Penalty Page: Focuses on Florida. http://
    law.fsu.edu/lawtech/deathpen/deathpen.html
The Death Penalty. http://www.amnesty.org.au/
    dp.html
Death Penalty Information. http://www.hotsites.net/
    fightback/jfa/DP.html
Death Penalty Statistics. http://
    www.theelectricchair.com/stats.htm
Death Penalty. http://miranda.bu.edu/~amaral/
    Personal/death.html
Death Penalty: the Ultimate Revenge. http://
    www.esslink.com/~brud/issues/deathpen/
    dpenpage.html
The Electric Chair. http://www.theelectricchair.com/
    index.htm
Executions. http://sashimi.wwa.com/~gregory/
    executions/
Girvies Davis Home Page: Death Row Inmate Tells
    His Story. http://www.mcs.net/~bkmurph/
    girvies.htm
The JusticeNet Prison Issues Desk. http://
    www.peacenet.apc.org/prisons/
Kentucky Department of Public Advocacy - Death
    Penalty Page. http://dpa.state.ky.us/~rwheeler/
    deathpen.htm
Links to Human Rights and Amnesty International
    Pages. http://www.derechos.org/human-rights/
    links.html
Mumia Abu-Jamal. http://www.calyx.net/~refuse/
    mumia/index.html
Texas Death Row. http://www.shsu.edu/~stdsls/hunt/
    tdcj/death_row/death_row.html
Tyburn Tree: Public Executions in Early Modern
    England. http://www.columbia.edu/~zll1/
    tyburn.html
Yahoo! - Death Penalty. http://www.yahoo.com/
    Society_and_Culture/Crime/Death_Penalty/

DRUGS, ALCOHOL, AND OTHER ADDICTIONS

AA's Big Book. http://www.global.org/bigbook/

Addiction Research Foundation. http://www.arf.org/

Alcohol and Drug Information: from NCADI. http://www.health.org/

CEDAR: Center for Education and Drug Abuse Research. http://www.pitt.edu/~mmv/cedar.html

CESAR: Center for Substance Abuse Research. http://www.bsos.umd.edu/cesar/cesar.html

Cocaine and Federal Sentencing Policy. http://www.bna.com/hub/bna/legal/crack.html

Cops Against the Drug War. http://www.drcnet.org/cops/cops.html

Dark Alliance: The Story Behind the Crack Explosion. http://www.sjmercury.com/drugs/

Drug and Alcohol Treatment Net. http://www.datnet.com/wesson/

Drug Info for DARE Officers. http://www.winternet.com/~publish/

Drug Information. http://www.paranoia.com:80/drugs/

Drug Price Report Project. http://www.hyperreal.com/drugs/price.report/index.html

Drug Reform Cordination Network. http://www.druglibrary.org/

Drug Text USA: Another Drug Text page is Located in http://www.xs4all.nl/~mlap/Holland. http://www.calyx.com/~mariolap/index.html

Drugs and Crime. http://www.ncjrs.org/drgshome.htm

Dual Diagnosis Web site. http://www.erols.com/ksciacca/

Focus on Crime and Drug Policy. http://www.rand.org/publications/RRR/Crime.Drugs/

Habitsmart Home Page. http://www.cts.com:80/~habtsmrt/

Hair Trac Technology: Hair Testing for Drugs. http://www.htrac.com/

Hazelden Recovery Page. Http://www.Hazelden.org/

The International Journal of Drug Testing. http://www.stpt.usf.edu/journal/index.html

LIBRA: UK Alcohol and Drug Awareness Site. http://www.brookes.ac.uk/health/index.html

Marijuana Archive. http://www.calyx.com/~olsen/

National Household Survey on Drug Abuse. http://www.health.org/hhs/93hhsrvy.htm

Netaholics Anonymous. http://simba.safari.net/~pam/netanon/

NIDA: National Institute on Drug Abuse. http://www.nida.nih.gov/

Office of National Drug Control Policy. http://www.whitehouse.gov/WH/EOP/ondcp/html/ondcp.html

Online Anonymous 12 Step Program. http://members.gnn.com/acbaird/index.htm

Quit Smoking Resource Page. http://ourworld.compuserve.com/homepages/bwprice/linkstoa.htm

Regulations Restricting the Sale and Distribution of Cigarettes and Smokeless Tobacco to Protect Children and Adolescents. http://www.access.gpo.gov/su_docs/fda/

Research Institute on Addictions. http://www.ria.org/

SAMHSA: The Substance Abuse and Mental Health Services Administration. http://www.samhsa.gov/

Steps for Recovery. http://www.pronex.com/steps/

Tobacco. http://charlotte.med.nyu.edu/woodr/tobacco.html

Tobacco Control Archives. http://www.library.ucsf.edu/tobacco/

Tulsa Drug Court. http://members.aol.com/bgrif/drugct.html

United Nations International Drug Control Program. http://www.undcp.org/index.htm

Web of Addictions. http://www.well.com:80/user/woa/

Webaholics. http://www.webaholics.com:80/

ELECTRONIC JOURNALS

The Activist Guide. http://www.drcnet.org/pubs/guide/10-95/guide10-95.html

American Police Beat. http://www.tiac.net/users/pdore/apb/

Cardozo Electronic Law Bulletin. http://www.gelso.unitn.it/card-adm/Welcome.html

Cornell Law Review. http://www.law.cornell.edu/clr/clr.htm

Crime Pays. http://www.kgbmedia.com/crime/index.html

The Critical Criminology ASA Section. http://sun.soci.niu.edu/~critcrim/

Elsevier Science Catalogue - Social / Behavioural Sciences and Humanities Section. http://www.elsevier.nl/catalogue/SAL/Menu.html

Federal Communications Law Journal. http://www.law.indiana.edu/fclj/fclj.html

Hastings Women's Law Journal. http://www.uchastings.edu/womenslj/womenslj.html

The International Journal of Drug Testing. http://www.stpt.usf.edu/journal/index.html

Internet Law and Security Reports. http://www.thinck.com/Publication.html

Journal of Criminal Justice and Popular Culture. http://www.scj.albany.edu:90/jcjpc/

Journal of Information, Law and Technology. http://elj.warwick.ac.uk/elj/jilt/

Journal of On-line Law. http://www.law.cornell.edu/jol/jol.table.html

Justice: CJ E-zine. http://198.105.232.7:80/industry/justice/

Law and Politics Book Review. http://www.polisci.nwu.edu:8001/

Law, Criminology, Justice: An Index of over 50 Mailing Lists. http://www.n2h2.com/KOVACS/S0039s.html

Law Journal Extra. http://www.ljx.com/

Law Publication Index from NUKOP Online. http://www.soton.ac.uk/~nukop/data/subject/law_indx.htm

Lee Grant's Criminal Justice Discussion Homepage. http://members.aol.com/grant2572/Lee.htm

The National Law Journal. http://www.ljextra.com/nlj/

Penn Library-Journals and Newspapers. http://www.library.upenn.edu/resources/ej/xej-index.html

Punch and Jurists: A Guide to Federal Criminal Law. http://www.fedcrimlaw.com/

Scholarly Journals Distributed Via the World-Wide Web. http://info.lib.uh.edu/wj/webjour.html

Secure News: Newsletter for Data and System Security. http://www.isecure.com/newslet

Sources e journal. http://www.dso.com/sources/

Stanford Law and Policy Review. http://www-leland.stanford.edu/group/SLPR/

The Terrorist Profile Weekly. http://www.site.gmu.edu:80/~cdibona/

U.S. Law Week: The Supreme Court. http://www.bna.com/supreme.html

University of Sydney - Sociology - Journals. http://www.arts.su.edu.au/Arts/departs/social/journal.html

Web Journal of Current Legal Issues. http://www.ncl.ac.uk:80/~nlawwww/

West's Legal News: Today's Top Stories. http://www.westpub.com/wlntop/front.htm

FEDERAL CRIMINAL JUSTICE AGENCIES

Alcohol, Tobacco, and Firearms. http://www.ustreas.gov/treasury/bureaus/atf/atf.html

Bureau of Justice Assistance. http://www.ojp.usdoj.gov/BJA/

Bureau of Justice Statistics. http://www.ojp.usdoj.gov/bjs/

Central Intelligence Agency. http://www.odci.gov/cia/

Civil Rights Division. http://gopher.usdoj.gov/crt/crt-home.html

Criminal Division. http://gopher.usdoj.gov/criminal/criminal-home.html

Department of Justice. http://www.usdoj.gov

Department of State Foreign Affairs Network. http://dosfan.lib.uic.edu/dosfan.html

Drug Enforcement Administration. http://www.usdoj.gov/dea/deahome.html

Federal Bureau of Investigation. http://www.fbi.gov/

Federal Bureau of Prisons. http://www.usdoj.gov/bop/bop.html

Federal Communication Commission. http://www.fcc.gov/

Federal Judicial Center. http://www.fjc.gov/

Federal Law Enforcement Careers Employment Guide. http://www.gnatnet.net/~fcfjobs/

Federal Law Enforcement Training Center. http://www.ustreas.gov/treasury/bureaus/fletc/fletc.html

Federal Protective Service. http://nletc.aspensys.com:83/nletchome.html

Federal Trade Commission. http://www.ftc.gov

Fedworld. http://www.fedworld.gov

Financial Crimes Enforcement Network. http://www.ustreas.gov/treasury/bureaus/fincen/

Government Printing Office. http://www.access.gpo.gov/su_docs/

House of Representatives. http://www.house.gov/

Internal Revenue Service. http://www.ustreas.gov/treasury/bureaus/irs/irs.html

Justice Technology Information Network. http://www.nlectc.org/E26T0/justnet.html

National Criminal Justice Reference Service. http://www.ncjrs.org/

National Institute of Justice. http://www.ojp.usdoj.gov/nij/

National Institute on Drug Abuse. http://www.nida.nih.gov/

National Law Enforcement Technology Center. http://nletc.aspensys.com:83/nletchome.html

National Security Agency. http://www.nsa.gov:8080/

Office of Juvenile Justice and Delinquency Prevention. http://www.ncjrs.org/ojjhome.html

Official Office of Justice Programs. http://www.ojp.usdoj.gov/

Punch and Jurists: A Guide to Federal Criminal Law. http://www.fedcrimlaw.com/

The White House. http://www.whitehouse.gov/

The World Factbook 1995. http://www.odci.gov/cia/publications/95fact/index.html

U.S. Coast Guard. http://www.dot.gov/dotinfo/uscg/

U.S. Customs Service. http://www.ustreas.gov/
treasury/bureaus/customs/customs.html

U.S. Customs Service, South Florida Section. http://
www.gate.net/~customs/Internal Revenue Service

U.S. Federal Judiciary. http://www.uscourts.gov/

U.S. Postal Inspection Service. http://www.usps.gov/
depart/inspect/Welcome.html

U.S. Secret Service. http://www.ustreas.gov/
treasury/bureaus/usss/usss.html

U.S. Senate. http://www.senate.gov/

U.S. Sentencing Commission. http://www.ussc.gov/

U.S. Treasury. http://www.ustreas.gov

FORENSICS

Borderline Personality Disorder. http://www.dds.nl/
~harwijn/

California Criminalistics Institute. http://
www.ns.net/cci/

Forensic Associates. http://www.asb.com/com/
forensic/home.html

Forensic Investigation and Human Identification
Society. http://www2.uncwil.edu/people/albertm/
fihis.htm

Forensic Science Resource Guide in a Criminal Fact
Investigation. http://www.usit.net/public/rscarp/
fsbindx.htm

Forensic Science Society and NetPage. http://
somt.nu.edu/~jdavis/Forensics/Forensicnet.html

Forensic Science Society. http://www.demon.co.uk/
forensic/index.html

GeoForensic Pattern Analysis. http://
ourworld.compuserve.com/homepages/
MauriceGodwinCriminalProfiling/

International Association of Bloodstain Pattern
Analysts. http://www.shadow.net/~noslow/
index.html

International Institute of Forensic Science. http://
www.iacnet.net/IIFS/

Recons-R-Us Collision Reconstructionists. http://
www.interlog.com/~robinl/

Zeno's Forensic Page. http://www.bart.nl/~geradts/
forensic.html

GUIDES TO CRIMINAL JUSTICE ON THE INTERNET

Cecil Greek's Criminal Justice Homepage. http://
www.stpt.usf.edu/~greek/cj.html

Guide to Internet Resources in Criminal Law and
Criminal Justice. http://www.law.ubc.ca/
international/guide.html

Sociology and Internet Resources. http://
147.26.186.101/areas/socres.htm

Sonoma State University Crime Related Links. http:/
/www.sonoma.edu/cja/info/infos.html

WWW VIRTUAL LIBRARY: SOCIOLOGY. http://
www.w3.org/hypertext/DataSources/bySubject/
Sociology/Overview.html

Yahoo - Social Science:Sociology. http://
www.yahoo.com/text/Social_Science/Sociology/

HUMAN RIGHTS

Criminal Justice Consortium Homepage. http://
www.peacenet.apc.org/justice/cjc

DIANA - An International Human Rights Database.
http://www.law.uc.edu:80/Diana/

Global Democracy Network. http://www.gdn.org/

Human Rights Gopher. gopher://
gopher.igc.apc.org:5000

The Human Rights Home Page. http://
www.traveller.com/~hrweb/hrweb.html

Institute for Law and Justice. http://ilj.org/index.htm

Institute for Law and Justice. http://www.ilj.org/

Network of Concerned Historians. http://
grid.let.rug.nl/ahc/nch/nch.htm

PeaceNet. http://www.peacenet.apc.org/

State of Emergency Database. http://
www.law.qub.ac.uk/human.htm

UN High Commission on Refugees. http://
www.unhcr.ch/

United States Institute of Peace. http://
www.usip.org/

Women of the World. http://www.echonyc.com/
~jmkm/wotw/

INTERNATIONAL AND FOREIGN CRIMINAL JUSTICE RESOURCES

Access to Justice Network Canada. http://
www.acjnet.org/acjnet/

Associated Institutes of the United Nations Crime
Prevention and Criminal Justice Programme.
http://www.ncjrs.org/unojust/

Australian Legal Information Institute. http://
austlii.law.uts.edu.au/

Cairo Conference on Population and Development.
http://www.iisd.ca/linkages/cairo.html

Canadian Crime Prevention Council. http://
www.web.apc.org/~ncpc/

Canadian Criminal Justice System. http://
www.criminaldefence.com/library/toc.html

Canadian Legal Resources on the Web. http://
www.mbnet.mb.ca/~psim/can_law.html

Central Adjudication Services (UK). http://
www.open.gov.uk/cas/cashome.htm

Centre for Defence and International Security Studies. http://www.cdiss.org/

CounterIntelligence and CounterTerrorism Page. http://www.tscm.com/

The CounterTerrorism Page. http://www.terrorism.com/

Country Information. gopher://library.berkeley.edu/11/resdbs/gove/foreign

Court Service. http://www.open.gov.uk/courts/court/cs_home.htm

Crime Stoppers On Line (Austrailia). http://www.crimestoppers.net.au/

Crisis Prevention Institute: An International Site of Violence Prevention Resources and Training. http://www.execpc.com/~cpi/index.html

CTI Law Technology Centre. http://ltc.law.warwick.ac.uk/

Europa. http://www.cec.lu/Welcome.html

European Association of Law and Economics. http://www.epas.utoronto.ca:8080/ecolaw/eale/eale.html

European Commission Legal Advisory Board. http://www2.echo.lu/legal/en/labhome.html

European Law Students Association (ELSA) UK Section. http://www.dur.ac.uk/~dla0www/elsa/elsa.html

Foreign Government Resources. http://www.lib.umich.edu/libhome/Documents.center/foreign.html

Forensic Science International. http://livor.oil.utu.fi/fsi/fsi.htm

HM Prison Service. http://www.open.gov.uk/prison/prisonhm.htm

Home Office of the United Kingdom. http://www.open.gov.uk/home_off/rsdhome.htm

International and Area Studies. http://www.clark.net/pub/lschank/web/country.html

International Association of Constitutional Law. http://www.eur.nl/iacl/index.html

International Association of Crime Analysts. http://web2.airmail.net/iaca/

International Association of Directors of Law Enforcement Standards and Training. http://midget.towson.edu:8001/IADLEST.HTML

International Association of Law Enforcement Intelligence Analysts, Inc. http://euphoria.mercy.edu/ialeia/index.html

International Association of Law Enforcement Planners. http://www.dps.state.ak.us:80/ialep/

International Center. http://flair.law.umb.ca/centres/icclr.html

International Centre for Commercial Law. http://www.link.org/EUROPE.HTM

International Centre for Criminal Law Reform and Criminal Justice Policy. http://www.law.ubc.ca/centres/crimjust.html

International Centre for the Prevention of Crime. http://www.web.apc.org/~cipc/

International Crime. http://www.sir.arizona.edu/govdocs/crime/intl.htm

International Criminal Justice References. http://www.ifs.univie.ac.at/~uncjin/country.html

International Rule of Law Clearinghouse. http://www.rol.org/

International Union of Police Associations. http://sddi.com/iupa.html

Law Society. http://www.lawsoc.org.uk/

Legal Aid Board (England and Wales). http://www.open.gov.uk/lab/legal.htm#index1

Maastricht Treaty. http://europa.eu.int/en/record/mt/top.html

Metropolitan Police Service, New Scotland Yard (UK). http://www.open.gov.uk/police/mps/home.htm

Migration and Ethnic Relations Virtual Library. http://www.ruu.nl/ercomer/wwwvl/wwwvlmer.html

Multilateral Conventions Project. http://www.tufts.edu/fletcher/multilaterals.html

National Criminal Intelligence Service (UK). http://www.open.gov.uk/ncis/ncishome.htm

North Atlantic Treaty Organization (NATO). gopher://gopher.nato.int/

Observatory on Criminality in Italy. http://www.securidata.it/osscarc.htm

Offender Profiles: Canada. http://www.web.apc.org/~ncpc/work/offpro_e.htm

Office of Fair Trading (UK). http://www.open.gov.uk/oft/ofthome.htm

OIJC: Office of International CJ. http://www.acsp.uic.edu/

On The Record - Official Documents from the EU. http://europa.eu.int/en/on_recor.html

Parliament. http://www.parliament.uk/

Peace Brigades International. http://www.igc.apc.org/pbi/index.html

Scandinavian Research Council for Criminology. http://rvik.ismennt.is/~tho/NSfK.html

Solicitor General of Canada. http://www.sgc.gc.ca/

Statewatch Database: The State and Civil Liberties in UK and Europe. http://www.poptel.org.uk/statewatch/

Striking the Balance: The Future of Legal Aid in England and Wales. http://www.open.gov.uk/lcd/lawp/lacont.htm

Systemic Racism: Ontario, Canada. http://www.yorku.ca/faculty/osgoode/owp/racism/contents.htm

Terrorist Group Index. http://www.site.gmu.edu/~cdibona/grpindex.html

UK Police and Forensic Web. http://www.innotts.co.uk/~mick2me/ukpolice.html

UN Crime and Justice Information Network. http://www.ifs.univie.ac.at/~uncjin/uncjin.html

UN Online Crime and Justice Clearinghouse. http://www.ncjrs.org/unojust/

UN Research Institute on Social Development (UNRISD). gopher://gopher.unv.ch:1250/

World Wide Legal Information Association. http://www.islandnet.com/~wwlia/wwlia.htm

JUVENILE DELINQUENCY

Adventure Bonding Parenting Page. http://www.imageplaza.com/parenting/

At-Risk Children and Youth. http://www.ncrel.org/ncrel/sdrs/areas/un0cont.htm

California State Juvenile Officers Association. http://www.csjoa.org/

Child Custody and Dependency Evaluation Web. http://forensic.nova.edu/

ERIC Gopher. gopher://ericps.ed.uiuc.edu:70/

Facts for Families. http://www.psych.med.umich.edu/web/aacap/factsFam/

Gutter Tribe: Kids on the Street. http://www.auschron.com/gallery/

Hotline Numbers. http://www.webshaker.com/directory/

Internships In Youth Development Agencies. http://www.cais.net/nonprofit/html/search.html

Juvenile Justice. http://www.ncjrs.org/jjhome.htm

Juvenile Justice Home Page. http://home.earthlink.net/~ehumes/homejuv.htm

Juvenile Justice in the 18th Century. http://www.pbs.org/williamsburg/justice/

Juvenile Justice Role Model Development Project. http://mailer.fsu.edu/~crimdo/cr-jjrole-model.html

Kathy's Resources on Parenting, Domestic Violence, Abuse, Trauma and Dissociation. http://www.mcs.net/~kathyw/home.html

Koch Crime Commission. http://www.kanzafoundation.org

Media Literacy Project. http://interact.uoregon.edu/MediaLit/HomePage

National Clearinghouse for Youth Studies. http://info.utas.edu.au/docs/ahugo/NCYS/

National Council of Juvenile and Family Court Judges. http://ncjfcj.unr.edu/

National Institute on the Education of At-Risk Students. http://www.ed.gov/prog_info/At-Risk/

National Youth Gang Center. http://www.iir.com/nygc/nygc.htm

Prevention Yellow Pages. http://www.tyc.state.tx.us/prevention/40001ref.html

School Violence. http://curry.edschool.virginia.edu/~rkb3b/Hal/SchoolViolence.html

Teen Help. http://www.vpp.com:80/teenhelp/index.html

TEENVUE: Teenage Driver Safety Program. http://www.goodnet.com/~teenvue/

Youth Link. http://ythlnk1.youthlink.net/wapy/index.html

THE LAW

Searchable (These Sites Provide a Search Engine)

'Lectric Law Library. http://www.lectlaw.com

1994 Crime Bill. http://gopher.usdoj.gov/crime/crime.html

Alaska Statutes. http://www.legis.state.ak.us/

California Law Code. http://www.leginfo.ca.gov/calaw.html

California Legislative Information. http://www.leginfo.ca.gov/

CataLaw: Metaindex of Law and Government. http://www.CataLaw.com/

The Code of Federal Regulations . http://www.access.gpo.gov/nara/cfr/index.html

Criminal Law Links. http://dpa.state.ky.us:80/~rwheeler/

The Declaration of Independence. http://www.law.emory.edu/FEDERAL/independ/declar.html

Federal Court Locator at Villanova. http://ming.law.vill.edu/Fed-Ct/

Find Law. http://www.findlaw.com/

Florida Government Locator. http://www.dos.state.fl.us/fgils/

Florida Legislature: Find Out About Pending Legislation. http://www.scri.fsu.edu/fla-leg/

Florida Statutes. http://www.scri.fsu.edu/fla-leg/statutes/

Full Text State Statutes and Legislation. http://www.prairienet.org/~scruffy/f.htm

The House of Representatives - Internet Law Library - Welcome! http://www.pls.com:8001/

Law Group Network. http://www.llr.com/

The Law Library of Congress. http://lcweb2.loc.gov/glin/lawhome.html

LAWS.COM: A Compendium of Law Resources.
http://www.laws.com/

The Legal List. http://www.lcp.com/The-Legal-List/
TLL-home.html

The Legal Pad. http://legal-pad.com/

Meta-Index for U.S. Legal Research.http://
gsulaw.gsu.edu/metaindex/

New York Court of Appeals. http://
www.law.cornell.edu/ny/ctap/overview.html

New York State Assembly. http://
assembly.state.ny.us/

The Oral Argument Page. http://oyez.at.nwu.edu/
oyez.html

Search Legal: Courts Search of Legal Sites. http://
www.intbc.com/sleuth/lega-c.html

Search Legal: News and Discussion Groups Search
of Usenet news.. http://www.intbc.com/sleuth/
lega-n.html

The U.S. Code. http://www.pls.com:8001/his/
usc.html

U.S. Constitution. http://www.law.emory.edu/
FEDERAL/usconst.html

The U.S. Court of Appeals, D. C. Circuit Cases.
http://www.ll.georgetown.edu/Fed-Ct/cafed.html

The U.S. Court of Appeals, Eleventh Circuit Cases.
http://www.law.emory.edu/11circuit/

The U.S. Court of Appeals, Fifth Circuit Cases.
http://www.law.utexas.edu/us5th/us5th.html

The U.S. Court of Appeals, First Circuit Cases. http:/
/www.law.emory.edu/1circuit/

The U.S. Court of Appeals, Fourth Circuit Cases.
http://www.law.emory.edu/4circuit/

The U.S. Court of Appeals, Ninth Circuit Cases.
http://ming.law.vill.edu/Fed-Ct/
ca09.html#usappeals

The U.S. Court of Appeals, Second Circuit Cases.
http://www.law.pace.edu/legal/us-legal/judiciary/
second-circuit.html

The U.S. Court of Appeals, Seventh Circuit Cases.
http://www.law.emory.edu/7circuit/

The U.S. Court of Appeals, Sixth Circuit Cases.
http://www.law.emory.edu/6circuit/

The U.S. Court of Appeals, Tenth Circuit Cases.
http://www.law.emory.edu/10circuit/

The U.S. Court of Appeals, Third Circuit Cases.
http://ming.law.vill.edu/Fed-Ct/
ca03.html#usappeals

The U.S. Government Printing Office. http://
www.access.gpo.gov/su_docs/

U.S. Supreme Court Decisions: Full Text;
Searchable by Subject; 1990–present. http://
www.law.cornell.edu:/supct/supct.table.html

U.S. Supreme Court Decisions: Full Text;
Searchable by Subject; 1937–1975. http://
www.fedworld.gov/supcourt/index.htm

Non-Searchable (These Sites Do Not Provide a Search Engine)

American Bar Association. http://www.abanet.org/

Association of Federal Defense Attorneys. http://
www.afda.org/

Association of Trial Lawyers of America. http://
www.atlanet.org/

Bill's Law Library: Canadian Sites. http://
www.io.org/~jgcom/librlaw.htm

Copyright Law. gopher://gopher.lib.virginia.edu:70/
11/alpha/copyright

CyberLawyer: On-line Legal Advice. http://
www.cyberlawyer.com

E-Law. http://www.murdoch.edu.au/elaw/

Electronic Legal Source. http://www.e-legal.com/

Emory University School of Law. http://
www.law.emory.edu/

Environmental Law. http://www.webcom.com/
~staber/welcome.html

Ethics on the WWW. http://www5.fullerton.edu/les/
ethics_list.html

International Law Page. http://
sray.wcl.american.edu/htm/intlaw.htm

Law Links. http://www.counsel.com/lawlinks

Law Marks: Legal Resource Database. http://
www.iwc.com/entropy/marks/bkmrk.html

Law-Related Internet Books and Newsletters. http://
www.abanet.org/lpm/magazine/booklist.html

Laws of Canada. http://canada.justice.gc.ca/Loireg/
index_en.html

Legal Domain Network. http://www.kentlaw.edu/
lawnet/lawnet.html

Legal Information Institute. http://
www.law.cornell.edu/lii.table.html

Legal Resource Locator. http://www.dorsai.org/p-
law/

Legal Resources. http://www.lsu.edu/~poli/
legal.html

LEGI-SLATE. gopher://gopher.legislate.com:70/1

LEXIS-NEXIS Communication Center. http://
www.lexis-nexis.com/

National Institute of Ethics. http://www.acc.net/
ethics/

RefLaw. http://lawlib.wuacc.edu/washlaw/reflaw/
reflaw.html

THE SEAMLESS WEBsite. http://seamless.com/

USA Law. http://www.usalaw.com/

Villanova Tax Law Compendium. http://
www.law.vill.edu/vill.tax.l.compen/index.html

Virtual Law Library. http://www.law.indiana.edu/law/lawindex.html

West Publishing. http://www.westpub.com/

MILITIAS, CULTS, BOMBERS, ARSONISTS, AND FEDERAL RESPONSES

1995 Index of Cults, Occult Organizations, New Age Groups, and New Religious Movements. http://rampages.onramp.net/~watchman/cat95.html

African-American Holocaust. http://www.tnp.com/holocaust/

Black Church Arsons. http://persephone.hampshire.edu/~mpm/arson.html

Black Church Fires—An Online Resource Guide. http://gbgm-umc.org/advance/Church-Burnings/index.html

Bombing of America: Includes the Unabomber. http://www.pbs.org/nova/bombing/index.html

The Conspiracy Pages. http://ROCK.SAN.UC.EDU/~TAYLORRM/

Cults A to Z. http://www.observer.co.uk/a-z-cults/index.html

David Koresh and the Branch Dividians. http://www.yahoo.com/Society_and_Culture/Religion/Christianity/Denominations_and_Sects/.David_Koresh_Branch_Davidians/

DOJ Report on Ruby Ridge. http://www.cs.cmu.edu/afs/cs.cmu.edu/user/wbardwel/public/nfalist/ruby.ridge1

Explosion in Oklahoma City. http://www.ionet.net/explode.shtml

Gonzo Links. http://www.capcon.net/users/lbenedet/gonzo.html

Guide to Hate Groups on the Internet. http://www.law.harvard.edu/library/guides/hateweb/hate.html

Information on Militias. http://www.well.com/user/srhodes/militia.html

Massacre of the Branch Dividians. http://www.shadeslanding.com/firearms/waco.massacre.html

Militia Watch. http://paul.spu.edu/~sinnfein/progressive.html

Montana Freemen. http://www.yahoo.com/Regional/U_S__States/Montana/Cities/Jordan/Organizations/. Montana_Freemen/

Oklahoma City Bombing. http://pegasus.acs.ttu.edu/~z3law/oklahoma.html

Overkill: Randy Weaver. http://www.playboy.com/expose/overkill.html

Patriot WWW Page. http://www.kaiwan.com:80/~patriot/

Project on Government Secrecy. http://www.fas.org/pub/gen/fas/sgp/

Published Works of Richard Kaczynski. http://www.rpi.edu/~bulloj/tjk/tjk.html

Randy Weaver. http://www.shadeslanding.com/firearms/waco.massacre.html#I.4

The Rise of the Militias: Why Are They so Angry? http://www.worldmedia.com/caq/militia.htm

The Unabomber Manifesto. http://www.netcenter.com/yellows/unabomb.html

Unabomber Suspect Arrested. http://www.yahoo.com/headlines/special/unabomber/.

Waco References. http://uts.cc.utexas.edu/~cwalker/waco/waco.html

OBSCENITY, CENSORSHIP, AND THE COMMUNICATIONS DECENCY ACT

The Battle Over Internet Censorship. http://www.zdnet.com/pcmag/special/reports/s960214a.htm

CAL-ACT: Californians Against Censorship Together. http://www.blowfish.com/calact.html

Center For Democracy and Technology. http://www.cdt.org/

Child Safety on the Internet. http://omni.voicenet.com/~cranmer/censorship.html

Constitutionality of the Communications Decency Act. http://journal.law.ufl.edu/~techlaw/1/sobel.html

The Cyberporn Fallout: from Computer-Mediated Communication Magazine. http://sunsite.unc.edu/cmc/mag/1995/aug/toc.html

Cyber-Rights and Civil Liberties (UK). http://www.leeds.ac.uk/law/pgs/yaman/yaman.htm

Cyber-Rights and Criminal Justice. http://avalon.caltech.edu/~thanne/law.html

Cybersitter. http://www.solidoak.com/

CyberSpace Law Center. http://www.cybersquirrel.com/clc/clcindex.html

Electronic Frontier Foundation. http://www.eff.org/

Electronic Privacy Information Center. http://epic.org/

The FileRoom: Fully Searchable Database of Censorship Attempts. http://fileroom.aaup.uic.edu:/FileRoom/documents/homepage.html

Free Expression Clearinghouse. http://www.freeexpression.org/

Freedom of the Press: Annotated Bibliography. http://www.lib.siu.edu/cni/toc.html

Internet Users' Association. http://www.dogtech.com/iua

Net Nanny. http://www.netnanny.com/netnanny/
home.html

New Age Comstockery: Exon vs the Internet. http://
www.cato.org/main/pa232.html

Platform for Internet Content Selection. http://
www.w3.org/pub/WWW/PICS/

The Privacy Pages. http://www.2020tech.com/
maildrop/privacy.html

Project 2000: The Cyberporn Debate. http://
www2000.ogsm.vanderbilt.edu/
cyberporn.debate.cgi

Project Censorship. http://www.tcom.ohiou.edu/
OU_Language/project-censorship.html

SafeSurf. http://www.safesurf.com/index.html

Safety-Net For Child Pornography and Illegal
Material on the Internet. http://dtiinfo1.dti.gov.uk/
safety-net/r3.htm

Surf Watch. http://www.surfwatch.com/

Telecommunications Act of 1996. http://
www.bell.com/

Temporary Injunction of the Communications
Decency Act. http://www.ionet.net/~mdyer/
decision.html

ORGANIZED CRIME

Asian Organized Crime: By the International
Association of Asian Crime Investigators. http://
www.deltanet.com/users/wcassidy/IAAOCI.html

POLICE AGENCIES AND RESOURCES

Anti-Police Sites: Actually, Citizens Watchdog
Groups. http://www.emergency.com/antipolc.htm

Bail Enforcement and Fugitive Recovery
Information Center. http://users.abcs.com:80/
drunyon/bail1.htm

Bolling's Police Pages. http://www.murlin.com/
~webfx/cops

Community Oriented Policing Office at DOJ. http://
www.usdoj.gov/cops/

Cop Links. http://www.freenet.msp.mn.us/people/
norstrem/coplinks.htm

Cop Net. http://police.sas.ab.ca/prl/index.html

Cops and Community. http://www.electriciti.com/
trisk/copscomm/

Crime Scene Training. http://members.gnn.com/
GRPD794/training.htm

Harris Criminal Justice Products. http://
www.harris.com/hcjp/

International Association of Chiefs of Police. http://
www.amdahl.com/ext/iacp/

Law Enforcement Agencies on the Web. http://
www.stpt.usf.edu/~greek/police.html

Law Enforcement (NCJRS). http://www.ncjrs.org/
lehome.htm

Law Enforcement Links. http://www.execulink.com/
~lbwilson/lel/

Law Enforcement Sites on the Web. http://
www.ih2000.net/ira/ira.htm

Maryland Community Crime Prevention Institute.
http://midget.towson.edu:8001/MDCP.HTML

Mr. Traffic. http://www.mrtraffic.com/

The National Center for Women and Policing. http://
www.feminist.org/welcome/police1.html

New York State Police. http://nyslgti.gen.ny.us/
nystate/NYSP/

Police Agency Official Home Pages. http://
police.sas.ab.ca/pdhome/index.html

Police Car Descriptions. http://eden.telalink.net/
zoomst/copcars/copcars.html

Police Central Dispatch. http://pages.prodigy.com/P/
O/C/police+public/pcd.htm

Police Complaint Center. http://netrunner.net/pcc/
index.htm

Police Officers' Internet Directory. http://
www.officer.com

Royal Canadian Mounted Police. http://www.rcmp-
grc.gc.ca/html/rcmp2.htm

Texas Street Beat. http://www.webwriter.com/street-
beat-1/index.htm

PRISONS

Alaska Department of Corrections. http://
www.state.ak.us/local/akpages/CORRECTIONS/
home.htm

Alcatraz. http://www.nps.gov/alcatraz/

American Correctional Association. http://
www.corrections.com/aca/

American Jail Association. http://
www.corrections.com/aja/

The Continuing Crime of Black Imprisonment. http:/
/www-unix.oit.umass.edu/~kastor/ceml_articles/
continuing.html

Control Unit Prisons. http://www-
unix.oit.umass.edu/~kastor/ceml_articles/
cu_in_us.html

Corrections Connection Network. http://
www.corrections.com/

Corrections (NCJRS). http://www.ncjrs.org/
corrhome.htm

Criminal Justice Reform: Focuses on California.
http://sonnet1.sonnet.com:80/
CriminalJusticeReform/

Esmor Correctional Services. http://www.esmor.com/

Federal Bureau of Prisons. http://www.usdoj.gov/bop/bop.html

Florida Corrections Commission. http://www.dos.state.fl.us/fgils/agencies/fcc/

Florida Department of Corrections. http://www.dos.state.fl.us/corrections/

Friends Outside. http://www.meer.net/users/taylor/frienout.htm

Inmate Classified. http://www.inmate.com/

The Keeper's Voice: The International Association of Correctional Officers. http://www.acsp.uic.edu/iaco/kv1603tc.htm

Maryland Department of Correctional Services. http://midget.towson.edu:8001.iadlest.html/DPSCS.HTML

Massachusetts Department of Corrections. http://www.magnet.state.ma.us:80/doc/

National Center on Institutions and Alternatives. http://www.ncianet.org/ncia

New York Commision on Corrections. http://crisny.org/government/ny/nysscoc/index.html

New York State Archives: Department of Correctional Services. http://unix6.nysed.gov/holding/aids/correct/intro.htm

North Carolina Department of Corrections. http://www.doc.state.nc.us/

Oregon Department of Community Corrections. http://www.multnomah.lib.or.us/div/correct.html

Paying the Price: The Rising Cost of Prison. http://www.mnplan.state.mn.us/press/prison.html

The Penal Lexicon: Focuses on England and Europe. http://www.demon.co.uk/penlex/

Pennsylvania Department of Corrections. http://www.state.pa.us/PA_Exec/Corrections/overview.html

Prison Connections. http://persephone.hampshire.edu/wmpig/prisoncon.html

Prison Documentary: Central Correctional Institution (SC). http://www.dgandf.com/bvc

Prison Ethnography Project. gopher://panda1.uottawa.ca:4011/11/.ethnography

Prison Fellowship International. http://www.goshen.net/PrisonFellowship/web/webhtm/pfihome.htm

Prison Issues Desk. http://www.igc.apc.org/prisons/

Prison Law Page. http://www.wco.com/~aerick/

Prison Legal News. http://weber.u.washington.edu/~lursa/PLN/pln.html

The Prison Project. http://168.216.210.13/mjhs/pproject/pproject.htm

Prison-Related Resources. http://www.cs.oberlin.edu/students/pjaques/prison/home.html

Prisoner-Related Resources. http://www.acsu.buffalo.edu/~heurich/prisoners.html

The Prisons Handbook: Focuses on England. http://www.tphbook.demon.co.uk/

Stop Prisoner Rape. http://www.igc.apc.org/spr/

Texas Youth Commission. http://www.tyc.state.tx.us/

Three Strikes: Focuses on California. gopher://gopher.well.sf.ca.us:70/11/Politics/three_strikes

Utah Department of Corrections. http://www.cr.ex.state.ut.us/home.htm

PROPERTY, WHITE-COLLAR, AND COMPUTER CRIMES

American Society for Industrial Security. http://www.asisaie.org/

Art Fraud: How to Avoid It. http://www.webcom.com/~lewrose/brochures/art.html

Computer Attacks at the Department of Defense. http://www.epic.org/computer_crime/gao_dod_security.html

Computer Crime. http://www.ifs.univie.ac.at/~pr2gq1/rev4344.html#crime

Copyright and E-Mail: Infringement on the Internet. http://www.mindspring.com/~isenberg/paper1.html

Copyright Guide. http://www.ilt.columbia.edu/projects/copyright/index.html

CRYPTO•LOG: The Internet Guide to Cryptography. http://www.enter.net/~chronos/cryptolog.html

DigiCrime. http://www.digicrime.com/

Electronic Frontier Outlaw Fringe: Cracking, Hacking, Bombs, Viruses, and Other Fringe Interests. http://www.virtualschool.edu/mon/Outlaws/

Executive Security International. http://www.esi-lifeforce.com/

Financial Scandals. http://www.ex.ac.uk/~RDavies/arian/scandals.html

Fraud Information Home Page. http://www.inforamp.net/~hyslo/

Information Law Alert. http://infolawalert.com/

James Randi Homepage: Exposed a Number of Fraud Artists. http://www.mamboland.com/randi/randi.html

Legal Resources Relating to Internet and World Wide Web Issues. http://www.crl.com/~philip/law/ilaw.html

Municipal Bond Scandals. http://lissack.com/

Pretty Good Privacy E-Mail Encryption. http://web.mit.edu/network/pgp.html

Securities Fraud and Investor Protection. http://www.securitieslaw.com/

Security Management Online. http://www.securitymanagement.com/

Stolen Web Page. http://www.rtt.ab.ca/rtt/personal/stolen.htm

Takedown: The Capture of Computer Hacker Kevin Mitnick. http://www.takedown.com/

U.S. Copyright Office. http://lcweb.loc.gov/copyright/

Virtual World of Spies and Intelligence. http://www.dreamscape.com/frankvad/covert.html

PROSTITUTION, PORNOGRAPHY, AND SATANIC CRIME

The Meese Commission Report. http://english-www.hss.cmu.edu/cultronix/Califia/meese.html

Prostitutes' Education Network. http://www.creative.net/~penet/

(Satanic) Ritual Abuse: The Biggest Crime Hoax of the Century. http://limestone.kosone.com/people/ocrt/ra.htm

Serial Murders and the Satanic/Ritualistic Crimes Myth. http://users.hol.gr/~diceman/serial.htm

UNSOLVED CRIMES AND FUGITIVES

The Bloodhound: Search for Anyone in the World. http://www.greatworld.com/public/bhound.htm

Crime Scene Evidence Files. http://www.quest.net/crime/crime.html

Fugitive Watch. http://www.fugitive.com/

Michael Moore's Investigative Database. http://world.std.com/~mmoore

Most Wanted Lists. http://www.gunyragg.com/crimes.htm

Solve Unsolved Crimes from Around the Country. http://www.emeraldcity.com/crimefiles/crimefiles.htm

U.S. Most Wanted Criminals. http://cpcug.org/user/jlacombe/wanted.html

World's Most Wanted List. http://www.mostwanted.com/

Index

Compiled by James Minkin